Brotherhood in Christ accomplishes three things of significance and current relevance. First, it introduces readers to the fascinating story of Baptist origins in the Russian empire in general and in Ukraine in particular, with a focus on how these Baptist communities understood their connections to the larger body of Christ. Second, the book offers an in-depth exploration of a core concept of the ecclesiology of Paul Fiddes, who is arguably the most important theologian among Baptists today. Third, Geychenko proposes a constructive theology of trans-local association that has wide applicability beyond the Ukrainian context. Any one of these things in isolation would make this book a noteworthy contribution to Baptist studies, but together they make *Brotherhood in Christ* a must-have volume for theological libraries, theologians, theological students and ministers – not only for Baptists, but also for their ecumenical dialogue partners.

Steven R. Harmon, PhD
Professor of Historical Theology,
Gardner-Webb University School of Divinity, North Carolina, USA

Brotherhood in Christ fills a gap in the theological literature by exploring associations of Ukrainian Baptist churches as ecclesial entities. Oleksandr Geychenko's historical-theological study is situated in the rich and complex history of Ukrainian Baptists from the Russian Empire in the late nineteenth-century to Ukraine in 2014. In addition to extensive interaction with published sources in Russian, Ukrainian and English, Geychenko interviewed key Ukrainian Baptists and engaged with Paul Fiddes's covenant ecclesiology and a wide range of Christian theologians to provide a theological assessment of associations of Baptist churches in Ukraine. Geychenko's study contributes significantly to the fields of Baptist theology and history, and I heartily recommend it.

Adam Harwood, PhD
McFarland Professor of Theology,
Associate Dean of Theological & Historical Studies,
New Orleans Baptist Theological Seminary, Louisiana, USA

This is an inspiring piece of work, focusing on Ukrainian Baptist ecclesiology, which is of central importance for evangelical identity. This research offers a point of comparison for further discussion relevant for wider theological conversation. A helpful source for students and scholars.

Toivo Pilli, PhD
Director of Baptist Studies,
International Baptist Theological Study Centre, Netherlands

Oleksandr Geychenko possesses a remarkable ability to bridge cultural and linguistic contexts towards the construction of an account of church life that is compelling, gospel-centred and deeply rooted in biblical teaching and Christian tradition. Geychenko's book offers an authoritative, detailed and judicious account of the theological foundations of church unity in the post-Soviet space. The book will appeal to anyone in search of original perspectives on how an emphasis on local church autonomy can be reconciled with the gospel imperative of Christian unity for the sake of fulfilling the Great Commission. At a time when the world's attention is focused on Ukraine, Geychenko is to be commended for making an outstanding contribution to the study of the evangelical movement in this key strategic region.

Joshua T. Searle, PhD
Professor of Mission Studies and Intercultural Theology,
Elstal Theological University, Germany
Co-Founder, Dnipro Hope Mission

This book is a reminder of how multifaceted and complex the development of a denomination can be. Tracing their life throughout different (and at times radically divergent) religious, political and cultural contexts, it presents a fascinating story of Ukrainian Baptist communities up to 2014, analysed through the lens of ecclesiology, and particularly focussing on regional associations. Drawing from the wider Baptist tradition, the book engages in a fruitful dialogue with Paul S. Fiddes's covenant ecclesiology, proposing a deepened theological understanding of the relationship between the life of the local church and the gift of trans-local fellowship.

Brotherhood in Christ examines not only the declared theology of Ukrainian Baptists, but also, importantly, probes their actual convictions and practices. It is an essential read for anyone interested in the life of Ukrainian Baptist communities, and indeed, wider Eastern European evangelical church scene.

Lina Toth, PhD
Assistant Principal and Lecturer,
Scottish Baptist College, UK
Senior Research Fellow,
International Baptist Theological Study Centre, Netherlands

Brotherhood in Christ

Towards a Ukrainian Baptist Perspective
on Associations of Churches

Oleksandr Geychenko

Langham
ACADEMIC

© 2024 Oleksandr Geychenko

Published 2024 by Langham Academic
An imprint of Langham Publishing
www.langhampublishing.org

Langham Publishing and its imprints are a ministry of Langham Partnership

Langham Partnership
PO Box 296, Carlisle, Cumbria, CA3 9WZ, UK
www.langham.org

ISBNs:
978-1-83973-789-3 Print
978-1-78641-019-1 ePub
978-1-78641-020-7 PDF

Oleksandr Geychenko has asserted his right under the Copyright, Designs and Patents Act, 1988 to be identified as the Author of this work.

All rights reserved. No part of this publication may be reproduced, stored in a retrieval system or transmitted, in any form or by any means, electronic, mechanical, photocopying, recording or otherwise, without the prior written permission of the publisher or the Copyright Licensing Agency.

Requests to reuse content from Langham Publishing are processed through PLSclear. Please visit www.plsclear.com to complete your request.

Scripture quotations are from The Holy Bible, English Standard Version® (ESV®), copyright © 2001 by Crossway, a publishing ministry of Good News Publishers. Used by permission. All rights reserved.

British Library Cataloguing-in-Publication Data
A catalogue record for this book is available from the British Library

ISBN: 978-1-83973-789-3

Cover & Book Design: projectluz.com

Langham Partnership actively supports theological dialogue and an author's right to publish but does not necessarily endorse the views and opinions set forth here or in works referenced within this publication, nor can we guarantee technical and grammatical correctness. Langham Partnership does not accept any responsibility or liability to persons or property as a consequence of the reading, use or interpretation of its published content.

To the bright memory of my mother
Nadezhda Petrovna Oleksenko
(1952–1991)

Contents

Abstract xiii

Acknowledgements xv

Foreword xvii

Abbreviations xxi

Introduction 1
    Context of the Monograph 1
    Survey of Literature 3
    Purpose and Scope of the Monograph 12
    Research Question and Subsidiary Questions 13
    Methodological Approach 14
    Content of the Monograph 15
    Transliteration 17

Chapter 1 19
    Baptist Origins in the Russian Empire
    1.1 Origins: Foreign, Indigenous or Hybrid? 19
    1.2 Stundists and Stundo-Baptists in Ukraine 20
    1.3 Baptists in Transcaucasia 25
    1.4 Evangelical Christians in St. Petersburg 30
    1.5 Summary 31

Chapter 2 33
    The Brotherhood Period (1880–1904)
    2.1 Introduction 33
    2.2 Formation and Structuring of Associations of Churches 35
        2.2.1 Early Attempts to Organise Union 35
        2.2.2 Consolidating the Brotherhood: Johann Wieler 39
        2.2.3 Structuring the Brotherhood: Dei Mazaev 41
    2.3 Associational Practices 45
        2.3.1 Conferences as Unifying Associational Practice 45
        2.3.2 The Unifying Role of Trans-Local Ministers 47
    2.4 Understanding the Nature of Associations of Churches 51
        2.4.1 Union as an Association of Churches 51
        2.4.2 Authority of the Local Church vs. Authority of an
            Association of Churches 52

  2.4.3 Brotherhood as Ecclesiological Category............................55
  2.4.4 Mission as Integrative Motif of Unity..................................60
  2.4.5 Union as Implementation of Unity......................................62
 2.5 Summary...65

Chapter 3 67
The Rise and Demise of the Union (1905–1935)
 3.1 Introduction..67
 3.2 Organisational Developments of Associations of Churches..........69
  3.2.1 Regionalisation and Branching of the Union......................69
  3.2.2 Ukrainian Union of Associations of Baptists: A Case
   of Regionalisation..72
  3.2.3 Discussions on the Configuration of the Union..................76
  3.2.4 Transformations of Leadership Structures...........................81
 3.3 Associational Practices 83
  3.3.1 Annual Edifying Conferences..83
  3.3.2 Trans-Local Ministers...85
 3.4 Understanding the Nature of Associations of Churches...............91
  3.4.1 Union as Voluntary Association..91
  3.4.2 Union as an Association of Churches..................................95
  3.4.3 Theological Foundations of the Union................................97
 3.5 Summary...106

Chapter 4 107
Restoration and Division of the Union (1944–1990)
 4.1 Introduction..107
 4.2 All-Union Council of Evangelical Christians-Baptists
  (AUCECB): Deviation from Baptist Principles and Practices....109
  4.2.1 Council of Ministers for Union of Churches.....................110
  4.2.2 Senior Presbyters as the Representatives of the Council..111
 4.3 Reaction: Reformist and Autonomous Movements.....................118
  4.3.1 Initiative Group (IG) and Council of Churches of
   Evangelical Christian-Baptists (CCECB)..............................118
  4.3.2 Autonomous Movement: Return to the Brotherhood.......121
  4.3.3 Transformations of Practices and Structures of
   AUCECB..124
 4.4 Understandings of the Nature of Associations of Churches.......130
  4.4.1 AUCECB: Association of Churches or the Church?.........131
  4.4.2 Biblical Images of the Union..133
 4.5 Summary...136

Chapter 5 139
The Union in Independent Ukraine (1991–2014)
    5.1 Introduction 139
    5.2 Organisational Structure 141
    5.3 Associational Practices 147
    5.4 Understandings of the Nature of Associations of Churches 149
        5.4.1 Images of the Union 149
        5.4.2 Local Church and Union 151
        5.4.3 The Ecclesiological Nature of Associations of Churches .. 160
    5.5 Summary 161

Chapter 6 163
Exploring Oral Tradition on Associations of Churches
    6.1 Introduction 163
    6.2 Interviews: A Descriptive Dimension 163
        6.2.1 Interviewees 163
        6.2.2 Interview Questions 164
        6.2.3 The Process of Interviewing 166
        6.2.4 Analysing Interviews 166
    6.3 Interviews: A Thematic Dimension 168
        6.3.1 The Nature of Associations of Churches 168
        6.3.2 The Necessity of Associations of Churches 176
        6.3.3 Biblical and Theological Arguments for
            Associations of Churches 180
        6.3.4 The Practices of Associations of Churches 184
        6.3.5 Local Churches and Associations of Churches 191
        6.3.6 The (Trans-Local) Leadership of Associations of
            Churches 194
    6.4 Summary 196

Chapter 7 199
Engaging Wider Tradition: Paul S. Fiddes's Covenant Ecclesiology
    7.1 Introduction 199
    7.2 Paul S. Fiddes's Ecclesiological Core 200
        7.2.1 Thinking Theologically about the Church 200
        7.2.2 Church Local, Universal and Wider Union 210
    7.3 Practical Implications for Associations of Churches 215
        7.3.1 Participation in Christ's Mission 215
        7.3.2 Theology of Trust 217
        7.3.3 Pastoral Oversight (*Episkope*) and Associations of
            Churches 220

    7.4 Significance for a Ukrainian Perspective on Associations
        of Churches 224
        7.4.1 Key Themes in Ukrainian Baptist Ecclesiology.............224
        7.4.2 Covenantal Language and the Practice of Covenanting ..226
        7.4.3 Participation in the Trinity..227
        7.4.4 Trustful Relations 229
    7.5 Summary 230

Chapter 8 233
Gathering Puzzles for a Theology of Associations of Churches
    8.1 Introduction 233
    8.2 Cases of Covenanting..234
        8.2.1 Joining to Constitute a Local Church: A Case of
            Tiflis Baptist Church 234
        8.2.2 Pledging for the Sake of Mission: A Case of Luchina
            Church 236
        8.2.3 Renewing the Covenant: A Case of Kyiv
            Autonomous Baptist Church 238
    8.3 Rethinking Local Church 241
        8.3.1 Intentional Community..242
        8.3.2 Covenant Community 246
        8.3.3 Freedom under the Lordship of Christ 249
    8.4 Rethinking Association of Churches 254
        8.4.1 Covenant Brotherhood in Christ 255
        8.4.2 Visualising Unity in Imperfect Forms 261
        8.4.3 Watching Over Each Other 265
        8.4.4 Participating in the Mission of God................................268
    8.5 Summary 270

Conclusion 273
    Results 273
    Contribution of the Monograph..276
    Areas for Further Study 277

Appendix 1 279
Interview Questions and Prompts

Appendix 2 281
Two Versions of the Interview Questions

Appendix 3 283
Initial Coding

Appendix 4 287
    Constitution of the Church

Appendix 5 291
    Equipping Stundist missionaries for Eastern Siberia

Appendix 6 297
    Church Covenant of the Community of Evangelical Christians-Baptists

Bibliography 303

Abstract

This monograph explores a Ukrainian Baptist understanding of the ecclesiological nature of associations of churches. The monograph reconstructs a historical understanding of the nature of associations, maps the current perspective on associations and suggests its further development through constructive dialogue with Paul S. Fiddes's covenant ecclesiology. In the process of reconstructing and mapping, special attention is paid to associational practices, organisational structures, and the theological language and imagery related to associations of churches. The monograph demonstrates that Ukrainian Baptists understand associations of churches as ecclesial entities. This is evident in associational practices and in the theological language and imagery used in regard to associations. Employing Fiddes's theology of trust, along with his concepts of covenant and participation in the Trinity, permits moving beyond pragmatic reasons for associating and presents associations as a covenantal brotherhood in Christ that represents the unity of the body of Christ, commits to mutual care through the ministry of trans-local ministers and participates in Christ's mission in the world.

Acknowledgements

This project would never have been accomplished without the contribution of many people. First of all, I want to thank my friends and colleagues, Taras N. Dyatlik, Roman P. Soloviy and Sergii V. Sannikov, who encouraged the project at its initial stage and were of great help as it was proceeding. Their sincere interest, attentive listening, wise recommendations and true friendship supported my journey.

The project could not have been accomplished without the financial contributions of many organisations and committed individuals. I am grateful to the Langham Partnership and the University of St. Andrews for selecting me for both the Thomas Chalmers Scholarship and St. Mary's Anniversary Scholarship. Without these generous gifts I wouldn't have been able to enjoy the wonderful research atmosphere or access the rich academic resources at the University of St. Andrews or been able to accomplish this project. The Euro-Asian Accrediting Association and Slavic Research and Resource Centre approved my research project and provided funds and guidance necessary for its completion. Overseas Council International granted financial support to my family while I was at St. Andrews. Gene Richards, Nell Sharkey and Charles Warner supplied necessary books for my research. Jim and Susan Gosney generously covered travel expenses for my first semester at St. Andrews.

Two churches have left a significant mark on my life. Leven Baptist Church became a temporary home and spiritual oasis for the years of my studies. This friendly Christian fellowship constantly encouraged me while I was away from my family. I am grateful to Mark Pexton, who was the minister of LBC, for his great preaching and the occasional conversations we had walking along the golf course. Home group at David and Sue's was always a refreshing spiritual experience. I can hardly express my thanks to Ian and Debbie Tinkler, whose hospitality exceeded even the boldest expectations. They exemplified the life of true disciples. Strathaven Evangelical Church took a risk to "adopt" me. Jeff and Susan, Drew and Lilian, Stuart and Debbie, David and Diane, and Ian and Christine have become not only fellow sojourners but dear friends. I also thank all those who constantly supported my family with their prayers and encouraged us with letters when life seemed very gloomy.

Steve Holmes was a wise supervisor. His encouragement and support during the final stages helped me overcome the customary Ukrainian proclivity to underestimate one's own work. He helped me gain the assurance so necessary for PhD work.

Ian Shaw was a good example of a scholar who loves the church and uses his gifts and talents for service in God's kingdom.

I thank Liz and Malcolm McGregor for being my spiritual directors. Conversations and prayers with Liz and Malcolm's advice were abundant and very much needed.

I am very grateful to Dr. John Jeacocke for his willingness to help with proofreading the thesis in the shortest period of time. This was a true labour of love. Cheryl Warner and Jeff Collison kindly agreed to check the abstract, acknowledgements and conclusion, and Mary Raber assisted with some aspects of English terminology. I am grateful to my colleague and friend Veaceslav Gherasimciuc for being an attentive listener and patient interlocutor during our discussions on some portions of the thesis.

I want to thank the interviewees for their openness and willingness to participate in the study and those Ukrainian Baptist ministers who kept asking me about the project, stimulating my efforts and assuring me of its necessity.

Special thanks to my family, my daughters Taia and Alice, and my dear wife, Tetiana. I thank Taia for helping to transcribe interviews when my time was tight. I thank Alice for loving and encouraging me when she herself was passing through a very uneasy period of life. My wife, Tetiana, took the heavy burden of raising our two teenage daughters. Without her this project would never have been finished. I cannot express how much I owe to her.

Most of all I thank God for granting me the opportunity to study, providing funds, connecting me with new friends and giving me strength to finish the project.

Foreword

"Look to the rock from which you were hewn," commands God, through the prophet Isaiah (Isa 51:1 ESV). The instruction is given to people in exile, contemplating their return to the ruins that once were Jerusalem. God asks them to remember Abraham and Sarah, who wandered homeless and childless for so long before God's promise to them was fulfilled. This example should give hope to the faithful remnant, few in number, who were wondering what life they might possibly create on the broken stones that littered Mount Zion.

Remembering our history, and remembering our history well – not just what happened, but the ways we can see the Lord leading us in the past – remains an important Christian task. God can create whatever He wills out of nothing, of course, but often God wills to be faithful to the stories that have been told, to renew some group of His people in a way that builds on, although perhaps transforms, their previous history.

Within the Scriptures, the two books of Chronicles might be the best example of this. Written after the exile, they retold the story of the nation, re-narrating events that had already been described in Samuel and Kings, to make sense of what had happened, and to give hope for the future. God is good; God remains good; God's goodness means that He might discipline His people for a time, but will never abandon them, and will lead them into 'broad places' where they can rest, look back, and see God's hand in all their story.

The Chronicler's example suggests that we do not just need to remember our history, but to reflect on it theologically to understand how God has been at work among us and where we might need to repent and refocus as we see that we have not quite understood. The books of Samuel and Kings are not untheological, of course, but the Chronicler hones the messages to make sure we cannot miss them in a whole series of ways: certain events of the history are emphasised far more than they are in Samuel/Kings (there is, for example, a sustained focus on the Temple, and the ministry of the Levites), whereas others are quietly passed over as part of the messiness of history which would detract from the clear messages the writer wants to give.

In this monograph Dr. Geychenko gives us valuable history, based on deep research into archival sources. This account of the origins and development of the Ukrainian Baptist denominations is certainly immeasurably more detailed and authoritative than anything previously available in English; more than that, it is now the definitive account in any language. Were this all we were given here, the book would be of immense value.

Like the Chronicler, however, Dr. Geychenko goes further, and interprets the history he tells. Chapter 7 gives us a perceptive account of Paul Fiddes's theology of association – and is in its own right a contribution to the growing literature surrounding Fiddes's work. This is then used as a theological lens to explore the questions and disputes that the history has raised up. This is valuable work for all Baptists, not just those in Ukraine, as we are offered worked examples of how historical examples might demonstrate theological themes – and of how theological themes might interrogate historical examples.

The question of association has always been difficult for Baptists: we seem, instinctively, to believe that we should associate, but we have regularly struggled to know what that means, and how it relates to the independence of the local church. There are famous disputes – notably the anti-missions controversy in the USA, which is still fossilised in the existence of separate Primitive Baptist associations and denominations – but any serious student of Baptist history anywhere in the world will know that the question is almost always present in one way or another. It is a great gift, therefore, to be offered a serious theological account of association, and perceptive readings of how that might work out in specific and real situations.

One final theme seems presently necessary, although I hope, pray and trust that soon it will not be. The interconnections and relationships between Ukrainian Baptists and Russian Baptists are ever present throughout this book; their past stories are shared, if now brutally fractured by the evil aggression of the present Russian regime. The Biblical Chronicler's treatment of the division of Israel after Solomon is perhaps interesting here, in that the split between the kingdoms is very obviously downplayed, when we compare the account in Chronicles to the account in Kings. The Chronicler believes that the Temple cult, and obedience to the Mosaic law, unifies the Twelve Tribes; if political divisions seem to obscure this, then the truth is to be re-asserted, and the politics condemned as a misleading lie. As a result, the Chronicler both minimises the division, and denounces those who pretend that it has theological justification, or remain cravenly silent in the face of such pretence.

Being involved with the European Baptist Federation, and knowing Oleksandr, I have some knowledge of the remarkable humanitarian work Ukrainian Baptists are presently doing – their present story will, once fully told, be one of the glories of our tradition. Their willingness to reach out to Russian sisters and brothers as the invasion began is a matter of record, and the author of this present work was actively involved in that. Baptists know that we are aliens and strangers in this present world, and so we sit somewhat lightly to governments, kingdoms, and empires: we know also that we are called to seek and demand justice, and that to fail in this is to fail in our discipleship. This book tells some of the story of how that orientation was negotiated with imagination and faithfulness under the Soviet regime; we must pray that our sisters and brothers who live under the present Russian nationalist regime, hardly less evil, will discover that same faithfulness.

Stephen R. Holmes
St. Mary's College,
St. Andrews, UK

Abbreviations

AC	association of churches
AUUCECB	All-Ukrainian Union of Churches of Evangelical Christians-Baptists
AUCECB	All-Union Council of Evangelical Christians-Baptists
BFSU	Baptists in the Former Soviet Union
BUGB	Baptist Union of Great Britain
BWA	Baptist World Alliance
CARC	Council for the Affairs of Religious Cults
CCECB	Council of Churches of Evangelical Christian-Baptists
E-AAA	Euro-Asian Accrediting Association
EBF	European Baptist Federation
FBU of USSR	Federated Baptist Union of the Union of Soviet Socialist Republics
LMG	League of the Militant Godless
IG	Initiative Group
NT	New Testament
OC	Organising Committee
OQ	operational question
OT	Old Testament
RQ	research question
RBU	Russian Baptist Union
TLMs	trans-local ministers
UUAB	Ukrainian Union of Associations of Baptists

Introduction

This monograph reconstructs the understanding of the nature of associations of churches (ACs) among Ukrainian Baptists affiliated with the All-Ukrainian Union of Churches of Evangelical Christians-Baptists (AUUCECB).[1] Ukrainian Baptists understand ACs as ecclesial entities, which is evident in their associational practices and the theological language and imagery used in regard to ACs. The monograph attempts to develop this understanding through constructive dialogue with Paul S. Fiddes's covenant ecclesiology.

Context of the Monograph

The current associational practice and organisational shape of the AUUCECB developed and matured in the twentieth century. It remained unchanged although the Ukrainian context changed tremendously. In the beginning of the twenty-first century, Catholics, evangelicals and some Orthodox are open to generous and trustful dialogue[2] and cooperation in educational[3]

---

1. This name was approved in 2006. Earlier, the union was known as the All-Ukrainian Union of Associations of Churches of Evangelical Christians-Baptists (1994–2006) and the Union of Evangelical Christians-Baptist of Ukraine (1990–1994). I will use AUUCECB to avoid confusion.

2. The Euro-Asian Accrediting Association (E-AAA) and National Pedagogical Dragomanov University's Religious Studies Department PhD programme (Kyiv, Ukraine) became a platform for presenting and discussing crucial theological and socially relevant subjects from representatives of evangelical, Catholic and Orthodox communions. Slavic Resource and Research Centre, a research arm of E-AAA, holds a series of seminars and conferences attracting participants and speakers from different denominations.

3. Mikhail Cherenkov, the executive director of Mission Eurasia Field Ministries, a well-known Baptist philosopher and public figure, is now professor of the Ukrainian Catholic University's Philosophy Department.

and social spheres.[4] Perhaps distrust and exclusion are slowly fading away. The opportunity for dialogue points to the need to reassess the ecclesiology inherited from earlier times in order to face this new situation.

In the middle of the first decade of the twenty-first century, the ministers of some prominent local churches challenged the existing structure of AUUCECB and its associational practices.[5] They launched Rukh za Zdorovu Tserkvu (Movement for the healthy church)[6] which, among other things, promoted local church autonomy.[7] Perhaps, by avoiding the cumbersome AUUCECB, they sought to react more effectively to the current Ukrainian situation. The crisis was one of the factors behind "Pervyi Simpozium: Vzaimootnosheniia Pomestnoi Tserkvi I Soiuza" (First symposium: Relations of a local church and the union).[8] The participants agreed that "different forms of associations (interchurch fellowship) have a *certain* ecclesiological nature (which has to be formulated more precisely)."[9]

A personal note is relevant here: for the last twenty-five years, I have been involved in AUUCECB as a member of the local church, lay preacher, and faculty member and academic dean (2007–2014) of one of the key Ukrainian Baptist theological seminaries. This means that this thesis is a work of the insider. Both the rapidly changing context and the tensions inside of AUUCECB point to the need for constructing a more viable understanding of the nature of ACs which the present research aims to provide.

---

4. Since the Revolution of Dignity (October 2013–February 2014) and the Russo-Ukrainian War in Eastern Ukraine (March 2014–present time), members of different churches have worked together in voluntary organisations and civic initiatives.

5. See Mokienko, "Vseukrains'kyi Soiuz Ob'ednan"; Honcharov, "Bibleiskoe Obosnovanie Avtonomii"; Panych, "Instytutsializatsiia Evangel's'koho Protestantyzmu."

6. See "Prezentatsiia Rukhu" for details. At the moment the movement is inactive. Some of the participants are active now in the Baptist Union programmes.

7. For the movement's values see "Opys Tsinnostei Rukhu" on the blog *Rukh "Za Zdorovu Tserkvu."*

8. The symposium was held 6–7 December 2007 in Kyiv, Ukraine. For the proceedings see *Avtonomiia Pomestnoi Tserkvi*. The content of this conference volume and its significance will be discussed in section 5.4.2.

9. "Obobshchenie Obsuzhdenii," 381.

Survey of Literature

The Baptist practice of associating is well researched in the West. Scholars have produced a number of historical-theological studies of associations among early English and American Baptists.[10] G. Hugh Wamble explores the motif of Christian fellowship beyond the local church among early English Baptists and concludes that for them valid faith and correct order are the grounds for Christian unity.[11] Winthrop S. Hudson criticises Baptist individualism and argues for congregational membership in associations.[12] Walter B. Shurden researches Baptist associations in America.[13] His most significant contribution is his differentiation of the origins of and justification for associations – where the former is usually practical, the latter is biblical, theological and practical.[14] F. Russell Bennett argues that association expresses the nature of the church and the Baptist belief in the interdependence of churches.[15] He views it as an ecclesiological organisation which allows the Spirit to act in an embodied and tangible form.[16]

Southern Baptist scholars focus on cooperation. Michael Waldrop proposes a theology of cooperation based on the idea of the unity of the people of God in the Old and New Testaments and on the local church's participation in the kingdom of God. He insists on "essential doctrinal truth as definer and limiter for interchurch cooperation."[17] Within this trajectory Dennis Wilkins explores intercongregational collaboration as a form of ecumenism and argues

---

10. May, "Role of Associations in Baptist History"; Carter, "Dealing with Doctrinal Conflict in Associational History"; Yarbrough, "Origin of Baptist Associations"; Randall, "Council and Help."

11. Wamble, "Concept and Practice," 532.

12. Hudson, "Associational Principle among Baptists," 15; see also Hudson, "Stumbling into Disorder"; Hudson, "Documents on the Association of Churches"; Hudson, "Prolegomena to a Theology of Church Order."

13. Shurden, "Associationalism among Baptists"; Shurden, "The Development of Baptist Associations in America, 1707–1814"; Shurden, "Baptist Associations"; Shurden, "Associational Principle, 1707–1814"; Shurden, "Church and Association"; Shurden, "The Advance of Baptist Associations across America"; Shurden, "The Historical Background of Baptist Associations"; Shurden, "The Authority of a Baptist Association"; Shurden, "Minutes of the Philadelphia Baptist Association"; Shurden, "Baptist Associations and the Turn toward Denominational Cooperation."

14. Shurden, "Associationalism among Baptists," 69–111; Shurden, "Associational Principle, 1707–1814."

15. Bennett, *Fellowship of Kindred Minds*; Bennett, "The Nature of the Baptist Association."

16. Bennett, *Fellowship of Kindred Minds*, 69.

17. Waldrop, "Toward a Theology," 176–81.

that it is justified when it is based on Scripture, prioritizes the local church and builds unity on the revealed truth in the Bible.[18] David Rogers explores the history of missionary cooperation with other denominations.[19] Samuel Tyson, focussing on the Philadelphia Baptist Association, argues for the necessity of confessing to local church autonomy and assuming dependence on the wider body of Christ beyond the local church. He calls to go beyond cooperation to inter-communion as a visible manifestation of the universal church.[20]

Steven Harmon, a Baptist ecumenical theologian affiliated with Cooperative Baptist Fellowship, suggests that Baptist "gathered church" ecclesiology has potential for ascribing ecclesial status to denominational and even ecumenical gatherings.[21] However, he opines that the existence of the Baptist denomination is only justifiable if placed within the goal of "full visible unity of the church."[22]

While most US scholars gravitate towards local church autonomy, their British peers approach the issue from the perspective of the universal church and insist on the simultaneous interdependence and freedom of local churches. Thus, Nigel G. Wright appeals to the notion of *koinonia* and insists on "being Church beyond the local church."[23] Brian Haymes, Ruth Gouldbourne and Anthony Cross build Baptist ecclesiology theologically and go beyond pragmatic reasons for associating.[24] Keith G. Jones did a significant work on Baptist interdependency focussing on the European Baptist Federation (EBF) as a case study.[25] Paul S. Fiddes developed "covenant ecclesiology," addressing the subject of wider union and the practice of associating from the perspective of covenant community, a perspective which was characteristic for early

---

18. Wilkins, "Southern Baptist Intercongregational Collaboration," 218–21.

19. Rogers, "A Critical Analysis."

20. Tyson, "Dependent Independence."

21. Harmon, "Ecumenical Dimensions," 42; see also Harmon, *Baptist Identity*, 135–64. For other perspectives on denomination as an ecclesiological category see Collins and Ensign-George, *Denomination*.

22. Harmon, *Baptist Identity*, 149.

23. Wright, "Koinonia"; Wright, *New Baptists, New Agenda*, 46–63; Wright, *Free Church, Free State*, 183–203; Wright, "Are Baptist Churches Autonomous?"

24. Haymes, Gouldbourne, and Cross, *On Being the Church*, 195–213.

25. Jones, *European Baptist Federation*; see also Jones, "Rethinking Baptist Ecclesiology"; Jones, *From Conflict to Communion*; Jones, "Spirituality and Structures"; Jones, "Re-Visiting the Web."

English Baptists.²⁶ Since Fiddes is the primary dialogue partner for this thesis, a detailed analysis of his ecclesiology is given in chapter 7.

As a leading Baptist theologian, Fiddes has been heavily involved in different inter-church projects among Baptists and ecumenical bilateral and multilateral theological dialogues.²⁷ He served as chairman of the Doctrine and Worship Committee of the Baptist Union of Great Britain (BUGB), convenor of the division for theology and education of the European Baptist Federation (EBF) and chair of the Baptist Doctrine and Inter-Church Cooperation Study Commission of the Baptist World Alliance (BWA).²⁸ He was a member of a number of ecumenical study commissions, such as the British Council of Churches/Churches Together in Britain and Ireland, and served as co-chairman of the Anglican Communion–BWA International Conversations (2000–2005) and co-moderator of the second series of the Roman Catholic–BWA International Conversations (2006–2010).

Fiddes has written extensively.²⁹ His theological interests encompass continental philosophy, modern English literature, films, and Baptist history and theology.³⁰ Participation in various ecumenical theological conversations re-

---

26. Born into a Baptist family in Upminster on 30 April 1947, Paul Fiddes was educated at Drayton Manor Grammar School and then St. Peter's College, Oxford, where he read English language and literature (1968) and theology (1970) for his double first. This double interest is ever present in his subsequent writings. After earning a DPhil in theology (1975) at the University of Oxford, he spent a year at the University of Tübingen, doing post-doctoral studies under Jürgen Moltmann and Eberhard Jüngel. Meanwhile, Fiddes was ordained a Baptist minister in 1972 and became a resident fellow in the Old Testament (1972–1975) and then a tutorial fellow in Christian doctrine (1975–1989) at Regent's Park College. In 1989, he was elected principal of Regent's Park College and served in this capacity until 2007 when he became principal emeritus, professorial research fellow and director of research. In 2002, he occupied the position of professor of systematic theology at the University of Oxford and delivered the Oxford Bampton Lectures which Oxford University Press published in 2013. See Fiddes, *Seeing the World*.

27. On Fiddes as ecumenical theologian, see Harmon, "Trinitarian Koinōnia."

28. Mulcahy, "Cause of Our Salvation," 117.

29. For the list of publications see https://www.rpc.ox.ac.uk/people/professor-paul-fiddes/; see also the chronological arrangement in Clarke, *For the Sake*, 232–42.

30. For analysis of Fiddes's soteriology, see Mulcahy, "Cause of Our Salvation," 117–217; for his doctrine of God, see Clarke, *Within the Love*; for his ecclesiology, see Clarke, *For the Sake*. For an interaction with the themes of Trinity and his participation at the Young Scholars in the Baptist Academy Colloquium (Regent's Park College, Oxford, UK, 2016), see *Perspectives in Religious Studies* 44, no. 1, containing papers by Haymes, "Trinity and Participation"; Harmon, "Trinitarian Koinōnia"; Peek, "Sacrifice"; Schelin, "All Are Alive"; Hanch, "Participation in God"; Glover, "Partakers of the Promise"; Wilmington, "Distinctly Harmonious." See also Fiddes's response in Fiddes, "Covenant and Participation."

sulted in a number of reports[31] and theological discussion papers prepared for EBF and the BUGB[32] that bear signs of Fiddes's theological imprint. The BUGB discussion paper *The Nature of the Assembly and the Council of the BUGB*, of which Paul Fiddes was the main writer, accumulates his understanding of the nature of ACs.[33] The most comprehensive and cumulative treatment of covenant ecclesiology and its implications for different ecclesiological concerns is found in *Tracks and Traces*.[34] In other publications Fiddes uses the notion of the covenant with regard to the authority of leaders,[35] baptism, church membership[36] and communion ecclesiology.[37] In a recent work, Fiddes and his long-time friends and colleagues Brian Haymes and Richard Kidd develop a Baptist understanding of the idea of the communion of saints, drawing from the Baptist theology of covenant.[38] Recently, Fiddes proposed to view covenant ecclesiology, the movement that encompassed various groups from English Separatists to continental Anabaptists and Mennonites, as the "fourth strand of the Reformation."[39] The key trait of the movement was their pledge to "walk together," a phrase that was emblematic of covenant relations with God and each other. This proposal was developed and argued for in a

---

31. Anglican Communion Office and Baptist World Alliance, *Conversations*; Baptist Union of Great Britain, Faith and Unity Executive Committee, and Council for Christian Unity, *Pushing at the Boundaries*; Catholic Church and Baptist World Alliance, "Word of God"; Baptist World Alliance, "Extended Response"; Fiddes, *Sharing the Faith*. On Fiddes's role in compiling these documents, see Harmon, "Trinitarian Koinōnia," 19–22.

32. European Baptist Federation, *What Are Baptists?*; Baptist Union of Great Britain, *Nature of the Assembly*; Baptist Union of Great Britain, *Forms of Ministry*; Baptist Union of Great Britain and Ireland, *Believing and Being Baptized*.

33. Baptist Union of Great Britain, *Nature of the Assembly*; Baptist Union of Great Britain, *Forms of Ministry*.

34. Fiddes, *Tracks and Traces*; see also Fiddes's response to the review in Carter and Fiddes, "Baptist Ecclesiology," 93–100. For a shorter version of his ecclesiology, see Fiddes, "Fourth Strand"; Fiddes, Brackney, and Yarnell, *Fourth Strand*; cf. Fiddes, "Christian Doctrine." Some of his later essays draw from *Tracks and Traces*. See Fiddes, "Church's Ecumenical Calling," 36–61.

35. Fiddes, *Leading Question*; Fiddes, "Authority," 59–63; Baptist Union of Great Britain, *Forms of Ministry among Baptists*.

36. Baptist Union of Great Britain and Ireland, *Believing and Being Baptized*; Fiddes, "Baptism," 48–65; Fiddes, "Receiving One Another," 65–105.

37. Fiddes, "Church, Trinity and Covenant," 37–54; Fiddes, "Church Local and Universal," 97–120.

38. Fiddes, Haymes, and Kidd, *Baptists*.

39. Fiddes, "Fourth Strand."

book written by Fiddes, Canadian Baptist theologian Willian H. Brackney and American Baptist theologian Malcolm B. Yarnell III.[40]

A significant event that focused on the issue of local church autonomy, relations between local churches and the wider union and authority of trans-local ministers was the BWA Symposium on Baptist Identity and Ecclesiology.[41] A number of scholars presented papers that represent the most recent perspectives on Baptist ecclesiology. Uwe Swarat, professor of systematic theology at the Theologisches Seminar (Elstal, Germany), argues for the ecclesiological nature of wider structures from the perspective of Reformation ecclesiology, appealing to concepts of *communio sanctorum, congregatio vere credendum, koinonia* and the body of Christ. He rejects traditional Baptist understanding of wider structures as necessary merely for practical purposes and states that the real question is whether they have an *"ecclesiological indispensability."*[42] Swarat also claims that fellowships of churches should have organisational and legal forms for "every visible fellowship needs structures."[43] Christoph Stenschke, professor at Missionshaus Bibelschule (Wiedenest, Germany), analyses the issue of power and interdependence in the Bible. Having explored cases of the exchange and sharing of material means, spiritual gifts, people and prayer support, as well as attempts to address doctrinal heterodoxy, he concludes that "there is evidence of the exercise of authority and power (by the church founders) beyond the local church in the New Testament."[44] Nigel Wright, principal of Spurgeon's College (London, UK), and William Brackney, professor of theology at Acadia Divinity College (Wolfville, Nova Scotia, Canada), address the issue of local church autonomy.[45] Both assert the importance for Baptists of the local church's freedom under the lordship of Christ and try to balance that with the associational principle and a proper understanding of the universal church. Ian M. Randall, senior research fellow

---

40. Fiddes, Brackney, and Yarnell, *Fourth Strand*.
41. Elstal, Germany, March 21–24, 2007. The papers are no longer available on the BWA website. For those by Uwe Swarat, Christoph Stenschke, Neville Callam, Nigel Wright, William Brackney on the statement "Are Baptist Churches Autonomous?" see *Avtonomiia Pomestnoi Tserkvi*. For Ian Randal's paper, see Randall, "Council and Help."
42. Swarat, "Local Churches," 48–53.
43. Swarat, "Local Churches," 50–51.
44. Stenschke, "Issues of Power," 147.
45. Wright, "Are Baptist Churches Autonomous?"; Brackney, "Historical Theologian."

at Spurgeon's College (London, UK), surveys the history of associating among European Baptists from the seventeenth to the twentieth century.[46]

A number of studies address Russian and Ukrainian Baptist movements from a historical perspective and provide necessary background. American Baptist historian Albert Wardin writes extensively on the origins and development of Baptists and other Evangelicals in the Russian Empire.[47] Wardin argues for a hybrid nature of the movement that incorporates external influences, a variety of local traditions and the input of local leadership.[48] His monograph *On the Edge* provides a very thorough and meticulously documented introduction to the evangelical movement in the Russian Empire from 1850 to 1917.[49] Heather Coleman addresses the period of spiritual searching from 1905 to 1929.[50] She does this through the lens of personal conversion narratives and by exploring the formation of new personal and social identities. Her study is important for understanding the Baptist movement as part of a general process encompassing the formation of a pluralist public sphere and the modernisation of the Russian Empire. The collective volume on the AUCECB and the works of Sergei Savinskii contain a very detailed description of the Ukrainian Baptist movement.[51] Ukrainian Baptist scholar Sergei Sannikov and Iurii Reshetnikov give a general survey of Baptist history in Ukraine.[52]

During the times of independence, a number of Ukrainian scholars researched the regional development of sectarian movements. Thus, Viacheslav Potots'kii in his thesis describes the development of religious sectarianism in Kharkiv province in 1861–1917[53] and argues that the factor of German

---

46. Randall, "Council and Help."

47. Wardin, "Continental European Baptists"; Wardin, "Baptist Influences"; Wardin, "Mennonite Brethren"; Wardin, "Penetration"; Wardin, "August G. A. Liebig"; Wardin, "Baptist Immersions."

48. Wardin, "How Indigenous."

49. Wardin, *On the Edge*.

50. Coleman, "Most Dangerous Sect." Published as Coleman, *Russian Baptists*.

51. VSEKhB, *Istoriia Evangelskikh Khristian-Baptistov v SSSR*; Savinskii, S. N. *Istoriia Evangelskikh Khristian-Baptistov Ukrainy, Rossii, Belorussii (1867–1917)*; Savinskii, *Istoriia Evangelskikh Khristian-Baptistov Ukrainy, Rossii, Belorussii (1917–1967)*.

52. Reshetnikov, *Ukrainskie Baptisty i Rossiiskaia Imperiia*; Reshetnikov and Sannikov, *Obzor Istorii*. For older surveys see Domashovets', *Narys Istorii*; Kmeta-Efimovich, "Zhyvye Kamni."

53. Potots'kii, "Rozvytok Relihiinoho Sectantstva."

funding was obvious but not decisive in its development.[54] Olga Beznosova documented history of the evangelical movement in Ekaterinoslav province, connecting it with the life and activities of German colonists.[55] Ievgenia Goloshchapova published a number of articles devoted to the quantitative dynamics,[56] organisational structure,[57] leadership[58] and activities[59] of Ukrainian Baptists in the southern provinces against the background of social transformations in the 1920s and 1930s.[60] Though her perspective is a historical one, she provides information relevant for the study of Ukrainian Baptists. Thus, she reaffirms the significance of local church autonomy for Ukrainian Baptists[61] and points to the structure of the Ukrainian Union of Associations of Baptists (UUAB) as one of the key factors in their significant growth in the 1920s and relatively quick demise in the 1930s.[62] Her research provides necessary background information for understanding the work of UUAB in this period. Roman Sitarchuk explores Protestant confessions against the background of state politics regarding religious associations.[63] Sitarchuk indirectly touches ecclesiological matters. Particularly, he claims that in the 1920s and 1930s, UUAB grew in its autonomy with regard to the wider national union and developed institutionally, evolving from a "sect" into a "traditional church."[64] This factor of developing church organisation became one of the reasons for the intrusion of the government into the life of

---

54. Potots'kii, "Rozvytok Relihiinoho Sectantstva," 13–14.

55. Beznosova, "Do Pytannia Zarodzhennia Protestantyzmu"; Beznosova, "Pozdnee Protestantskoe Sektantstvo"; Beznosova, O. V., ed. *Evangel'skoe Dvizhenie v Rossiiskoi Imperii, 1850–1917*.

56. Goloshchapova, "Dynamika Tchysel'nosti Hromad."

57. Goloshchapova, "Organisatsiina Budova Baptysts'kykh Hromad."

58. Goloshchapova, "Lidery Hromad Evangels'kykh Krystyian-Baptystiv Ukrainy 1920–1930-kh rr."

59. Goloshchapova, "Osnovni Vektory Diial'nosti."

60. Goloshchapova, "Hromady Evnagel'skikh Khrystyian-Baptistiv"; Goloshchapova, "Baptysty Ukrainy v Umovakh Suspil'nykh Transformatsii."

61. Goloshchapova, "Organisatsiina Budova Baptysts'kykh Hromad," 153–57.

62. Goloshchapova, "Dynamika Tchysel'nosti Hromad," 151–52; Goloshchapova, "Organisatsiina Budova Baptysts'kykh Hromad," 158–59. Ukrainian Union of Associations of Baptists (UUAB) existed from 1918 to 1930 and ceased to exist due to the government repressions.

63. Sitarchuk, "Diial'nist' Protestants'kykh Konfesii"; Sitarchuk, "Represii shchodo Protestants'kykh Tserkov"; see also Pashchenko and Sitarchuk, "Deiaki Aspekty Derzhavno-Tserkovnykh Vidnosyn."

64. Sitarchuk, "Diial'nist' Protestants'kykh Konfesii," 2, 8–9.

the UUAB, which eventually destroyed its original structures and transformed them into copies of "party and Soviet organisations."[65]

Only a handful of studies have focused on ecclesiology and associations. Johannes Dyck explores the ecclesiological concept of *bratstvo* (brotherhood),[66] which was significant during the early years of the Baptist movement in the Russian Empire.[67] Based on Colonel Pashkov's archive, Dyck reconstructs the life and structure of the Bratstvo. He suggests that the concept was borrowed from Free Church tradition through Mennonite Brethren. Dyck's claim that "the concept is not so much doctrinal as operational representing how individual local congregations and different traditions wished to relate to one another"[68] evidences that he underestimates the theological significance of the concept. This monograph will demonstrate that the concept was not only operational but also formative for the ecclesiological self-identification of Baptists in the Russian Empire.

Paul D. Steeves's older study of the history of the Russian Baptist Union provided a documented story of its emergence and development and, in the second part, surveyed their theological views. Although the section on ecclesiology is brief and somewhat outdated in terms of sources, it covers such sections as theological views on the church, sacraments, ordination and offices, church polity, church discipline and the union of churches, and it is a good starting point for understanding ecclesiology prior to the 1930s.[69] Steeves pointed out that Baptists understood union as "a voluntary 'brotherhood' of like-minded believers and congregations"[70] but admitted that there were various views on associations and an ambivalent attitude towards them.[71]

---

65. Sitarchuk, "Diial'nist' Protestants'kykh Konfesii," 2.

66. Russian word *bratstvo* (brotherhood) refers both to a concept and as a shorthand to the association of churches. When the former is implied, the word is italicised, when the latter it starts with capital letter. It also should be pointed out that quite often the Bratstvo was used as an informal generic title for Baptist churches.

67. Dyck, "Fresh Skins"; Dyck, "Moulding the Brotherhood"; Dyck, "Zavisimost Nezavisimosti."

68. Dyck, "Moulding the Brotherhood."

69. Steeves, "Russian Baptist Union," 448–85. Russian Baptist Union existed from 1917 to 1935 when it formally ceased to exist due to the government repressions.

70. Steeves, "Russian Baptist Union," 484.

71. Steeves, "Russian Baptist Union," 481–84.

Ukrainian scholar Iurii Reshetnikov addresses the historical experience of unification and the intrinsic tensions between union and autonomy.[72] His analysis of the stadial development of Baptist churches from "new religious movements" into "established religions" is particularly helpful for understanding the historical development of the UUAB.[73] Religious studies scholars Mikhail Mokienko and Olena Panych address the processes of the institutionalisation and democratisation of AUUCECB in the independent Ukraine.[74] Both scholars pointed out that AUUCECB inherited a developed ecclesiastical structure which was subject to the processes of reform in 1991–2001.

Perhaps the most significant work that explores ecclesiology in the Soviet period (1960–1990) is the unpublished PhD thesis defended by Ukrainian Baptist theologian Yaroslav Pyzh in Southwestern Baptist Theological Seminary (Fort Worth, TX).[75] He argues that confessing community was the key characteristic of Soviet Baptist ecclesiology that helped them to survive persecutions and distinguished them from Western fellow-believers.[76] Confessing community is "a fellowship of believers who submit to the Lordship of Jesus Christ and the authority of the Bible, preserve the distinctives of their faith in contrast to the ideology and values of the culture, and maintain doctrinal purity among their members and express their beliefs through communal confession of faith."[77] Besides tracing the sources and reconstructing the shape of the concept, Pyzh inscribes it in the wider discussion on communal ecclesiology, dialoguing with the works of Tönnies,

---

72. Reshetnikov, "Ob'edinitel'naia Tendentsiia"; Reshetnikov, "Zahal'ni Problemni Pytannia."

73. Reshetnikov, "Zahal'ni Problemni Pytannia," 324.

74. Mokienko, "Vseukrains'kyi Soiuz Ob'ednan"; Panych, "Instytutsializatsiia Evangel's'koho Protestantyzmu."

75. Pyzh, "Confessing Community." The text contains a number of factual mistakes and typos. For instance, the emergence of the Evangelical Christians Union is dated to after the Second World War (pp. 16, 43), while in fact it was founded by Ivan S. Prokhanov in 1907 as the Russian Evangelical Alliance and in 1909 changed to the Russian Union of Evangelical Christians; Prokanov's ministry is dated to the early nineteenth century or the Second World War (pp. 43, 57); and a quote from *Pravila Veroispovedaniia*, composed by Ratushny, is ascribed to Prokhanov (pp. 98, 180). Apart from these and other minute mistakes, the thesis is a serious contribution to the study of Baptist ecclesiology in the USSR.

76. Pyzh, "Confessing Community," 8–10. Pyzh is dealing with the post WWII union of Baptists called All-Union Council of Evangelical Christians-Baptists (1944–1991).

77. Pyzh, "Confessing Community," 4–5.

Bonhoeffer and Volf.[78] Unfortunately, he only briefly touches the problem of ecclesial structures beyond the local level, stating that "the fundamental principle of church organisation for the BFSU was to preserve ecclesiological and communal unity within the brotherhood," and that the notion that local church is inseparable from the universal church maintained "a balance between the autonomy of the local church and interdependence with larger ecclesial Baptist body."[79] I suggest that the proposed concept of confessing community may be extended to a wider group of believers, for just as individual believers are gathered into a community of faith so are local churches united into "gathered church" beyond the level of a local community and representing another way of being the church together.

This overview demonstrates the need for research aimed at the theological understanding of the ecclesiological nature of ACs. This monograph aims to fill this gap. It draws from historical studies, especially those that indirectly address the issue of ecclesial structures and practices among Ukrainian Baptists, but differs in that it attempts to reconstruct the theological perspectives on ACs and their associational practices. This monograph approximates the work of Keith Jones on the EBF[80] in that it is a case study on the theology of ACs expressed in the views and embodied in the practices of the All-Ukrainian Union of Churches of Evangelical Christians-Baptists.

Purpose and Scope of the Monograph

The original intention of this project was to study the understanding of the nature of ACs among three Ukrainian Baptist unions.[81] This was driven by a desire to map an understanding of ACs and from this to proceed to a constructive proposal for a local theology of ACs done in dialogue with wider ecclesiological tradition. As the work proceeded, several issues prevented the original design. First, the leaders of one of the unions were suspicious of

---

78. Tönnies and Harris, *Community and Civil Society*; Bonhoeffer and Green, *Sanctorum Communio*; Volf, *After Our Likeness*.

79. Pyzh, "Confessing Community," 124.

80. See footnote @@25, above.

81. These are the All-Ukrainian Union of Churches of Evangelical Christians-Baptists, Council of Churches of Evangelical Christians-Baptists and the Brotherhood of Independent Churches and Missions of Ukraine. On the formation and relations of these, see sections 4.3.1. and 4.3.3.

attempts to explore their past and have it presented by outsiders. Interviewing them proved to be impossible. Second, although originally all three unions related to one tradition, two of them lost any ties and developed into distinct versions of the tradition that could hardly be fitted into one folder. The project ended up concentrating on AUUCECB, which is in historical continuity with AUCECB (1944–1990), FBU of USSR (1926–1935), Union of Baptists of the USSR (1924–1926), Union of Russian Baptists (1905–1924) and Union of Russian Baptists of Southern Russia and the Caucasus (1884–1904).[82] When I refer to Ukrainian Baptists, I assume this complex and long tradition.

The overall purpose of the monograph is to (re)construct a Ukrainian Baptist understanding of the nature of ACs and develop it through critical and constructive dialogue with Paul S. Fiddes.

Research Question and Subsidiary Questions

This monograph is driven by the following question: What is the Ukrainian Baptist understanding of the ecclesiological nature of ACs as it is reflected in their practices, organisational structure and key theological documents?

To answer the research question, I need to find answers to a number of subsidiary questions:

1. How is the understanding of the nature of ACs reflected in Ukrainian Baptist historical and current practices, structures and documents?
2. How do the representatives of the AUUCECB understand the nature of ACs?
3. Upon what theological ideas does this understanding of the nature of ACs rest?
4. How does this understanding of the nature of ACs relate to local church autonomy?

---

82. In 1870, the first Baptists in the Russian Empire formed Novoobraschennoe Russkoe Bratstvo (Newly Converted Russian Brotherhood), a loose association of churches situated in the territory which now comprises Ukraine, and since that time it has been part of all the unions listed above in the form of a regional union. Participation in these unions shaped Ukrainian Baptist tradition as it is now.

5. What are the important and also problematic, conflicting or underdeveloped elements in the understanding of the AC of Ukrainian Baptists?
6. Which constructive elements from wider ecclesiological tradition may potentially fill the gaps and improve problematic areas in the Ukrainian understanding of ACs?

Methodological Approach

The project rests on the supposition that practices reflect significant convictions that constitute the character and identity of a given community.[83] This points to the necessity of investigating community practices since they represent a way of living that both exemplifies convictions and forms them. The methodology of this project follows three basic stages.[84]

Stage 1: Reconstruction of the historical understanding of ACs among Ukrainian Baptists. At this stage the project focuses on rediscovering an understanding of the ecclesiological nature of ACs as reflected in organisational structure, associational practices and significant theological texts. The main sources at this stage are minutes and resolutions of the associational conferences, statutes, official statements, circular letters, confessional texts, publications in church periodicals, memoires and diaries. The primary method is that of historical theology. I analyse sources against the subsidiary questions 1, 3 and 4.

Stage 2: Mapping current understanding of ACs. At this stage the project focuses on mapping current understandings of the ecclesiological nature of ACs as held by key Ukrainian Baptist ministers and reflected in official documents and denominational publications. At this stage of the research, a method of research interview is employed. A questionnaire builds on subsidiary questions 2, 3 and 4.[85] The data is analysed according to the procedures proposed by Bill Gillham, honorary senior lecturer in the Department of

---

83. McClendon, *Biography as Theology*, 14–23; McClendon, *Ethics*, 169–82; cf. Parushev, "Carrying Out."

84. This approach was inspired by the work of a Catholic theologian Robert J. Schreiter. See Schreiter, *Constructing Local Theologies*, 22–38.

85. See appendix 1.

Psychology at the University of Strathclyde, UK, and Sharan B. Merriam, professor of adult education at the University of Georgia, USA.[86]

Stage 3: Development of a local tradition through engagement and dialogue with wider tradition. The process of rediscovering and mapping tradition in the present context brings forth recurring theological ideas, images and concepts. It also indicates problematic, conflicting or underdeveloped elements in the understanding of the ecclesiological nature of ACs. At this stage the project turns to wider Baptist tradition, represented by Paul S. Fiddes. I analyse his primary ecclesiological writings in search of constructive elements that may throw light on, critique or fill gaps in the Ukrainian understanding of the nature of ACs. A Ukrainian understanding of ACs is put in dialogue with Paul S. Fiddes for the purpose of developing and enriching local tradition through his covenant ecclesiology.

This approach combines empirical study with a historical-theological reading of significant documents and proceeds to a constructive dialogue on a theology of AC with the selected dialogue partner. The methodology is restricted by the sources this thesis uses. The historical part is limited by the sources available for the relevant periods. Newly discovered materials may expand, add to or clarify some aspects of the thesis. Human sources are limited to a group of expert practitioners, represented by the leaders of AUUCECB.

Content of the Monograph

The monograph consists of three logical parts: chapters 1–4 are historical, traversing the understanding of ACs from 1880 to 1990; chapters 5–6 explore an understanding of ACs from 1991 to 2014; chapters 7–8 are constructive, exploring Paul S. Fiddes's covenant ecclesiology and putting it into dialogue with the findings of chapters 1–6.

Chapter 1 surveys the Baptist origins in the Russian Empire and demonstrates the hybrid nature of the movement evident in the influence of Pietist, evangelical and Baptist traditions on its shape.

Chapter 2 explores the Baptist Union in the period of its semi-official existence as an association of churches (1880–1904). It focuses on how

---

86. Gillham, *Research Interview*; Gillham, *Research Interviewing*; Merriam, *Qualitative Research*.

associational life was consolidated and structured under the leadership of Johan Wieler and Dei Mazaev. The shaping role of two associational practices – annual conferences and trans-local ministers – is highlighted. Special attention is paid to associational convictions expressed through the concept of *bratstvo* and the desire to see churches united in one mission and rooted in the unity of the Godhead.

Chapter 3 focuses on the period of geographical and organisational growth (1905–1935) which impacted organisational and leadership models, caused new forms of associational practices (annual edifying conferences) and strengthened the role of trans-local ministers. The status and role of trans-local ministers is discussed against the transformations of the Union. Indirect debates on the nature of ACs between Vasilii Pavlov (union as association of individuals) and Dei Mazaev, Vasilii Ivanov and others (union as association of churches), and the maturation of theological perspectives on ACs, are analysed against the Baptist traditions of the time.

Chapter 4 explores the period from the Second World War to the collapse of the USSR (1944–1990) when the restored AUCECB significantly departed from Baptist associational practices. Special attention is paid to the minimizing of local church involvement in associational life, the functioning of the union as the council of ministers and the mutation of trans-local ministers into denominational functionaries.

Chapter 5 sketches associational practices, organisational structure and the understanding and theological representation of ACs in the independent Ukraine (1991–2014). It demonstrates that AUUCECB in general stays in continuity with the understanding of ACs shaped at the end of the Soviet period. Special attention is paid to theological discussions on the nature of ACs and local church autonomy.

Chapter 6 outlines the ecclesiological nature of ACs as understood by the key leaders of the AUUCECB. The data is analysed under the rubrics of nature, necessity, biblical and theological arguments, the practices of ACs, the relations of local churches and ACs, and the status of trans-local ministers. I point out that pragmatic reasons occupy the central place although there are some appeals to ACs as manifestation of the universal church, the body of Christ.

Chapter 7 engages Paul S. Fiddes's covenant ecclesiology. After summarising the historical and qualitative findings, and hinting at the further development of these elements, the chapter introduces Fiddes's ecclesiological core: concepts of covenant, *koinonia* and the body of Christ. The concluding part points to which elements of Fiddes's thought could help Ukrainian Baptists develop their understanding of the nature of ACs, and in what ways.

Chapter 8 brings together a Ukrainian understanding of ACs and covenant ecclesiology. It uses cases of covenanting as the touchpoint of local tradition with Fiddes's covenant ecclesiology. It reconsiders local church as intentional and covenantal community which is free under the rule of Christ and interrelated with other churches. Then local understandings of ACs are developed through covenant ecclesiology, interpreting *bratstvo* (brotherhood) as a covenant communion of churches that visualises unity of the body of Christ in forms of associations and union, commits to mutual care through the ministry of trans-local ministers and participates in Christ's mission in the world.

Transliteration

In this monograph I follow the transliteration rules of the US Board on Geographic Names. Cities situated in historic Ukrainian territory are transliterated according to the current Ukrainian pronunciation (Kyiv not Kiev; Odesa not Odessa; Donets'k not Donetsk).

CHAPTER 1

Baptist Origins in the Russian Empire

1.1 Origins: Foreign, Indigenous or Hybrid?

Baptist origins in the Russian Empire are the subject of debates even after more than a century of research. Russian Orthodox polemicists of the nineteenth century laid responsibility for the emergence of the movement predominantly on foreign missionaries.[1] On the other hand, attempts to explain Baptist origins by providential factors look rather naïve and deserve a critique.[2] Recent scholarship seems to have reached a consensus that the Baptist movement in the Russian Empire was of neither "western" nor "indigenous" origin but "hybrid" in nature.[3]

American Baptist historian Albert Wardin argues for a complex story of Baptist origins in the Russian Empire.[4] He admits significant foreign influence from Reformed and Lutheran pietist revivals among German colonists

---

1. Ushinskii, *O Prichinakh Poiavleniia*; Aleksii Ia. (Dorodnitsyn), *Iuzhno-Russkii Neobaptizm*. For a more deliberated version see Rozhdestvenskii, *Iuzhnorusskii Shtundizm*.

2. For a providential view, see Kmeta-Efimovich, "Zhyvye Kamni"; Domashovets', *Narys Istorii*; Savinskii, *Istoriia Evangelskikh Khristian-Baptistov Ukrainy, Rossii, Belorussii (1867–1917)*; and Savinskii, *Istoriia Evangelskikh Khristian-Baptistov Ukrainy, Rossii, Belorussii (1917–1967)*. For a moderate version, see Reshetnikov and Sannikov, *Obzor Istorii*. For modifications of the self-identifying story, see Puzynin, *Tradition*, 121, 149–69, 192–212.

3. The concept of "hybridity" is widely used in post-colonial theory. Borrowed from horticulture, where cross-pollination produces "hybrid" variety, in post-colonial theory it refers to transcultural linguistic, cultural, political or racial forms that emerge in the areas dominated by colonization. See Ashcroft et al., *Postcolonial Studies*, 108–11; see also Prabhu, *Hybridity*; Acheraïou, *Questioning Hybridity*.

4. See Wardin, *On the Edge*.

while also recognizing the importance of such factors as the translation and circulation of Scriptures, emancipation of serfs and the failure of the Orthodox Church to meet the needs of the people. All these amalgamated into a movement containing bits of various traditions. Heather Coleman admits the formative role of foreign tradition but points out that "although Russian Baptists constantly engaged foreign ideas and models, these were not accepted without challenge, and, indeed, much soul-searching."[5] Thus, here "hybridity" simply points to the historical processes that produced a distinct version of Baptists through the interplay of foreign and local strands of tradition.[6]

The movement originated in the southern provinces of Ukraine, Transcaucasia, and St Petersburg. It touched different social groups, and this determined the role respective communities played in the process of the movement's formation in the Russian Empire. These streams developed independently for some time, absorbing and crystallizing various foreign and local influences, but then began "gradually finding one another, acknowledging their spiritual kinship, and, by the early 1880s, seeking paths to joint activity."[7]

1.2 Stundists and Stundo-Baptists in Ukraine

In Ukraine the revival spread in Kherson, Ekaterinoslav, Tavrida and Kyiv *gubernii* (provinces), among the moderately well-to-do or the poorest landless peasants who worked seasonally in German colonies and growing cities.[8]

---

5. Coleman, "Baptist Beginnings," 31.

6. For such a use of "hybridity," see Wardin, "How Indigenous," 31–32. For a stronger emphasis on the foreign role, see Steeves, "Russian Baptist Union"; Beznosova, "Pozdnee Protestantskoe Sektantstvo"; and Coleman, "Most Dangerous Sect." For a stronger emphasis on the indigenous role, see Zhuk, *Russia's Lost Reformation*.

7. Coleman, "Baptist Beginnings," 24.

8. Russian Empress Catherine II (1729–1796) initiated the process of the foreign colonisation of Ukraine in the second half of the eighteenth century, trying to attract different religious nonconformist groups from Europe. By the middle of the nineteenth century, diverse ethnic and religious groups populated the territories of the northern Black Sea area between the rivers of Danube and Dnipro. Colonists of different religious traditions (Lutherans, Reformed, Moravians, and Mennonites) were granted broad privileges: the right of self-government inside of the colonies and the freedom to worship according to their custom with only one reservation – attempts to convert native Orthodox people were illegal. On this complex story, see Friesen and Toews, *Mennonite Brotherhood*, 201–574; see also Plokhy, *Gates of Europe*, 140–46; Hrytsak, *Narysy z Istorii Ukraiiny*, 35. For Marxist interpretation of the revival, see Klibanov, *Istoria Religioznogo Sektantstva*, 190–201. For recent analysis of the Ukrainian movement, see Beznosova, "Pozdnee Protestantskoe Sektantstvo," 108–15.

The lower social status and insufficient level of literacy of the first converts explains why leadership and formative ideas came from outside sources.[9]

The first conversions, formation of communities and growth occurred from the end of the 1850s to the middle of the 1860s. Early centres of revival were in the villages adjacent to the German colonies of Rohrbach and Worms in Odesa *uezd* (district) and Alt-Danzig in Elisavetgrad *uezd*.[10] Earlier, Reformed pastor Johannes Bonekemper (1795–1857), his son Karl Bonekemper (1817–1893) and a separatist Lutheran minister Eduard Wüst (1818–1859) worked there. Both Bonekempers discouraged separatism from existing parishes, while Wüst advocated creating separatist communities of "true believers."[11]

The first group of Ukrainian converts was reported to emerge in Osnova village around 1861–1862.[12] They were labelled "Stundists" after the German practice of pious gatherings (*Stunden*) in private houses. The dispatch of a local conciliator to the Odesa governor on 12 March 1866 reported a group of peasants who were

> constantly in touch with the local colonists and some of them worked for colonists for several years, being simple and uneducated, got used to the colonists' customs and practically learned the German language and, probably because of the German Reformed Stundists turned to their teaching. This opinion is based on that fact that the Reformed colonists are also gathering at night in one house to sing hymns and read books of sacred content.[13]

The movement was very complex.[14] Some groups maintained Orthodox practices, while others were more critical towards them. Local priest Stoikov

---

9. Aleksii Ia. (Dorodnitsyn), *Materialy*, 60–64.

10. Osnova, Riasnopol' and Ignatovka, and Karlovka and Liubomyrka, respectively.

11. VSEKhB, *Istoriia Evangelskikh Khristian-Baptistov v SSSR*, 41–42.

12. Aleksii Ia. (Dorodnitsyn), *Iuzhno-Russkii Neobaptizm*, 118–21. Klippenstein says Johann Wieler began preaching to Ukrainians in 1860; see Klippenstein, "Johann Wieler," 48.

13. Aleksii Ia. (Dorodnitsyn), *Materialy*, 47. All translations from Russian or Ukrainian are original translations by the author unless indicated otherwise.

14. For distinctions between indigenous quasi-Orthodox groups and the groups ignited by foreigners, see Beznosova, "Pozdnee Protestantskoe Sektantstvo," 67–74. Aleksii calls the latter *neo-baptist* (see Aleksii Ia. (Dorodnitsyn), *Iuzhno-Russkii Neobaptizm*, passim). Klibanov calls the former *stundists* and the latter *stundo-baptists*. See Klibanov, *Istoria Religioznogo*

reported in 1865 that he often visited Osnova and saw icons in every sectarian house and during his prayers "every suspect family paid due veneration to the icons."[15] On 16 February 1867, the Odesa captain of the police reported to the Kherson governor that groups of Stundists in Ignatovka, Riasnopol' and Osnova

> gather in premises selected by them, read Church-Slavonic books and discuss their meaning and content under the guidance, nevertheless, of some Reformed sectarians, Germans from the neighbouring colony of Rohrbach. As a result, the peasants, followers of the sect, formed strong opinions which prevent them from going to the Orthodox Church, venerating holy icons and performing any Orthodox rite.[16]

These reports refer to one locale, Osnova. Perhaps initially these groups remained in the Orthodox Church, at the same time practicing what resembled a traditional Pietistic model of *ecclesiola in ecclesia*, encouraged by Bonnekemper.[17] This model worked well in the Lutheran and Reformed parish church system but could not sustain a revival in the Orthodox Church for the obvious reason that the practice of *Stunden* was alien to the Orthodox community. Neither Orthodox priests nor the majority of the population were ready to accept this practice as part of their everyday piety. Thus, a cumulative force of pressure from Orthodox priests and population, the administrative measures of local authorities, contact with Germans who had converted to become Baptists and a growing self-awareness gradually transformed Stundist

---

Sektantstva, 188; cf. Wardin, *On the Edge*, 116–20. Domashovets' differentiates quasi-Orthodox *stundists* and Ukrainian Baptists, dissociating the latter from the extreme sectarian tendencies of the former and pointing to the "strong organisation, democratic order and high moral requirements for their members" among the Baptists (Domashovets', *Narys Istorii*, 110–11). See comment on other Stundists in Klippenstein, "Johann Wieler," 53–54.

15. Aleksii Ia. (Dorodnitsyn), *Iuzhno-Russkii Neobaptizm*, 119.

16. Aleksii Ia. (Dorodnitsyn), *Materialy*, 47–48.

17. Responding to a charge of converting Ukrainians, Karl Bonekemper wrote in *Odesskii Vestnik* (Odesa Herald): "The Stundist brotherhood existing in the colonies of Rohrbach and Worms in the Kherson *guberniia* is neither a sect nor a schism but a community of parishioners who love religious mood in daily life. Stundists were always sincere worshippers in common service." Aleksii Ia. (Dorodnitsyn), *Iuzhno-Russkii Neobaptizm*, 123.

groups into Protestant churches. However, it seems Ukrainian converts did not formally break away from the Orthodox Church until 1869.[18]

Several baptisms of Ukrainian peasants occurred prior to 1869,[19] but only the baptism of Efim Tsymbal in 1869 ignited a Baptist movement among other Ukrainian Stundists. Tsymbal baptised Trifon Khlystun and the brothers Gavrilenkov and Ivan Riaboshapka.[20] By 1873 communities in Ignatovka, Karlovka and Liubomyrka were organised into Baptist churches with ordained ministers, who baptised new converts and performed the Lord's Supper, marriages and funerals. As will be demonstrated below, Mennonite Brethren assisted Ukrainians in organising into an association and crystallizing their confession of faith.[21] Mennonite Brethren themselves trod the way from an ethno-confessional group of German colonists in the Russian Empire to a mission-minded one due to the formative influence of Wüst's brotherhoods[22] and German Baptists.[23] This Mennonite group separated from German Mennonite colonists and eventually managed to acquire recognition from the Russian government by 1862.[24] German Baptists influenced Mennonite

---

18. See notes @@12 and 13 above. Perhaps, that fact that Efim Tsymbal was baptised was considered by the Orthodox priests as the formal break with the Orthodox Church. Karl Bonekemper grieved that Ukrainians left the Orthodox Church: "I . . . did not want at all to make Russians followers of our brotherhood apostate from the Orthodox Church and create a sect of them. . . . I always refrained from this great evil." Ushinskii, *O Prichinakh Poiavleniia*, 10–11.

19. Savinskii, *Istoriia Evangelskikh Khristian-Baptistov Ukrainy, Rossii, Belorussii (1867–1917)*, 112–13.

20. Savinskii, *Istoriia Evangelskikh Khristian-Baptistov Ukrainy, Rossii, Belorussii (1867–1917)*, 112–13.

21. The Mennonite Brethren was a group that emerged on the wave of revival among German colonists inspired by Eduard Wüst in the 1850s. On the origin and development of Mennonite Brethren in the Russian Empire see Friesen and Toews, *Mennonite Brotherhood*, 87–200; Bondar, *Sekta Mennonitov v Rossii*; Toews, "Russian Origin," 78–107; Wardin, *On the Edge*, 55–92.

22. On Wüst, see Doerksen, "Second Menno?"; Doerksen, "Eduard Wüst and Jerusalem"; Jantz, "Pietist Pastor."

23. J. A. Toews admits affinity in closed communion, evangelism and the mode of baptism between German colonists and Ukrainians but registers dissimilarities in non-resistance, foot washing, abstinence from alcohol and tobacco, and church polity. See Toews, "Baptists and Mennonite Brethren," 92–93; cf. Wardin, "Baptist Influences," 205–10; Wardin, "Mennonite Brethren," 97–112.

24. Kreider, "Anabaptist Conception," 25.

Brethren in such aspects as believer's baptism,[25] their organisational model and church polity.[26]

One of the most noticeable figures in the process of transforming Stundist groups into Protestant communities was Johann Wieler (1839–1889) from Khortitsa, who acquired a good command of both Russian and Ukrainian languages. In 1860 he joined the Mennonite Brethren and actively evangelised German colonists and Ukrainians.[27] On 7 November 1884, in a letter to German donors, Wieler tells the story of his early missionary efforts among the Ukrainian population in Odesa and Ekaterinoslav and of involvement in the movement among the native population.[28] This document throws light on the formative years of the movement among Ukrainians. Its promotional nature and the somewhat magnified role of Wieler should be admitted.[29] Nevertheless, it fits into historiographical consensus and coincides with other witnesses. Thus, Mikhail Ratushnyi,[30] in his letter to Hermann Fast,[31] recalls Iakov Deliakov's help in edifying new converts in 1866–1867,[32] along with Wieler who "introduced the order of how to admit into community, taught the presbyters, preachers and so on."[33] Wieler helped Ukrainians understand the importance of believer's baptism,[34] encouraged them to withdraw from the

---

25. Toews, "Baptists and Mennonite Brethren," 85.

26. In 1866, August Liebig arrived from Romania to organise the Einlage community according to Baptist order and resolve tensions. A two-week visit proved to be successful. Later, Karl Benzien introduced new organisational principles, ordained elders and established missionary stations according to the German Baptist model. See VSEKhB, *Istoriia Evangelskikh Khristian-Baptistov v SSSR*, 459–61; Val'kevich, *Zapiska*, 57, 114; Val'kevich, *Zapiska*, Appendix 1, 45–47.

27. Wardin, *On the Edge*, 114–16; Klippenstein, "Johann Wieler," 45.

28. Klippenstein, "Johann Wieler," 48.

29. Wieler incorrectly calls Ratushnyi the first Ukrainian convert, when in fact he was influenced by Feodor Onischchenko. See Wardin, *On the Edge*, 104–5; Domashovets', *Narys Istorii*, 114–19. Ratushnyi recalls Onishchenko's influence on his conversion. See Val'kevich, *Zapiska*, Appendix 5, 133–34.

30. Mikhail Ratushnyi (1830–c. 1915) was one of the first Ukrainian converts, leader of the church in Osnova and one of the leaders of the Baptist movement in Ukraine. See Wardin, *On the Edge*, 102–7.

31. Hermann I. Fast (1880–1935) was a German Mennonite who trained in a missionary school in Switzerland and was one of the leaders of the evangelical movement in the Russian Empire. See Wardin, 243.

32. Iakov Deliakov or Jakob D. Delyakov (1833–1898) was an evangelical Nestorian from Persia, working as a colporteur and independent missionary in Russia. See Wardin, 152–53.

33. Val'kevich, *Zapiska*, Appendix 5, 135.

34. Klippenstein, "Johann Wieler," 49.

Orthodox Church and form their own congregations,[35] and assisted in composing a confession of faith that "agreed with the statement used by Baptists in Germany" and a petition to Alexander II, to be presented by Riaboshapka, Ratushnyi and Kapustian.[36] Wieler also took an active role in organising communities in Ukraine, Southern Russia and the Caucasus into a union.[37]

Thus, it is hard to imagine what the movement would have looked like without the help and advice provided by Mennonite Brethren and, indirectly, by German Baptists. This influence is obvious if the social portrait and literacy level of the first Ukrainian converts is considered. It is impossible to imagine the formation of stable communities and the subsequent organisation of the communities into one union without Ukrainian Baptists' acquaintance with the Western models.

1.3 Baptists in Transcaucasia

In Transcaucasia, revival predominantly touched the affluent or middle merchant Molokan[38] families.[39] The first convert, Nikita Isaevich Voronin (1840–1905), a Molokan believer and presbyter, was baptised on 20 August 1867 by Martin Kalweit (1833–1918), a Lithuanian-born German Lutheran who became a Baptist.[40] In 1871, Voronin baptised Vasilii G. Pavlov (1854–1924) and Vasilii V. Ivanov (1846–1919) who became key Russian Baptist leaders.

---

35. Klippenstein, "Johann Wieler," 49–50.

36. Klippenstein, 49–50. This is *Pravila Veroispovedaniia Novoobraschennogo Russkogo Bratstva* [Rules of Confession of Faith of the Newly Converted Russian Brotherhood]. Perhaps, "the statement used by Baptists in Germany" stands for the Hamburg Confession of Faith (1847). For the text of the confession see Aleksii Ia. (Dorodnitsyn), *Materialy*, 477–82; cf. analysis of the principal points of the Mennonite Brethren Confession of Faith and the Hamburg Confession of Faith in Aleksii Ia. (Dorodnitsyn), *Iuzhno-Russkii Neobaptizm*, 107–16.

37. See section 2.1.2.

38. The Molokans ("milk drinkers") are a Russian non-conformist group named after the practice of drinking milk during Lent. This group emerged in the 1770s in Tambov *gubernia*, adhered to the authority of the Bible, salvation by Christ's sacrifice and priesthood of all believers. They rejected priests and saints and understood the sacraments spiritually. They sought to restore New Testament church practices and only recognised elders. During worship services they read Scriptures and sang Psalms. See Karetnikova, "Russkoe Bogoiskatel'stvo," 66–72. They obtained official permission to practice their faith by 1805. On their origin, beliefs and practices, see Iuzov, *Russkie Dissidenty*, 144–71; and Bolshakoff, *Russian Nonconformity*, 105–9.

39. Breyfogle, "Heretics and Colonizers," 282–83.

40. According to Vasilii V. Ivanov, the first conversions in Transcaucasia were through personal Bible study, and the German influence through Vasilii Pavlov and Johann Wieler was

Tiflis church, which consisted only of twelve members in 1871 and twenty in 1879, existed as a loose community. Voronin developed *Ustav Bogosluzheniia i Dogmaty Very* (Divine service order and doctrines of faith) which perished in the fire of 1879 together with the church building.[41] In 1875 Pavlov went to Hamburg to the missionary school where he was ordained by Gerhard Oncken as a missionary. Pavlov mastered English, German, Hebrew, Azerbaijani and other languages. The knowledge of Baptist doctrines and polity equipped him to order communities in Transcaucasia according to German tradition. He translated the Hamburg Confession of Faith, the basis of Russian Baptists' beliefs, and in 1907 prepared a draft of the statute for the Russian Baptist Union. In 1876 Pavlov returned. He was elected as presbyter in 1879 and in 1880 was ordained by Johann Kargel (c. 1846–1933) and August Liebig (1836–1914), German Baptist ministers in St. Petersburg and Odessa.[42] All this time Voronin was acting as presbyter and led the community perhaps because of his Molokan presbytership.

The Tiflis church became an influential early Baptist centre in the Russian Empire. Orthodox scholars and government officials accumulated a significant share of the documents that help to reconstruct the beliefs and practices of this community.[43] These documents show the influence of German Baptists on the Tiflis church. Val'kevich names Vasilii G. Pavlov as one of the key leaders who attempted to unify the nascent Russian Baptist movement along

---

not significant. See Ivanov, "Kniga Episkopa Aleksiia," 24–25; see also Breyfogle, "Heretics and Colonizers," 298–302.

41. Savinskii, *Istoriia Evangelskikh Khristian-Baptistov Ukrainy, Rossii, Belorussii (1867–1917)*, 135. Malkhaz Songulashvili translated into English a very important document, "Russian Baptist Congregation in Tiflis," composed by the Orthodox priest Nikolai Kallistov. This document mentions Vasilii N. Treskovskii, a former teacher at the local classic school and Orthodox seminary who was educated at St. Petersburg University and had wide knowledge of classical and modern languages, as the one who "started organisational work of the congregation." Songulashvili, *Evangelical Christian*, 345–46. On the conversion of Treskovskii, see V. Pavlov's letter to V. Ivanov in Val'kevich, *Zapiska*, Appendix 5, 1.

42. Savinskii, *Istoriia Evangelskikh Khristian-Baptistov Ukrainy, Rossii, Belorussii (1867–1917)*, 137; Val'kevich, *Zapiska*, Appendix 1, 45–47. Soon a conflict between Voronin and Pavlov emerged: Voronin was charged with getting interest on loans and excommunicated. See Songulashvili, *Evangelical Christian*, 350–51.

43. For minutes of church meetings for 1879–1885, see Val'kevich, *Zapiska*, Appendix 1, 32–64, and Aleksii Ia. (Dorodnitsyn), *Materialy*, 601–77. For catechisms and regulations on community practices, see Val'kevich, *Zapiska*, Appendix 2, 1–14, and Aleksii Ia. (Dorodnitsyn), *Materialy*, 677–86. For excerpts from early periodicals, see Val'kevich, *Zapiska*, Appendix 3, 1–69, 119–29. For Vasilii V. Ivanov's diaries and reports for 1883–1889, see Val'kevich, Appendix 4, 1–39. For selected correspondence, see Val'kevich, *Zapiska*, Appendix 5, 1–176.

German Baptist lines. Pavlov was familiar with Western publications and drew from them in his teaching. In his letter to Ivanov written in November 1873, Pavlov refers to Spurgeon's sermons[44] and Robert Haldane's commentary on Romans.[45] He mentioned ordering from Odesa a history of Baptists and a Baptist confession of faith in German which he planned to translate.[46] His attempts intensified after his return from Hamburg. One case is exemplary of these attempts. On 17 August 1880, Pavlov, on behalf of Tiflis Baptist Church, invited August Liebig and Johannes Kargel to properly constitute the Tiflis community and ordain Pavlov as presbyter. During the procedure, Liebig and Kargel even offered for the Tiflis Baptist Church to join the German Baptist Union.[47]

The opposing group tried to retain such aspects of Molokan spirituality as the singing of the Psalms and even creatively drew from the Orthodox ecclesial practices. This group is represented by Voronin, and to some extent, Vasilii Ivanov, who compiled the proposal on reorganisation of Baptist communities in the Caucasus (hereafter "O Reorganisatsii").[48] This aligns with the fact that after 1880, when Pavlov became presbyter, the Tiflis church moved to the German Baptist model.[49] According to Ivanov, all communi-

---

44. "Kak deti Bozh'i mogut dostigat uverennosti v proshchenii" (How God's children may reach assurance of salvation) and "Sokhranenie Tserkvi" (Protection of the church). See Val'kevich, *Zapiska*, Appendix 5, 2. Perhaps, "Full Assurance" (28 April 1861) and "Security of the Church" (1 November 1857), respectively.

45. Val'kevich, *Zapiska*, Appendix 5, 5.

46. Val'kevich, *Zapiska*, Appendix 5, 4.

47. Val'kevich, *Zapiska*, Appendix 1, 45–47. Bishop Aleksii *contra* Val'kevich believes it never happened, though they maintained close relations. See for comparison, Aleksii Ia. (Dorodnitsyn), *Materialy*, 689; Val'kevich, *Zapiska*, 62.

48. Val'kevich, *Zapiska*, Appendix 2, 12–14; Aleksii Ia. (Dorodnitsyn), *Materialy*, 686–90. For an English translation, see Songulashvili, *Evangelical Christian*, 361–66. It was confiscated during a search on 7 June 1884 but was actually composed before 1879. Songulashvili incorrectly ascribes it to an unknown author and dates it to around 1890, while Aleksii and Val'kevich firmly point to Ivanov's authorship. Val'kevich dates the document to before 1879. See Aleksii Ia. (Dorodnitsyn), *Vnutrenniaia Organisatsiia*, 9; Val'kevich, *Zapiska*, Appendix 2, 12. The document reflects on the mission of the church (introduction and section 6), moral concerns aimed at the contextualization of Russian Baptists preaching in the Caucasus (sections 1–4), the organisational model (section 5), the salary of ministers and missionaries (section 7) and the washing of feet (section 8; see Aleksii Ia. [Dorodnitsyn], *Materialy*, 601–77). For a comparison between Tiflis church's organisational model and polity and that of German Baptists, see Val'kevich, *Zapiska*, 57, 59–61. For a detailed analysis of the document, see Songulashvili, *Evangelical Christian Baptists*, 70–78.

49. Tensions between the "German" and "Russian" model were still in the air even in the 1910s. See Coleman, "Most Dangerous Sect," 50–53; O[dintsov], "S'ezd Baptistov v S.-

ties in Transcaucasia should unite into one Tiflis church or Transcaucasia community.[50] Smaller communities, which were dependent on Tiflis, Ivanov called "locales" (*mesta*) or "stations" (*stantsii*).[51] Tiflis church should elect a presbyter, a presbyter's assistant, two deacons and a treasurer and the "stations" should elect teachers or deacons, if the membership was even smaller.[52] He also called the "stations" under teachers' leadership, "departments of the community or the church," and those which were under deacons leadership, "stations of the department."[53] Commenting on the use of finances at the end of section 5, he spoke of the "union's treasury" and explained that money could be taken from this fund only with the presbyter's approval.[54]

According to Ivanov, a presbyter was responsible for leading worship and performing sacraments and such rites as weddings and funerals. He oversaw "the right actions of the teachers who [were] responsible to him, and his deacons and treasurers" and considered complaints concerning teachers, deciding "them according to his discretion, in terms of decision which should be accepted by all if it [was] not contrary to God's Word."[55] Assistants, teachers or deacons could also do all this if the presbyter delegated his rights to them. Teachers had the same rights in their communities as the presbyter in Tiflis with only one restriction: they should teach "not from the pulpit (cathedra) but from a simple table."[56] Deacons did not have these rights; they could lead worship and read the Scriptures with a short explanation but could only have the responsibilities of a teacher if such were delegated to them.

The structure of the Transcaucasia community looks hierarchical: teachers are subject to a presbyter and deacons to the nearby teacher. The presbyter controls the "union's treasury," and teachers control the "stations' treasury."[57] The presbyter could only be removed if all teachers agreed with this decision. Teachers could be removed only with the approval of the presbyter, and

---

Peterburge," 304; Breyfogle, "Heretics and Colonizers," 325.
    50. Aleksii Ia. (Dorodnitsyn), *Materialy*, 689.
    51. Aleksii Ia. (Dorodnitsyn), *Materialy*, 690.
    52. Aleksii Ia. (Dorodnitsyn), *Materialy*, 689.
    53. Aleksii Ia. (Dorodnitsyn), *Materialy*, 690.
    54. Songulashvili overlooks this in his analysis of the document.
    55. Aleksii Ia. (Dorodnitsyn), *Materialy*, 690.
    56. Aleksii Ia. (Dorodnitsyn), *Materialy*, 689.
    57. Aleksii Ia. (Dorodnitsyn), *Materialy*, 690.

deacons with the teachers' approval.⁵⁸ Songulashivli calls this ecclesiological model "Proto-Orthodox Patriarchate," similar to those of Jerusalem or Antioch.⁵⁹ He also assumes that this structure was partially aimed at meeting the need for proper superintendence of the newly established communities of faith.⁶⁰ He is certainly right in supposing that the author of the document manifests an attempt to combine Orthodox and Western Baptist ecclesiology. However, the terminology of the text is underdeveloped and even confusing: from "community/church" and "stations," Ivanov turns to "union" and "departments." It seems that thinking of "Tiflis church" as a union of local churches rather than a territorial local church, as in the Orthodox tradition, was more natural for him. The model proposed in the document manifested itself in the decision of the Tiflis conference "of election of one presbyter and constituting of one community in the Caucasus and Transcaucasia."⁶¹ However, we do not have evidence confirming that this model lasted for any significant time.

Pavlov's perspective prevailed over the autochthonous one. Tiflis Baptists strongly held to believer's baptism and opposed open communion with pedo-baptists. They placed confessional and doctrinal consistency over the common experience of regeneration. Their rigid position on the issue of communion caused significant tensions with evangelical Christians.⁶² In the 1910s, Pavlov introduced Russian Baptists to the American Baptist ecclesial models by translating and publishing excerpts from Edward Hiscox's influential manual.⁶³ His influence was formative for Russian and Soviet Baptists, and its repercussions are felt even now.

---

58. Aleksii Ia. (Dorodnitsyn), *Materialy*, 689.

59. Songulashvili, *Evangelical Christian Baptists*, 72–73.

60. Songulashvili, 71–72. See Ivanov on the necessity of supervision in Val'kevich, *Zapiska*, Appendix 1, 38. See details in section 2.3.2.

61. Aleksii Ia. (Dorodnitsyn), *Materialy*, 622; Val'kevich, *Zapiska*, Appendix 1, 38.

62. Evangelical Christians or Gospel Christians are the believers associated with the St. Petersburg revival. See section 1.4. The conflict occurred in 1884 during a meeting in St. Petersburg. See VSEKhB, *Istoriia Evangelskikh Khristian-Baptistov v SSSR*, 99–100. Minutes from 1885 and 1889 meetings witness to this strict position. See Aleksii Ia. (Dorodnitsyn), *Materialy*, 590–91, 608.

63. This aspect will be discussed in section 3.4.1.

1.4 Evangelical Christians in St. Petersburg[64]

In St. Petersburg, conversions occurred among high-ranking society and the nobility and only later reached the lower classes. The revival drew on British evangelicalism represented by such personalities as Granville A. W. Waldgrave, 3rd Baron Radstock (1833–1913); Reginald Radcliffe (1825–1895); Dr. Frederick Baedeker (1823–1906); and George Müller (1805–1898).

Lord Radstock's arrival in St. Petersburg in 1873 sparked a so-called "drawing-room revival" among nobility.[65] He converted Colonel Vasilii Pashkov (1831–1902), Count Modest Korf (1842–1933) and Count Aleksei Bobrinskii (1826–1894), who became key leaders of the movement later labelled "Pashkovism."[66] Radstock was a typical representative of nineteenth century British evangelicalism. He belonged to the "low wing" of the Church of England. At the same time, not being a member of a particular local church, he joined the Evangelical Alliance in 1865. He also associated for some time with the Open Brethren but severed these relations before his trip to Russia.[67] Radstock seems to have been instrumental in acquainting the converted nobility with the Evangelical Alliance model, a tradition that characterised the Pashkovite movement and distinguished it from Stundo-Baptist and Baptist fellow believers in Southern Russia.

On the other hand, Dr. Baedeker, a traveling evangelist of distinctly Open Brethren heritage,[68] and George Müller, one of the founders of the Open Brethren church, were likely instrumental in introducing St. Petersburg believers to the practice of open communion characteristic of this group. Baedeker also had close ties with the Evangelical Alliance[69] and was actively involved in preparations for the first congress in St. Petersburg in 1884.[70]

---

64. Here English "Evangelical" stands for Russian *Evangel'skii*, sometimes rendered as "Gospel," and refers to the revival movement among Orthodox high-ranking society associated with St-Petersburg. See Puzynin, *Tradition*.

65. On Radstock's ministry, see Leskov and Muckle, *Schism in High Society*; Fountain, *Lord Radstock*; McCarthy, "Religious Conflict."

66. On Paskovism, see Heier, *Religious Schism*; Surer, "Colonel V. A. Pashkov"; Corrado, "Philosophy."

67. For analysis of Radstock's theological trajectory, see Puzynin, *Tradition*, 1–52. Kuznetsova points to Radstock's connections with Open Brethren. Kuznetsova, "Early Russian Evangelicals," 104–6.

68. Kuznetsova, "Early Russian Evangelicals," 119–25.

69. Latimer, *Dr. Baedeker*, 209.

70. VSEKhB, *Istoriia Evangelskikh Khristian-Baptistov v SSSR*, 99–100.

These leaders contributed to the distinctly ecumenical stance and the weak ecclesiology of the St. Petersburg stream of the evangelical movement.[71] The representatives of this tradition sought unity in the personal experience of conversion and did not require believer's baptism as a condition for fellowship. The key expression of the ecumenical spirit of the Evangelical Alliance was the practice of open communion. Later Evangelical Christians to some extent influenced Russian Baptists who "turned into evangelicals losing some measure of their closedness, intolerance, formalism and fixation on rites."[72]

1.5 Summary

The origins and early development of the Baptist movement in the Russian Empire points to an amalgamation of multiple factors and traditions, forms of spirituality (Pietism) and confessional, ecclesial and organisational shapes (German Baptist via Mennonite Brethren) into a complex and adaptable movement. The hybrid character of the movement manifests itself in the way Russian Baptists appropriated and adapted both the confessional stance and ecclesial forms of their Western brethren. It is particularly evident in the adoption of the Hamburg Confession of Faith by Transcaucasia Baptists, and its formative influence on the Ukrainian *Pravila Veroispovedaniia Novoobraschennogo Russkogo Bratstva* (Rules of confession of faith of the newly converted Russian brotherhood). The hybridity points to the necessity of interaction with wider tradition. As will be demonstrated in the next chapter, this outside influence encompasses not only confessional components but practices – associational practices in particular.

---

71. Heier, *Religious Schism*, 145. In this, Pashkovism resembled Pietism in the German colonies, which was dependent on charismatic persons and was not ecclesiologically sustainable. Cf. Val'kevich, *Zapiska*, 38.

72. Val'kevich, *Zapiska*, 157–58.

CHAPTER 2

The Brotherhood Period (1880–1904)

2.1 Introduction

Between 1880 and 1904 a handful of churches, scattered throughout the southern part of Ukraine, Russia and the Caucasus, grew into a movement which encompassed the whole south of the Russian Empire, including Ukraine, the Caucasus, Transcaucasia and the lower course of the Volga River, and even reaching St. Petersburg in the north and the Amur River in the Rusian Far East.[1]

The expansion usually followed a certain pattern. After initial conversions and a period of dependence on external leadership, there followed installation of a local presbyter, teachers and deacons. Evangelisation of the nearby villages continued and missionary stations, depending on the established church, were formed. The stations grew into churches and continued the work further. Later stations, together with central community, formed local associations.[2]

---

1. The Orthodox priests reported 2,000 Baptists in Kyiv by 1884 and 3,000 in Kherson *gubernia*, who by 1891 had grown by 5,000 (Klibanov, *Istoria Religioznogo Sektantstva*, 208). The area expanded: in 1884 Baptists were in 95 villages in Kherson *gubernia* and by 1891 spread to 167 villages. By the 1890s, Baptists were present in 30 *gubernias* of the Russian Empire (Klibanov, 207). In 1905, at the first World Baptist Congress in London, Dei Mazaev reported 20,000 Baptists among Russians. See Mitrokhin, *Baptizm*, 250.

2. Val'kevich explains the growth by (1) the active role of German ministers in constituting communities; (2) the preparatory role of Stundist or evangelical preaching; (3) the indecision and inconsistency of the local governor; (4) the constitution of communities and arrangement of inter-church ties for the sake of missions. Val'kevich, *Zapiska*, 59–62; cf. Dyck, "Zavisimost Nezavisimosti," 285.

This was a period of mixed hopes. Thus, on 27 March 1879, the Governing Senate granted to Baptists legal right to practice their faith.[3] In 1882, the Ober-Procurator of the Holy Synod, Konstanitn Pobedonostsev (1827–1907), restricted application of this regulation to German Baptists.[4] On 3 May 1883, another document granted to the sectarians the right to worship but forbade dissemination of their faith among the Orthodox population. In 1882–1896, persecution, administrative banishment and even deportation of some leaders of the movement was usual.[5] Legal and administrative measures were coupled with a series of anti-sectarian conferences led by Orthodox missionaries and aimed at sectarians.[6] These efforts slowed down the quantitative and organisational growth of Baptists, but they also enhanced the transition of leadership from German to Russian believers.

At this period, different Baptist churches began consolidating to unite the dispersed communities for the sake of mission and survival.[7] Other groups, especially the Pashkovites, whose leadership was expelled from the country by 1884,[8] sought to join the union. Under the persecutions, Baptists and evangelical Christians could not develop official structures beyond local communities. They maintained unofficial relations grounded in a common understanding of faith and mission, and these initial contacts and loose

---

3. Reshetnikov, *Ukrainskie Baptisty i Rossiiskaia Imperiia*, 45–50. Because of the initial confusion as to the meaning of the document, Russian and Ukrainian Baptists enjoyed relative freedom by 1882.

4. Savinskii, *Istoriia Evangelskikh Khristian-Baptistov Ukrainy, Rossii, Belorussii (1867–1917)*, 176.

5. For evidence, see *Istoriia Evangel'skogo Dvizheniia* 1.1. Russan Baptist historians call the years from 1882 to 1905 "the Pobedonostsev's period" after the name of the chief procurator of the Holy Synod. See also Savinskii, *Istoriia Evangelskikh Khristian-Baptistov Ukrainy, Rossii, Belorussii (1867–1917)*, 170–232.

6. For an example of published materials that produced such conferences, see Kal'nev, *Russkie Sektanty*.

7. Johannes Dyck frames the period between composing *Pravila Veroispovedania* (c. 1870) and the election of Dei Mazaev as supervisor of the union's affairs (1887; Dyck, "Zavisimost Nezavisimosti," 277). Joining existing unions or forming a new one began in the mid-1870s and intensified by 1880. On participation of Mennonites and Russian Baptists in the 1874 meeting of the South-West Russian and Bulgarian [Baptist] Association, see reference to Pritzkau in Dyck, "Moulding the Brotherhood," 62–63. Beznosova, "Germanskii vopros," 412. Minutes of Tiflis Baptist Church date attempts to establish a missionary union to 1878 (see Val'kevich, *Zapiska*, Appendix 1, 33–34). For the meeting in 1880 in Novo-Vasil'evka, see Plett, *Zarozhdenie Tserkvei EkhB*; cf. Pavlov, "Pravda o Baptistakh," 345.

8. Heier, *Religious Schism*, 145.

organisational forms laid the foundation for the Baptist Union after the Edict of Toleration (1905).[9]

2.2 Formation and Structuring of Associations of Churches

The formation of Baptist organisational and associational practices evolved around annual conferences that laid the foundation for organisational and confessional unity.[10] The meetings led to the establishment of the Union of Believers, Baptized Christians, or so-called Baptists of Southern Russia and the Caucasus (1884), which later transformed into the Union of Evangelical Christians-Baptists (1903).[11]

2.2.1 Early Attempts to Organise Union

Several documents witness live and intense communication between different churches in the late 1870s. The minutes of Tiflis Baptist Church from 13 May 1879 record discussion of the letter sent by Mikhail Rathushnyi, presbyter of Osnova church, asking to admit the community into the missionary union but allow them to retain their donations to the mission fund in their church treasury and use it at their discretion. This request was declined on the grounds that membership in the union involved donation into the missionary fund.[12] The first conference of Russian Baptists occurred in Tiflis (1879).[13] The participants approved two important decisions. The first was to establish a missions committee and appoint a missionary. The committee

---

9. According to this document, published on 17 April 1905, Russian Baptists and other sectarian groups received religious freedom. For more on the significance of the document, see *105 Let Legalizatsii Russkogo Baptizma*, and Savinskii, *Istoriia Evangelskikh Khristian-Baptistov Ukrainy, Rossii, Belorussii (1867–1917)*, 247–52.

10. Data on the conferences in 1888, 1892–1894, 1896, 1898 and 1899–1900 are unavailable. Heather Coleman refers to minutes of the 1897, 1902, 1903, and 1904 meetings in Coleman, "Most Dangerous Sect," 140n10.

11. This name was a compromise one which was formally approved only at the 1905 congress in response to the request of the Evangelical Christians. Later this name was again changed into Russian Baptist Union.

12. Val'kevich, *Zapiska*, Appendix 1, 33–34.

13. Val'kevich, *Zpaiska*, Appendix 1, 35, 37–38; cf. Songulashvili, *Evangelical Christian Baptists*, 346. Val'kevich contradicts himself, dating the consolidation of Russian Baptist communities into a missionary organisation to 1879 and the joining of the German Missionary Union to 1880, then admitting that the earliest date for establishing a missionary union among

included Nikita I. Voronin, Martin Kalweit and Vasilii G. Pavlov, who was overseeing the work of the missionary. This shows that the initial impulse to create a union was missionary. The second was to elect a presbyter and organise one community in the Caucasus and Transcaucasia.[14] This decision was accomplished a year later. Two documents evidence that there was at least some form of association in 1879. It lacked yet a formal organisation, but it already had formal requirements for those churches that wanted to associate with Tiflis Baptist Church. This attempt failed due to poor representation at the assembly in Tiflis in 1879 and preoccupation with insignificant moral issues.[15] But the idea was not abandoned.

The Tiflis church also interacted with German Baptists. In 1880 Pavlov invited two Baptist ministers, Johann Kargel and August Liebig, to constitute a Baptist church in Tiflis and ordain a presbyter. This is a significant fact because by 1880 the community in Tiflis had already existed and functioned for at least ten years. They baptised believers, held church meetings and sent evangelists to nearby towns and villages. What were the reasons behind this decision to formally constitute a Baptist church in Tiflis?

Perhaps, this was dictated by the change of religious climate in the Russian Empire. In 1879 German Baptist churches received freedom of worship as stipulated in the Makovskii Circular.[16] The local officials in the Caucasus initially applied this law to Baptists regardless of their ethnic composition, considering Russian Baptists "a split within the community of 'Russian sectarians-Molokans.'"[17] Later, when it became clear that the Makovskii Circular applied only to German Baptists, not their Russian co-believers, Tiflis Baptist Church lost its legal status. Pavlov's election for presbyter and ordination by two German Baptist preachers, along with the constitution of the church, met

---

Russian believers was 1882 (Val'kevich, *Zapiska*, 61–62, 63). Perhaps the first date concerns Caucasus and the second date concerns Ukraine.

14. For one church consisting of many congregations, see Mazaev, "Eshche po Povodu Stat'i," 5–6; cf. Wamble, "Concept and Practice," 255–74; Shurden, "Development," 32–33.

15. They discussed the acceptability of riding draft animals on Sundays, usury and unsupported promissory notes, introducing anointing and foot-washing into the communities, the marriages and burial of the excommunicated and non-believers, kissing members of the opposite sex, head-coverings and the use of luxury food and drink items that caused others to stumble. See Val'kevich, *Zapiska*, Appendix 1, 35, 37–38.

16. This is the document named after the minister of internal affairs, Lev Savvich Makov (1830–1883).

17. Breyfogle, "Heretics and Colonizers," 332–33.

formal governmental requirements formulated by the Makovskii Circular and gave it the right to operate officially. Besides that, Pavlov might have sought to strengthen his position as a leader. There were tensions between Pavlov, a representative of Western tradition, Voronin and, perhaps, Ivanov, proponents of more autochthonous tradition.[18] Finally, only properly constituted Baptist churches could be in fellowship with other communities.[19] The election and ordination of Pavlov was a form of recognition by wider Baptist circles which opened the doors for contact and cooperation.[20]

Liebig and Kargel arrived on 10 August,[21] and the church was constituted on 17 August 1880.[22] Liebig chaired the meeting and Kargel assisted him. They addressed the congregation in German, and Vasilii Pavlov translated into Russian.[23] This is the earliest description of the constitution of a Baptist church in the Russian Empire. Liebig and Kargel asked, and the church answered. Besides constituting the church, Liebig and Kargel proposed for it to join the German Union of Communities of Baptised Christians.[24] The text of the protocol reads,

> The chair: Do you want to join our German Union of Communities of Baptised Christians in Germany, Denmark, Switzerland, Russia etc.?
>
> Brother V. Pavlov asks to explain the aim of this union.
>
> The chair: The aim of the aforementioned union is, firstly, in support and spread of missionary activity; then for mutual help between the churches and in order to fulfil Saviour's word "*that*

---

18. Coleman, "Most Dangerous Sect," 50–53.

19. See how the Novo-Vasil'evka conference addresses the church in Novo-Sofievka as not an "autonomous church yet for it has neither a presbyter, nor self-government, but it is considered a part of Einlage Russian Church." Aleksii Ia. (Dorodnitsyn), *Materialy*, 581–82; cf. Payne, *Fellowship of Believers*, 52.

20. The surviving protocols of Tiflis Baptist Church describe the event, and this description deserves the closer analysis which is given in chapter 8. Val'kevich, Appendix 1, 45–47; Aleksii Ia. (Dorodnitsyn), *Materialy*, 637–40.

21. Val'kevich, *Zapiska*, Appendix 1, 45.

22. Val'kevich, *Zapiska*, Appendix 1, 45.

23. Val'kevich, *Zapiska*, Appendix 1, 47.

24. Bishop Aleksii *contra* Val'kevich believes the Tiflis church never joined the German Union of Communities of Baptised Christians. See Aleksii Ia. (Dorodnitsyn), *Materialy*, 689; cf. Val'kevich, *Zapiska*, 62.

all be one" and demonstrate unity to the world. Thus, do you want to join this union?

The community's unanimous response: yes.

The chair: At the future conference the community may send from its side a suggestion to admit it into union.[25]

This interchange manifests the church's interdependency and belonging to a wider ecclesial body. Liebig, answering Pavlov's question, points to these aims of the German Baptist Union: (1) missionary activity; (2) mutual help; and (3) fulfilment of Christ's High Priestly Prayer about unity as the witness to the world. These three elements are the most important motifs for joining the union. Though the first two elements could be interpreted pragmatically, unity for the sake of witness is rooted in Christ's prayer for and command to his disciples and intrinsically related to Christ's unity with the Father and the church's mission in Christ's way. The subsequent narrative points to what extent these elements inform Russian and Ukrainian Baptist understanding of the nature of ACs.

Other early attempts came from St. Petersburg where Lord Radstock's converts, Colonel Vasilii Pashkov and Count Modest Korff, attempted to unite Russian evangelicals in the form of the Evangelical Alliance. High social status and active involvement in and support of evangelistic initiatives made them highly influential among Russian evangelicals. Pashkov was in correspondence with the Evangelical Alliance in the UK.[26] In 1884 they convoked the first conference on the issue of unity in St. Petersburg. The event attracted more than seventy participants from different evangelical groups. These attempts failed due to the inability of different groups to overcome theological differences. The situation was further complicated by Pashkov's exile from Russia later in 1884.[27]

In Ukraine and Southern Russia, Johann Wieler, a member of the Mennonite Brethren church in Rückenau,[28] tried to unite diverse com-

---

25. Val'kevich, *Zapiska*, Appendix 1, 45–47; Aleksii Ia. (Dorodnitsyn), *Materialy*, 640.

26. Puzynin, *Tradition*, 72–73; see also Nichols, *Development*, 121–24, 243–45; Val'kevich, *Zapiska*, 157–58, 188–90.

27. Heier, *Religious Schism*, 145.

28. Klippenstein, "Johann Wieler," 44–60; Dyck, "Moulding the Brotherhood"; Val'kevich, *Zapiska*, 62, 66.

munities through common missionary work. In 1881, Wieler and Peter M. Friesen (1849–1914) visited Colonel Vasilii Pashkov in St. Petersburg to acquire support for establishing a missionary training school in Bulgaria and a mission among Armenians and to discuss theological issues, particularly open communion.[29] Although originally Wieler's views were closer to those of German Baptists, his contact with Pashkov widened his perspective on unity. This initial contact brought Pashkov to Ukraine in 1882 where he met with Wieler and other evangelicals, including Baptists and evangelical Molokans.[30] Pashkov offered Wieler funding and the position of evangelist with the purpose of establishing a union of churches. He accepted the offer.[31]

2.2.2 Consolidating the Brotherhood: Johann Wieler

Wieler was prepared for this ministry because, in 1872, the conference of the Mennonite Brethren Church elected him to chair the Missions Committee and serve as itinerant preacher.[32] He had a clear vision for the union, its operations and purpose. His views were summarised in the letter to potential donors of the newly-established union.[33] The primary task of the union was "the carrying out of the missionary mandate in a systematic way."[34] Wieler's programme included (1) visiting scattered churches and mission stations; (2) fostering a sense of mission among the believers; (3) promoting unity and love among the congregations; and (4) evangelizing the lost.[35] This programme was fulfilled in a series of conferences held between 1882 and 1904 in the southern provinces of the Russian Empire.[36]

---

29. Dyck, "Moulding the Brotherhood," 76. The question of open communion centered on the conflicting views around believer's baptism held by Pashkovites and Baptists. The latter required rebaptism, while the former did not. The issue was raised unsuccessfully at the conferences in Rückenau (1882), St. Petersburg (1884) and Novo-Vasil'evka (1884). Only in 1907 did Baptists and Pashkovites officially have a common table. Wieler's experience of Wüst's brotherhoods made him open to this view.

30. "Deiatel'nost' Pashkova." Wardin dates Pashkov's visit to 1879 and Count Korf to 1874 (see Wardin, *On the Edge*, 192).

31. Dyck, "Moulding the Brotherhood," 77.

32. Dyck, "Moulding the Brotherhood," 46, 60.

33. Klippenstein, "Johann Wieler."

34. Klippenstein, "Johann Wieler," 52.

35. Klippenstein, "Johann Wieler," 55.

36. Meetings were held in Rückenau (20–23 May 1882), Novo-Vasil'evka (30 April–1 May 1884), Vladikavkaz (3–6 April 1885), Kuban' (26–30 December 1886), Nikol'skoe (29 December 1887–1 January 1888), Nikol'skoe (1889), Nikol'skoe (1–10 January 1890), Gor'kaia

Established in Novo-Vasil'evka from 30 April to 1 May 1884, this loose union of churches assumed the name Konferentsiia Veruuishchikh Kreshchenykh Khristian, Tak Nazyvaemykh Baptistov Iuga Rossii i Kavkaza (Conference of believing baptised Christians, so-called Baptists, of Southern Russia and the Caucasus)[37] and the short name Bratstvo (Brotherhood). It mostly included representatives from Russian and Ukrainian churches.[38] Two resolutions of the conference throw light on the nature of the Bratstvo and the way it worked. First, Wieler proposed to arrange all resolutions according to their significance: resolutions related to mission would be obligatory for all Bratstvo churches; resolutions related to dogmatic and confessional rules were desirable for the sake of dogmatic unity; and resolutions concerning general issues, not covered in the confessional rules, would be left at the discretion of the churches.[39] Thus, mission was the driving force and constituting principle behind the union. Second, the conference decided that the churches that wanted to be in the union with other churches must send their representatives to the conference.[40] This laid the pattern of interaction: Bratstvo presupposed fellowship and constant involvement in its affairs. The practice of associating was clearly elevated as a necessary condition for the existence of a healthy union, but it did not interfere with local church autonomy.

Wieler chaired the Missions Committee from 1882[41] to 1885, when he fled Russia escaping arrest.[42] Under Wieler's leadership, organisational structure

---

Balka (10–18 January 1891), Rostov-on-Don (1895), Tsaritsyn (1898), Rostov-on-Don (1902), Tsaritsyn (1903) and Rostov-on-Don (1904).

37. Aleksii Ia. (Dorodnitsyn), *Materialy*, 569. Russian and Ukrainian Baptist historians treat this event as the official date for establishing the Russian Baptist Union. See Savinskii, *Istoriia Evangelskikh Khristian-Baptistov Ukrainy, Rossii, Belorussii (1867–1917)*, 200.

38. They represented Tavrida *guberniia*, Ekaterinoslav *guberniia*, Kherson *guberniia* and St. Petersburg. The Tiflis church only sent a written proposal on mission issues. Six guests represented the evangelical Molokans (Zakhar'evtsy).

39. Aleksii Ia. (Dorodnitsyn), *Materialy*, 580–81.

40. Aleksii Ia. (Dorodnitsyn), *Materialy*, 582–83.

41. Aleksii Ia. (Dorodnitsyn), *Materialy*, 557–69. This was the only joint conference. German believers were afraid of charges of proselytizing. See Dyck, "Moulding the Brotherhood," 80.

42. Dyck, "Moulding the Brotherhood," 91. Klippenstein says Wieler had to leave the country in 1885, travelling to Romania and to Hamburg. Upon his return to Molochna in February 1886, he had immediately to flee to Germany. See Klippenstein, "Johann Wieler," 57.

of the union was simple: horizontal and egalitarian.⁴³ The primary building blocks of Bratstvo were the local communities that delegated representatives to annual meetings. At annual meetings delegates made decisions on different mission and church issues on behalf of their churches, appointed missionaries, and elected the chair and members of the Missions Committee who oversaw the work in between conferences. A local church could approve or disapprove any of the decisions. The function of the missionaries was not only to disseminate the gospel among non-believers but also to homogenise practice and strengthen fellowship among existing communities of faith.⁴⁴ The overall purpose of *Bratstvo* was to assemble existing human and financial resources for the promotion and support of missionary work. In this model, without strong local churches and good relations among them, the task could not be accomplished.

2.2.3 Structuring the Brotherhood: Dei Mazaev

Government measures against well-known Ukrainian and German leaders conditioned the transition of leadership to Russian believers beginning in 1885.⁴⁵ Perhaps the fruits of missionary efforts did not pass unnoticed by the local government.⁴⁶ The majority of Ukrainian converts were of Orthodox background, and the government considered change of faith illegal. Consequently, they were either persecuted or under strict police surveillance.⁴⁷ Worsening relations between Russia and Germany led to the growth of Germanophobia⁴⁸ and stricter government measures against German colonists involved in spreading the gospel among Ukrainians. All this brought

---

43. Reidar Aasgaard in his study of siblingship metaphors in Paul points out that though he uses siblingship language to establish common identity, this does not presuppose equality in power or rank. See Aasgaard, *My Beloved*, 261–64, 285–95.

44. Aleksii Ia. (Dorodnitsyn), *Materialy*, 559, 560, 564, 565.

45. Riaboshapka, Ratushnyi and Khlystun were under strict police surveillance. Aleksii Ia. (Dorodnitsyn), *Materialy*, 325–26, 600.

46. Mitrokhin, *Baptizm*, 222.

47. The conference considered the fact of persecutions and resolved to keep a missionary's remuneration in case of arrest, supported the idea of hiring lawyers for brothers under arrest, and established a fund for prisoners and the persecuted. See Aleksii Ia. (Dorodnitsyn), *Materialy*, 601, 603. The inability of well-known and experienced missionaries to serve pushed the conference to appoint new personalities, who were granted authority only to evangelise not baptise. See Aleksii Ia. (Dorodnitsyn), 601; cf. Val'kevich, *Zapiska*, 77.

48. Wardin, *On the Edge*, 208.

Baptists of Molokan origin to the fore.[49] At the time, they enjoyed relative freedom, and Tiflis Baptist Church even attained legal status in 1879 and retained it until 1886.[50]

In 1885, when Wieler left the country, the conference elected Dei Mazaev,[51] a son of a well-known Molokan sheep rancher, to be first Wieler's assistant and then the chair of the Missions Committee. Mazaev was a very capable person and strong leader. For the next thirty years, with a short interruption in 1909–1911, he served as president of the Baptist union and used his finances, along with his organisational and leadership skills, for its development, flourishing and structuring.

Under Mazaev, Bratstvo underwent transformations that led to a more structured and centralised organisation. In 1886, the conference transferred the right to elect members of the Missions Committee to the local churches, reduced the committee from nineteen to nine members and enlarged the regions they represented.[52] This contributed to a more intensive interaction of churches in the regions and the formation of sub-regional groups of churches that later formed regional associations. Val'kevich emphasises this step, saying, "As the number of members of the Committee was reducing and the number of missionaries was expanding, influence of members of the Committee, who became important leaders of pretty significant local organisations which were slowly approximating associations similar to German Baptist brotherhoods, was growing too."[53] This had a positive influence on the efficiency of the Missions Committee's work but reduced the direct input of local churches on its decisions. Perhaps to balance this disparity, both the chair and treasurer were restricted in their independent use of funds.[54]

The regionalisation of the Missions Committee was coupled with a centralisation of leadership embodied in the decision of the next conference (Nikol'skoe, 29 December 1887–1 January 1888), when Mazaev was not only

---

49. The government considered Molokans non-Orthodox and was permissive when they changed religious affiliation.

50. Pavlov, "Pravda o Baptistakh," no. 44, 345.

51. On Dei Mazaev, see Steeves, "Russian Baptist Union," 30–33; Levindanto, "Pamiati Deia Ivanovicha Mazaeva"; Nahirniak, "Dei Mazaev."

52. The members of the committee represented the Caucasus, Transcaucasia, Tavrida *guberniia*, Kuban', Kherson *guberniia*, Kyiv *guberniia* and Ekaterinoslav *guberniia*.

53. Val'kevich, *Zapiska*, 71, 109–11.

54. Aleksii Ia. (Dorodnitsyn), *Materialy*, 603.

re-elected chair of the Missions Committee but acquired the title "Supervisor of Union Affairs."[55] The responsibilities of this new position were not specified. The decision of 1889 indicated that Mazaev acquired the right to appoint short-term missionaries but could not use the general mission fund for this. The union was changing from a loose horizontal fellowship of churches that could exercise their authority through delegates and members of the Missions Committee to a more organised and structured entity where churches had a more limited influence. Iohannes Dyck deems this development a sign of the end of the Bratstvo period.[56] Indeed, Mazaev contributed to the formation of a centralised structure, but perhaps the development of centripetal forces was also a response to geographical expansion and the quantitative growth of Baptist churches. Dyck is also right in assuming that the persecutions organised by Pobedonostsev influenced Bratstvo, but he overlooks the fact that it was almost impossible to continue annual assemblies under such circumstances.[57]

The available information indicates that meetings in Nikol'skoe (1–10 January 1890),[58] Gor'kaia Balka (10–18 January 1891)[59] and Rostov-on-Don (1895) followed the traditional pattern of mission fund audit, appointment of evangelists and distribution of funds for prisoners. It is striking that in 1891 some of the missionaries refused to commit to service for the next year due to persecutions.[60] In fact, the semi-official activities of the union were almost totally paralysed after 1891. From 1886 to 1889, the union expanded its ministry to the Far East, the region of Amur River[61] and new regions within Ukraine and Russia. Val'kevich, analysing developments after 1890, points to three tendencies: (1) the consolidation of Russian sectarians around Baptists; (2) the development of ties with foreign Pietistic and evangelical Protestant groups and their influence on Russian Baptists; (3) the transformation of

---

55. VSEKhB, *Istoriia Evangelskikh Khristian-Baptistov v SSSR*, 129.

56. Dyck, "Zavisimost Nezavisimosti," 277.

57. Pobedonostsev occupied the position of Ober-Procurator of the Holy Synod from 1880 to 1905. While in power, Pobedonostsev initiated a number of legislatory acts restricting activities of Russian sectarians. See Mitrokhin, *Baptizm*, 241–46.

58. Aleksii Ia. (Dorodnitsyn), *Materialy*, 609–10.

59. VSEKhB, *Istoriia Evangelskikh Khristian-Baptistov v SSSR*, 130–31.

60. This is mentioned in the coded letter of evangelist Pavel Demakin. See Savinskii, *Istoriia Evangelskikh Khristian-Baptistov Ukrainy, Rossii, Belorussii (1867–1917)*, 206.

61. Aleksii Ia. (Dorodnitsyn), *Materialy*, 604.

Baptist practices through the influence of Russian and foreign evangelicals and the influx of educated converts who gravitated towards the more open position of Evangelical Christians.[62]

In 1898, when persecution eased, Mazaev convoked the annual meeting in Tsaritsyn and invited representatives of the remaining Pashkovite movement. According to Nikolai Levindanto,[63] in 1898 "a spiritual union"[64] and agreement on cooperation for the kingdom of God was reached.[65] This opened up a new page in very uneasy relations between the two groups.[66] In 1902, in Rostov-on-Don, Pashkovites from St. Petersburg, Kyiv, Konotop and Sevastopol came and discussed with the Baptists the issues of unity and joint ministry. Annual meeting in Tsaritsyn (1903)[67] formally approved the appeal of the Pashkovites to be included into the union, and its name was changed to "Evangelical Christians-Baptists" upon their request.[68] In Rostov-on-Don (1904), some delegates from Kyiv asked Baptists to include them into the union.[69] Usually Baptists abstained from eucharistic fellowship with evangelical Christians because of difference in baptismal practices. Perhaps "spiritual union" referred to eucharistic fellowship. Dei Mazaev recalled that in the Kyiv, the church, Evangelical Christians "gave [the] hand of fellowship" to the Baptist and "received a fraternal kiss of peace in return,"[70] which is a typical verbal formula for entering into fellowship with someone, sometimes in a eucharistic context.[71]

The Union of Russian Baptist of Southern Russia and Caucasus from 1888 to 1904 reflects the genius of Dei Mazaev. Amid persecutions, Mazaev managed to make the union work, expanding the gospel outreach and strengthening existing churches. He was a proponent of a strong centre model that

---

62. Val'kevich, *Zapiska*, 157–58.

63. Nikolai A. Levindanto (1896–1966) was an influential Baptist minister, senior presbyter in the Baltic Soviet republics (1945–1966) and the first vice-president of AUCECB.

64. Levindanto, "Pamiati Deia Ivanovicha Mazaeva," 97.

65. VSEKhB, *Istoriia Evangelskikh Khristian-Baptistov v SSSR*, 130.

66. On uneasy relations with the Evangelical Christians, see Steeves, "Russian Baptist Union".

67. Mazaev, "Ne ta Doroga!," 268.

68. Mazaev, "Ne ta Doroga!," 268.

69. Belousov, "Pervyi Nazidatel'nyi S'ezd," 39.

70. Mazaev, "Ne ta Doroga!," 268.

71. Jones, "Kiss of Peace," 290.

differed from the egalitarian approach of Wieler. But the challenges the two men faced were different. While Wieler was trying to consolidate existing churches and redirect their human and financial resources towards mission in the south of the Russian Empire, Mazaev had to work on a much bigger scale, coping with the imprisonment of key leaders, the appointment of new missionaries and the structuring of the union's work.

2.3 Associational Practices

At this stage, during the Union of Russian Baptists of Southern Russia and Caucasus, two associational practices played significant roles in the consolidation and support of the union. These were the annual mission conferences that regularly gathered representatives of the churches and the ministry of evangelists who, besides preaching the gospel, exercised the function of translocal ministers.

2.3.1 Conferences as Unifying Associational Practice

The Bratstvo conferences were initiated around, and for the purpose of, common missionary work. They implemented Wieler's understanding of the purpose and the major tasks of the union, as discussed above. The union was based on the principles of brotherhood – a loose horizontal, non-hierarchical association of churches. The member churches shared responsibility for mission, mutual support and encouragement. The model of Bratstvo resembles voluntary association but has deeper theological overtones.

Bratstvo presupposed the participation of local churches in the annual conferences. At Novo-Vasil'evka, in response to the question of whether participation of member churches could be reduced to just sending suggestions in written form, the deputies replied: "If the communities want to stay in union with other communities, they should certainly send their deputies for the conference; however, there could be exceptions for good reasons."[72] The initiative to join the union belonged to the local church. Membership in the union could not be simply a formality; it required active participation in making decisions, sharing responsibilities and fellowshipping with other

---

72. Aleksii Ia. (Dorodnitsyn), *Materialy*, 582–83.

churches.⁷³ The key goal for which the union existed was mission, which required obedience to the collegial decisions of the union from the member churches. Nevertheless, this obedience was not blind; any local church was free to disapprove the resolutions.⁷⁴

Besides mission, delegates discussed different theological and practical issues. Agreement in the dogmatic issues was "desirable" while practical issues were left at local churches' discretion. However, the protocols evidence serious preoccupation with matters of doctrine and practice, which may indicate that conferences operated as local church councils. For instance, in Novo-Vasil'evka, the deputies discussed fifteen issues encompassing the area of theological opinions (e.g. attitudes towards Jumpers[75]), church practice (e.g. marriage, the limits of a minister's authority, ordination, the Lord's Supper, the washing of feet, church discipline), Christian ethics (e.g. debts and usury, parents' authority over children). In this regard the conferences operated as regional church councils. One of the major purposes of discussions on theological and practical issues was the consolidation and unification of the beliefs and practices of these dispersed and varied communities of faith. Similar issues were also in focus in Vladikavkaz on 3–6 April 1885.[76] Vasilii G. Pavlov led the sessions when Johann Wieler and Riaboshapka left the meeting due to police surveillance.[77] The delegates of Tiflis Baptist Church raised the question of homogeneity of doctrine and practice among the missionaries, complaining that some missionaries taught foot washing and open

---

73. The delegates designated new areas for ministry (Aleskii Ia. [Dorodnitsyn], *Materialy*, 561–62) and distributed finances according to the term of ministry (Aleskii Ia. [Dorodnitsyn], 564–65). Other issues they addressed: a tri-monthly collection of money for the missionary fund (Aleskii Ia. [Dorodnitsyn], 574, 603, 608) and missionary reports and obedience (Aleskii Ia. [Dorodnitsyn], *Materialy*, 575–76).

74. Aleksii Ia. (Dorodnitsyn), *Materialy*, 581.

75. Jumpers or Hüpfers was a charismatic group that emerged among Mennonites in response to Eduard Wüst's preaching and whose worship was characterized by joyful singing in a major key with dancing, jumping, clapping and the shouting of "glory" or "halelujah." See Bondar, *Sekta Mennonitov v Rossii*, 107–41.

76. Traveling by steamers, riding horses on Sundays, etc. were probably, signs of social inequality that was a concern to Molokans. See Val'kevich, *Zapiska*, Appendix 1, 37; Aleskii Ia. (Dorodnitsyn), *Materialy*, 687–88.

77. Later Wieler disapproved decisions made after his departure. See his message to Tiflis on sending minutes to member churches. Val'kevich, *Zapiska*, Appendix 1, 63.

communion with pedo-baptists.[78] A stricter dogmatic position and separation from other kindred groups, characteristic of a Caucasus group of Baptists, resulted in the rejection of a joint conference with evangelical Molokans with this explanation: "because of differences in doctrine there can be no chance of joint missionary activity."[79] Conference protocols after 1886 demonstrate a relative shrinking of doctrinal and practical issues and the emergence of procedural and disciplinary matters.[80] This can be interpreted as a sign of the unification of churches under Bratstvo.

2.3.2 The Unifying Role of Trans-Local Ministers

Newly established Baptist communities often suffered from a lack of sound teaching or ordering of their communal life. Songulashvili refers to an article published by a Presbyterian missionary who, after visiting Tiflis in 1875 and 1879, concluded that "the little congregations which Herr Pavlov had planted were suffering for lack of proper superintendence."[81] This was true even in 1895, when Vasilii Ivanov, in his letter to Elena Kirchner,[82] clearly formulated the problem:

> All communities of our brotherhood (Baptists) which number not by tens but, perhaps, already by hundreds, are sufficiently ordered, and spiritual life moves forward. There are many of thirsty and revived souls, the growth increases every year, praise the Lord! But it should be said that all these communities, consisting of common undeveloped people, need tutelage and true apostolic care for them. All these newly planted churches cannot stand on their feet without outer help – they need someone constantly visiting them. There often emerge disputes among

---

78. This obviously assumed Mennonite practices. The minutes leave an impression of tensions between the Tiflis group and the Kherson and Tavrida group. See Aleksii Ia. (Dorodnitsyn), *Materialy*, 590–91.

79. Aleksii Ia. (Dorodnitsyn), *Materialy*, 591.

80. Aleksii Ia. (Dorodnitsyn), *Materialy*, 608.

81. Songulashvili, *Evangelical Christian Baptists*, 71.

82. Elena V. Kirchner was one of the leaders of the evangelical movement in the Russian Empire and participated in the publishing of *Beseda* (Conversation) and the establishing of the missionary school in Tulcha, Bulgaria, in 1896. See Val'kevich, *Zapiska*, 46, 50, 120–21. *Beseda* was an evangelical publication established by Hermann Fast and Ivan Prokhanov around 1889. See Wardin, *On the Edge*, 253, 267–68.

them, some heresies, which they cannot deal with on their own. I receive so many invitations from different communities that I have to stay at home for two or three months only.[83]

The churches suffered from disputes on doctrine and misunderstandings of practice. Ivanov points to the fact that most of the converts were new to faith and of lower educational status. Ivanov's statement that Baptist communities were "sufficiently ordered, and spiritual life moves forward" somewhat contradicts their inability to cope with inner tensions and heresies. Perhaps he refers here to the newly planted churches which were not mature enough to deal with these issues.[84] These problems could only be resolved with the outside help provided by more knowledgeable and experienced ministers, whose actions Ivanov labels "apostolic," perhaps referring to Apostle Paul's regular visits to the churches planted in Asia Minor and Greece.

Another aspect of the problem is hinted at in an article published about the same time, probably by Johann Kargel.[85] His observation points to the practice of visiting dispersed communities for the sake of strengthening them and establishing ties between them. Recollecting how changes in society impact the spreading of God's kingdom, the author states that "many brethren suffer from rare visitations and brotherly support"[86] caused by the low financial capacities of ministers. The author hopes that price-cutting on railway transportation will stimulate brethren to "undertake travels for the spiritual purpose, which, in their turn, will have positive impact upon the whole Church" and "could be one of the reasons reviving general ties."[87] He regrets that the poor motivation of ministers prevents visits to the dispersed brethren.[88] As shown above (section 2.2.3), this was a period of severe persecutions from the government

---

83. Val'kevich, *Zapiska*, Appendix 3, 26. Perhaps the E. V. ("E. B." in Russian) in the letter stands for Elena Valer'evna.

84. In later writings, Ivanov insists on the necessity of proper church order for the steady growth of the church and its capacity to be the instrument of God's kingdom. See Ivanov, "Zabota o Vsekh Tserkvakh"; Ivanov, "Obshchiny i Presvitery."

85. Kargel was one of the regular contributors to *Beseda*. According to Gregory Nichols, Kargel and his family lived in Finland from 1891 to 1895. See Nichols, *Development*, 145. The author of the article shows familiarity with the religious situation in Bulgaria and Romania and writes from Finland. I assume that the "K" at the end of article stands for Kargel. See Val'kevich, *Zapiska*, 50, 120–21.

86. Val'kevich, *Zapiska*, Appendix 3, 31.

87. Val'kevich, *Zapiska*, Appendix 3, 31.

88. Val'kevich, *Zapiska*, Appendix 3, 31.

and low motivation could be explained by fear of imprisonment or expulsion from the country. Absence of structure and insufficient funds were among the key reasons for a lack of "proper superintendence."[89] There were attempts to meet this need in at least two different ways: Ivanov's vision of reorganising churches in Transcaucasia and Wieler's programme of mission mobilisation through Bratstvo.

As was demonstrated in chapter 1, Ivanov suggested a model aimed at better organising the church in Transcaucasia with a view to mission,[90] with all churches uniting into one community headed by a presbyter with a teacher, two deacons and a treasurer.[91] Analysing Ivanov's "O Reorganisatsii," Malkhaz Songulashvili supposes that the document introduces the threefold ministry dealing with the issue of *episkope*. He reads the document through the lens of "a proto-Orthodox, patriarchate-type infrastructure."[92] He admits that the vocabulary of the document obviously comes from the German Baptist tradition with its presbyter (*der Älteste*), teacher (*Lehrer*) and deacon (*Diakon*) but tries to relate these to the Orthodox bishop, priest and deacon, respectively.[93] Songulashvili substantiates this interpretation with analysis of the ministerial practices of the presbyter who had the exclusive right to lead the service from *kafedra* (cathedra or pulpit). Songulashvili opines that the document uses *kafedra* in the Orthodox sense of the bishop's seat and a sign of teaching authority.[94] The text of "O Reorganisatsii" does restrict the teaching authority of ministers from the top down, granting the highest right only to the presbyter. Perhaps this scheme did not take hold, though the Tiflis conference elected one presbyter and constituted one community in the Caucasus and Transcaucasia in 1879.[95]

Wieler's programme of systematic missionary work presupposed the unification of widely scattered churches and stations through visitations, fostering

---

89. Songulashvili, *Evangelical Christian Baptists*, 71.
90. Aleksii Ia. (Dorodnitsyn), *Materialy*, 686–87.
91. Aleksii Ia. (Dorodnitsyn), *Materialy*, 689. See section 1.3.
92. Songulashvili, *Evangelical Christian Baptists*, 72.
93. Songulashvili, *Evangelical Christian Baptists* 72.
94. Songulashvili, *Evangelical Christian Baptists* 73–74. Perhaps, he is right in pointing to the *kafedra* as a sign of authority. Teachers can preach in their communities only from the table rather than the pulpit. See Aleksii Ia. (Dorodnitsyn), *Materialy*, 689.
95. Aleksii Ia. (Dorodnitsyn), *Materialy*, 622; Val'kevich, *Zapiska*, Appendix 1, 38.

a sense of mission and promoting unity and love among congregations.[96] Practically this was accomplished by way of evangelists visiting churches and stations. Thus, at the 1882 conference, Ratushnyi reported that visiting villages around Osnova, he found that some brothers lived in discrepancies on many issues. He then proposed "more frequent visits to these brethren *in order to unify them into one thought* according to the teaching of the Gospel."[97] The protocol of the 1884 conference witnesses that Riaboshapka was involved in the ordering of community in Kyiv *gubernia* (province) while Kushnerenko was appointed to serve in the Caucasus to oppose "the heresy of *khlysty*."[98] Another way to strengthen churches was through the visits of brethren from nearby churches which supplemented the rare visitations of trans-local ministers and encouraged the fellowship of local churches.[99]

Unfortunately, the text of the protocol does not describe evangelists' functions, though it does point out that there were two types of evangelists: "with authority"[100] and "without authority."[101] This designation relates to their right to baptise. Val'kevich adds that "authority" means that these evangelists could also install ministers in the churches.[102] Those "without authority" could only preach. The introduction of evangelists "without authority" coincides with the inability of such leaders as Riaboshapka, Ratushnyi and Khlystun to join the conference and work as evangelists due to close police surveillance and severe restrictions on travel.[103] Perhaps this prompted Mazaev to propose, as a temporary measure, for evangelists to be less known and experienced brethren; those who had not yet proved themselves to be reliable ministers.

Both models of trans-local ministry were aimed at helping churches to grow in maturity and unity, with the result of more active and healthier

---

96. Klippenstein, "Johann Wieler," 55.

97. Aleksii Ia. (Dorodnitsyn), *Materialy*, 560. Emphasis added.

98. Aleksii Ia. (Dorodnitsyn), 572. Emphasis original. *Khlysty* is a Russian mystical sect that emerged between the 1730s and 40s. Details on their beliefs and practices are in Bolshakoff, *Russian Nonconformity*, 83–91.

99. Aleksii Ia. (Dorodnitsyn), *Materialy*, 564–5.

100. Aleksii Ia. (Dorodnitsyn), *Materialy*, 606.

101. Aleksii Ia. (Dorodnitsyn), *Materialy*, 601.

102. Val'kevich, *Zapiska*, 77. This claim is unsupported. Minutes of the 1889 conference contain a resolution to satisfy the church in Nikol'skoe's request to ordain brother Fomin for presbyter, which means that the church just elected a person, while the right to ordain and install belonged to the union. See Aleksii Ia. (Dorodnitsyn), *Materialy*, 608.

103. Aleksii Ia. (Dorodnitsyn), *Materialy*, 600.

missionary activity. Together with regular conferences, they assisted in the implementation of ecclesial relations beyond the local level.

2.4 Understanding the Nature of Associations of Churches

Only a handful of the documents mentioned above contain information that may inform our search for an understanding of the nature and theological representation of ACs among Baptists in the Russian Empire. These are "O Reorganisatsii," "O Bratskom Soiuze," *Pravila Veroispovedaniia* and protocols of Tiflis Baptist Church and Bratstvo. In what follows, I will demonstrate that a basic understanding of the union was that of an association of churches which was theologically represented as *Bratstvo* and driven by unity and mission.

2.4.1 Union as an Association of Churches

The article "O Bratskom Soiuze" was the first attempt to describe the union, its relations to local churches, and its authority and limits of authority. Its compiler points out that Baptists always had a "tendency to unite their communities" in associations and unions,[104] which led to the establishment of the unions in Great Britain and Germany.[105]

The unions function as associations of churches. Local churches may freely join or leave them: "there must be no imposition, for the local church should be according to God's Word autonomous and independent."[106] Liebig's proposal for Tiflis Baptist Church to join the German Union of Churches of Baptised Christians fits this model: if the local church accepts the invitation, it sends a request to the union to be admitted into fellowship and formally joins the union after sending delegates to the annual assembly at which it could be accepted into the fellowship.[107] However, Liebig's explanation of the purpose of union has deeper theological motives than the model presented in "O Bratskom Soiuze."

---

104. Val'kevich, *Zapiska*, Appendix 3, 2.
105. Val'kevich, *Zapiska*, Appendix 3, 3.
106. Val'kevich, *Zapiska*, Appendix 3, 2.
107. Aleksii Ia. (Dorodnitsyn), *Materialy*, 640.

The author of "O Bratskom Soiuze" just points to the pragmatic reasons for union. First, uniting local churches and their resources for the implementation of missions inside and outside of the motherland is the chief task of the union.[108] Second, the author admits that the task of consolidating scattered brotherhoods and their ministers is especially important during the initial stages of union formation.[109] Membership in the association of churches presupposes not only a formal connection, with local communities delegating part of their authority to the elected ministers, empowering them to serve for the benefit of God's kingdom,[110] but something deeper. When a decision of a local church concerns the brotherhood, it should communicate this decision to the nearby churches, acting on the basis of mutual respect.[111]

2.4.2 Authority of the Local Church vs. Authority of an Association of Churches

The concept of the union as an association of churches is tightly related to the idea of local church autonomy. Another side of this is the tension between these concepts. The earliest discussion about local church authority versus the union's authority appears in the protocols of Tiflis Baptist Church in 1879. When some members challenged the legitimacy of the conference due to poor representation (just two churches), Pavlov responded,

> [I do] not see why the conference should be considered illegitimate, even more so that resolutions of the conference are for the communities not more than advice and the communities may or may not accept them at their discretion; for we do not ascribe to the resolutions of the conference the authority of ecumenical councils.[112]

Then Pavlov asked what should be done to those not supporting the majority's opinion. Voronin proposed to ask the conference; Pavlov declined this proposal for "communities are superior than the conference and, therefore, it depends on them whether its resolutions would be accepted or not. Other

---

108. Val'kevich, *Zapiska*, Appendix 3, 2.
109. Val'kevich, *Zapiska*, Appendix 3, 3.
110. Val'kevich, *Zapiska*, Appendix 3, 3.
111. Val'kevich, *Zapiska*, Appendix 3, 4.
112. Val'kevich, *Zapiska*, Appendix 1, 37; Aleksii Ia. (Dorodnitsyn), *Materialy*, 621.

brothers approved his opinion."[113] In this discussion local church is placed over the conference.

Another situation illustrating the democratic way the union interacted with churches occurred at the Novo-Vasil'evka conference (1884), when Wieler read a letter by someone named Sofron. Sofron expressed the grievance that his church was not invited and a concern that the conference would appoint a presbyter they did not want. He stated that any "decision or affirmation of our Russian conference cannot have the power of the laws set by the Russian government."[114] The participants reply: "the conference *does not interfere in the inner affairs of a church*; therefore, it does not need to appoint a presbyter to another church, especially against that church's desire."[115] They explained that resolutions never engage civil law and need not to be approved by it. They commissioned the Missions Committee to elect a group of ministers to explore this issue together with the representatives of the local church and to plead with the local ministers "to maintain the unity of peace with the brothers of all other churches."[116] It is likely that here the conference encountered misunderstanding about the conference's authority complicated by personal opposition. This was dealt with through the local church and the appointed deputies in a way that demonstrated that the union did not exercise power over the local church.

The issue of authority was also addressed in a short article, "O Bratskom Soiuze" (On the brotherly union), in the 1891 November–December issue of the semi-underground evangelical magazine *Beseda*.[117] It explains "the meaning of the annual meeting and the union in general."[118] The publication claims that local churches are free to join or leave union: "there must be no imposition, for the local church should be according to God's Word

---

113. Val'kevich, *Zapiska*, Appendix 1, 38; Aleksii Ia. (Dorodnitsyn), *Materialy*, 623. The Russian word "*starshe*" could be rendered as "elder, order, senior" or "superior, higher." The former concerns age and the latter authority.

114. Aleksii Ia. (Dorodnitsyn), *Materialy*, 581.

115. Aleksii Ia. (Dorodnitsyn), *Materialy*, 581. Emphasis added.

116. Aleksii Ia. (Dorodnitsyn), *Materialy*, 582. This is the standard practice for conflict resolution. Aleksii Ia. (Dorodnitsyn), *Materialy*, 588, 604.

117. Val'kevich, *Zapiska*, Appendix 3, 2–4.

118. Val'kevich, *Zapiska*, Appendix 3, 2. Based on unidentified German and English publications.

autonomous and independent."[119] The annual conferences gather *propovedniki* (preachers) and deputies elected by the churches. They can only give advice to the churches, not dictate. The text of the article points to the usefulness of gatherings but warns of the danger of usurping power over local churches, which, on their part, should guard autonomy and prevent the intrusion of the union into their affairs.[120] Nevertheless, the churches may delegate their authority to certain brothers who, upon election, should work according to strictly determined boundaries; churches may withdraw this authority at the next assembly.[121] These reflections set the pattern that reappears time and again in Russian Baptist thought with regard to local churches and ACs. The decisive power is in the hands of the local church, as the examples of conflict resolution and the removal and installation of ministers demonstrate.[122]

These examples concern local church actions in resolving conflicts that threaten its existence and the proper procedure for removing and installing ministers. The text of "O Bratskom Soiuze" insists that when a situation is aggravated by tensions and an inability to resolve conflict, or if it concerns the moral fall of a minister, the church should invite respected ministers from other churches and present the case. These ministers step in as arbiters whose advice should be taken as a recommendation, but final decision belongs to the local church.[123] The anonymous author is consistent in placing local church authority over other external authorities.

However, a local church may reach the limits of its autonomy in these two areas – local church conflict and the moral fall of a minister. In the case of local church conflict, when sides are in clear opposition, the invitation of external arbiters is an act of common sense. But the moral fall of a minister goes beyond the concept of local church autonomy. The text states that a minister is "a guardian on the walls of Sion" and servant of the word, loved and respected among many communities; his fall is "a lamentable incident

---

119. Val'kevich, *Zapiska*, Appendix 3, 2. Though the article is anonymous it could have been written by Vasily G. Pavlov because the views presented there resemble his later writings. See section 3.4.1.

120. Val'kevich, *Zapiska*, Appendix 3, 3.

121. Val'kevich, *Zapiska*, Appendix 3, 3.

122. Val'kevich, *Zapiska*, Appendix 3, 3–4.

123. Val'kevich, *Zapiska*, Appendix 3, 3–4.

for all communities" and similar to "a dying celestial body."[124] The invitation of other local ministers is needed but, again, their decision, insists the author, is only a recommendation which the local church should approve and implement. Similar logic applies to those situations which concern common interests, namely the installation of ministers. The local church informs surrounding churches and convokes an advisory meeting of ministers who "should have right to previously get acquainted with the character, knowledge and capabilities of the brother to have been installed."[125] Although the church may disagree with advisors' final recommendation, the author says "it is hard to imagine a case when the brotherhood would install presbyter contrary to the recommendation of such advisory meeting."[126] Thus, in both situations participation of other ministers is crucial but is not decisive. The final decision comes from the local church. Though the case of removal of a minister involves other local ministers it lacks theological explanation and may be interpreted as exercise of common sense and good practice. Such a view is pragmatic and appears to be shallow because it only appeals to common sense and is devoid of theological explanation.

2.4.3 Brotherhood as Ecclesiological Category

Theologically, newly established union was represented as *bratstvo* (brotherhood). *Bratstvo* expressed the self-identity of the union, rooted in Free Church ecclesiology and in the Bible, and pointed to the union's type of structure. According to Joachim Wach's sociology of religion, brotherhood occupies an intermediary position between a circle of disciples, gathered around the charismatic founder of the movement, and an established ecclesiastical body.[127] It retains spiritual conditions of membership and aims at the restoration of a "primitive state."[128] Brotherhood also gravitates towards ecclesiastical organisation expressed in more mature doctrine, religious practices and structure

---

124. Val'kevich, *Zapiska*, Appendix 3, 3.
125. Val'kevich, *Zapiska*, Appendix 3, 3.
126. Val'kevich, *Zapiska*, Appendix 3, 3.
127. Wach, *Sociology of Religion*, 137–41.
128. Wach, *Sociology of Religion*, 139.

but retains characteristics of freedom and simplicity.[129] Religious practices (*cultus*, according to Wach), not doctrine, unite the brotherhood.[130]

Johannes Dyck traces the Russian Baptist concept of *bratstvo* to its use among the Mennonites, the first community "with a realised deep self-perception as a brotherhood."[131] For Mennonites, *bratstvo* was an ethno-confessional group restricted to German Mennonite colonists. It avoided "clergy-laity" divisions and comprised "all the mature male members of the individual congregation."[132] Mennonite Brethren moved beyond ethno-confessional limits and turned into a community of faith similar to *Gemeinde* or *Brüderschaft* and characteristic of the Anabaptist communities of Schleitheim Confession of Faith.[133] This distinctive was originally introduced and encouraged by Pietist preachers Johann Bonekemper and Eduard Wüst, who taught that belonging to brotherhood depends on shared faith, conversion and new birth. Out of these experience, new unity of God's children and true fellowship follows.[134]

The first use of *bratstvo* among Baptist churches in the Russian Empire dates to 1873 when an Odesa police captain [*ispravnik*] found *Pravila Veroispovedaniia* during a search of Mikhail Ratushnyi's house.[135] This document was composed earlier (c. 1870) with the help of Johann Wieler,[136] who describes it in a letter to potential donors:

> Finally, the brethren decided to make a complete break with the Orthodox Church and form a fellowship of their own according to God's Word. A number of brethren met in Wieler's home especially to seek guidance on this matter through prayer and the reading of God's Word. From this resulted the drawing up

---

129. Wach, *Sociology of Religion*, 139–40. Cf. Fiddes's reflections on church and sect in Fiddes, "Church and Sect."

130. Wach, *Sociology of Religion*, 141.

131. Dyck, "Moulding the Brotherhood," 11.

132. Aleksii Ia. (Dorodnitsyn), *Materialy*, 12–13.

133. Lumpkin, *Baptist Confessions of Faith*, 25–26. On the relationship between the concept of *bratstvo* and the Hamburg Confession of Faith and Anabaptist confessions, see Pyzh, "Confessing Community," 62–65.

134. Dyck, "Moulding the Brotherhood," 15–16.

135. Aleksii Ia. (Dorodnitsyn), *Materialy*, 477–82.

136. Bishop Aleksii mistakenly ascribes it to Bonekemper. See Aleksii Ia. (Dorodnitsyn), *Materialy*, 477.

of a confession of faith including ten articles which set out the principal points of the Christian faith. It agreed essentially with the statement used by Baptists in Germany. The brethren then submitted copies of the statement to all their groups for discussion and approval. With few exceptions, all the members agreed to form a Baptist fellowship on the basis of this declaration.[137]

The narrative points out that the composition of the document was preceded by the decision of Ukrainian believers to break away from the Orthodox Church, and it was followed by their writing a petition to the tsar to obtain legal status. The document, together with the petition, had to include the community's basic confessional statements and assure its loyalty to the empire. It also had to point to continuity with similar groups, in this case Baptists in Germany.

The most revealing statement is that this confession was composed by representatives of different congregations (Ratushnyi: Osnova; Riaboshapka: Liubomyrka; Kapustian: Ignatovka; Kushnerenko: Poltavka) who sent it to the members of their congregations, who then, in their turn, "agreed to form a Baptist fellowship on the basis of this declaration."[138] Thus, here *bratstvo* resembles the early English Baptist associations that united communities in a geographical locality[139] or Ivanov's "Baptist community in Transcaucasia."[140] Technically, Bratstvo as an organised group was established in 1884, but even in 1873 there existed an intentional fellowship of churches, united around common confessional core. After 1884, the term *bratstvo* was applied indiscriminately, sometimes in the same document, to different groups of people. It could refer to a local community of faith ("deputy of the same *brotherhood*"),[141] a regional group of churches ("all Transcaucasian *brotherhood*"),[142] a confessional society ("in the communities of believing Mennonite *brotherhood*")[143]

---

137. Klippenstein, "Johann Wieler," 50; cf. Val'kevich, *Zapiska*, Appendix 5, 135.
138. Klippenstein, "Johann Wieler," 50. Altogether, 103 members.
139. White, *English Baptists*, 64–70; McBeth, *Baptist Heritage*, 95–98; Bennett, *Fellowship of Kindred Minds*, 12.
140. Aleksii Ia. (Dorodnitsyn), *Materialy*, 689.
141. Aleksii Ia. (Dorodnitsyn), *Materialy*, 561, 564, 565, 575. Emphasis added.
142. Aleksii Ia. (Dorodnitsyn), *Materialy*, 565. Emphasis added.
143. Aleksii Ia. (Dorodnitsyn), *Materialy*, 578. Emphasis added. The speaker referred to practices of Mennonite Brethren.

and all Baptist churches ("all communities of our [Baptist] *brotherhood*").[144] Such use of the term is devoid of ethno-confessional German Mennonite overtones but, instead, is full of confessional ones. Russian-Ukrainian *bratstvo*, as an association of churches, was united around common experience of conversion, new faith and shared practices, while doctrinal differences demarcated the lines between "us" and "them."

As was demonstrated above, the structure of Bratstvo was horizontal and open, but as it grew numerically and geographically, it tended to become more structured.[145]

Pravila Veroispovedaniia contains the ecclesiological principles on which *bratstvo* rested. The text consists of ten sections, four of which deal with ecclesiological issues: the sacraments of baptism and communion (4),[146] admission into the church through baptism (5), ministers and their function (6) and church discipline (7).[147]

The document refers to local and universal – or visible and invisible – church, though differentiation is absent.[148] It equates *bratstvo* and visible church:

> Through baptism we admit into the visible church of Christ on earth, which should consist only of true believing members following the example of the first Apostolic Church; it should be built as living stones, having been affirmed on the foundation of the apostles and prophets, Jesus Christ himself being the cornerstone in whom the whole building is joined and grows into a holy temple in the Lord, in whom we are built into a dwelling of God through the Spirit (Eph 2:20–22; 1 Pet 2:5).[149]

---

144. Val'kevich, *Zapiska*, Appendix 3, 20.

145. See sections 2.2.2 and 2.2.3.

146. The Russian word *tainstva* (sacraments) is somewhat unusual for describing baptism and the Lord's Supper in Baptist documents which usually use *ustanovleniia* (ordinances) instead of *tainstva* (sacraments). See Prokhanov, "Izlozhenie Evangel'skoi Very," 450–52.

147. Aleksii Ia. (Dorodnitsyn), *Materialy*, 479–81.

148. The universal church only comes into focus in section 10, which is on the Second Coming. For more nuanced ecclesiology, see Prokhanov, "Izlozhenie Evangel'skoi Very," 448–54. For an analysis of *Pravila Veroispovedaniia* against the Orthodox critique of the concept of the visible church, see Pyzh, "Confessing Community," 65–70. Pyzh sets *Pravila* in the framework of the Anabaptist notion of "gathered church." See Pyzh, "Confessing Community," 75–77.

149. Aleksii Ia. (Dorodnitsyn), *Materialy*, 480.

This visible church is part of something larger. First, it should be arranged according to the ideal apostolic church, which precedes it chronologically. Second, the biblical texts and images used in the quote point to the universal church, of which, it seems, the visible church is a part. The section on visible church (5), together with the paragraphs on ministers (6) and church discipline (7), resembles believer's church ecclesiology, especially in that the church is made up of believers only, who are admitted through baptism on the basis of their true repentance and profession of faith.[150]

Sections 4 and 10 go beyond the concept of visible church, referring to "the community of the saints." This phrase is used in the context of the Lord's Supper (4) and Christ's second coming (10). Explaining the meaning of the Lord's Supper, the text states: "The Holy Communion has this meaning: as we all are participants of one bread, we are also the members of Christ's Body, which is the *community of saints* [*obshchestvo sviatykh*], and as we drink from one cup we are also witnesses of His Blood purifying us from our sins."[151] The text combines the image of the body of Christ and the community of saints. Though the Eucharist is served locally, it exceeds the limits of visible community and witnesses to the wider body of Christ not limited by time and space. The text also designates the Lord's Supper as communion, or partaking (*priobshchenie*),[152] when the believers "take Christ's sacraments in remembrance of Christ's suffering and death, as a token of communion [*v znak soobshcheniia*] with Christ and a token of communion [*v znak soobshcheniia*] of believers with each other."[153] Thus, members of all visible communities of faith have communion with Christ and each other, and through this they transcend limits of local church.

The ultimate unity of the people of God is expected at the second coming, which is

> the crown of salvation (1 Cor 1:7, 8), for at that day all the peoples will see this truth and His marvellous majesty and His Bride, that is the assembly of saints (Rev 19:6–9), for those asleep

---

150. Aleksii Ia. (Dorodnitsyn), *Materialy*, 479; cf. Little, "The Concept of the Believer's Church," 27–32; Durnbaugh, *Believers' Church*, 32–33.

151. Aleksii Ia. (Dorodnitsyn), *Materialy*, 479. Emphasis added.

152. Aleksii Ia. (Dorodnitsyn), *Materialy*, 479.

153. Aleksii Ia. (Dorodnitsyn), *Materialy*, 480.

in Christ will be risen in imperishable glory and will see Him as He is and become like Him and will be reigning with Him.[154]

In this paragraph the total number of the saints appears in glory being "the assembly" [*sobranie*] of the people of God devoid of any divisions or limits.

2.4.4 Mission as Integrative Motif of Unity

Mission as an integrative motif of unity is one of the key ideas that prompted Baptists in the Russian Empire to form ACs. Any significant effort to draw churches together is inspired by this motif, which can be found in "O Reorganisatsii," the minutes of Tiflis Baptist Church, "O Bratskov Soiuze" and the protocols of Bratstvo.

Ivanov's proposal "O Reorganisatsii" represents a programmatic and contextual approach to the organisation of the churches and their mission against the background of the dominant target group of their missionary activity – the Molokans.[155] Mission is the driving force behind all suggestions Ivanov makes with regard to ethical behaviour, church discipline, structure and order. He places it within the context of the "calling, task and purpose" of Christian action for God's kingdom.[156] Believers are *called* to be Christians and adopted children of God due to Christ's death. This status places high responsibility on their involvement in the kingdom of God.[157] Their *task* is to obey the will of God directed inside and outside of believers. The former requires the restoration of moral strength and sanctification, aimed at combating the lusts of the flesh and guarding oneself. The latter is the implementation of "loving one's neighbour" and involves commitment to converting peoples to Christ. This also requires the use of various means and "a general, holy zeal of united efforts."[158] Neglecting the *task* makes one unworthy of this high

---

154. Aleksii Ia. (Dorodnitsyn), *Materialy*, 482.

155. Sections 1–4 mention usury, smoking and sniffing tobacco, eating pork, luxury and celebrating Sunday. Aleksii Ia. (Dorodnitsyn), 587–88; cf. Val'kevich, *Zapiska*, Appendix 1, 37. See also Ivanov's letter to Mazaev in Coleman, "Most Dangerous Sect," 52. These issues may also point to the Muslim context, as Azerbaijanis, Dagestanis and other traditionally Muslim ethnic groups were settled in Transcaucasia.

156. Aleksii Ia. (Dorodnitsyn), *Materialy*, 686, 687.

157. Aleksii Ia. (Dorodnitsyn), *Materialy*, 686, 687.

158. Aleksii Ia. (Dorodnitsyn), *Materialy*, 686, 687.

calling. For Ivanov the ultimate *purpose* of all Christian activity is the coming of God's kingdom:

> [The purpose] is such that the kingdom of this world will soon become the kingdom of our Lord and his Christ (Rev 11:15). That all peoples may be enlightened by God's word and believe in Christ; that all ignorance, superstition, and untruth may be destroyed; that the government, rulers, and judges may be filled with wisdom and the fear of God; that all communities may be improved; that God-pleasing institutions may be established; that inexhaustible funds may be collected for the support of the suffering, the poor, orphans, and widows; for the enlightenment of youth and for the expansion of God's Kingdom on the earth in all places, countries and tribes: that our country may be filled with all peace, calmness, and safety, and that God's name would be glorified everywhere by everyone. This is the final goal of our cry: "Thy Kingdom come!"[159]

Setting aside its enthusiasm, this holistic vision encompasses the peoples of the world and the improvement of state and society, eliminating social inequality and ignorance in society. The overall goal of this vision is glorifying God's name. All practical suggestions are subject to this grand vision.

In section 5, Ivanov proposes to unite all the local communities of Transcaucasia into one church with its centre in Tiflis.[160] The proposal betrays familiarity with the organisational model of the German Baptist Union,[161] though later he denied any significant German influence on Baptist origins in Transcaucasia.[162] His vision for this church was underdeveloped; it oscillated between a highly centralised model and a concept of a union of churches.

---

159. Aleksii Ia. (Dorodnitsyn), *Materialy*, 687.

160. Aleksii Ia. (Dorodnitsyn), *Materialy*, 689–90. See two paragraphs taken from section 5 of the document.

161. For the German model, see Val'kevich, *Zapiska*, 45–46.

162. In his review of Aleksii's "Vnutrenniaia Organisatsiia Obshchin" (Inner organisation of the communities), Ivanov denies that Baptism in Russia was planted by German missionaries. He insists on "perfect indigenousness" (*sovershennoi samobytnosti*) of the movement, ignited by independent Bible study and the sincere search for God's will among Molokans. He admits that German Baptists "(randomly) rendered a great service to the Russian Baptists in the sphere of organisation and spread of teaching," but claims that Mazaev's contribution far superseded that of Johann Wieler. See Ivanov, "Kniga Episkopa Aleksiia," 24–25.

Nevertheless, for Ivanov this structure was an instrument for uniting churches for God's mission. In subsequent years he returns to the idea of unity for the sake of mission.[163]

The description of constituting Tiflis Baptist Church and "O Bratskov Soiuze" mention mission as the key reason for uniting local churches into union. Liebig and Kargel, explaining the purpose of the union, refer to mission as its first task,[164] and the author of "O Bratskov Soiuze" agrees with that.[165] This idea motivated Wieler, when he united Baptist communities into Bratstvo and proposed to divide its decisions according to the level of priority, where mission-related resolutions occupied the highest position and should be accepted by all member churches. However, the way the missionary motif is formulated in the documents lacks theological depth and could be interpreted pragmatically. Ivanov's attempt to place missions and the unity of churches in the wider context of God's kingdom is worth further development.

2.4.5 Union as Implementation of Unity

For early Russian Baptists, unity was not something abstract but something to be implemented in the visible and tangible form of the union. The earliest occurrence of the idea dates to 17 August 1880 when Liebig and Kargel constituted the Tiflis community. Their explanation mentions that among other things the purpose of the union was "to fulfil the Saviour's word 'that all may be one' and demonstrate this unity to the world."[166] Here Liebig and Kargel formulated their concept of unity as a testimony to the world and grounded it in Christ's prayer about unity (John 17:21, 23).

This theme was actively employed by representatives of the evangelical Christian camp, particularly in a letter sent by Pashkov and Korff to the delegates of the first congress of Russian believers on 24 March 1884 (St Petersburg).[167] This is probably the earliest public document containing theological ideas on unity. The authors admit that, although their great vision of

---

163. See discussion of his contribution in section 3.4.3.2.
164. Val'kevich, *Zapiska*, Appendix 1, 45–47; cf. Aleksii Ia. (Dorodnitsyn), *Materialy*, 640.
165. Val'kevich, *Zapiska*, Appendix 3, 2.
166. Val'kevich, *Zapiska*, Appendix 1, 45–47; cf. Aleksii Ia. (Dorodnitsyn), *Materialy*, 640.
167. See in VSEKhB, *Istoriia Evangelskikh Khristian-Baptistov v SSSR*, 98–99; M[otorin], "Pervyi S'ezd Russkikh Veruiushchikh," 24–25. Some sources state that the congress occurred in 1883. See Holovashchenko, *Istoriia Evangel'sko-Baptistskogo Dvizheniia v Ukraine*, 251, 252.

unity cannot be fulfilled worldwide, it does not relieve them of the responsibility to enhance it locally: "If the completion of unity of all the earthly Church does not depend on us, then at least we are obliged to enhance the unity of the Church where the Lord has placed us."[168]

Pashkov and Korff use multiple quotations and allusions to biblical texts (John 17:21, 23; 1 Cor 12:12–13; 1 John 1:3; John 11:52; 10:16; Eph 4:3) and images (Christ's body, the mustard seed,[169] one flock). These are not just proof texts; they are organised into a coherent argument, which the authors intended to use to convince delegates of the necessity of such a meeting and to succinctly present their theological vision of unity. The key Bible text is John 17:21, 23, which has the obligatory force of a commandment or even a task to perform. Pashkov and Korff see Christ's prayer as his testament and will which is not yet fulfilled. This aspect adds significance and urgency to the task of unity and strengthens its obligatory force.[170] The authors refer to the biblical images that support their vision of unity. For instance, comparing Christ to a mustard seed, they point to the original intentions of Christ, the actual results of Christ's death and the subsequent growth of the kingdom. Appealing to the body of Christ, they point to the unity that already exists among believers and summon their readers to fulfil Christ's will. Recalling one flock and Shepherd, they strengthen the motive for unity, pointing out that it was one of Christ's original purposes.

Pashkov and Korff set the task of unity in the context of Christ's redemptive death, which is the foundation of unity. Christ is said to have "laid himself down for the Church"[171] and "died 'also for the scattered children of God to bring them together and make them one' and to bring them into one flock with one Shepherd."[172] He is the centre around which unity is formed.[173] Besides soteriological consequences, Christ's death also has ecclesiological

---

168. VSEKhB, *Istoriia Evangelskikh Khristian-Baptistov v SSSR*, 98.

169. The authors conflate images of the seed (John 12:24) and the mustard seed (Matt 13:31–32).

170. For Russians, someone's last will has obligatory power over those to whom it is pronounced.

171. VSEKhB, *Istoriia Evangelskikh Khristian-Baptistov v SSSR*, 98.

172. VSEKhB, *Istoriia Evangelskikh Khristian-Baptistov v SSSR*, 98–99.

173. VSEKhB, *Istoriia Evangelskikh Khristian-Baptistov v SSSR*, 99. On Korff recalling attempts to stop discussions on baptism with appeals to unity in Christ, see M[otorin], "Pervyi S'ezd Russkikh Veruiushchikh," 25.

implications, since believers become members of one body, the church, and are filled with one Holy Spirit.[174] Therefore, the task of unity is unavoidable. Members of one body filled with one Holy Spirit cannot be divided and have to find ways to express this unity visibly. The thought that believers are admitted into fellowship with the Father and the Son,[175] when placed next to the idea of believers belonging to the body of Christ and being filled with one Spirit, resembles the traditional Orthodox concept of *theosis*, although it is doubtful that the authors intended it. Perhaps they referred to the experience of conversion and resulting union with Christ typical to evangelical thinking.

The ideas expressed in Pashkov and Korff's letter find some repercussions in the minutes of the Novo-Vasil'evka conference. At this meeting, the issue of open communion with other evangelical fellow believers was raised. Wieler formulated it in a way similar to that of Pashkov and Korff:

> Since 1) all the believers all over the earth comprise one body of Christ; 2) Christ pleads in his farewell prayer: 'And now I am no longer in the world, but they are in the world, and I am coming to you. Holy Father, protect them in your name that you have given me, so that they may be one, as we are one' (John 17:11), – sincere desire and longing for unity in Christ should be the holy task of all believers. If it is not possible in the rite of baptism, one should seek to make it possible in the breaking of bread, i.e., in the Lord's Table.[176]

Appeals to the image of the body of Christ and Christ's prayer summon for implementation of the unity of all believers. Although the union is not mentioned, Wieler appealed to the delegates of the annual conference, calling them to implement unity with other Christians in such visible and tangible form as the Lord's Supper.[177]

---

174. VSEKhB, *Istoriia Evangelskikh Khristian-Baptistov v SSSR*, 98.

175. VSEKhB, *Istoriia Evangelskikh Khristian-Baptistov v SSSR*, 98.

176. Aleksii Ia. (Dorodnitsyn), *Materialy*, 580.

177. The majority of deputies were ready for a common table with those who after examination proved to be true believers but decided to leave the problem unresolved. Disapproval of open communion caused the withdrawal of Pashkov's financial support by 1890. Dyck, "Moulding the Brotherhood," 91.

2.5 Summary

This chapter demonstrates that Baptist churches associated with those who shared their conversion experience, their faith and their practices. The key reasons were survival, fellowship, mutual support and mission. Mission motivated Tiflis Baptist Church, Pashkov and Korff, Wieler and Mazaev. Even the vision of unity inspired by John 17:23 was subjected to mission. *Bratstvo* was the key theological concept. This ecclesiological category encompassed local communities and wider groups united by conversion experience, faith and practice. It incorporated believers' church ecclesiology that bridged concepts of visible church and universal church. It implied mission and union as visible implementations of unity. Bratstvo had a horizontal, open and non-hierarchical structure. In this model, the local church was primary, while the union was derivative and could not rule over local churches. However, it was incapable of resolving severe local conflict or dealing with the installation or removal of ministers. Organisationally, Bratstvo was an association which local churches joined or left freely. Thus, the motif for this was pragmatic: accumulating resources for effective missions. Two associational practices – annual conferences and trans-local ministers – homogenised beliefs and practices. The conferences resembled early church councils. How the understanding of ACs evolved in the context of relative religious freedom will be examined in the next chapter.

CHAPTER 3

The Rise and Demise of the Union (1905–1935)

3.1 Introduction

The Edict of Toleration (17 April 1905) opened a new page in the history of the Baptist union. Baptists enjoyed relative freedom and used it for missionary work and for the development of the union. In 1911 religious freedom was restricted again, and the outbreak of the First World War further slowed down development of the union. After the February Revolution (1917), freedom was restored and continued until the late 1920s. Baptist historians call this period "the golden age" of Soviet Baptists.[1] Vasilii Ivanov calls the years after 1905 an "epoch of open assault,"[2] alluding to the numerical growth and active evangelistic strategy of Baptists. The "golden age" ended in 1928 when the Soviet government changed its religious politics.[3] Roman Sitarchuk provides

---

1. Steeves, "Russian Baptist Union," 99–100; see also Prokhorov, "Golden Age." According to Prokhorov, quantitative growth during the "Golden Age" was an indirect result of the Bolsheviks' efforts to demolish the Russian Orthodox Church. Evangelical Christians and Baptists enjoyed freedom only until the Bolsheviks were done with the Orthodox Church.

2. Ivanov, "Polozhenie Baptistov," 69.

3. Mitrokhin, *Baptizm*, 389–91. Freedom began shrinking even in the early 1920s when Soviet officials began requesting the mandatory registration of religious communities. In 1923, the government made Baptist and Evangelical Christians change position on military service. See *Tserkov' Dolzhna Ostavat'sa Tserkov'iu*, 36–49; Coleman, "Most Dangerous Sect," 295–97. In 1924, Bolsheviks formed the League of the Militant Godless (LMG) to win the public through mass atheistic propaganda. For more on the LMG, see Pospielovsky, *History*, 49–68. For the Ukrainian context, see Pashchenko and Sitarchuk, "Deiaki Aspekty Derzhavno-Tserkovnykh

a detailed analysis of the Soviet government's policies towards evangelical sectarians in Ukraine. He points to two periods with distinct policies: the Soviet government's externally loyal attitude with secret measures against believers in 1920–1928 and the open campaign against Protestants in 1929–1939.[4]

In 1929 the Soviet government issued a resolution "On Religious Associations" that significantly limited religious freedom. Suffice it to point out that local officials could recall members of religious communities' executive committees; religious activities were limited to meeting the religious needs of the community inside of buildings; all forms of mutual support and grassroots organisations were forbidden; preachers and evangelists were to operate only in the area of the community or communities where they were registered; and regional and national assemblies were convened only with the permission of Soviet officials.[5] The level of interference of the government was so intense that, according to Sitarchuk, "after intrusion of the government into development of protestant churches, distinctives in their organisational structure are wiped away and it becomes similar to the structures of Communist Party and Soviet organisations."[6] It was numerical growth and the development of organisational forms that caused anti-Protestant campaigns in the 1920s and 1930s.[7] The leaders were imprisoned or killed by Communists.[8] As a result, regional Baptist unions disappeared by 1930 and the Federated Baptist Union of the USSR (FBU) ceased to exist by 1935.[9] As Albert Boiter aptly summarises: "It suffices to note that by 1939 only a few hundred churches remained open, tens of thousands having been forcibly

---

Vidnosyn"; Sitarchuk, "Represii shchodo Protestants'kykh Tserkov"; Goloshchapova, "Hromady Evnagel'skikh Khrystyian-Baptistiv."

4. Sitarchuk, "Diial'nist' Protestants'kykh Konfesii," 3.

5. For a detailed analysis, see Gsovski, "Legal Status," 7–23.

6. Sitarchuk, "Diial'nist' Protestants'kykh Konfesii," 2. In chapter 4, I shall demonstrate how these transformations were embodied in AUCECB structure and practices after the Second World War. See, for example, a notice in the protocol of the council of UUAB on the presence of someone named Katunin, a representative of NKVD (the Soviet secret police), during a meeting of the council. See Aleshko, "O Zasedanii Soveta," 50; cf. "Plenum Soveta Vseukrainskogo Soiuza," 57.

7. Sitarchuk, "Diial'nist' Protestants'kykh Konfesii," 9.

8. VSEKhB, *Istoriia Evangelskikh Khristian-Baptistov v SSSR*, 398; Mitrokhin, *Baptizm*, 393–96; see also Gsovski, "Legal Status," 23–25.

9. Boiter, "Law and Religion," 109–11; see also Savinskii, *Istoriia Evangelskikh Khristian-Baptistov Ukrainy, Rossii, Belorussii (1917–1967)*, 116–18.

closed in successive waves of antireligious fervor, along with all seminaries, monasteries, and religious publications. No religion had a functioning administrative centre."[10] Against this background, the rise and demise of the Baptist union took place.

3.2 Organisational Developments of Associations of Churches

The initial years of this period are characterised by quantitative growth, continuing geographic expansion, the organisational development of the union and active dialogue with the Evangelical Christians on the merger of their unions. Geographically, the Baptists spread to Siberia, the Far East and Central Asia. Nevertheless, the period of 1917–1921 was complicated by the collapse of normal communication between the centre of the empire and its periphery due to the Russian Civil War. Geographical remoteness prompted Russian Baptists to seek better models for fellowship and evangelisation.

3.2.1 Regionalisation and Branching of the Union

Congresses during this period (1907–1911) addressed new challenges. The union of churches began branching into departments (*otdely*) that united churches scattered over the vast territories and belonging to several administrative and territorial units.

At Rostov-on-Don (1907), responding to the report of a local congress in Omsk, delegates established "department [*otdel*] of the Union and the Missionary Society in Blagoveshchensk" and encouraged Odesa churches to gather for a district (*raionnaia*) conference, for "such conferences that help acquainting with each other, are rather desirable in that sense that they assist to eradicate local misunderstandings and satisfy needs of this district; the decisions of this conference should be in harmony with the direction of general conferences and their resolutions."[11] The congress in Kyiv (30 April–6 May 1908) permitted departments (*otdely*) to be organised with the condition that "they should not act contrary to the general direction of the Union, to have maintained unity between themselves and be in concord with all churches

---

10. Boiter, "Law and Religion," 111.
11. "Protokol Zasedanii Konferentsii," 21.

of the Baptist Union."[12] This development follows logically the development of relations between local churches and promotion of local missions.[13] In Moscow (25 September–1 October 1911), I. A. Goliaev, a former president of the union, proposed to unite local communities in the European part of Russia into districts (*raiony*) and appoint senior presbyters (*starshii presviter*) to oversee them.[14] Districts coincide with administrative borders of provinces (*gubernia*) or regions (*oblast*).[15] After some debates, the idea was approved with recommendation to districts to concentrate on inner improvement to avoid damage to the union.[16] Districts represent another structural level of the union.[17] Stevees correctly assumes that the catalyst of this step was two-fold: the growth of relations and initiatives on the grassroots level that "threaten to disrupt the work of the Russian Baptist Union" and shrinking of freedom that might block the administrative efforts of the union.[18] The union needed a model that would regulate a haphazard process of branching by subordinating local bodies and ensuring they were in tune. The Vladikavkaz congress (1917) abrogated districts, but they continued to exist and grow. The delegates recognised "the Siberian and Far Eastern Departments and one general Union in Russia without districts,"[19] and commissioned the board to establish the Turkestan Department.[20] Both steps addressed geographical remoteness and a lack of good communication with the regions complicated by general post-revolutionary disorder. These factors would play a key role in the drift towards a federated model.

Between 1908 and 1926, the union was in poor order: local churches could be part of a district, department or even the union itself. By 1925, the

---

12. "Protokol Zasedanii S'ezda," 18.

13. "Raionnyi S'ezd," 19–20.

14. Timoshenko, "S'ezd Baptistov v Moskve," 367; Levindanto, "O Sluzhenii Starshego Presvitera," 48.

15. Mazaev, "O Nashikh Nuzhdakh," 11.

16. Timoshenko, "S'ezd Baptistov v Moskve," 367.

17. See minutes or summary of congresses in Odesa and Oms'k (1907) in *Baptist*, no. 4, 8–9, 12–17; Novouzen'sk and Khar'kiv (1908) in *Baptist*, no. 2, 18–19, 28–29; Peski (1908) in *Baptist*, no. 8, 19–20; Rostov-on-Don, Kyiv and Poltava (1908) in *Baptist*, no. 10, 19–20; Nikolaevka (1909) in *Baptist*, no. 8, 11–12; Stavropol'e (1909) in *Baptist*, no. 13, 17–20; and Konstantinovka (1909) in *Baptist*, no. 2, 13–14.

18. Steeves, "Russian Baptist Union," 82–83.

19. *Pervyi Svobodnyi S'ezd Russkikh Baptistov*, 13–14.

20. *Pervyi Svobodnyi S'ezd Russkikh Baptistov*, 15.

union comprised six departments, twenty-nine districts that did not belong to the departments and twenty-five local congregations that did not belong to districts.[21] Geographical expansion of the union made a centralised organisational system invalid. Interaction with the centre was slow and ineffective. This was also aggravated by the different numerical and organisational size of departments and legal dissimilarities in Soviet republics. Relations and responsibilities of district associations, departments or the union itself were foggy. Steeves aptly illustrates this with a metaphor of "an old house to which additions and alterations had been made over the years in a haphazard manner."[22]

The situation was resolved at the Twenty-Sixth Congress of Baptists in the USSR (Moscow, 14–18 December 1926) when the federative model was approved.[23] This was "an association of several independent unions into one Union with some spheres of activity singled-out under the centre's authority."[24] The official report reads: "Our overgrown brotherhood cannot be directed by the old centralised approach when management of all affairs concentrated in one place. The life itself brought forward the emergence of the local Unions that met spiritual needs of the Brotherhood within the limits of their territory."[25] The FBU consisted of eight regional unions: the Far Eastern Baptist Union, Siberian Baptist Union, Central Asian Baptist Union, North Caucasian Baptist Union, Transcaucasian Baptist Union, Ukrainian Union of Associations of Baptists (with a German section), Crimean Baptist Union and North Russian Baptist Union (with a Latvian section).[26] All district associations and local churches that were not part of districts or departments, should either join regional unions or establish a new regional union. In 1927, two regional unions were formed and joined the FBU: the Volga-Kama Union of Baptists[27] and the Baptist Union of Central Regions of Russia.[28]

---

21. "Spisok Otdelov, Raionov Soiuza Baptistov," 22; *Zapis' Zasedanii Plenuma*, 28.
22. Steeves, "Russian Baptist Union," 218.
23. "26-i Vsesoiuznyi S'ezd Baptistov SSSR," 24.
24. *26 Vsesoiuznyi S'ezd Baptistov*, 2.
25. "26-i Vsesoiuznyi S'ezd Baptistov SSSR," 24.
26. *26 Vsesoiuznyi S'ezd Baptistov*, 99.
27. *Protokoly i Materialy*; Filadelfiiskii, "Polozhennoe Nachalo."
28. "Pervyi s'ezd Tsentral'nogo Soiuza Baptistov."

3.2.2 Ukrainian Union of Associations of Baptists: A Case of Regionalisation

Against this background occurred emergence and growth of Ukrainian Union of Associations of Baptists (UUAB). The aftermath of the Bolshevik takeover in St. Petersburg and Moscow (1917) and the Russian Civil War (1917–1922) prevented the convening of the annual Baptist congress in 1918. Meanwhile, Ukraine declared its independence from Russia and established the Ukrainian People's Republic.[29]

On 1–8 October 1918, about 130 delegates of more than seventy churches gathered for the First All-Ukrainian Baptist Congress in Kyiv.[30] They approved the committee for developing a statute and confession of faith and voted for establishing a periodical publication in Ukraine.[31] By 1930, Ukrainian Baptists had convened four congresses: in Zinov'evsk (May 1921)[32]; in Kyiv (1922); and in Khar'kiv (12–17 May 1925 and 10–13 May 1928).[33] Ukrainian Baptist minister and editor of *Baptist Ukrainy* (Ukrainian Baptist), Ivan Kmeta-Efimovich (1901–1997), described these in terms of the slow growth and maturation of Ukrainian Baptists' self-awareness. He also mentions the constant attempts of the Russian Baptist leaders to discourage the independent existence of the UUAB.[34]

The growth and significance of the Ukrainian Baptist churches was recognised by the plenum of the All-Russian Union of Baptists in 1924 that

---

29. On these complex political events, see Plokhy, *Gates of Europe*, 204–27.

30. *Pervyi Vseurkainskii S'ezd Baptistov*. Reshetnikov and Sannikov mention 110 delegates. See Reshetnikov and Sannikov, *Obzor Istorii*, 144. The leadership of the Russian Baptist Union approved this congress. However, the delegates left the case of Ukrainian union for the next all-Russian congress. See *Pervyi Vseurkainskii S'ezd Baptistov*, 7, 15.

31. *Pervyi Vseurkainskii S'ezd Baptistov*, 9–10, 11–12, 14. On other regional congresses in this period, see Savinskii, *Istoriia Evangelskikh Khristian-Baptistov Ukrainy, Rossii, Belorussii (1917–1967)*, 87–88.

32. Zinov'evsk (1924–1934) was a city in Central Ukraine, formerly Elisavetgrad (1784–1924), then Kyrovograd (1934–2016), and now Kropyvnytskyi.

33. Unfortunately, the documents of the Second and Third All-Ukrainian Baptist Congresses did not survive. We can only rely on short summaries provided in Kmeta-Efimovich, "Do Istorii Z'izdiv," 40–41. Initially, the fifth congress was planned for 1927, but it was postponed until 1928. See Kostiukov, "Vsem Obshchinam," 43. All-Ukrainian Congresses occurred approximately every three years.

34. Kmeta-Efimovich, "Do Istorii Z'izdiv," 40–41. He reminds his readers that in 1922 Ukrainian Baptists even agreed to liquidate the Ukrainian Baptist Union. See Kmeta-Efimovich, "Do Istorii Z'izdiv," 41; see also Savinskii, *Istoriia Evangelskikh Khristian-Baptistov Ukrainy, Rossii, Belorussii (1917–1967)*, 88–89.

approved the establishment of the Ukrainian Department "in consideration of felt necessity."³⁵ This obviously was a concession to the reality of the maturing UUAB. The Fourth Congress of UUAB (1925) was of such significance that almost all the Council of the Union of Baptists of the USSR attended the meeting.³⁶ The most important question on the agenda was the "organisation of All-Ukrainian Union of Baptist Communities [sic!],"³⁷ which was driven by several different reasons. First, the Ukrainian legislation significantly differed from that of the Russian Federation. Second, the solutions of all the issues of Baptist communities in relation to the state were concentrated in Khar'kiv not in Moscow.³⁸ Finally, Ukrainian was not only the official language of the Ukrainian Soviet Socialist Republic but was also the language of worship for many Ukrainians. As Pavel Ia. Datsko, a Baptist minister and vice-president of UUAB, formulated it later, "we live in the moment of the revival of national self-awareness that influences the life of our brotherhood."³⁹ UUAB conceded to follow the guidance of the Baptist centre in Moscow in all the important aspects of spiritual life.⁴⁰

According to Sitarchuk, all Ukrainian Protestant associations, including Baptists, by 1930s "had characteristics of independent ecclesiastical organisation: institution of power, clear organisational structure, unified rituals, separate from the general union finances, own publishing houses, youth organisations, cultural and educational institutions etc."⁴¹ These characteristics

---

35. Baptist [pseudo], "S'ezd Plenuma Soveta," 5. All-Russian Union of Baptists was renamed in the Union of Baptist of the USSR in 1924.

36. "Chetvertyi Vseukrainskii S'ezd," 1. The official report of the congress published in *Baptist* points to the hot debates over the Ukrainian Baptist Union. See "Chetvertyi Vseukrainskii S'ezd," 4; see also Kostiukov, "K Zasedaniiu Soveta," 32–33.

37. "Chetvertyi Vseukrainskii S'ezd," 2. Kharkiv was the capital of Ukraine from 1919 to 1934. This is a variation of the name of the Ukrainian Union of Associations of Baptists.

38. "Chetvertyi Vseukrainskii S'ezd," 4.

39. Datsko, "Soiuz Baptistov i Ego Deiatel'nost," 43.

40. The Moscow centre retained some power over Ukrainian Baptists through contacting Ukrainian communities, sending evangelists and collecting money for mission directly from local churches with only one concession: these acts should be previously negotiated with the Ukrainian Baptist Union. See "Chetvertyi Vseukrainskii S'ezd," 4.

41. Sitarchuk, "Diial'nist' Protestants'kykh Konfesii," 8–9. Goloshchapova comes to similar conclusions. See Goloshchapova, "Organisatsiina Budova Baptysts'kykh Hromad," 320.

led Sitarchuk to conclude that this "evidences for their eventual overcoming of the limits of classical 'sectarianism.'"[42]

In 1925, all UUAB churches were organised into eleven district associations (*raiony*)[43] that by 1926 were reorganised into fourteen regional (*oblast*) associations.[44] In 1926, UUAB consisted of more than sixty thousand members in one thousand churches and groups,[45] two hundred ministers and thirty-four permanent evangelists.[46] UUAB established departments of evangelism, legal affairs, finances, publishing, the training of evangelists and choir directors, and organisation and statistics.[47]

Structurally, UUAB consisted of three levels: local communities, regional associations and the national union.[48] In this structure, local communities played the most significant role.[49] They collected funds to support permanent evangelists and the executive board of the UUAB. Regional associations met

---

42. Sitarchuk, "Diial'nist' Protestants'kykh Konfesii," 9. For a similar proposal regarding early English Baptists, see Fiddes, "Church and Sect." Goloshchapova points out that "in 1930, the structure of the all-Ukrainian association of Baptists was crushed under the pressure of totalitarian power. The absence of the centre made local communities defend themselves on their own and led to their dispersion, isolation and the severance of ties between communities, *de facto* returning the confession to the level of a sect and leaving it defenceless in the face of pressure and repressions." See Goloshchapova, "Osnovni Vektory Diial'nosti," 261.

43. Kostiukov, "Ot Pravleniia Vseukrainskogo Soiuza Baptistov," 31–32.

44. Kostiukov, "Doklad Pravleniia Vseukrainskogo Soiuza Baptistov," 67–68; Pravlenie, "Ot Soiuza k Obshchinam," 53.

45. Kostiukov, "Doklad Pravleniia Vseukrainskogo Soiuza Baptistov," 69. Goloshchapova, referring to Sitarchuk, says that in 1925 UUAB consisted of 34,000 members united into 511 communities and groups. See Goloshchapova, "Dynamika Tchysel'nosti Hromad," 128. In 1926, the council of UUAB reported a 15 to 20 percent increase in membership. See Aleshko, "Aven-Ezer," 55. Goloshchapova confirms the significant quantitative growth of UUAB in the 1920s and 30s with some regional peculiarities. This statistical data does not account for Baptist churches in Galychyna, Volyn' and Besarabia, since they were only included into the USSR's territory in 1939. See Reshetnikov and Sannikov, *Obzor Istorii*, 149–69; Domashovets', *Narys Istorii*, 161–226.

46. Kostiukov, "Doklad Pravleniia Vseukrainskogo Soiuza Baptistov," 69. Domashovets mentions four hundred ministers and forty-six permanent evangelists. See Domashovets', *Narys Istorii*, 155; see also Reshetnikov and Sannikov, *Obzor Istorii*, 147.

47. Kostiukov, "Doklad Pravleniia Vseukrainskogo Soiuza Baptistov," 65.

48. Goloshchapova, "Organisatsiina Budova Baptysts'kykh Hromad," 153.

49. Goloshchapova, "Organisatsiina Budova Baptysts'kykh Hromad," 153–55.

annually.[50] They took responsibility for evangelism[51] and the education of ministers in their respective regions.[52] Presidents of associations were members of the council of UUAB which also included the executive board and some personal members.[53] The board (the president, vice-president, treasurer and secretary) was responsible for operative leadership. The council met at least twice annually.[54] During such meetings participants discussed overall strategy, acute problems, planned next steps, appointed permanent evangelists and heard reports from regional associations and from the board for the previous period.[55] Protocols and official informational reports in *Baptist Ukrainy* (Ukrainian Baptist) depict the very intensive and highly organised ministry of UUAB. The official report of the Fifth Congress of UUAB resolves:

> The congress, having heard reports of the presidents of regional associations, recognises that associations which were established by the life itself are very fruitful and there are achievements in evangelism, music and singing. This fruitfulness is accounted for proximity of associational boards to their communities and [serving as] liaisons between communities and the centre of the Union.[56]

The case of UUAB could be extrapolated to a degree to other regional unions. No doubt this situation caused discussions on the form of the union.

---

50. For reports of typical regional congresses, see Ziubanov, "Na Nive Bozhiei"; Shalamov, "Do Sego Mesta Pomog Nam Gospod'"; Krashtan, "Godovoi Prazdnik"; Tret'iakov, "S'ezd v Konotope"; Ziubanov, "Trinnadtsatyi S'ezd Sredne-Iuzhnogo Ob'edineniia"; Dranyi, "S'ezd Zaporozhskogo Oblastnogo Ob'edinenia."

51. It seems that from 1925, evangelistic activities were concentrated in the regional associations. This practice changed in 1927, when UUAB decided to form thirty-three missionary locations, reckoning twenty-five to thirty communities each, and assign thirty-three permanent evangelists for these locations. The council of UUAB also assigned thirteen senior and experienced ministers for the work of "economy" [*domostroitelstvo*], that is, the inner arrangement of churches, the ordination of new ministers, conflict resolution, etc., in their regional associations. See Kostiukov, "Vsem Obshchinam," 44–45.

52. For a report about such meetings and the discussed themes, see "Na Nive Bozhiei" (1926); Siora, "Oblastnaia Dukhovnaia Konferentsiia."

53. Kostiukov, "Ot Pravleniia Vseukrainskogo Soiuza Baptistov," 31–32; Aleshko, "Aven-Ezer," 52–53; "5-i Vseurkainskii S'ezd," 36–38.

54. Kostiukov, "Ot Pravleniia Vseukrainskogo Soiuza Baptistov"; Pravlenie, "Ot Soiuza k Obshchinam."

55. Aleshko, "Aven-Ezer"; Aleshko, "O Zasedanii Soveta."

56. "5-i Vseurkainskii S'ezd," 35.

3.2.3 Discussions on the Configuration of the Union

Two rounds of hot discussions, in 1909–1912 and 1924–1925, preceded approval of the federative model. There were attempts to keep processes under control with old tested models and slow but inevitable recognition that new situations required new models.

Goliaev's proposal,[57] which addressed the processes of branching and regionalisation, invited some criticism. The most consistent opponent of forming grassroots districts and departments was Dei Mazaev, who opted for the centralisation of the process. In 1909, commenting on the minutes of the Caucasus district congress, which organised into the Caucasus Department,[58] he wrote: "Formation of departments can be recognised as justified, seems to me, only if the Union establishes them and they are its brainchild; in that case when a region establishes departments without Union's approval and participation of its representatives such cannot be recognised as rightful."[59] He countered the opinion that the union could simply approve departments, stating that it should generate departments, which are "flesh of its flesh and bones of its bones, and not adopt them as something foreign."[60]

In 1912, Mazaev discussed the agenda of the coming congress[61] with Feodor P. Balikhin (1854–1919), an influential Baptist minister, and someone referred to as "Baptist."[62] Balikhin proposed that district congresses should define what should be done, and in which geographical limits, by local churches in terms of mission.[63] He maintained that districts should fit administrative-territorial units of the empire. Mazaev opposed such division claiming that some churches would be remote from the administrative centre and lack constant relations with it. He proposed that districts should follow the principle of accessibility of communities, which required fewer expenses for visiting evangelists. Mazaev distinguished "artificial" and "natural

---

57. See "Protokol Zasedanii Konferentsii," 21.

58. "Protokol S'ezda Predstavitelei," 17.

59. Mazaev, "K Protokolu," 20.

60. Mazaev, "K Protokolu," 20. Ivanov rejects departments and districts for one union but supports "local autonomous unions" responsible for local mission. See Ivanov, "O Soiuze (okonchanie)," 399.

61. Mazaev, "O Nashikh Nuzhdakh"; Mazaev, "O Nashikh Nuzhdakh (prodolzhenie)."

62. This unnamed constrisbutor may have been Mikhail Timoshenko. See Baptist [pseudo], "Nashy Nuzhdy"; Baptist [pseudo], "Nashy Nuzhdy (prodolzhenie)."

63. Balikhin, "Mysli po Voprosam Programmy."

or organic" districts. The former resulted from a formal decision of the union, executive board or district congress and were "lacking spiritual connection and, thus, useless."[64] The latter emerged from "gravity of communities towards their centre and such a district is natural and organic."[65] Mazaev seemingly changed his earlier position which in fact was just a rhetorical concession to his opponents. He claimed that "district associations will do more harm than help"[66] because they would divide union into parts, begin manifesting their leaders' preferences and run into the danger of contradictions and tensions that undercut common ministry. He thought districts stemmed from the ambitions of local leaders striving to build their own authority rather than keep unity with the centre. Such associations, prognosed Mazaev, would grow into local unions and "threaten not only the unity of the Union but its very existence and . . . swallow the gross body of our Union as did the skinny Egyptian cows."[67] If, instead of supplying funds to the union, districts withdraw funds from the union, then, resolved Mazaev, let "rather districts perish than the Union."[68] In 1917, Mazaev claimed that formation of districts "turned our once closely-related union, one whole, into a wandering flock,"[69] and praised the congress for "restitution of the Union in its previous form and definitive elimination of the Union's division into districts that had caused us so much harm."[70]

The next round of discussions was partially stirred by worsening relations between Baptist and Evangelical Christian unions and the significant strengthening of regional departments. Key participants of this discussion were Mikhail D. Timoshenko (1885–c. 1938), member of the Union of Baptists of the USSR's executive board, and Iakov Ia. Vins (d. 1940), president of Far Eastern Baptist Union, Pavel Ia. Datsko (1884–1941), and Alexander S. Anan'in (1894–c. 1940), president of Siberian Baptist Union.[71] Vins and

---

64. Mazaev, "O Nashikh Nuzhdakh," 11.
65. Mazaev, "O Nashikh Nuzhdakh," 11.
66. Mazaev, "O Nashikh Nuzhdakh," 11.
67. Mazaev, "O Nashikh Nuzhdakh," 11.
68. Mazaev, "O Nashikh Nuzhdakh," 11.
69. Mazaev, "Nechto o S'ezde," 13.
70. Mazaev, 14. On elimination of districts, see Anan'in, "Ob'edinenie Obshchin Baptistov," 16.
71. Timoshenko, "Soglasovannost' Raboty"; Belousov, "Pervyi Nazidatel'nyi S'ezd."

Datsko supported federated union while Anan'in and Timoshenko opted for one union with districts and departments but wanted to see clearer demarcation lines in their authority and responsibilities.

At the plenum of the union in Moscow (5–12 December 1925), Iakov Vins proposed to develop a federated scheme of relations between the departments and the centre and requested to join the Far Eastern Baptist Union to the Union of Baptists of the USSR on the basis of these relations.[72] The request was accepted but relations with the centre left intact.[73] Earlier in 1925, Ukrainian Baptists assumed the status of a union. These changes were left unnoticed in the draft of the new statutes, presented by Nikolai V. Odintsov (c. 1886–1939), a member of the Executive Board of the Union of Baptists of the USSR, at the plenum, which admitted regional associations, departments and unions without clarifying their relations.[74]

Pavel Datsko addresses the question "What is better: five–six smaller autonomous unions united on the basis of federation or one powerful union?"[75] He opts for federation and points to pragmatic and organisational reasons.[76] For him, the union is a means of serving the major goals of spreading the gospel, encouraging spiritual growth and establishing a gospel-based economy (*domostroitel'stvo*) in Baptist churches.[77] These purposes could be reached efficiently only through several unions.[78] He refers to the necessity of decentralisation to better serve local needs and mentions regional legal and cultural peculiarities.[79] In the paper read at the congress in Moscow (1926), Datsko pointed to outer and inner reasons for decentralisation. The outer include the geographical spread of churches and remoteness from one centre; the administrative divisions of the USSR along territorial and ethnic lines; and the constant growth of the membership. The inner reasons include poor communication between the centre and churches for spiritual fellowship

---

72. *Zapis' Zasedanii Plenuma*, 16.
73. *Zapis' Zasedanii Plenuma*, 22; cf. Baptist [pseudo], "S'ezd Plenuma Soveta," 5.
74. *Zapis' Zasedanii Plenuma*, 72–74.
75. Datsko, "Soiuz Baptistov i Ego Deiatel'nost," 41.
76. Datsko, "Soiuz Baptistov i Ego Deiatel'nost," 41–43; Datsko, "O Forme Upravleniia Delami Soiuza," 93–98.
77. Datsko, "Soiuz Baptistov i Ego Deiatel'nost," 41–42.
78. Datsko, "Soiuz Baptistov i Ego Deiatel'nost," 42.
79. Datsko, "Soiuz Baptistov i Ego Deiatel'nost," 42–43.

and practical Christian activity; low spiritual level of church members; and deficient organisation and gospel-based order in the communities.[80] Datsko implies that only local unions could effectively help churches in spiritual development and proper church order. He concludes,

> federation of many unions is the best form of our union organisation for it presupposes such administrative machinery that will best serve the needs of communities and significantly expand the cause of evangelisation in our country; this will be what we are longing for and what the Lord requires of us.[81]

In 1926 an extensive article on the union by Alexander Anan'in was published,[82] as well as Timoshenko's response to Datsko and Anan'in.[83] Anan'in's article deals with the foundations, historical experience and purposes of associating among Baptists.[84] The article not only described the current state of affairs, traced the historical development of districts and departments and justified the necessity of associating but contained a proposal for the configuration of the union. Anan'in attempted to dispel confusion over the rights and responsibilities of the union and its departments and districts.[85] He organised these around four purposes: mission, nurture, economy (*domostroitel'stvo*) and mutual help.[86] In spite of good intentions, Anan'nin failed to clarify the issue. In his scheme, the union would supply Central Russia with evangelists and send organised units of three evangelists (two from the union and one from a department) and a choir; departments would provide evangelists for their churches; and districts would have unpaid evangelists who work from door to door.[87] The union would operate as a department. Anan'in secures to the union the exclusive responsibility to run a school for preachers and publish edifying literature.[88] Departments occupy

---

80. Datsko, "O Forme Upravleniia Delami Soiuza," 95–97.
81. Datsko, "Soiuz Baptistov i Ego Deiatel'nost'," 42.
82. Anan'in, "Ob'edinenie Obshchin Baptistov," 12–19.
83. Timoshenko, "Soiuz Baptistov i Ego Deiatel'nost'." He alludes to Datsko and critiques Anan'in.
84. Anan'in, "Ob'edinenie Obshchin Baptistov," 12.
85. Anan'in, "Ob'edinenie Obshchin Baptistov," 18.
86. Anan'in, "Ob'edinenie Obshchin Baptistov," 18.
87. Anan'in, "Ob'edinenie Obshchin Baptistov," 18–19.
88. Anan'in, "Ob'edinenie Obshchin Baptistov," 18.

the central place, and the scheme is closer to that of a federated union but is not identical with it.

Timoshenko also argues, *contra* Vins and Datsko, for a centralised model: "The division of the Baptists into separate unions according to political or national borders in our country will not be helpful to the cause of unity and conformity."[89] He proposes to delegate organisational and administrative responsibilities to the centre while districts and departments focus on convening local congresses for spiritual fellowship and edification in faith and Christian life. The centre's plenipotentiary representatives would implement general decisions and resolutions in districts and departments.[90] Timoshenko thinks this scheme makes the work harmonious and releases additional funds and workers' energy.

Timoshenko's second article addresses the central management of the union and its relations with departments and districts. He strives for *via media* between a centralised union without districts and departments and strong and large departments that turn into independent unions, connected only by common interests.[91] He admits the inadequacy of a model where "all complex and responsible activity of the Union could be delegated to one or even two–three persons, putting on them all responsibility for running the affairs whereas they are incapable physically to delve into all the work."[92] To solve the crux of the relationship between the centre, the departments and the districts, Timoshenko proposes to concentrate missionary work, publishing and the training of preachers in the centre. Departments should be governed by representatives from the centre and should carry on evangelism according to a generally approved plan. Districts should stop centralised evangelistic work, delegating it to the local level, and concentrate on deepening the spiritual life of local churches by strengthening spiritual connections, convoking edifying congresses and business meetings, and putting into practice the resolutions and assignments of the all-union congress.[93] Timoshenko rightly criticises Anan'in for downplaying the union and turning it into a department.

---

89. Timoshenko, "Soglasovannost' Raboty," 29.
90. Timoshenko, "Soglasovannost' Raboty," 29.
91. Timoshenko, "Soiuz Baptistov i Ego Deiatel'nost'," 20.
92. Timoshenko, "Soiuz Baptistov i Ego Deiatel'nost'," 20.
93. Timoshenko, "Soiuz Baptistov i Ego Deiatel'nost'," 20, 21.

Timoshenko's administrative model looks as follows: The highest organ would be the all-union congress which would elect the executive board (three to five persons) and members of the council of the union (fifteen persons). Between the congresses, the council would meet at least two times a year. The plenum would consist of the heads of departments and districts, permanent evangelists and personal members recommended by the council or board. Decisions of the congress would be mandatory for the executive board, the council and the plenum. The congress would define the form of government of the union and approve or disapprove all the decisions made between congresses.[94] This scheme was accepted in 1926; with some amendments it still exists among Ukrainian Baptists.[95]

These discussions demonstrate that the proponents of the centralised model gave way to the new reality and modified their position in attempts to address the issues the union faced at this stage. The transformations touched not only the configuration of the union but also its leadership structures.

3.2.4 Transformations of Leadership Structures

Structural changes of the union also involved transformations of the form of government. It changed at least three times: presidential (1905–1917), collegial (1918–1923) and presidential (1924–1935).

In 1907 Vasilii Pavlov was commissioned to draft the statute. The first draft, known as "Proposal No.1," was based on the statutes of the German Baptist Union.[96] An alternative version, known as "Proposal No. 2," was composed in 1909 by a council gathered in Rostov-on-Don.[97] They differed on the constituency, goals and governance of the union. The St. Petersburg congress (1910) discussed these proposals and approved an amended version. The highest organ was the annual congress. It would elect an executive board for a year (president, vice-president, secretary, vice-secretary, treasurer and

---

94. Timoshenko, "Soiuz Baptistov i Ego Deiatel'nost'," 20, 21.
95. See section 5.2.
96. Pavlov, "K Reorganisatsii Nashego Soiuza," 26–30; Pavlov, "Besedy 'Baptista,'" 276.
97. "Protokol Ocherednogo Zasedaniia Missionerskogo Obschestva," 18–19; Pavlov, "Besedy 'Baptista,'" 276. It is not clear what meeting Pavlov means. See Pavlov, "Nam Pishut," 21. The minutes of the Rostov-on-Don congress (27 September–7 October 1909) have no resolution on the statute. See "Protokol S'ezda Predstavitelei." A report on the St. Petersburg congress indicates that Proposal No. 2 was discussed in Rostov-on-Don. See O[dintsov], "S'ezd Baptistov v S.-Peterburge," 304.

three candidates).[98] The board would meet at least two times a year and was authorised to invite, accept and remove evangelists, define the ministry of districts and prepare agendas for annual congresses.[99]

The period of 1917–1919 required a major change from a presidential to collegial model of leadership. This was forced by the Russian Civil War that divided the country and prevented travel and the communication of the board. Mikhail D. Timoshenko and Pavel V. Pavlov (1883–1936), son of the well-known Baptist pioneer Vasily G. Pavlov, organised "a leadership core," the interim board, in the centre of Russia until the next congress convened. They invited such respected Baptist ministers as Vasilii G. Pavlov and Ivan N. Shilov (1887–1942) to join the board.[100] The "core" coordinated all the activities of the union and merger negotiations with the Russian Evangelical Alliance. In 1920 the deputies officially moved to the collegial model.[101] The congress was the highest organ of the union. It elected an executive board consisting of three members and five candidates, two of them having an advisory role but no vote, and the council consisting of twenty members. This model operated until 1924 when the plenum decided to switch again to the presidential model.[102]

When in 1926 the Baptist union switched to a federative model it retained the presidential form of governance. This influenced membership of the council which included members of the executive board (president, secretary and treasurer), representatives of local Baptist unions (one representative from unions of over fifteen thousand members and three from unions of over forty thousand members) and seven of "the most spiritually experienced and respected" personal members.[103] The congress elected members of the board and personal members of the council. The councils of local unions elected and delegated their representatives.[104] Members of the council were plenipo-

---

98. "Proekt Ustava Soiuza," 350; *IV Vserossiiskii S'ezd*, 25.

99. "Proekt Ustava Soiuza," 351. In 1917, the board comprised twelve members including the president. See *Pervyi Svobodnyi S'ezd Russkikh Baptistov*, 14.

100. *Otchet Vserossiiskogo S'ezda*, 8–9.

101. *Otchet Vserossiiskogo S'ezda*, 18–19.

102. Baptist [pseudo], "S'ezd Plenuma Soveta," 5; "26 Vsesoiuznyi S'ezd Baptistov," 29.

103. "26 Vsesoiuznyi S'ezd Baptistov," 102.

104. "26 Vsesoiuznyi S'ezd Baptistov," 29.

tentiary representatives of the union, responsible for the implementation of the resolutions of the congress and the purposes of the union.[105]

3.3 Associational Practices

The expansion and growth of Baptists duirng this period of their history brought to the fore the need to keep up with it and provide spiritual nurture to the converted and proper supervision of church economy (*domostroitel'stvo*). These needs were addressed through edifying conferences and senior presbyters.

3.3.1 Annual Edifying Conferences

The idea of edifying conferences emerged in 1909 to sustain the growth and spiritual vitality of the churches. The delegates of the Caucasus Department of the union resolved to organise annual meetings for those in the immediate vicinity of each other for "better acquaintance with God's Word and fellowship with each other."[106]

In 1912, Wilgelm A. Fetler (1883–1954) and Ivan V. Neprash published an article on the subject accompanied by Dei Mazaev's comments.[107] The authors ascribed the pitiful state of spiritual immaturity in Baptist churches to the prevailing evangelistic character of worship services which aimed at conversion but failed to edify new believers. They claimed that a key Christian purpose was "spiritual nurture, inner sanctification and perfection."[108] Since this purpose could not be accomplished through general congresses that "discuss issues of dogmatic nature, inner theological order of communities,"[109] annual edifying conferences should be arranged. These should gather preachers, evangelists and those believers "who seek to serve the Lord."[110] The congresses could last for one or two weeks, with three or four gatherings a day, and focus on Bible studies and prayers. Fetler and Neprash suggested focussing on "death with Christ, baptism of the Holy Spirit, sanctification, victory over

---

105. "26 Vsesoiuznyi S'ezd Baptistov," 102.
106. "Protokol S'ezda Predstavitelei," 18.
107. Fetler, Neprash, and Mazaev, "Nazidatel'nye S'ezdy," 9–11.
108. Fetler, Neprash, and Mazaev, "Nazidatel'nye S'ezdy," 9.
109. Fetler, Neprash, and Mazaev, "Nazidatel'nye S'ezdy," 9.
110. Fetler, Neprash, and Mazaev, "Nazidatel'nye S'ezdy," 10.

sin" or on studying Bible books or chapters.[111] Experienced spiritual brothers should present these topics in practical and applicable ways. They also proposed giving significant time to solitary and common prayer to strengthen participants "in their hearts."[112] Even a quick glance over the themes and format is inevitably reminiscent of Keswick's characteristic features.[113]

In the following issues of *Baptist*, several authors suggested their versions of edifying congresses.[114] Thus, Balikhin proposed to organise edifying gatherings for church members. These could occur in central churches on the occasion of celebrations, with the participation of invited preachers and open for members of other churches.[115] Dei Mazaev positively evaluated this proposal as giving the chance to edify church members and whole communities and not only selected representatives.[116] Perhaps external factors prevented the realisation of the idea on a national scale for the necessity of such conferences is emphasised again in 1917 and 1924.[117] The extant documents witness that edifying conferences were used as effective instrument of instruction and mobilisation on the level of districts and departments after 1917.[118] Alongside pragmatic goals, conferences maintained and expressed fraternal relations between churches on district and regional levels through worship, edification and participation in the Lord's Supper.[119] While edifying congresses addressed the spiritual needs and mobilisation of Christians, the need for proper order and the installation of ministers was resolved through trans-local ministers.

---

111. Fetler, Neprash, and Mazaev, "Nazidatel'nye S'ezdy," 10.
112. Fetler, Neprash, and Mazaev, "Nazidatel'nye S'ezdy," 10.
113. See Pierson, *Keswick Movement*, 63–80.
114. The text of these programmes did not survive, and the congresses never occurred.
115. Balikhin, "Mysli po Voprosam Programmy," 11.
116. Mazaev, "O Nashikh Nuzhdakh," 12.
117. *Pervyi Svobodnyi S'ezd Russkikh Baptistov*, 19; Baptist [pseudo], "S'ezd Plenuma Soveta," 5.
118. *Pervyi Svobodnyi S'ezd Sibirskogo Otdela*, 9, 15–16, 85–86; "Chetvertyi Vseukrainskii S'ezd," 4; Belousov, "Pervyi Nazidatel'nyi S'ezd"; "Na Nive Bozhiei" (1925), 34; Kostiukov, "K Zasedaniiu Soveta," 34; "Na Nive Bozhiei" (1926), 43–47; "Piatyi Vseurkainskii S'ezd," 9.
119. For instance, the official report from the Thirteenth Congress of Sredne-Iuzhnyi Association of Baptists says: "At the last day of the congress during the solemn divine service with the breaking of the bread brother M. D. Zagora, whose fevor and blessings in the ministry call for thanksgivings to the Lord, was ordaining evangelists." Ziubanov, "Trinnadtsatyi S'ezd Sredne-Iuzhnogo Ob'edineniia," 49. Perhaps here the Lord's Supper expresses the unity of the churches, while the ordination of evangelists during the congress is a way to commission evangelists for trans-local ministry. Cf. *Pervyi Svobodnyi S'ezd Sibirskogo Otdela*, 9, 15–16.

3.3.2 Trans-Local Ministers

In 1884–1904, evangelists not only spread the gospel but also unified local churches in doctrine and practice. In 1905–1935, under conditions of branching, expansion, the growing complexity of the union's ministry and changing relations with the state, the role of trans-local ministers only grew in significance. Besides traditional teacher-evangelists, Russian Baptists introduced "senior presbyters" who had slightly different functions. In this section I shall consider types of trans-local ministers and their role in ordination and church-state relations.

3.3.2.1 Types of trans-local ministers

Goliaev's proposal to introduce "senior presbyters" faced disagreement because their functions resembled those of bishops: oversight, control and communication.[120] Historian Sergei Savinskii, summarising their functions, states that they visited local churches to watch over them, oversee correct order and its improvement, encourage active participation in the union through offerings in the union's missionary work and support of the executive board. They also communicated correct understanding of government prescriptions in the churches. Senior presbyters reported to the congress.[121] According to Savinskii, this system existed until 1916.[122]

Baptists also had teachers or evangelists. In his fundamental article on ecclesiology, Nikolai Odintsov pointed to two categories of ministers in the church:[123] (1) apostles, prophets and teachers (or evangelists)[124] (2) and presbyters (or bishops) and deacons.[125] The latter meet local needs for ordinances,

---

120. Timoshenko, "S'ezd Baptistov v Moskve," 367. See A. E. Leushkin, "Pis'ma k Bratiam Evangel'skim Khristianam Baptistam" in Klibanov, *Istoria Religioznogo Sektantstva*, 238; cf. "A. E. Leushkin."

121. Savinskii, *Istoriia Evangel'skikh Khristian-Baptistov Ukrainy, Rossii, Belorussii (1867–1917)*, 273.

122. Savinskii, *Istoriia Evangel'skikh Khristian-Baptistov Ukrainy, Rossii, Belorussii (1917–1967)*, 133.

123. Odintsov, "O Tserkvi," 6–7.

124. Besides the twelve and those who saw the Lord, the circle of apostles includes all who "received from Him authority and power to proclaim the Gospel"; prophets are those who have the gift of inspired speech; and teachers are those who have special gift of teaching, as recognised by the church (Odintsov, "O Tserkvi," 6).

125. Odintsov, "O Tserkvi," 7. He equates presbyters and bishops; the former is status and the latter, function.

discipline and administration.[126] To the former God entrusted ministry of the word and prayer in the universal church because they are called by the Spirit (1) to preach God's word to lost sinners; (2) to strengthen the spiritual growth of disciples; and (3) to order churches through ordaining presbyters.[127] For Odintsov, only this group of apostles, prophets and teachers were free of "civilian affairs" and might live on the church's support. He elevated them, calling them "messengers of God's name," who "prepare a pristine sacrifice, sanctified by the Holy Spirit, and pleasing to God" and perform "the priestly duty."[128] Their status of "priests and shepherds" was not local; they were ministers of the universal church.[129] He concluded,

> according to God's word, the Lord has two categories of ministers in the Church: ministry of apostles, prophets and teachers is significant for the whole Church in its entirety, they hold the right, entrusted to them by the Lord, everywhere, they are God's ministers for *every* local church; ministry of the bishops (presbyters) and deacons has *local* significance: they have the rights through election by a local church in that church not everywhere: presbyter in Jerusalem cannot be presbyter in Antioch.[130]

Odintsov's distinction of two categories fit his understanding of the church as both universal society of all true people of God on earth and in heaven and as visible local gatherings.[131] What Odintsov failed to demonstrate was how trans-local ministers fit into his understanding of union where churches united "for mutual help and better success in missions" and were tied together by "mutual respect and love, characteristic to the disciples of one Teacher" and not by "interdependence in church life and actions."[132] It is unclear then how the ministry of teachers and evangelists correlated with this vision.

---

126. Odintsov, "O Tserkvi," 6.

127. Odintsov, "O Tserkvi," 6. For equating presbyters and teachers, see Sapozhnikov, "Sluzhiteli Tserkvi," 7; Levindanto, "O Pravakh Sluzhitelei Tserkvi," 20–21. For the need of trans-local ministers to order communities, see *Pervyi Svobodnyi S'ezd Sibirskogo Otdela*, 42.

128. Odintsov, "O Tserkvi," 6.

129. Odintsov, "O Tserkvi," 6.

130. Odintsov, "O Tserkvi," 7. Emphasis original.

131. Odintsov, "O Tserkvi," 4–5.

132. Odintsov, "O Tserkvi," 7. Odintsov's definition resembles Hiscox, and six of nine sections of the article follow Hiscox.

Perhaps by differentiating between local and trans-local ministers, Odintsov attempted to distinguish their functions to resolve tensions.[133] Nikolai Levindanto (1896–1966), an influential Baptist minister, turned to a similar problem, inquiring whether presbyters and teachers (i.e. evangelists) had similar ministerial status and equal rights "in economy" (*domostroitel'stvo*)[134] – that is, the "right of ordination, enquiring of complains against presbyters, working as presidents in districts, unions etc."[135] His question was prompted by an opinion that presbyters had exclusive rights both in local churches and "in economy."[136] Levindanto appealed to the confession of faith that equated the ministerial status of ordained evangelists and teachers with that of local presbyters, except presbyters had exclusive rights in the local church.[137] He grounded the right of teachers and evangelists "not on the nature of their ministry or title but on availability of the gifts of pastoral ministry and teaching (Eph 4:11) with outstanding spiritual strengths, proven faithfulness (1 Cor 4:2) and experience" and "on the level of trust and favour of God's people towards them as personalities, individual Christians and ministers in economy."[138] They were "worthy of double honour (1 Tim 5:17),"[139] which he interpreted as the honour in economy. His conclusion was straightforward: there is no need to divert a presbyter from a local church if "there is available a teacher-evangelist with recognised honour, who could successfully accomplish mission of ordering churches, ordination of presbyters and other ministers or work as the president of district or union."[140] Teachers and evangelists were not tied to one church and had particular roles in the ordering of churches and installation of ministers.

3.3.2.2 Trans-local ministers and the installation of ministers

The participation of ministers from other churches in the process of election and ordination was a standard practice among Baptists. Here the responsibility

---

133. See evidences in "Protokol Zasedanii Pervogo Ocherednogo Sobraniia," 24; *Ob'edinennyi S'ezd*, 15.
134. Levindanto, "O Pravakh Sluzhitelei Tserkvi," 20–21.
135. Levindanto, "O Pravakh Sluzhitelei Tserkvi," 21.
136. Levindanto, "O Pravakh Sluzhitelei Tserkvi," 21.
137. Levindanto, "O Pravakh Sluzhitelei Tserkvi," 20; cf. "Ispovedanie Very Khristian-Baptistov," 429.
138. Levindanto, "O Pravakh Sluzhitelei Tserkvi," 20.
139. Levindanto, "O Pravakh Sluzhitelei Tserkvi," 20.
140. Levindanto, "O Pravakh Sluzhitelei Tserkvi," 21.

for ordination shifts from local to trans-local ministers who assumed full responsibility for ordination and the ordering of churches. Thus, the conference of the Caucasus Department (1909) recommended that elders (*startsy*) and presbyters from other churches be present at the election or removal of ministers.[141] The department played the key role in the process of ordination by assuming responsibility for this.[142] The most significant rationale for having ministers from other churches present was "that with their [presbyters'] participation to maintain complete fellowship with each other and test those elected for ministry."[143] Thus, the participation of other ministers was an expression and instrument of fellowship between local churches. The testing of candidates before ordination could also be interpreted theologically as an examination of a candidate's standing in the Baptist and universal tradition.

Vasilii Ivanov based the presence of senior presbyters during election and ordination of ministers in local churches on Acts 7, which depicts the election of seven deacons in Jerusalem.[144] When apostles passed away, they were substituted for senior presbyters, whom Ivanov identified with "the elders who rule well" (1 Tim 5:17), putting them on par with bishops and calling them "ruling presbyters-bishops."[145] Ivanov's comparison of the function of senior presbyters with that of apostles seems to hint at their function of representing the wider church at the local level.

Dei Mazaev provided further insight into the role of external presbyters in the election and ordination of ministers.[146] He mediated Balikhin and "Baptist" on the question of who might judge the presbyter. Where Balikhin opted for judgement by those who ordained the presbyter, "Baptist" claimed that those who elected the presbyter might judge him. Mazaev replied that the Scriptures testify that presbyters are not only elected but also installed. Only the church may elect, but the right to install belongs to "special persons, who do not belong to this church, such as the apostles and the ministers whom they installed, for instance, Timothy or Titus."[147] The elected candidates are

---

141. "Protokol S'ezda Predstavitelei," 18.
142. "Protokol S'ezda Predstavitelei," 18; cf. *Pervyi Vseurkainskii S'ezd Baptistov*, 13–14.
143. "Protokol S'ezda Predstavitelei," 18; cf. *IV Vserossiiskii S'ezd*, 31. This lacks rationale.
144. Ivanov, "Zabota o Vsekh Tserkvakh," 8.
145. Ivanov, "Zabota o Vsekh Tserkvakh," 8.
146. Mazaev, "O Nashikh Nuzhdakh (prodolzhenie)," 8–9.
147. Mazaev, "O Nashikh Nuzhdakh (prodolzhenie)," 8.

"tested and admitted into ministry by these special persons who 'know how one ought to behave in the household of God.'"[148] The external presbyters are present at the election and ordination not as "observers or witnesses but as the primary actors, who have the right and authority to approve or disapprove candidates elected by the church in the dignity of presbyters or deacons."[149] Thus, a presbyter can only be judged by "that authority which 'tests' him and 'admits into ministry' – installs."[150] Mazaev certainly hinted at the special status of trans-local ministers who were also keepers of tradition and might test a candidate's standing.

The opponents, represented by Vasilii Pavlov and Mikhail Timoshenko, consistently argued for local church autonomy and the advisory nature of all external bodies.[151] In 1911, Pavlov translated and published an excerpt from Hiscox on an accused minister.[152] It insisted on the advisory role of committees and retained final authority for the local church. Read against the publications of Ivanov and Mazaev, this piece stands out as an attempt to counterbalance emphasis on trans-local ministers and external bodies. However, it ran contrary to Levindanto's later explanation of judgements on accused ministers which became normative for Russian Baptists.[153] Hiscox suggested that convening a committee of the local church was desirable and wise, while Levindanto deemed it mandatory.[154] Levindanto pointed to the key role of "the elders who rule well," which for him did not indicate the quality of their service but their status as trans-local ministers.[155]

By 1918, ordination by trans-local ministers seems to become a normative practice, as seen in the minutes of the congress of the Siberian Department

---

148. Mazaev, "O Nashikh Nuzhdakh (prodolzhenie)," 9; cf. Kudelia, "Tserkov', Vozniknovenie Ee i Organisatsiia," 2–3.

149. Mazaev, "O Nashikh Nuzhdakh (prodolzhenie)," 9.

150. Mazaev, "O Nashikh Nuzhdakh (prodolzhenie)," 9. In 1917, Mazaev's paper on ordination was approved and recommended for publication. See *Pervyi Svobodnyi S'ezd Russkikh Baptistov*, 16.

151. Baptist [pseudo], "Nashy Nuzhdy"; Baptist [pseudo], "Nashy Nuzhdy (prodolzhenie)." For details on tensions, see Steeves, "The Russian Baptist Union," 465.

152. Hiscox, "Obvinenie na Presvitera"; cf. Hiscox, *New Directory*, 206–13.

153. Levindanto, "Blagochinie Pomestnykh Tserkvei," 8.

154. Hiscox, "Obvinenie na Presvitera," 314, 315; cf. Levindanto, "Blagochinie Pomestnykh Tserkvei," 8–9.

155. Levindanto, "O Pravakh Sluzhitelei Tserkvi," 20; cf. Ivanov, "Zabota o Vsekh Tserkvakh," 8.

where Andrei L. Evstratenko, evangelist and presbyter of Omsk district, mentioned the need for ordaining local ministers and proposed to select "special organisers for ordering communities."[156] He stated that "this job should be laid upon special proven and vested with the trust of the Union and the Executive Board brothers-organisers."[157] Proper constitution of the church was a very important aspect, without which Russian Baptists considered local church incomplete.[158]

3.3.2.3 Trans-local ministers and church-state relations

Legalisation of Russian Baptists after 1905 introduced church-state relations into their routine. That is, the needs of local communities, districts, departments and the union should be represented to the state and the state regulations communicated to churches. The Kyiv congress delegated this responsibility to senior presbyters.[159] Early versions of the statutes delegated representation in all judicial, administrative and governmental institutions to the executive board.[160] The statutes of 1910 and 1925 did not specify who represented churches to the state. We may assume that previous practices were left unaltered. The statutes of 1926 assigned representation on the national scale to FBU of USSR without specifying which institution of the union was responsible for this representation.[161] Since FBU was a union of local unions, it is probable that the function was delegated to the executive boards of the local unions and their constitutive associations. The government's tendency to interact with a few authoritative representatives of the Baptist associations rather than local pastors further solidified the position of such ministers and contributed to the emergence of a denomination.

---

156. *Pervyi Svobodnyi S'ezd Sibirskogo Otdela*, 42.
157. *Pervyi Svobodnyi S'ezd Sibirskogo Otdela*, 42.
158. Ivanov, "Obshchiny i Presvitery," 9.
159. Savinskii, *Istoriia Evangelskikh Khristian-Baptistov Ukrainy, Rossii, Belorussii (1867–1917)*, 273; Savinskii, *Istoriia Evangelskikh Khristian-Baptistov Ukrainy, Rossii, Belorussii (1917–1967)*, 133.
160. "Proekt Ustava," 278–79.
161. "26 Vsesoiuznyi S'ezd Baptistov," 100.

3.4 Understanding the Nature of Associations of Churches

Denominational publications and documents contain two understandings of the nature of unions. The most common was union as an association of churches, and this understanding is found in the majority of Baptist publications and official documents.[162] However, there were attempts, exemplified by the publications of Vasilii G. Pavlov, which promoted an alternative model of union as the voluntary association of individuals. In what follows, I first focus on the peculiarities of the latter and then turn to the former.

3.4.1 Union as Voluntary Association

The idea of union as voluntary association means that it consists not of churches but individuals who associate together, establishing "separate societies that exist by themselves with their own statutes and resolutions that are not mandatory for the local churches."[163]

Pavlov follows Hiscox who promoted individualism and warned against the interdependence of churches.[164] This becomes obvious if Pavlov's essay is read in the context Hiscox's notions of the church,[165] associations,[166] and their relations. Pavlov says that Baptists follow a congregational principle when "every local, properly constituted church or community has independent governance, headed by presbyter, and is not in organic union with other communities."[167] His formulation has dissonance with the rich concept of the visible community of the saints in *Pravila Veroispovedania*.[168] Pavlov reduced it to a local community of believers based on the principle of self-governance. From this conviction follows a very important disclaimer: "Baptists do not recognise national churches; there cannot be one church in one country

---

162. "Union of unions" in "26 Vsesoiuznyi S'ezd Baptistov," 100; cf. Clifford, "Vsemirnyi Soiuz Baptistov," 234.

163. Pavlov, "Pravda o Baptistakh," no. 46, 361–62.

164. Jeffrey Mask puts Hiscox in line with such Baptists as John Newton Brown and James M. Pendleton who is characterised as "a protagonist in the Landmark movement" in Mask, "At Liberty under God," 120–21; see also Thompson, "Toward Baptist Ecclesiology," 182–83.

165. Hiscox, "Khristianskaia Tserkov," *Baptist*, no. 23, 24, 25, 26, 27 (1910); cf. Hiscox, *New Directory*, 20–60.

166. Hiscox, "O Soiuzakh"; cf. Hiscox, *New Directory*, 330–39.

167. Pavlov, "Pravda o Baptistakh," no. 46, 361; cf. Vins, *Nashi Baptistkie Printsipy*, 35.

168. Aleksii Ia. (Dorodnitsyn), *Materialy*, 477–82.

united under the leadership of one person or collegium. Thus, we see in the New Testament *churches* in Galatia, not *the church*, but *churches* in Macedonia etc."[169] Pavlov distinguished a Baptist understanding of the church from those associated with the state church. Perhaps this could be explained by the apologetic thrust of Pavlov's document that prompted him to present the most characteristic traits of Baptist polity, but the influence of American individualism should not be discarded either.

Chronologically, Pavlov's essay followed the publication of Hiscox's piece on the church which Pavlov probably translated himself. First, he imitates Hiscox's elevation of local gatherings of disciples over "invisible universal company,"[170] which includes all true people of God in heaven and on earth but for Hiscox is not a historic concept and only has "figurative and secondary" meaning.[171] Second, Pavlov almost verbatim follows Hiscox in his insistence on the existence of only "churches" not "church."[172] This results in a view of "autonomous" or "independent" local church. Finally, Pavlov, in harmony with Hiscox, advocates for Baptist associations on a sheerly pragmatic basis:

> All Baptist communities have fraternal relations but are not subject to each other. They try working jointly on large projects, such as education of preachers, publishing and home and overseas missions, and for this establish associations. But unions are in essence particular societies which exist by themselves with their own statutes and resolutions and which do not have mandatory force for the communities.[173]

This resembles Hiscox's view of organisational forms beyond local church.[174] For Hiscox, an association is a small body comprising limited areas (a state or several states) and local churches in the geographical vicinity of each other. They unite on the "simple basis of association for mutual help and counsel."[175]

---

169. Pavlov, "Pravda o Baptistakh," no. 46, 361–62. Emphasis original.

170. Hiscox, "Khristianskaia Tserkov," no. 23, 178.

171. Hiscox, "Khristianskaia Tserkov," no. 23, 178; cf. Graves, *Old Landmarkism*, 38.

172. Cf. Pavlov, "Pravda o Baptistakh," no, 46, 361–62; Hiscox, "Khristianskaia Tserkov," no. 23, 178.

173. Pavlov, "Pravda o Baptistakh," no. 46, 361–62.

174. Hiscox, "O Soiuzakh," 396–99; cf. Hiscox, *New Directory*, 330–43. Only a section on associations was published.

175. Hiscox, "O Soiuzakh," 396.

"Association" stands for two realities: (1) an organised body of pastors and messengers meeting annually for business matters and (2) churches and the geographical territory where they are situated.[176] An association exists for mutual help and the benefits of wider society. It emerges out of desire for Christian fellowship and mutual support for needs and has human, not divine, authority.[177] For Hiscox associations are "convenient" for Christian work while the church is "essential."[178]

Differentiation between organisation and territory is important because it allows one to postulate that an association consists of ministers and messengers not churches.[179] Hiscox's opinion on individual membership is based on the conviction that a "Baptist church cannot be a member of any other body whatever,"[180] otherwise it "violates its sacred charter, and loses its identity as the body of Christ."[181] He thinks that by becoming a member of a union, a church is adsorbed into a wider body and loses its independence and control over local issues.[182] This notion follows a strict either/or logic: local church is either a member of Christ's body or of another body. He misses the fact that other local churches are manifestations of the body of Christ, and it is impossible to be a local manifestation thereof and not maintain visible unity with other local manifestations.

Another difficulty is that a local church has virtually no connection with independent associations of individuals. Decisions of association are binding only for participants of the assembly. For Hiscox, an association is not a representative gathering, and churches cannot delegate their authority even if they want to.[183] This means an association is neither the instrument of local churches' vision nor an expression of fellowship in the body of Christ. Rather, it is an instrument of associated individuals. Hiscox softens this by introducing distinction between "membership" in an association and "fellowship and

---

176. Hiscox, "O Soiuzakh," 397.
177. Hiscox, "O Soiuzakh," 397.
178. Hiscox, "O Soiuzakh," 396.
179. Hiscox, "O Soiuzakh," 396.
180. Hiscox, "O Soiuzakh," 397.
181. Hiscox, "O Soiuzakh," 397.
182. Hiscox, "O Soiuzakh," 397.
183. Hiscox, "O Soiuzakh," 397–98.

cooperation."[184] Membership belongs only to individuals while local churches are admitted into fellowship for cooperation. Nevertheless, his vision of ACs is pragmatic and ecclesiologically reductionist. Pavlov refers to Hiscox's view positively in the translator's postscript, which explains that publication of the section of Hiscox's book is aimed at reaching a healthy balance between the union's decisions and local church autonomy:[185]

> We published this article on unions to give to the members of our communities a clear understanding of the purposes and the tasks of Baptist unions in general, for we are in danger on the one hand, of overestimating the significance of our Union, considering all its resolutions of such mandatory essence for the congregations that all congregations or persons disagreeing with them should be expelled from the Union and treated as Gentiles and tax collectors; while on the other hand, by insisting on the autonomy of any single congregation, we are in danger of dispersing our strength to such a degree that, being small units, we would not be able to create by the efforts of our congregations anything great in the milieu of God's Kingdom.[186]

Hiscox's concept differs from that of Baptists in the Russian Empire who treated union as an association of churches. A variation of the view was formulated by Vins, who presented an ambiguous view on the mutual relations of churches. Local churches are connected only by "mutual love and respect for all believers are made to drink of one Spirit who teaches every member to pay each other mutual help, love and preference (Acts 11:23)."[187] Vins also claimed that churches have organic relations with each other because they are rooted in relationship with Christ, the head of the church, and interested in the well-being of all sister churches.[188] On the other hand, missionary unions, in which local churches may unite for pooling resources

---

184. Hiscox, "O Soiuzakh," 397.

185. These precautions seem to be timely because some regional congresses went beyond the authority of the meeting, excommunicating members of the local church. See *Otchet Vserossiiskogo S'ezda*, 4.

186. Pavlov, "O Souzakh," 399.

187. Vins, *Nashi Baptistskie Printsipy*, 20. This is a nod to the necessity of relations between the churches, yet is weak and insufficient as an expression of the *esse* of the church.

188. Vins, *Nashi Baptistskie Printsipy*, 39–40.

and mutual help, are "exclusively voluntary associations of local churches,"[189] "valuable and desirable."[190] His former statement goes further than Pavlov's and Hiscox's concept of association by rooting association in participation in God's nature obtained through repentance and faith,[191] while the latter is in harmony with theirs. However, Vins clearly differed in his view on the status and role of committees in the instance of a local church going astray and falling into heresy or failing to exercise church discipline properly. A special committee should be elected from the representatives of at least five nearby churches. Their decision is "final and cannot be protested by one of the sides since through [the committee], *God's universal Church, gathered for this in its representatives, had its say.*"[192] This clause steps over the pragmatic common sense and good practice ideas typical of Hiscox and Pavlov, pointing to the ministers as representatives of the universal church.

3.4.2 Union as an Association of Churches

Another perspective on the union was to view it as an association of churches. Together with the affirmation of local church autonomy, this is the perspective represented in the official documents, denominational publications and associational practices of the union.

The earliest statutes of the union defined it as "the Union of Russian Baptist churches that consists of those churches which have requested and have been admitted into it by the general assembly of the union on the basis of such request."[193] Local churches delegated representatives to participate in the annual assembly and empowered delegates to act on their behalf. This was one of the key characteristics of the understanding of union among Russian Baptists. In 1926, when the union transformed into a federation, this definition changed into a "Union of autonomous and equal local associations (unions) of Baptists."[194]

---

189. Vins, *Nashi Baptistskie Printsipy*, 41.
190. Vins, *Nashi Baptistskie Printsipy*, 40–41.
191. Vins, *Nashi Baptistskie Printsipy*, 39.
192. Vins, *Nashi Baptistskie Printsipy*, 41–42. Emphasis added.
193. Pavlov, "Proekt Ustava Soiuza," 26; cf. "Protokol," 18; "Proekt Ustava," 278; "Proekt Ustava Soiuza," 350; *Zapis' Zasedanii Plenuma*, 72.
194. "26 Vsesoiuznyi S'ezd Baptistov," 99.

Most of the leaders saw the union as an association of churches. For instance, N. E. Iakimenko said that the union was an "association of churches for the service in God's field."[195] Vasilii P. Stepanov (1874–1938), a member of the executive board of the Union of Baptists of the USSR, agreed with this definition: "Union is association of churches."[196] Dei Mazaev, discussing the agenda of the congress in 1912, emphatically stated: "assembly is not a gathering of individual members but of communities which participate in it through their representatives, and it is, of course, necessary that the right to vote is given in these cases only to the representatives of the communities."[197]

Vasilii Ivanov formulated his views in a series of essays that strongly criticise the union of Evangelical Christians.[198] This explains why he defended the use of the name "Baptist"[199] and promoted "union." For him "union" simply meant an "alliance" uniting churches not individual believers.[200] All alliances should be evaluated according to their purposes and actions to discern "whether they are helpful or not."[201] He understood "helpfulness" as accomplishing the great and important Christian tasks that prompted the formation of the alliance.[202] Ivanov believed that since the tasks of the union were spiritual and aimed at accomplishing God's purposes, "distrust towards the Union is disgusting to God and insulting to all who love God's cause."[203] Ivanov assigned all misunderstandings of the union and its purposes to the

---

195. Belousov, "Pervyi Nazidatel'nyi S'ezd," 38.

196. Belousov, "Pervyi Nazidatel'nyi S'ezd," 38.

197. Mazaev, "O Nashikh Nuzhdakh," 10.

198. Ivanov, "Chto Takoe Baptisty"; Ivanov, "O Soiuze (okonchanie)"; Ivanov, "O Soiuze." See summary of the discussion in Coleman, "Most Dangerous Sect," 45–49.

199. The name summarises the primary statements of faith, connects with the worldwide community, and helps outsiders to identify the Russian Baptist movement and its teaching. Ivanov, "Chto Takoe Baptisty," 2.

200. Ivanov, "Chto Takoe Baptisty," 1, 3. Elsewhere he seems to support voluntary association: "The union should consist of the representatives of communities and local unions who during annual conferences should elect the president of the union, his assistant and several members of the Board for not more than three years. . . . The union should resolve different quarrels both in spiritual and material issues through the representatives of communities and local unions at the annual conferences" (Ivanov, "O Soiuze (okonchanie)," 399). This may mislead as to Ivanov's view of the union, but a closer analysis of the statement demonstrates that he sees representatives as acting on behalf of their churches not independently. The union acts as an arbiter for its members. This is absent in Hiscox or Pavlov.

201. Ivanov, "Chto Takoe Baptisty," 3.

202. Ivanov, "Chto Takoe Baptisty," 3.

203. Ivanov, "Chto Takoe Baptisty," 3.

lack of an officially written and approved statute.²⁰⁴ The union presupposed rights and responsibilities for all members: the elected leaders exercised the *governing* of the union, while all members should support and obey them. For Ivanov, governing was a realisation of spiritual gifts and offices in the church (1 Cor 12:28; Eph 4:11–12), while the support and obedience of all the communities was backed by 1 Peter 5:1–5 and 1 Timothy 5:17.²⁰⁵

Ivanov also held to the prevailing view of local church autonomy, which was a church's right to disagree with resolutions of the annual conference. The union's power consisted in the "moral authoritativeness and wisdom of its leaders."²⁰⁶ The association of churches never assumed power over local churches, and the ecclesiological statements and tracts balanced the ideas of associating and autonomy. The statutes of 1907 stated that the "Union's assembly makes resolutions related to the issues of administration of the union. Other reasonings have for the churches value of instructions and recommendations."²⁰⁷ Balancing unity in the form of the union and local church autonomy was typical within the model of union as an association of churches.²⁰⁸ Now I turn to theological ideas and images supporting the idea of union.

3.4.3 Theological Foundations of the Union

Arguing for the necessity of the union, Baptist leaders often employed pragmatic arguments. Pavel Datsko reasoned for a federative model for the union. Vasilii Ivanov, Mikhail Timoshenko and Nikolai Odintsov pointed to pooling resources for efficient missionary work and development of churches.²⁰⁹ Even the church's mission or unity was sometimes seen from the perspective of accumulating resources, human and material. Vasilii Stepanov, explaining relations between the churches in apostolic times, said:

---

204. Ivanov, "O Soiuze (okonchanie)," 399.
205. Ivanov, "Chto Takoe Baptisty," 3.
206. Ivanov, "Chto Takoe Baptisty," 3.
207. Pavlov, "Proekt Ustava Soiuza," 26.
208. See Odintsov, "O Tserkvi," 7; Sinitsyn, "Tserkov Khristova," 22; "Voprosy po Domostroitelstvu," 23.
209. Ivanov, "Chto Takoe Baptisty," 3; Ivanov, "O Soiuze," 317; Timoshenko, "Soglasovannost' Raboty," 29; Odintsov, "O Tserkvi," 7.

[union] emerged by necessity because one or two cannot uplift the weight. The first union was in the apostolic times (Acts 15:1–31; 18:4–5; Gal 2:1–10). Here was the first organisation of Christians from where they went: Paul to Gentiles, Cephas and others to Israel. The highest purpose of the union is evangelisation.[210]

Stepanov reinterpreted the book of Acts in terms of the organisational development and missionary activity of the primitive churches, pointing out that preaching the gospel was too massive for any independent local church. Others thought about the union apart from pragmatic reasons.

3.4.3.1 Unity as a sign of spiritual maturity

Some authors arguing for unity or associating pointed out that this was a natural outcome for a regenerated person. Thus, Ivanov distinguished between spiritually mature and immature persons.[211] The spiritually mature cannot be satisfied with personal happiness and naturally strive to see their neighbours happy. They unite to achieve the great Christian tasks which are unachievable individually. The immature live for themselves, following their egotistic, sinful and corrupt nature that suppresses the good seeds of God's love. For Ivanov, joining into union stemed from new life in Christ. He referred to the early church and first Russian evangelicals, who, motivated by the Holy Spirit, strove to work for other people and to bring them true happiness through preaching the gospel. According to Ivanov, a desire to serve others proceeds from the Holy Spirit, leads Christians to unity and is itself a natural consequence of the restoration of God's image and the pouring out of God's love in the believers.[212]

Mazaev formulated a similar thought in response to "Baptist."[213] Discussing the local church's right to remove a presbyter, he added an interesting twist to the idea of unity as a sign of spiritual maturity. Mazaev claimed that those who insisted on local church independency do not really understand what the church is. A group of people, not unified in thoughts and actions, could not

---

210. Belousov, "Pervyi Nazidatel'nyi S'ezd," 38.
211. Ivanov, "O Soiuze," 316.
212. Ivanov, "O Soiuze," 316.
213. Mazaev, "O Nashikh Nuzhdakh (prodolzhenie)," 9.

be called "church" because they lacked "unity in the spirit." Mazaev alluded to Ephesians 4, claiming that the church is "something joint with mutually connecting ties and where every member contributes in their measure to the unity of the spirit, purpose and actions."[214] Only such churches could be independent from external power: "the church that stands higher in its calling speaks less of its independence and, conversely, the more a church torn apart with quarrels and looks like a crowd, not a church, the more it screams for independence, self-government and so on."[215] Mazaev criticised autonomy and local unions as "coming not from Christ but from the false prophet and aimed at fragmentation of God's children and hostile and internecine actions among the disjoint army."[216] Unlike Mazaev, Sinitsyn in his article on the church balanced autonomy and unity, quoting Dr Rushbrooke: "Voluntary fellowship of churches together with full autonomy is a remarkable token of the presence of the Holy Spirit."[217] Thus, the Holy Spirit produces harmony of autonomy and unity. Sinitsyn agreed with Ivanov and Mazaev that "only illness in the Church may persuade in unwillingness to have fellowship with other churches. 'For if we walk in the light we have fellowship with each other' (1 John 1:7)."[218] New life in Christ expresses itself also in the passion for mission.

3.4.3.2 Missions as the foundation and goal of the union

Missions led to the formation of Bratstvo and the Baptist union.[219] The Baptist leaders agreed that mission was the foundation and goal of the union. Thus, Iakimenko said that the union is an "association of churches for the work in God's field. Ministers in the union lead the work of evangelisation and ordain presbyters."[220] Anan'in agreed that the task of the union is missionary.[221] Writing about the unity of Baptist churches, he pointed to inner and outer

---

214. Mazaev, "O Nashikh Nuzhdakh (prodolzhenie)," 9.
215. Mazaev, "O Nashikh Nuzhdakh (prodolzhenie)," 9; cf. Haymes, Gouldbourne, and Cross, *On Being the Church*, 27.
216. Mazaev, "O Nashikh Nuzhdakh (prodolzhenie)," 8; cf. section 3.2.3.
217. Sinitsyn, "Tserkov Khristova," 22.
218. Sinitsyn, "Tserkov Khristova," 23.
219. See chapter 2.
220. Belousov, "Pervyi Nazidatel'nyi S'ezd," 38.
221. Belousov, "Pervyi Nazidatel'nyi S'ezd," 38.

unity, where inner unity consists in belonging to the one Spirit and being baptised in the Spirit in love, but outer unity is the goal – the participation of all churches in one mission.²²² Missions led to establishing missionary organisations in England and the USA and Baptist associations in the Russian Empire.²²³ Another consistent advocate of this view was Vasilii Ivanov who saw the tasks of the Russian Baptist union in the wider context of God's kingdom and speeding up its coming.²²⁴ For him, such great vision could only be accomplished with the help of the Holy Spirit.²²⁵ Ivanov ascribed the unity of the first evangelicals in the Russian Empire to their passion for preaching the gospel, which naturally resulted from their conversion and new life in Christ and prompted them to establish a union for the evangelisation of the Russian Empire.²²⁶ Ivanov saw resemblance between the apostolic church and Russian Baptists in this regard.²²⁷ Mission corresponds to the unity of the church.

3.4.3.3 Unity in the form of union

Discussions on unity occurred even before Bratstvo emerged.²²⁸ They intensified in the first decade of the twentieth century when the union of Evangelical Christians was established (1909) and continued with different intensity until 1920, when an attempt to merge two unions failed.²²⁹ The discussions revolved around John 17:21–23 and Ephesians 4:5–6 and theological ideas proceeding from these texts.²³⁰

John 17:21–23 is part of what is known as Jesus's High Priestly Prayer and refers to the unity of the disciples. Many authors have treated Jesus's prayer as a last will or commandment with obligatory force.²³¹ Vasilii Ivanov called

---

222. Anan'in, "Ob'edinenie Obshchin Baptistov," 13; cf. Mazaev's thought on the unity of origin and purpose in Mazaev, "Edinstvo i Razdelenie," 6.

223. Anan'in, "Ob'edinenie Obshchin Baptistov," 13–15.

224. Ivanov, "O Soiuze (okonchanie)," 398, 399.

225. Ivanov, "Chto Takoe Baptisty," 3.

226. Ivanov, "O Soiuze," 316.

227. Ivanov, "O Soiuze," 316.

228. See section 2.4.4.

229. Steeves, "Russian Baptist Union," 137–93.

230. The treatment of this topic is beyond the scope of this thesis. See on this in Reshetnikov, "Ob'edinitel'naia Tendentsiia"; Borodyns'ka, "Dosvid Ob'ednavchykh Protsesiv"; Sinichkin, *Vozrozhdenie Vopreki Bezbozhiiu*, 110–14, 171–95; Geychenko, "On the Use of Scripture."

231. "Edinaia tserkov' Bozhiia," 11, 12; Belousov, "Pervyi Nazidatel'nyi S'ezd," 38.

to unite efforts and resources, appealing to Jesus's prayer and pointing out that unity is a condition for fulfilment of the church's task of speeding up God's kingdom:

> The Lord Jesus Christ prayed about believers' unity: "so that they may be brought to complete unity. Then the world will know that you sent me and have loved them even as you have loved me." (John 17:23). The world, according to Christ's word, will only then know the truth, when it sees unity of the believers – the union. And this unity of God's children we should understand not only as the unity of faith and doctrine, it should be real in life and actions. Two forces, spiritual and material, should be manifested inseparably all together.[232]

Unity validates the church's message. Ivanov also read the unity of Baptist churches into God's economy: "all congregations all over Russia should be united in one strong All-Russian Union so that there is one Church of Christ in the whole country as 'His body, joined and held together by every supporting ligament, grows and builds itself up as *each member* does its work.'"[233]

Gavriil Mazaev (1858–1937), presbyter, evangelist and treasurer of the Russian Baptist Union,[234] in discussing John 17:21, went beyond the commanded trajectory and pointed to the union of and with the Father and the Son not only as an example but as the way of unity:

> If we consider the text that speaks of unity then we see that it speaks more seriously, that is, deeper and more fundamentally; it reads "*that* all of them may be one, Father, just as you are in me and I am in you." That is, it is necessary to abide in Father and his Son Jesus Christ and then this unity takes place not directly among people but first with the Father and his Son Jesus Christ, and this unity lays the foundation for uniting all people in one. Here and only here no more Jew or Greek, barbarian, Scythian,

---

232. Ivanov, "O Soiuze (okonchanie)," 399.
233. Ivanov, "O Soiuze," 317. Emphasis original.
234. For Mazaev's biography, see Prokhorov, "Kakoi Bogach Spasetsa."

slave or free, no male or female but Christ all in all. Such unity is firm, foundational and justified and it was, is and always will be.[235]

For Mazaev, Christ was the cause of divisions among Jews, Gentiles and Christians and the point around which they could be united for he destroyed the dividing wall (Eph 2:14).[236] Through Christ different groups of people enter into unbreakable unity, first with God and then with each other. However, Mazaev read both John 17:21 and the discussion about unity with the Evangelical Christians through the lens of Ephesians 4:5–6, 11–12.[237] Ephesians 4:5–6 is known as the Baptist motto – "One Lord, one faith, one baptism" – and Ephesians 4:11–12 points to different offices in the church. Baptism and the ordination of ministers are the points on which the Evangelical Christians and Baptists disagreed. Thus, Mazaev proposed a distinctly Baptist interpretation of John 17:21 based on confessional foundations and common practices.[238]

Russian Baptists predominantly saw unity in the form of confessional union. Ivanov thought that "all congregations all over Russia should be united in one strong All-Russian Union so that there would be one Church of Christ in the whole country as 'His body, joined and held together by every supporting ligament, grows and builds itself up as *each member* does its work.'"[239] For Ivanov, the Baptist Union was an expression of the universal church and a form of unity without which fulfilment of the vision when "the kingdom of this world becomes the kingdom of our Lord and his Christ and he will reign for ever and ever" (Rev 11:15) is impossible.

Unity in form of a union presupposes visible expression.[240] For Ivanov, unity involved not only commonality in the matters of faith and doctrines but also in life and actions. This meant unity in the form of the union which could be seen by the world and convince it to believe the church's message.[241]

---

235. Mazaev, "O Edinstve," 9.
236. Mazaev, "O Edinstve," 9.
237. Mazaev, "O Edinstve," 9.
238. See Timoshenko, "Soglasovannost' Raboty," 28.
239. Ivanov, "O Soiuze," 317. Empasis original.
240. For an alternative perspective, see Vins saying that God's church is one organism spread all over the earth and is "invisible Church for it is not a visible organisation" (Vins, *Nashi Baptistskie Printsipy*, 20).
241. Ivanov, "O Soiuze (okonchanie)," 399.

Alexander Anan'in, answering the question about where Scripture speaks about union pointed to John 17:21, emphasising that unity is rooted in the relations of the Son and the Father, and Ephesians 4:3 that calls to unity of the Spirit in the bond of peace. He disagreed with the "strange Molokan notion" of spiritual kinship only. As baptism and Lord's Supper are visible, so "our union should also express itself in a visible organisation: congresses, council, preachers."[242] Russian Baptists, following German and English Baptists, saw baptism and the Lord's Supper as the means of grace, ordained by God "to draw sinners to himself and impart to them salvation obtained by Christ."[243] They believed that through baptism a person joins the visible church on earth[244] and that the Lord's Supper is a means of witnessing for Christ, experiencing close fellowship with him and visibly representing the communion of saints.[245] Thus visible form is both the expression of and the means for participation in the invisible.

3.4.3.4 *Images of the union*

There are several recurring images in the Baptist publications. Among them are *bratstvo* and the body of Christ. *Bratstvo* is one of the key images of the union. Georgii I. Shipkov developed his ecclesiological vision around it.[246] His article states that godliness, evangelism and deeds of mercy could only be kept together if the church is thought of as *bratstvo*.[247] Shipkov traced the image to Petrine thought (1 Pet 2:17; 3:8; 4:8; Johannine community, whose chief responsibility is brotherly love towards each other; and Paul, for whom "Church is a synonym of brotherhood" built around the commandment of love.[248] Jesus exemplified love by washing his disciples' feet and praying for their unity in love.[249] Shipkov criticised historical definitions for their identification of the church with hierarchy and sacraments or preaching and

---

242. Belousov, "Pervyi Nazidatel'nyi S'ezd," 38; cf. Pyzh reflecting on Pilgram Marpeck's notion of visible church in Pyzh, "Confessing Community," 75–77, 87–88.
243. "Ispovedanie Very Khristian-Baptistov," 425.
244. "Kratkoe Verouchenie Baptistov. Chlen X," 1.
245. "Ispovedanie Very Khristian-Baptistov," 425, 427–28.
246. Shipkov, "Bratstvo vo Khriste"; Shipkov, "Bratstvo vo Khriste (continued)." For a recent study of sibling language and its significance in Paul's letters, see Aasgaard, *My Beloved*.
247. Shipkov, "Bratstvo vo Khriste," 5.
248. Shipkov, "Bratstvo vo Khriste," 5.
249. Shipkov, "Bratstvo vo Khriste," 5–6.

the administering of sacraments. Only love could be the criterion of the church's genuineness.[250] Love is first directed at the community of disciples and only then to the world, thus, the minister is to foster the "Christlike spirit of brotherhood."[251] Shipkov opposed the idea of human brotherhood as abstract and claimed that true brotherhood is based on the fatherhood of God and conditioned by love.[252] Since the church is God's building and the temple in which the new altar is erected, which is the cross of Christ, then Christians bring new sacrifices (evangelism, thanksgiving and charity) that are burnt by the fire of the Holy Spirit.[253]

Another popular image was the body of Christ. Reflections on the union often employed this image. In most of the cases its use is occasional or substantiates an important aspect of church doctrine or practice. For instance, Dei Mazaev appealed to it supporting his idea of common origin and purpose grounded in one God.[254] In another case he used the image to show continuity of Russian and European Baptist doctrine.[255] Similar use is found in the publications of Gavriil Mazaev and Vasilii Ivanov who demonstrated the foundations of unity[256] and were convinced of the necessity of associating in one union.[257] Ivanov, possibly inspired by the image, even called it "one Church of Christ in Russia,"[258] a very unusual understanding of the church for a Baptist. Anan'in used the image to illustrate the inner unity of the church and to build his argument for the association of churches in the form of a union.[259] All these authors build their concept of the union on the image of the body.

Sometimes the image was applied to the Baptist union directly. Dei Mazaev, discussing the election of members of the board and their relations with the

---

250. Shipkov, "Bratstvo vo Khriste," 7–8.

251. Shipkov, "Bratstvo vo Khriste (continued)," 1.

252. Shipkov, "Bratstvo vo Khriste (continued)," 2.

253. Shipkov, "Bratstvo vo Khriste (continued)," 3–4.

254. Mazaev, "Edinstvo i Razdelenie," 6.

255. Mazaev, "Imia 'Baptisty,'" 3. Mazaev points out that the church actually preexists individual churches, and Russian Baptists join to something larger and more ancient than themselves.

256. Mazaev, "O Edinstve," 9.

257. Ivanov, "O Soiuze," 317.

258. Ivanov, "O Soiuze," 317.

259. Anan'in, "Ob'edinenie Obshchin Baptistov," 12–13.

union and the status of delegates of local churches and their participation in annual congresses, pointed out that they should value the unity of the union. Otherwise, to be consistent, they should reject the honour of being elected. To justify this, he employed the image of the body and rhetoric of unity:

> The members of one body should gather and reason as brothers and participants of common cause that should be equally valuable for all and they should defend not their honour and name but the Lord's cause, in humility considering for better to be at the threshold of the temple where great works of God are discussed. . . .
>
> Therefore, I insist that for members of the Board should be elected those brothers, who understand and defend moral significance of the Union as the voice of the fullness of God's people, who by word and personal example protect its wholeness and strive with all their strengths to unite all believers in one general organisation and make this strong and unshakable. Any thought of autonomy and specific brotherly unions should be condemned and put to shame as coming not from Christ but from the false prophet and aimed at fragmentation of God's children and hostile and internecine actions among the disjoint army.[260]

Here Mazaev thought of the union's leadership and Baptist churches united in one union in terms of the universal Church. The participants of the congress were "members of one body" – a clear reference to the image of the body; the union itself was "the fullness of God's people." Mazaev's view starkly contrasted to that of Pavlov who thought of the union in terms of a voluntary association of individuals.[261] Pavel Datsko thought of the federative model as enhancing growth in "unity of faith and the measure of the full stature of Christ," which is a direct citation of Ephesians 4:13. The federation of the unions implements the tasks the Lord set before his church by having granted gifts and offices – apostles, prophets, evangelists, pastors and

---

260. Mazaev, "O Nashikh Nuzhdakh (prodolzhenie)," 8.

261. Earlier Mazaev differentiated community and the church, claiming that in one locality there could be several communities with presbyters but still one church like in Jerusalem. See Mazaev, "Eshche po Povodu Stat'i," 5.

teachers – for building up the body of Christ. This resonates with Ivanov's use of 1 Corinthians 12:38 and Ephesians 4:11–12 when he justified the necessity of leadership in the Union: "There 'God has appointed some first apostles, second prophets, third teachers,' there has established '*leadership*' which should accomplish its responsibilities and there must be obedience to it."[262] For Ivanov gifts and ministries given to the church were in some form manifested and implemented in the Baptist union. Application of the image of the body of Christ to the union of churches points to the conclusion that some Russian Baptists thought of their Union in ecclesiological terms, but this understanding was not well developed and had multiple lacunae that demand further theological thinking.

3.5 Summary

The reality of growth and expansion caused organisational and leadership changes. The centralised model formed by Mazaev could not cope with the new reality and gave way to the federative model where regional associations of churches assumed more responsibility for evangelization and spiritual nurture. Association of churches became the dominant model. The alternative model of association of individuals proposed by Pavlov did not take root among Russian Baptists. Practices of edifying congresses and trans-local ministers were also aimed at coping with the need to build up members of churches and the churches themselves. The congresses were the instrument of spiritual invigoration of church members and provincial lay preachers and ministers. Trans-local ministers established churches and ordained local presbyters. The status and role of trans-local ministers in Baptist ecclesiology received theological explanation. They were identified with teachers and evangelists (Eph 4:13) and were considered the ministers of the universal church who assumed rights in testing the elected ministers and their ordination. According to Ivanov and Mazaev, unity in the AC was a sign of spiritual maturity, grounded in new life produced by the Holy Spirit and expressed in a visible form of union. The notion of visible unity was consonant with Christ's High Priestly Prayer (John 17) and the understanding of the Union as an expression of the body of Christ.

---

262. Ivanov, "Chto Takoe Baptisty," 3. Emphasis original.

CHAPTER 4

Restoration and Division of the Union (1944–1990)

4.1 Introduction

The Second World War unexpectedly gave Baptist churches in the occupied territories a chance to restore their relations and vitality. Ukrainian Baptists convened congresses on the occupied territories in Dnipropetrovs'k (1942) and Kyrovograd (18-20 July 1943).[1] These meetings helped to restore the Ukrainian Baptist Union but had consequences for its leadership – they were imprisoned in Siberia.

Attitude towards religion changed by 1943.[2] Sergei Savinskii cites the opinion of Soviet historian Dmitrii Volkogonov that Stalin changed his attitude towards religion due to "political pragmatism" driven by desire to reward the church's patriotic activities and to win the benevolence of allies in anticipation

---

1. Reshetnikov and Sannikov, *Obzor Istorii*, 180. For Dnipropetrovs'k congress, see Savinskii, *Istoriia Evangelskikh Khristian-Baptistov Ukrainy, Rossii, Belorussii (1917-1967)*, 148; Domashovets', *Narys Istorii*, 222; Nyshchyk, *Shliakh Viry*, 79-86; Sinichkin, *Vozrozhdenie Vopreki Bezbozhiiu*, 125-26. For other local congresses, see Liubomyrenko, *Z Khrystom v Ukraini*; Borodyns'ka, "Dosvid Ob'ednavchykh Protsesiv," 55.

2. There is a widespread myth that this change was due to the pressure of the USSR's allies. However, Savinskii points out that by May of 1942, Baptist communities, groups and even some individual believers received letters from the Temporary All-Union Council of Evangelical Christians-Baptists. See Savinskii, *Istoriia Evangelskikh Khristian-Baptistov Ukrainy, Rossii, Belorussii (1917-1967)*, 150-51; see also "Obrashchenie Rukovoditelei." On the role of security services consult Savinskii, *Istoriia Evangelskikh Khristian-Baptistov Ukrainy, Rossii, Belorussii (1917-1967)*, 150; Mitrokhin, *Baptizm*, 400-401; Borodyns'ka, "Dosvid Ob'ednavchykh Protsesiv," 55-58. See also "Obrashchenie Rukovoditelei" and "Obrashchenie VSEKhiB."

of the Teheran meeting.³ Thus, the state allowed the Local Council of the Russian Orthodox Church to elect the patriarch for the first time since 1925.⁴ Baptists and evangelical Christians also enjoyed a relative alleviation of persecution. There is a consensus among Baptist historians that the Soviet government was highly interested in uniting dispersed evangelical groups into a body that would be easily controlled.⁵ It is against this background that the Moscow Consultation (26–29 October 1944) gathered forty-five evangelical Christians and Baptists from most regions of the USSR, who met to merge two traditions and resolve issues related to the functioning of the union. None of the participants was delegated by regional congresses. This raises questions about the legitimacy of the consultation,⁶ and the newly established Baptist magazine *Bratskii Vestnik* (Fraternal herald) attempted to disavow these charges:⁷ "Not the great number of participants but their authoritativeness resolves the issue from a biblical and societal point of view."⁸ The merger was preceded by grassroots regional unification meetings to lay

---

3. As quoted in Savinskii, *Istoriia Evangelskikh Khristian-Baptistov Ukrainy, Rossii, Belorussii (1917–1967)*, 152. An Orthodox historian, Dimitry Pospielovsky, opines: "The reopening of churches in the German-occupied territories required the Soviet Government to make some concessions to the believers at home, in order to rally them to the defense of the country." Pospielovsky, *History*, 67.

4. On 4 September 1943, Stalin met with the orthodox metropolitans and conceded that the council gather for electing the patriarch. See Pospielovsky, *Pravoslavnaia Tserkov' v Istorii Rusi, Rossii i SSSR*, 297–302; see also Stricker, *Russkaia Pravoslavnaia Tserkov' v Sovetskoe Vremia*, 1:337–40.

5. Reshetnikov and Sannikov, *Obzor Istorii*, 182–83; Savinskii, *Istoriia Evangelskikh Khristian-Baptistov Ukrainy, Rossii, Belorussii (1917–1967)*, 156; Kriuchkov, *Velikoe Probuzhdenie*, 15–16; Borodyns'ka, "Dosvid Ob'ednavchykh Protsesiv," 57–58; Sinichkin, *Vozrozhdenie Vopreki Bezbozhiiu*, 128–32.

6. Sawatsky, *Soviet Evangelicals*, 85–86; Savinskii, *Istoriia Evangelskikh Khristian-Baptistov Ukrainy, Rossii, Belorussii (1917–1967)*, 157–58. Sinichkin refers to a letter from the chair of the Council for the Affairs of Religious Cults (CARC), I. V. Polianskii, to V. M. Molotov, where the former points out that the organisation of a united centre of Evangelical Christians and Baptists without utilising proper Baptist procedures "causes dissatisfaction among the communities, especially in Ukraine, and leads to certain complications in the practical operations of this centre." Sinichkin, *Vozrozhdenie Vopreki Bezbozhiiu*, 131–32.

7. The arguments: (1) The consultation fulfilled Jesus's prayer (John 17:21) and God's will; (2) it recapitulated previous efforts to reach unity; (3) it was participated in by the elderly and respected ministers; (4) the decision was unanimous; (5) it was celebrated by BWA and other organisations; (6) it was recognised by the state and publicised in the major newspaper *Izvestiia* 10 (November 1944). "Avtoritetnost' Vsesoiuznogo Soveshchaniia," 18–20.

8. "Avtoritetnost' Vsesoiuznogo Soveshchaniia," 18.

the groundwork for acceptance of the merger.⁹ The representatives of the evangelical camp occupied the highest positions in the union but accepted Baptist church polity.¹⁰

In spite of these concessions, the pressure on religion renewed in 1947, turned into an offensive by the early 1950s¹¹ and flourished during the notorious "godless decade" under Khrushchev (1954–1964).¹²'

4.2 All-Union Council of Evangelical Christians-Baptists (AUCECB): Deviation from Baptist Principles and Practices

Formation of the All-Union Council of Evangelical Christians-Baptists (AUCECB)¹³ as a centralised organisation eventually influenced Baptist churches via introduction of the system of plenipotentiary representatives (*upolnomochennye*) or senior presbyters (*starshie presvitera*) and via approval of statutes that reflected government regulations rather than traditional Baptist polity. These steps had serious consequences for the practices and structures of Russian Baptists: the central office substituted for the union of local churches, loyal ministers were appointed by the centre and top-down instructions bound local initiatives. A network of appointed senior presbyters played a significant role in this new organisational machinery.

---

9. See Borodyns'ka, "Dosvid Ob'ednavchykh Protsesiv," 55. The only exception was a group of the so-called "pure Baptists." See Reshetnikov and Sannikov, *Obzor Istorii*, 184, 190; "Vystuplenie Starshego Presvitera po Ukraine," 35–36.

10. Baptisms, communion services and wedding ceremonies were performed by ordained ministers. "Polozhenie o Soiuze (1944)," 34. For comparison with the agreement reached in 1920, see *Otchet Vserossiiskogo S'ezda*, 7.

11. Pospielovsky, *History*, 69–82; Pospielovsky, *Soviet Antireligious Campaigns*, 91–97.

12. Sawatsky, *Soviet Evangelicals*, 131–56; Pospielovsky, *History*, 82–97.

13. The All-Union Council of Evangelical Christians-Baptists referred both to the governing organ (the council of ministers) and the union of churches. I suggest that the council effectively assumed the role of representing the union. For the government, the council ("the governing body") was the legitimate representative of the union.

4.2.1 Council of Ministers for Union of Churches

AUCECB *de facto* replaced the union of churches and eliminated associational practices characteristic to Baptists from 1905 to 1930. This is reflected in the statutes of AUCECB which underwent a series of revisions in 1948 and 1960.[14]

The statutes of 1944 described the churches of Evangelical Christians and Baptists merged into one body as a "union."[15] AUCECB was "the governing body."[16] All the officers were elected from the members of AUCECB council and the procedure of adding new members was not described.[17]

The statutes of 1948 reflected attempts to reintroduce some changes which were in line with Baptist practices. The union was defined as an "association of churches of Evangelical Christians-Baptists admitting water baptism by faith,"[18] while AUCECB was still "the central and governing body."[19] It "governs activity of all churches . . . installs presbyters by approving, appoints, removes and transfers senior presbyters, controls their activity and financial operations."[20] The members of the AUCECB committee should be elected by local church representatives at the congresses. However, the statutes do not clarify how often the congresses are convened, though the tenure of an AUCECB member was five years.[21] New members could be co-opted into AUCECB at the plenum.[22] All this was just on paper and had never been realised in practice.

In 1959 the state made AUCECB change statutes again. In this modified version the union became an "association of believers" instead of churches.[23] AUCECB retained the status of "the central governing body" which "appoints and removes senior presbyters and audits their general and financial activities."[24] The members of AUCECB and senior presbyters were excluded

---

14. See "Polozhenie o Soiuze (1948)"; "Polozhenie o Soiuze (1960)."
15. "Polozhenie o Soiuze (1944)," 33; Zhidkov, "Tserkov Khristova i Ee Poriadki," 5.
16. "Polozhenie o Soiuze (1944)," 33.
17. "Polozhenie o Soiuze (1944)," 33–34.
18. "Polozhenie o Soiuze (1948)," para. 1.1.
19. "Polozhenie o Soiuze (1948)," para. 2.4.
20. "Polozhenie o Soiuze (1948)," para. 2.11.
21. "Polozhenie o Soiuze (1948)," para. 2.18.
22. "Polozhenie o Soiuze (1948)," para. 2.19.
23. "Polozhenie o Soiuze (1960)," para. 1.1.
24. "Polozhenie o Soiuze (1960)," paras. 2.3, 2.11.

from the right to perform "spiritual rituals being only senior spiritual overseers for complying with the established order in the churches."[25] The right to elect members of AUCECB was limited to "special consultations of the representatives of the union by a simple majority."[26] Perhaps these consultations encompassed only senior presbyters and the leadership of AUCECB, restricting the influence of local churches on the process. The statute was circulated with *Instruktivnoe Pis'mo* (Instructive letter),[27] sent to senior presbyters as inner instruction.[28] Approval of these documents by AUCECB's plenum in 1959[29] sparked some churches to openly resist and others to sabotage these decisions.[30]

As will be demonstrated below, the leaders of AUCECB justified the existing structure and practices with biblical precedents. This legitimised the existing structure and leadership order (AUCECB, then senior presbyters, then local churches). The biblical examples were routinely reinterpreted in the light of contemporary church experience and practice.

4.2.2 Senior Presbyters as the Representatives of the Council

To implement all significant decisions of the "spiritual centre" and consolidate local churches, AUCECB opted for the system of plenipotentiary representatives. This section explores their status and functions, their ministry seen through the lens of the Bible and their place in the overall structure of AUCECB.

---

25. "Polozhenie o Soiuze (1960)," para. 2.12.
26. "Polozhenie o Soiuze (1960)," para. 2.18.
27. "'Instruktivnoe Pis'mo,'" 321–27.
28. Shaptala calls them "anti-Gospel" (Shaptala, *Kak Eto Bylo*, 41). On disclosure of the document, see "Otchet o Rabote Orgkomiteta," 2. *Instruktivnoe Pis'mo* consists of eight sections which expand paragraphs 3.21–3.24 of Statutes 1960. Sections 1–2 define the status, functions and responsibility of senior presbyters. Sections 3–6 instruct on relations with subordinates and ordained and non-ordained ministers. Sections 7–8 regulate the admission of new members and conduct of worship services. *Instruktivnoe Pis'mo*, Statutes 1960 and the Soviet law on religious associations (1929) were defined as the foundation of all church activities. See "Instruktivnoe Pis'mo," 321, 322, 323, 324, 327.
29. Mitskevich calls this "a mistake." See Mitskevich, *Istoriia Evangelskikh Khristian-Baptistov*, 325–26.
30. "Basic traits of the blessed inner-church movement developed by 1958" (Kriuchkov, *Velikoe Probuzhdenie*, 24).

The system, status and functions of plenipotentiary representatives, or senior presbyters,[31] is expounded in a number of documents[32] and articles in *Bratskii Vestnik*.[33] Mikhail Orlov (1887–1962), presbyter of the Moscow church of Evangelical Christians, introduced the consultation to the idea in an address that explains the system and traces its history back to 1931.[34] Orlov contraposed administration of the communities through councils and plenipotentiaries, arguing that the system fit the extraordinary circumstances of Baptists in the USSR and had proved its effectiveness in the past.[35] It allowed the most experienced and tested ministers to be appointed to make decisions without prolonged discussions in the regional councils, putting all responsibility on one person.[36]

Most of the leaders of the AUCECB equated senior presbyters to bishops. Thus, Iakov Zhidkov pointed out that they functioned as bishops though they did not hold the title.[37] They were "presbyters-overseers,"[38] which was a description of their status. Nikolai Levindanto, giving a theological perspective on senior presbyters, said that they were first among equals in their regions and ministered to many churches.[39] He admitted that this did not presuppose hierarchical status. Nikolai Mel'nikov, a vice-president of AUCECB, added that as pastors over many churches, senior presbyters were not mere administrators but "spiritual ministers, guardians and instructors of local churches."[40] This means they were trans-local ministers, whose responsibility exceeded the limits of a local church. It means they functioned as classical

---

31. On change of the title, see "Izveshcheniia VSEKhB," 61; Savinskii, *Istoriia Evangelskikh Khristian-Baptistov Ukrainy, Rossii, Belorussii (1917–1967)*, 178.

32. "Instruktsiia dlia Upolnomochennykh"; "Polozhenie o Soiuze (1948)"; "Polozhenie o Soiuze (1960)."

33. Zhidkov, "Neskol'ko slov o rabote VSEKhB," 34; Zhidkov, "Nash Otchet," 14; Levindanto, "O Sluzhenii Starshikh Presviterov," 48–52; Klimenko, "Otvetstvennost Presviterov," 47.

34. Orlov, "Soobshchenie o Sisteme Upolnomochennykh," 35–36. In this address, Orlov mistakenly conflated two plenums. See Levindanto, "O Sluzhenii Starshikh Presviterov," 48–52.

35. Orlov, "Soobshchenie o Sisteme Upolnomochennykh," 35–36.

36. Orlov, "Soobshchenie o Sisteme Upolnomochennykh," 35–36.

37. Zhidkov, "Neskol'ko slov o rabote VSEKhB," 34; Zhidkov, "Otradnoe v Zhizni," 11; cf. Bychkov, "Otchetnyi Doklad VSEKhB" (1980), 19. On "bishops" among Latvian Baptists, see Teraudkalns, "Episcopacy."

38. Zhidkov, "Vzgliad Nazad," 8.

39. Levindanto, "O Sluzhenii Starshikh Presviterov," 49–50.

40. Mel'nikov, "O Rabote Starshikh Presviterov," 68.

bishops in holding churches in unity of faith and fellowship.[41] In 1980, Iakov Dukhonchenko, senior presbyter for Ukraine (1974–1990), in his report on statute amendments, mentioned that some regional conferences proposed to change "senior presbyter" to "bishop" but this suggestion was declined by the Statutes Committee because such a practice was foreign to Bratstvo.[42] Attempts to avoid the title "bishop" while retaining episcopal functions may hint that for many recognising "bishops" would have been too obvious a departure from the traditional Baptist congregationalism and for the inherited fear of centralised structures invested with authority over local churches.

The functions of senior presbyters changed over time due to some external factors. In 1985, the president of AUCECB, Andrei Klimenko, commenting on the origin and functions of senior presbyters, remarked:

> In the initial period of their emergence senior presbyters visited churches with the purpose of evangelism, joyful fellowship with God's children and for their instruction, not for scrutiny of conflicts and disorders.
>
> Later organisational and administrative work in churches prevailed. This was caused by the necessity to organise and register churches after the war.[43]

Thus, under the state pressure, what originally were evangelistic and ministerial functions were limited to organisational and administrative ones.

A document titled *Instruktsiia dlia Upolnomochennykh* (Instruction for plenipotentiaries) stipulates that senior presbyters watch over the activities of local churches and communicate with them, participate in church ordinances and services, resolve local conflicts, represent before state officials and enhance the unity of Baptist and Pentecostal churches.[44] The statutes of 1948 specify that senior presbyters help local ministers "in the correct implementation of their ministry," control the installation and ordination of new presbyters and approve deacons.[45] This overlaps with the spheres that were under local church authority. The statutes of 1960 limit the activity

---

41. Pyzh, "Confessing Community," 117–19.
42. Dukhonchenko, "Ob Izmeneniiakh v Ustav," 41.
43. Klimenko, "Otvetstvennost Presviterov," 47.
44. "Instruktsiia dlia Upolnomochennykh."
45. "Polozhenie o Soiuze (1948)," para. 2.24.

of senior presbyters to registered churches only[46] and put them in charge of the "enrolment of new members and the character of church services."[47] They were responsible for "observing strict church discipline."[48] This description resonates with the functions explicated by Iakov Zhidkov earlier: (1) to arrange registration of churches according to legislation; (2) to arrange church discipline (*blagochinie*) and (3) to connect churches with the centre in Moscow.[49] The handing of church discipline over to senior presbyters was the most symptomatic evidence of the shift towards the authoritarian rule of the senior presbyters over the spheres that traditionally belonged to the local churches only. Zhidkov's comment betrays this:

> They, of course, have to, as the Apostle Paul says, "warn those who are unruly" (1 Thess 5:14; 2 Thess 3:6–14), barring such from brotherly fellowship or even excommunicating them from the church. They have to "speak, exhort and reprove with all authority" (Titus 2:15) turning away from the heretic, "after the first and second admonition" (Titus 3:10). Of course, they have to do so henceforth.[50]

Contrary to the traditional Baptist views on church discipline, he sees it as a legitimate responsibility of senior presbyters.

Nikolai Levindanto represents a slightly different approach. His significant article "O Sluzhenii Starshikh Presviterov" presented senior presbyters from a historical, theological, functional and moral perspective. His theological discussion on the status and functions of senior presbyters drew heavily from Odintsov's article on the church.[51] Levindanto employed Odintsov's concept of the teacher as a trans-local minister standing next to apostles

---

46. "Polozhenie o Soiuze (1960)," para. 2.22. Official registration meant that a community had legal status and was recognized by the government. Refusal to register or revocation of registration led to the closing of communities. Unregistered communities became subjects of severe measures by the Soviet government. See Reshetnikov and Sannikov, *Obzor Istorii*, 191–92; Savinskii, *Istoriia Evangelskikh Khristian-Baptistov Ukrainy, Rossii, Belorussii (1917–1967)*, 68–69; 193–95.

47. "Polozhenie o Soiuze (1960)," para. 2.22.

48. "Polozhenie o Soiuze (1960)," para. 2.22.

49. Zhidkov, "Neskol'ko slov o rabote VSEKhB," 34. For a descriptive account, see Zhidkov, "Nash Otchet," 14.

50. Zhidkov, "Vzgliad Nazad," 8.

51. Odintsov, "O Tserkvi."

and prophets.[52] The concept applies to those in whom the gifts of teaching and shepherding are successfully joined, making them capable "to equip the body of Christ and through this enter the number of Christianity's leaders receiving 'double honour' (1 Tim 5:17)."[53] Similarly to apostles and prophets, teachers (evangelists) preach the word to the unsaved, strengthen the souls of disciples (enhancing their growth) and establish churches through ordination of presbyters.[54] Levindanto held on to Odintsov's differentiation between local and trans-local ministers and put senior presbyters among the latter.[55] While admitting the similarity of their functions to those of teachers, Levindanto claims that the title "teacher" does not fully describe their status and role. The meaning of "teacher" is too "earthbound" and "civilian not spiritual," and a minister's role could be misunderstood.[56] "Senior presbyter" better describes "the spiritual ministry and status of such a minister" for the secular and Christian audience.[57] Such a minister combines the gifts of teaching and shepherding, acting as teacher and presbyter.[58] Levindanto concludes: "The title – senior presbyter – rather points to his activities than to his status, to his spiritual and moral authority but not to his official (hierarchical) authority."[59]

Levindanto located the ministry of senior presbyters in AUCECB's structure and defined it according to the documents of the union. They operated as "evangelists (teachers) and equippers [*domostroiteli*] of churches,"[60] enriching the spiritual life of churches, protecting and strengthening Christian unity, observing correctness of church activities and helping churches. They participated in the elections of presbyters and ordained or removed them from the ministry. In case of conflicts, they negotiated trying to reconcile the opponents. Senior presbyters communicated with and visited churches, encouraged financial donations for AUCECB and served as instruments of

---

52. Levindanto, "O Sluzhenii Starshikh Presviterov," 49. See section 3.3.2.
53. Levindanto, "O Sluzhenii Starshikh Presviterov," 49.
54. Levindanto, "O Sluzhenii Starshikh Presviterov," 49.
55. See section 3.3.2.
56. Levindanto, "O Sluzhenii Starshikh Presviterov," 49.
57. Levindanto, "O Sluzhenii Starshikh Presviterov," 49.
58. Levindanto, "O Sluzhenii Starshikh Presviterov," 50.
59. Levindanto, "O Sluzhenii Starshikh Presviterov," 50.
60. Levindanto, "O Sluzhenii Starshikh Presviterov," 50.

control over the implementation of AUCECB decisions.⁶¹ Levindanto's article is in line with the official regulations on senior presbyters but adds spiritual and evangelistic dimensions.

The status and functions of senior presbyters was substantiated by biblical texts, usually from the Pastoral Epistles. Orlov appealed to Titus 1:5.⁶² In this text, Paul reminds Titus to accomplish the ordering of churches on Crete by installing presbyters for local churches. Iakov Zhidkov turned to 1 Timothy 5:17 and Titus 1:5 and equated senior presbyters to those whom Paul called "the elders who rule well" (1 Tim 5:17) and who actually exercised the role of "bishops."⁶³ Quoting 1 Timothy 5:17, Zhidkov emphasised the idea of "rule," which for him meant the special status of a minister. He maintained that their role was similar to that of Timothy and Titus, who "oversee churches, installing presbyters and teachers in them" (Titus 1:5).⁶⁴ Zhidkov did not state straightforwardly that senior presbyters appointed presbyters but seemingly implied this, alluding to Timothy and Titus as Paul's close companions and ministerial plenipotentiaries.

In the overall system of AUCECB, senior presbyters supervised churches in the regions. Originally plenipotentiary representatives and senior presbyters may have occupied different levels on the administrative ladder. In 1944, the system of regional divisions was not yet developed and only two levels of divisions existed: republican (*republics*) and regional (*oblast*) levels.⁶⁵ In 1944, the consultation appointed only three plenipotentiaries: A. L. Andreev for Ukraine, V. N. Chechnev for Belarus and N. I. Kornaukhov for North Caucasus.⁶⁶ In 1947 the district (*raion*) level was added.⁶⁷ The statutes of 1948 described the three-storeyed system of authority: AUCECB, then senior

---

61. Levindanto, "O Sluzhenii Starshikh Presviterov," 50.

62. Orlov, "Soobshchenie o Sisteme Upolnomochennykh," 35–36. Orlov does not provide interpretation of this text, perhaps assuming that its meaning is self-evident.

63. Zhidkov, "Otradnoe v Zhizni," 11.

64. Zhidkov, "Neskol'ko slov o rabote VSEKhB," 34.

65. "Izveshcheniia VSEKhiB," 42–44.

66. "Vsesoiuznoe Soveshchanie," 37. Fifty were appointed after 1944. See Zhidkov, "Neskol'ko slov o rabote VSEKhB," 34.

67. Zhidkov, "Otradnoe v Zhizni," 11. The article states that senior presbyters on the level of area were just an experiment, particularly in the Kursk region.

presbyters of republics, then senior presbyters of regions.[68] This layered pyramid of authority encompassed almost all registered Baptist churches in the USSR.

Operation of this system was from the top down and from centre to periphery.[69] It was built around an administrative command approach that concentrated power in the hands of a minority.[70] A striking example of this is seen in the AUCECB letter to the senior presbyters on sending circular letters:

> We received from some areas copies of circular letters, sent by our plenipotentiaries/senior presbyters to the communities of their regions. These letters contain such statements that represent personal opinions of our brothers and in no case should be presented as the rules for all communities of this or that region. Such circular letters, sent by our plenipotentiaries/senior presbyters bring great disorder into directives, sent to our communities. An undesired effect happens – every region has its own rules.
>
> To stop all this Presidium of AUCECB requests to send all circular letters as drafts to the All-Union Council for a preliminary assessment and only when they approved multiply and circulate them in a republic or region.[71]

It appears that neither republican nor regional senior presbyters had freedom to circulate ideas not approved by the centre. Strings were attached to all three levels of the structure. Even the highly polished and scrupulously neutral style of *Bratskii Vestnik* betrays the administrative essence of the system, informing readers that new senior presbyters "were appointed"[72] or

---

68. See "Polozhenie o Soiuze (1948)," para. 3.22.b.

69. See "Pismo VSEKhB Starshim Presviteram"; "Pismo VSEKhB Presviteram Obshchin"; "Pismo VSEKhB o Pravilakh Prepodavaniia Krescheniia"; "Pismo VSEKhB Starshim Presviteram o Sobliudenii Polozheniia."

70. An example of this is Karev's report on the incorporation of Pentecostals into AUCECB on 24 August 1945, which was reached organisationally and administratively and only later would transit into "unity of hearts – to flaming brotherly love among Christ's disciples and full mutual understanding among themselves" (Karev, "Eshche Odin Shag," 8).

71. "Pismo VSEKhB Starshim Presviteram o Poriadke Rassylki." The document uses both "plenipotentiaries" and "senior presbyters," but the former is crossed out by pencil.

72. "Izveshcheniia VSEKhiB," 42.

"summoned to Moscow for consultations."[73] The practice of appointment of senior presbyters led to many distortions, and even Iakov Zhidkov admitted that some exercised dominion over churches instead of serving them.[74]

4.3 Reaction: Reformist and Autonomous Movements

4.3.1 Initiative Group (IG) and Council of Churches of Evangelical Christian-Baptists (CCECB)

In April 1961, the Baptist church in Uzlovaia, Tula region, delegated a group of brothers "to lead the work of summoning all believers to prayer and common actions for the cause of protecting the truth."[75] The group assumed the title Initsiativnaia Gruppa (Initiative Group [IG]). On 13 August 1961, at the meeting with AUCECB's presidium, members of IG presented an address[76] where they blamed the leadership for the elimination of the principle that the local church decides all vital issues on the basis of God's word; for the installation of ministers who hindered God's cause; and for compiling, circulating and imposing documents contradictory to God's word and the will of the churches.[77] The usurpation of power and submission to the state's dictate underlines these. IG pointed to AUCECB's failure to help churches obtain registered status.[78] IG proposed to treat all Baptist churches, registered and unregistered, as one brotherhood and elect unified central leadership for all churches on the basis of God's word. IG summoned AUCECB to convene an

---

73. "Izveshcheniia VSEKhiB," 43.

74. Zhidkov, "Tserkov Khristova i Ee Poriadki," 6. For exercising authority over local churches, see Zhidkov, 7.

75. The group included Gennadii K. Kriuckov (1926–2007), Aleksei F. Prokofiev (1915–1995), Pavel A. Iakimenkov (1926–2009), Georgii P. Vins (1928–1998) and Boris M. Zdorovets (1929–). Kriuchkov, *Velikoe Probuzhdenie*, 25. Boris Zdorovets, an original member of IG, refutes that the church delegated the group. He attributes the subsequent schism and establishment of CCECB to Kriuchkov's personal ambitions. See Zdorovets, "Kakim Sudom Sudite"; Zdorovets, "Kakim Sudom Sudite 2."

76. "Poslanie Prezidiumu VSEKhB."

77. "Poslanie Prezidiumu VSEKhB."

78. IG estimated that two-thirds of churches were unregistered. See Kriuchkov, *Velikoe Probuzhdenie*, 81, 88, 178.

extraordinary congress.[79] After two more unsuccessful meetings[80] and a written appeal,[81] IG decided to act independently and gathered in consultation (25 February 1962) and formed Orgkomitet (Organising Committee [OC]) for the preparing and convening of congress.[82] Later, this group and churches that joined it formed Sovet Tserkvei Evangelskikh Khristian-Baptistov (Council of Churches of Evangelical Christian-Baptists [CCECB]) in 1965.[83] Instead of uniting all Baptist churches,[84] CCECB only succeeded in establishing another union.

The situation among Baptists in the USSR was further complicated in the late 1960s and early 1970s, when the government allowed churches to have legal status apart from membership in a denomination.[85] Perhaps this step was driven by a desire of the Council for the Affairs of Religious Cults (CARC) to drive a wedge between unregistered churches and weaken them.[86] Initially CCECB reacted positively.[87] However, very soon the leadership realised that this might threaten their union.[88] In 1975, they cancelled the previous regulation[89] and even began stigmatising those registered as "traitors."[90] Avoiding registration became the test for orthodoxy and even the eternal salvation of a believer.[91]

---

79. "Poslanie Prezidiumu VSEKhB."
80. On 23 August and 26 November 1961.
81. Kriuchkov, *Velikoe Probuzhdenie*, 58.
82. Kriuchkov, 59; "Izveshchenie ob Obrazovanii Orgkomiteta."
83. The momentum for reconciliation and reunion was lost in 1965, when OC evolved into CCECB and approved constitution (*Bratskii Listok*, 33–40; 44–48). In spite of a number of meetings between leaders of CCECB and the AUCECB Commission on Unification, established in 1966, reconciliation did not occur. For a detailed description of meetings and analysis, see Sinichkin, "Dialog mezhdu STsEKhB i VSEKhB" (2004); Sinichkin, "Dialog mezhdu STsEKhB i VSEKhB" (2005). AUCECB and CCECB existed in more or less parallel worlds. In 1969, CCECB convened its first congress in Tula, but even this did not lead to official recognition by the Soviet government. For report, see *Bratskii Listok*, 171–77; Kriuchkov, *Velikoe Probuzhdenie*, 366–70; Sawatsky, *Soviet Evangelicals*, 243–45.
84. See *Bratskii Listok*, 43.
85. Such churches received a nickname "autonomous." See Shaptala, *Kak Eto Bylo*, 88.
86. Reshetnikov and Sannikov, *Obzor Istorii*, 197–98; Shaptala, *Kak Eto Bylo*, 89.
87. *Bratskii Listok*, 41–42, 97–98, 173–76, 187.
88. Thus, Shaptala, *Kak Eto Bylo*, 88–89; cf. *Bratskii Listok*, 226, 230.
89. *Bratskii Listok*, 258, 263–66, 269–70.
90. Reshetnikov, "Ob'edinitel'naia Tendentsiia," 58; Shaptala, *Kak Eto Bylo*, 89, 121.
91. *Bratskii Listok*, 263–66, 269–70.

The structure of CCECB resembled that of AUCECB except for the system of senior presbyters.[92] Mikhail Shaptala, one of the leaders of the movement, pointed to the signs of centralisation and authoritarianism within the CCECB.[93] By 1976, two influential Baptist ministers, Joseph Bondarenko and Stepan Dubovoi, proposed granting more authority and freedom to regional associations and restructuring CCECB into a federation. Bondarenko pointed to the extreme separatism of CCECB, its unwillingness to forgive and reconcile with AUCECB and its intolerance towards alternative positions.[94] The tension reached its peak at the consultation of ministers in Khartsyz'k, Donets'k region (22 May 1976),[95] when Gennadii Kriuchkov, president of CCECB, accused Bondarenko and Dubovoi of collaboration with the KGB and financial dishonesty.[96] They were effectively removed from the council but the tensions remained.[97] Inability to deal with these tensions caused antagonisms within the movement and eventually led to what Ukrainian scholar Oleksandr Lakhno called "a schism within the schism."[98] The gap between autonomous churches[99] and CCECB deepened and led to the emergence of another movement.

---

92. The union consisted of regional associations. The assembly was the supreme body that convened every three years. It elected a council of churches, a supervisory body. The council of churches consisted of eleven respected ministers who made the most crucial decisions. Members of the council were liaisons between the churches and associations. Associations were comprised of the churches in a geographic location. Associations met regularly for consultations, elected their councils and organised departments (evangelism, printing, youth, etc.). See "Ustav Soiuza Tserkvei Evangel'skikh Khristian-Baptistov v SSSR"; cf. *Ustav Mezhdunarodnogo Soiuza Tserkvei*; Shaptala, *Kak Eto Bylo*, 73–74. Development of regional associations, formation of departments and expansion was complicated by the imprisonment of some members of the council, and the necessity of operating underground meant the council was unable to cope with local challenges and slowed down its reactions.

93. Shaptala, *Kak Eto Bylo*, 98, 100, 110; Velichko, "Istoriia Avtonomnogo Bratstva," 7. He even compared it to Politburo, the central governing body of the Communist Party of the USSR. See Shaptala, *Kak Eto Bylo*, 100.

94. Obviously, Bondarenko and Dubovoi represented a wider circle of ministers and churches striving for changes within the movement. See, for example, Kovalenko, "Otkrytoe Pis'mo," 74–76.

95. Lakhno, "Rozkol u Rozkoli," 51; Shaptala, *Kak Eto Bylo*, 93–95.

96. He recorded a speech that was played during the meeting. See Shaptala, *Kak Eto Bylo*, 93–94.

97. It is reflected in Kriuchkov's clash with Central Asia association of churches (Shaptala, *Kak Eto Bylo*, 100–121).

98. Lakhno, "Opozytsiia v Evangel's'ko-Baptysts'komu Rusi"; Lakhno, "Rozkol u Rozkoli."

99. In Russian and Ukrainian historiography, this term refers to the Baptist churches that obtained state registration as autonomous religious communities not belonging to a larger union

4.3.2 Autonomous Movement: Return to the Brotherhood

Facing the suspicion and detachment of CCECB, and disappointed by the growing centralisation and authoritarianism of leadership,[100] autonomous churches established informal and then more formal ways to organise and promote key values. By the time of Consultation of autonomous churches (12 November 1983), there were sixty-seven communities and approximately seven thousand members in the USSR.[101] Mikhail Shaptala dates emergence of a loosely consolidated group to 10 July 1984, when representatives of churches issued and circulated *Bratskoe Soglasie* (Fraternal agreement).[102] These churches "united for fellowship in prayers and edifying consultations."[103] Formally, Bratstsvo Nezavisimykh Tserkvei EKhB (Brotherhood of Independent Churches of ECB) emerged in May 1989 when Baptist churches from Donets'k (Ukraine), Voroshylovgrad (now Luhansk, Ukraine), Rostov-on-Don and Krasnodar (Russia) joined in association.[104] With the collapse of the USSR, it was discontinued, and in 1993, thirteen Ukrainian churches established Bratstvo Nezavisimykh Tserkvei i Missii EKhB Ukrainy (Brotherhood of Independent Churches and Mission of ECB of Ukraine).[105]

Bratskoe Soglasie was a theological manifesto, addressed to all fellow believers. Its seven sections evaluate the causes and results of renewal of 1960s (1–2); depict the current situation in CCECB (3); formulate a position on unity (4), church-state relations (5) and local church autonomy (6); and offer practical suggestions (7). Sections 4–6 expound the key concepts on which autonomous churches based their association.

First, unity is distinguished from unification.[106] The document claims allegiance to the original intent of *Initsiativniki*: "to remove sin and ... maintain

---

of churches. On the formation of the autonomous movement, see section 4.3.2. These churches positioned themselves as a bridge between AUCECB and CCECB and aimed at reconciling the two groups.

100. Velichko, "Istoriia Avtonomnogo Bratstva," 7; Velichko, *Uzok Put'*, 148–49.

101. Lakhno, "Rozkol u Rozkoli," 53.

102. For the full text, see Shaptala, *Kak Eto Bylo*, 128–34.

103. Shaptala, *Kak Eto Bylo*, 134.

104. Shaptala, *Kak Eto Bylo*, 135.

105. Shaptala, *Kak Eto Bylo*, 135; cf. Velichko, "Istoriia Avtonomnogo Bratstva," 8; Nazarkina, "Protestants'ki Konfesii Ukrainy," 73.

106. Shaptala, *Kak Eto Bylo*, 131.

full unity of all God's people and return all the Church to the way of truth and under the lordship of her Head – Christ Jesus."[107] The compilers concede the existence of two parts of Baptist brotherhood but envision a situation when separated churches would be registered and be able to maintain relations with AUCECB and Baptists worldwide.[108]

Second, the understanding of church-state relations follows a traditional Baptist concern for the separation of church and state and obedience to the state only if it does not limit faith.[109] The state should not exercise its power over the church, interfering with the confessional life of a community. This statement also touches on the registration of local communities.[110] Since the church belongs to "Christ's Kingdom, which is not of this world,"[111] it should not "interfere with civic affairs, seek patronage of the state and to make a compromise with it."[112]

Third, the document holds on to radical local church autonomy: "We recognise that every local church is [an] independent, autonomous and self-governing community of believers."[113] Only Christ as the head of the church rules and governs local churches. Two conclusions follow: (1) local churches elect ministers, admit new members and exercise discipline, not allowing another church or church unions to intrude; (2) all members are equal and have equal rights. Presbyters have leading but not dominating positions and

---

107. Shaptala, *Kak Eto Bylo*, 131.

108. Shaptala, *Kak Eto Bylo*, 131. This differs from the position of Leonid E. Kovalenko expressed in *Otkrytoe Pismo o Edinstve* [Open Letter on Unity] in 1970 (Kovalenko, "Otkrytoe Pis'mo," 74–76.). Kovalenko was part of the *Initsiativniki* movement and a preacher and deacon in the Kyiv Autonomous Church (Velichko, *Uzok Put,'* 39–40). He evaluates changes in AUCECB positively and is intolerant towards division. Kovalenko builds on two ideas: God strives to sanctify his people by the truth (John 17:6, 8, 12, 14, 19) and to make them one through love (John 17:11, 15, 20–23, 26) (Kovalenko, "Otkrytoe Pis'mo," 74–75.). The church and every member should lean on both principles: "based on the commanded will of Christ on indissoluble connection of truth and love, considering admission by AUCECB of their guilt and a big correction in their churches done according to God's Word, I claim that maintaining division in our brotherhood is a gross crime against Christ and His Kingdom in our country" (Kovalenko, 76.). This voice signifies desire among representatives of the autonomous churches to step over the past insults and restore unity as the major value of the church. *Bratskoe Soglasie* is not as irenic and contains a portion of contempt that the transformations in AUCECB are irreversible.

109. Shaptala, *Kak Eto Bylo*, 132.

110. Shaptala, *Kak Eto Bylo*, 132.

111. Shaptala, *Kak Eto Bylo*, 132.

112. Shaptala, *Kak Eto Bylo*, 132.

113. Shaptala, *Kak Eto Bylo*, 132.

exercise their ministry on the basis of the consensus of all members. The church of Christ has no hierarchy.[114]

Such a concept of local church autonomy raises a question: what role should church unions and associations play? *Bratskoe Soglasie* denies governing over the churches and restricts the activity of unions to the "strengthening of interchurch relations and development of common mission in the Lord's work."[115] The document is silent as to the practical steps of implementing these tasks. The last paragraph alludes to regular meetings of church representatives for "fellowship in prayers and instructive dialogues" and "election of representatives from their midst for interchurch relations."[116] It resembles the horizontal structure of Bratstvo.[117] Shaptala admits that churches are free "to establish among themselves necessary forms of fraternal fellowship and joining ligaments."[118] However, it is unclear how this model would work if the quantity of autonomous churches increases significantly. Early Baptist history makes it clear that growth and expansion lead to the development of organisational structures for union.

The autonomous churches' self-definition as a mediatory group between AUCECB and CCECB, striving to bridge the sad division, provides a constitutive narrative that forms their identity up to recent times. Sadly, the autonomous project of reconciliation failed for CCECB did not have relations either with AUCECB or with the autonomous movement.[119] However, the efforts of IG were not in vain. Commenting on AUCECB's reaction to IG, Sawatsky states, "Instead of dealing with the *Initsiativniki* directly and working out a joint reform program as requested by the *Initsiativniki*, the AUCECB now launched a program for reunification which, step by step, included more and more of the *Initsiativniki* suggestions."[120] These reforms affected the practices and, to some extent, the structures of AUCECB.

---

114. Shaptala, *Kak Eto Bylo*, 133.
115. Shaptala, *Kak Eto Bylo*, 133.
116. Shaptala, *Kak Eto Bylo*, 134.
117. See section 2.1.2.
118. Shaptala, *Kak Eto Bylo*, 135.
119. There are signs of convergence between AUUCECB and Brotherhood of Independent Churches and Mission of ECB of Ukraine. See Reshetnikov, "Ob'edinitel'naia Tendentsiia," 58–60.
120. Sawatsky, *Soviet Evangelicals*, 202.

4.3.3 Transformations of Practices and Structures of AUCECB

The plenum of AUCECB (29 November–3 December 1961) admitted the need for a congress.[121] After the plenum, Artur Mitskevich compared *Polozhenie (1960)*, *Instruktivnoe Pis'mo*, Orgkomitet's proposal of statutes and the Soviet law on religious associations (1929)[122] and presented the results to CARC on 15 December 1961, appealing for the necessity of statutes that account for traditional Baptist beliefs and practices.[123] On 19 December 1962, he received an offer to compile a programme of congress, which was submitted to CARC on 16 January 1963, and new statutes, which were submitted on 31 January 1963. CARC allowed the convening of congress on 24 July 1963.[124]

The new statutes (1963) incorporated most suggestions made by OC.[125] Michael Bourdeaux, commenting on the amendments to the statutes, states:

> A careful study of the text of the new constitution as compared with the new *Statutes* of 1960 is the most revealing, and the wide-spread nature of concessions to the reformers is a matter of some surprise, considering the refusal to co-operate with the new movement on the part of AUCECB. Indeed, there are so many concessions, at some points even with verbal correspondence, that not only do we have proof of the extreme pressure which the reformers had exerted, but we must also postulate a genuine desire, at least on the part of some of AUCECB officials, to meet the reformers half-way.[126]

It restored the union as association of churches[127] which was omitted in the statutes of 1960.[128] The congress is the supreme authority, while AUCECB

---

121. Mitskevich, *Istoriia Evangelskikh Khristian-Baptistov*, 339–40.

122. Mitskevich, 342–55. For the English text and analysis and comparison of Statutes 1960, the OC proposal and Statutes 1963, see Bourdeaux, *Religious Ferment in Russia*, 68–71, 190–210.

123. Mitskevich, *Istoriia Evangelskikh Khristian-Baptistov*, 341; cf. Reshetnikov and Sannikov, *Obzor Istorii*, 200.

124. Mitskevich, *Istoriia Evangelskikh Khristian-Baptistov*, 356.

125. See comparison in Bourdeaux, *Religious Ferment in Russia*, Appendix 1, 190–210.

126. Bourdeaux, *Religious Ferment in Russia*, 68–69.

127. "Ustav Soiuza (1963)," para. 1.1.

128. "Polozhenie o Soiuze (1960)," para. 1.1.

as executive body operates between the congresses.[129] AUCECB and senior presbyters assume the role of spiritual leaders, not only observers watching over correct implementation of Soviet legislation and statutes. Senior presbyters are appointed with the agreement of local churches where they are members. They "help the churches situated in their territories, both spiritually . . . and from an organisational standpoint."[130] The congress eliminated a three-year probation for baptismal candidates,[131] restriction on choirs in worship services[132] and removed the phrase limiting membership in the union to the registered churches.[133] The congress in Moscow (15–17 October 1963) approved the changes, a significant shift to traditional practices.[134]

The members of OC were not satisfied and continued criticising AUCECB for violation of Baptist principles.[135] In a letter to AUCECB's presidium, they pointed to the violation of the principle of separation of church and state, which led to abandonment of the main purposes of the church: "preaching the Gospel and witness for Christ."[136] They referred to the statutes of the unions of Evangelical Christians and Baptists.[137] Perhaps in response, the congress of 1966 modified the statutes.

---

129. "Ustav Soiuza (1963)," para. 2.3.

130. "Ustav Soiuza (1963)," para. 2.1, 3.15. Bourdeaux's analysis is based on an incorrect rendering of paragraph 3.22.c of Statutes 1960, which reads, "watching over installation of new worthy presbyters and ordaining them," while Bourdeaux gives, "to see that new worthy ministers are made available and to ordain them" (Bourdeaux, *Religious Ferment in Russia*, 70, 199).

131. "Ustav Soiuza (1963)," para. 4.17; cf. "Polozhenie o Soiuze (1960)," para. 4.25.

132. "Ustav Soiuza (1963)," para. 4.26; cf. "Polozhenie o Soiuze (1960)," para. 4.37. According to the statute (1960), the choir could not visit other local churches and its performance should be "in modest forms and should not turn into spiritual concerts"; local churches could only use the organ, harmonium or, in exclusive cases, piano. Statutes 1963 eliminates all this.

133. "Ustav Soiuza (1963)," para. 2.6; cf. "Polozhenie o Soiuze (1960)," para. 2.10.

134. Official account in "Vsesoiuznyi Se'zd," 7–54; cf. Sawatsky, *Soviet Evangelicals*, 202–10.

135. For a historical survey of Baptist principles and their significance, see Sannikov, "Istoriia i Analiz Baptistskikh Printsipov"; Vins, *Nashi Baptistskie Printsipy*; cf. Mitskevich, "Osnovnye Printsipy."

136. *Bratskii Listok*, 12–13.

137. *Bratskii Listok*, 13.

Some estimated the congress of 1966 to be "the most democratic congress,"[138] which "finally completed the positive reformation of the AUCECB into a growth-oriented, forward-looking free church union."[139] The statutes of 1966 state that the union has "to enhance implementation of Baptist principles and doctrines in life and activities of local churches; to promote unity among the member churches and other churches, which confess new birth from God's Word and the Holy Spirit and water baptism by faith (John 17:21–23); to keep local churches in sound Gospel doctrines (Titus 2:7)."[140] Local churches have the tasks of "preaching the Gospel (Acts 20:24); discipling believers for growth in holiness, devotion and obedience to Christ's commands (Matt 28:20; 1 Tim 2:1–4); developing and strengthening of Christian love and unity of believers (John 17:21–23)."[141] The congress affirmed the independence and self-determination of local churches[142] and introduced regional councils and consultations of ministers.[143] Regional councils were to assist senior presbyters, strengthen their authority and introduce collective decision-making processes.[144] Perhaps the most significant implementation was that regional consultations of ministers assumed the right to elect senior presbyters, resolve the most vital issues[145] and hold senior presbyters accountable.[146] Decisions of the next four congresses were not as radical. In 1969 the congress extended the interval between congresses to five years, which strengthened the influence of AUCECB.[147]

In 1974 the congress did not change the statutes or structures of the union,[148] but two Plenums of AUCECB concentrated on the status, ministry

---

138. Sawatsky ascribes this to regional congresses' election of "outspoken persons to ensure that congregations' complaints would be heard in faraway Moscow" (Sawatsky, *Soviet Evangelicals*, 211).

139. Sawatsky, *Soviet Evangelicals*, 215.

140. Paragraph 1.3 in "Ustav Soiuza (1966)," 50.

141. Paragraph 4.19 in "Ustav Soiuza (1966)," 53.

142. "Ustav Soiuza (1966)," 53.

143. Karev, "Dokald," 23; "Ustav Soiuza (1966)," 51.

144. Karev, "Dokald," 32–33; "Ustav Soiuza (1966)," 52.

145. Karev, "Dokald," 32–33; "Ustav Soiuza (1966)," 52.

146. For implementation, see Chernopiatov, "Presviterskoe Soveshchanie v Kurske," 72.

147. "Tretii Den' S'ezda," 74; cf. Sawatsky, *Soviet Evangelicals*, 217, 219. For an example of a biased treatment of the Statutes 1969 by CCECB, see *Bratskii Listok*, 233–34.

148. Sawatsky, "Russian Evangelicals," 12–15; Pospielovsky, "Forty-First," 246–53.

and role of senior presbyters in the spiritual formation of believers.[149] The issue was addressed from different angles.[150] Almost all papers remarked on the role of senior presbyters in carrying out the task of implementing Baptist principles and doctrines and enhancing the unity and protection of pure Baptist teaching in the context of formation. Senior presbyters were spiritual leaders and not only administrators. One of the most significant aspects was that senior presbyters received help from presbyters' councils introduced in 1969. They consisted of "experienced church ministers" who "help with their wise collective advice."[151] The papers still betrayed residuals of the controlling and ruling role of senior presbyters.[152]

The congress in 1979[153] introduced departments to implement the decisions of the congress under the guidance of AUCECB's presidium[154] and pastoral consultations to discuss and resolve vital issues.[155]

In 1985,[156] AUCECB approved a new statement of faith[157] which surprisingly lacked any mention of the union of churches. Section 7, "On the Church," remained within the boundaries of universal (invisible) church and local church.[158]

At the end of 1980s processes of democratisation under the slogans of *perestroika* (reconstruction) and *glasnost* (openness) influenced Baptists. Discussions on the reform of AUCECB intensified and splashed out on the pages of denominational newspapers and magazines. Thus, Anatolii Rudenko, the secretary of the Russian Bible Society,[159] and Andrei Melnikov, a Christian publisher from Novosibirsk,[160] criticised the centralisation of AUCECB and

---

149. Bychkov, "Otchetnyi Doklad VSEKhB" (1980), 31, 43–47; Mel'nikov, "O Rabote Starshikh Presviterov," 67–72.

150. Borodinov, "O Vospitanii Veruiushchikh"; Kolesnikov, "O Vospitanii Veruiushchikh"; Mitskevich, "O Vospitanii Veruiushchikh"; Dukhonchenko, "O Dukhovnom Vospitanii."

151. Mel'nikov, "O Rabote Starshikh Presviterov," 69.

152. Mel'nikov, "O Rabote Starshikh Presviterov," 69.

153. Rowe, "1979 Baptist Congress," 188–200; "News in Brief," 329–30.

154. Paragraph 2.7 in "Ustav Soiuza (1979)," 61.

155. Paragraph 3.18 in "Ustav Soiuza (1979)," 63.

156. Rowe, "USSR Baptist Congress," 333–34.

157. "Verouchenie," 33–49; "Proekt Verouchenia," 32–52.

158. "Verouchenie," 43–46.

159. Rudenko, "Preodolet Administrativnyi Gypnoz" in Nazarkina, "Protestants'ki Konfesii Ukrainy," 66–67.

160. Mel'nikov, "V Plenu u Proshlogo," 6; Mel'nikov, "Tsentralizatsia ili Edinstvo?," 3.

argued for the democratisation of its structure. Rudenko differentiated unity from strong centralised administration:

> Unity is mutual understanding, essentially similar views on the most important issues of faith. . . . Unity should be exercised not by the will of administrators but via regularly occurring fellowships of the believers on all levels: assemblies, consultations, conferences, congresses of representatives of the churches with free and just mechanism of elections. These fellowships should become legislative bodies of the brotherhood; . . . they should decide all principal issues of faith.[161]

Melnikov argued for coordination instead of the administrative regulation of missionary work[162] and for the restoration of local church autonomy expressed in the form of regional associations.[163]

Baptist historian Sergei Savinskii criticised senior presbyters as being imposed by the system, pyramidal and authoritarian in nature and incapable of addressing the chief goal of the union: mission.[164] He put forward an elaborate proposal of reforms which included the elimination of senior presbyters and the centralised administrative structure; the idea of autonomous regional associations or departments uniting local churches around evangelism, spiritual unity, spiritual edification and assistance in the installing of ministers; and the restoration of the union of churches. He thought that regional conferences should elect Board and Council of associations who should be accountable to them. His structure reminds one of the Union of the 1920s.

Iakov Dukhonchenko (1931–1993), at the time senior presbyter in Ukraine, cautiously expressed similar ideas. He admitted that AUCECB should transform into union and form associations, explaining this as a desire "to unleash all administrative ties, which restricted, and give more space to spirit, personality, in resolving crucial issues."[165] Speaking on senior presbyters, Dukhonchenko stressed that they should quit being "arms of the

---

161. Rudenko, "Preodolet Administrativnyi Gypnoz" in Nazarkina, "Protestants'ki Konfesii Ukrainy," 66–67.
162. Mel'nikov, "Tsentralizatsia ili Edinstvo?," 3.
163. Mel'nikov, "V Plenu u Proshlogo," 6.
164. Savinskii, "K Voprosu o Structure," 5.
165. Kornilov and Rudenko, "Beseda s Ia.K. Dukhonchenko," 7.

AUCECB" and should be instead elected in the regions and be accountable to the associations where they serve.[166] Caution and slowness of reforms could be ascribed to the centrifugal processes in the union and the leadership's fear of losing control over these processes.[167]

In 1989, Vasily Logvinenko (1925–2009), president of AUCECB (1985–1990), in a report to the Plenum admitted existing dissatisfaction with AUCECB. He proposed two models of solution. In the first model, unions in republics should be strengthened to become autonomous bodies responsible for planting new churches, training ministers, evangelising, publishing, and international and interdenominational relations. The council in Moscow should carry responsibility for printing and importing literature, training ministers and teachers at the seminary, and distributing human and financial resources for inner mission. The second model resembled the first but retained the existing "hierarchical spiritual ladder of power: local church elects presbyter, regional association – senior pastor, republican union – senior presbyter in republic, the Union – president or senior presbyter, his assistants, secretary general and others."[168] The statutes of 1990 embodied the latter. In 1994, at the extraordinary Congress of the Ukrainian Baptist Union, Veniamin Honcharov, vice president of the Ukrainian Baptist Union, remarked in a report that the union's structure "should have already been changed several years ago and you all know it too well."[169]

The statutes of 1990 demonstrated that Savinskii's proposal was taken seriously and incorporated in the document.[170] It differed from all previous versions by reverting the order of the articles. Statutes from 1948 to 1979 were

---

166. Kornilov and Rudenko, 7. The statements and practice differed: "a) Senior presbyters and their assistants are installed by All-Union Council with endorsement of the churches, where they are members, and through their election at the regional (area), interregional and republican presbyters' conferences; b) In assistance to senior presbyters the conferences elect councils out of experienced church ministers; senior presbyters preside over councils" ("Ustav Soiuza (1966)," 51–52).

167. Kornilov and Rudenko, "Beseda s Ia.K. Dukhonchenko," 7; cf. K. R., "Ocherednoi Plenum," 60. At the end of the 1980s, Pentecostal churches left AUCECB and established their own unions. See K. R., 63.

168. K. R., 62.

169. Honcharov, "O Rabote Soiuza EKhB," 2.

170. "Ustav Soiuza (1990)," 82–94.

constructed "from above": from AUCECB to local church.¹⁷¹ The statutes of 1990 were built "from below": from local church to national union.¹⁷²

The collapse of the USSR prevented further transformations. In spite of the obvious processes of disintegration of the USSR, Baptists were slow to acknowledge that. Thus, the participants of the consultation of the union (Moscow, 3–5 December 1991) expressed their concern with the fact of the emergence of new independent states and their impact on the future of the union.¹⁷³ They confirmed desire to keep the union's spiritual centre in Moscow but also agreed to change the name, structure and statutes of the union.¹⁷⁴ The Euro-Asian Federation of the Unions of ECB replaced AUCECB at the Edifying Congress of ECB (Moscow, 9–14 November 1992).¹⁷⁵ Baptist churches had a strong feeling of belonging to one union and, perhaps, could not envision that the collapse of the USSR would bring the AUCECB to an end. Leaders of the new independent unions continued maintaining relations and hoped that the ties would be retained and even strengthened. They appealed to the image of the body of Christ and unity as an expression of the church's nature and organic ties.¹⁷⁶ Nevertheless, AUCECB had disintegrated into independent Baptist unions by 1994.

4.4 Understandings of the Nature of Associations of Churches

Deviations in the structure and practice of AUCECB were accompanied by the emergence of some new theological perspectives – or rather ecclesiological emphases – on ACs which coexisted with more traditional ones.

---

171. Statutes of the CCECB follow the same model. See "Ustav Soiuza Tserkvei Evangel'skikh Khristian-Baptistov v SSSR"; Mezhdunarodnyi Soiuz Tserkvei Evangel'skikh Khristian-Baptistov, *Ustav Mezhdunarodnogo Soiuza Tserkvei*.

172. The new approach of statutes of 1990 provides the model according to which AUUCECB still operates. The statutes of AUUCECB are legal documents that regulate operation of the union and its structural units, while the statutes of 1966–1990 were an amalgamation of legal provisions and church order.

173. Kadaeva, "Zasedanie Soveta Soiuza," 52.

174. "Obrashchenie Uchastnikov" (1992), 63; also, Kadaeva, "Zasedanie Soveta Soiuza," 52, 61.

175. "Obrashchenie Uchastnikov" (1993), 77–79; "Ustav Evro-Aziatskoi Federatsii," 72–75.

176. More on the theological underpinnings of this are given in section 5.4.1.

4.4.1 AUCECB: Association of Churches or the Church?

At the end of the 1940s, some Baptist authors began using the word "church" with regard to the union. Ivan Motorin, in his extensive article on unity, labeled unions of evangelical Christians and Baptists "churches" that merged into one "church."[177] The usage of the word relates neither to local church nor to the universal church. For Motorin, the church universal

> is not a particular church organisation united by certain ritual, dogmas, canon or tradition. It is something bigger. Christ's Church is the assembly of believers of all ages, tribes and peoples, redeemed by the blood of Christ. The Church is spiritual body of Christ, and Christ is the Head of the Church.[178]

Motorin referred to the traditional concept of invisible church. Labelling the unions "churches," he used the word in a restrictive, denominational way.[179] The church is bigger and not encapsulated by the denominational borders of AUCECB, but in some way it is present there. Such usage became rather common at this period. Iakov Zhidkov spoke of "the church of Evangelical Christians-Baptists" which was planted by God in the USSR along with "other so-called historical churches."[180] He specified that "this church consists of multiple churches spread over the vast space of our motherland."[181] Again, "the church of Evangelical Christians-Baptists" could be interpreted as a drift towards the denominationalism of AUCECB.

In another article, Zhidkov explained the leadership structure of AUCECB, comparing the presidium with "bright lamps in the house of God and pillars of our church, holding all her edifice on the great foundation, the cornerstone – Jesus Christ."[182] In this passage, the titles "house of God" and "church" apply to the union of churches which stands on the shoulders of AUCECB leaders. These statements could be the signs of ecclesiasticism, but they could

---

177. M[otorin], "Edinstvo Veruiushchikh," 19. On the traditional notion of union in AUCECB, see "Polozhenie o Soiuze (1944)"; "Polozhenie o Soiuze (1948)"; "Ustav Soiuza (1966)"; "Ustav Soiuza (1979)"; "Ustav Soiuza (1990)."

178. M[otorin], "Edinstvo Veruiushchikh," 20. On using the term "church" beyond the local level among English General Baptists, see Payne, *Fellowship of Believers*, 119.

179. Cf. Somov, "Odno Stado," 32, 33.

180. Zhidkov, "Nash Otchet," 13.

181. Zhidkov, "Nash Otchet," 13.

182. Zhidkov, "Nash Otchet," 14.

also be interpreted as mere eloquence and rhetoric that has nothing to do with transformations of Baptist self-identity. Notwithstanding this reservation, changed practices and the strong centralised structure of AUCECB prompt one to incline to the first supposition.

The leadership legitimised AUCECB with biblical examples. Thus, Iakov Zhidkov (1885–1966), president of the AUCECB, in his article on the Day of Transfiguration claimed that Baptist and evangelical churches in the USSR were "the most proximate in form and spirit of life to the transfigured Christianity."[183] By "transfigured Christianity," he meant Christian churches that have Jesus Christ as their centre and are built according to the commands of the Lord and his apostles.[184] He saw affinity to transfigured Christianity in an unprecedented spirit of unity and in simple church organisation and worship.[185] Zhidkov stressed the second element, contraposing the simplicity and familial relations of Soviet Baptist churches to the complexity and sluggishness of Western churches with their committees and councils: "The spirit of Christ's life is more important than all rules, forms and ordinances."[186] Going beyond the local church, he mentions the Jerusalem Council, "authoritative for the Apostles themselves and for local churches."[187] He drew an analogy between the Jerusalem Council and AUCECB:

> We likewise have All-Union Council with Presidium in Moscow, consisting of the most authoritative brethren – representatives of three former evangelical movements now united into one Union. All-Union Council of Evangelical Christians-Baptists is not the uncontrollable "elite" of God's people, not commanders, but a friendly community of the most mature in faith brothers, who love the Lord Jesus Christ and His holy cause and, in their turn, are loved by God's people. These are the people who have behind them many years of ministry to God and His people.[188]

---

183. Zhidkov, "Preobrazhenie," 10.
184. Zhidkov, "Preobrazhenie," 11, 12.
185. Zhidkov, "Preobrazhenie," 10–11.
186. Zhidkov, "Preobrazhenie," 10.
187. Zhidkov, "Preobrazhenie," 11; cf. Zhidkov, "Vzgliad Nazad," 9. See also Mitskevich, "Tserkov, Sviashchennosluzhiteli i Chleny Tserkvi," 31; Mitskevich, "Osnovnye Printsipy," 49.
188. Zhidkov, "Preobrazhenie," 11. For another example, see Zhidkov, "Vzgliad Nazad," 9.

The reference to the authority of the Jerusalem Council, to which even the apostles submitted, plays a significant role in establishing the case for the authority of AUCECB over other local churches. Zhidkov also compared senior presbyters to Titus and Timothy, for they "oversee life of local churches and their ministers"[189] and are "the most authoritative ministers in their republics, areas and regions."[190] Appealing to biblical examples, Zhidkov demonstrates that AUCECB's model is rooted in NT practices which should legitimise it in the eyes of those who were dissatisfied with centralisation and its significant departure from the traditional way of Baptist associating. Indeed, AUCECB betrays signs of episcopalian rather than traditional congregational church polity. However, having said that, I admit that these novelties do not represent the majority view but rather are the views of some officials of AUCECB.

4.4.2 Biblical Images of the Union

Traditional self-designation as "brotherhood" remained the most popular depiction of union in the official sources. It usually meant "union," designating the union of Evangelical Christians and Baptists, any national Baptist union[191] or a "confession," all Baptists worldwide. Unfortunately, this concept was used but hardly ever explained. Two publications turned to the motif of "brotherhood," using it with regard to ACs: (1) Aleksei Bychkov, general secretary of AUCECB (1971–1990), in his address to the Forty-Third Congress of ECB, referred to the concept's relation to Christian unity;[192] and (2) Janis Tervits, Latvian bishop and a member of AUCECB (1979–1992), provided a brief biblical and theological study of the concept.[193]

Bychkov defined the concept:

> Apostle Peter in his epistle says: 'love brotherhood' – 1 Pet 2:17. Brotherhood defines inner essence of the church and means unity in Christ. That is how it was at the times of apostles. But in our days the concept of 'brotherhood' more often concerns the believers united by common confession of major dogmatic

---

189. Zhidkov, "Preobrazhenie," 11.
190. Zhidkov, "Preobrazhenie," 11.
191. Zhidkov, "Tserkov Khristova i Ee Poriadki," 5.
192. Bychkov, "Otchetnyi Doklad VSEKhB" (1985).
193. Tervits, "Bratstvo Liubite."

statements, having single statement of faith and the Statutes of church order.[194]

Bychkov equated "brotherhood" with unity in Christ and claimed that this defines the essence of the church while also admitting that at his time "brotherhood" was confined by confessional and dogmatic limits. His reflections on the term are preceded by a reminder of the centennial celebration of the first conference on unity in St. Petersburg (1884) and followed by reference to the work for unity through the World Council of Churches. Bychkov recalled Korff and Pashkov's appeal: "Recall, brothers, that Christ died 'also for the scattered children of God to bring them together and make them one' [John 11:52] and to create of them one flock which has one Shepherd [John 10:16]." He also referred to the Apostles' Creed – "I believe in . . . the holy Christian [sic] Church, the communion of saints"[195] – and alluded to the three major purposes of ECB: preaching the gospel, spiritual nurture and keeping unity.[196] This hints that he saw the concept of "brotherhood" somehow related to the implementation of the idea of unity among the believers.

Tervits's more nuanced study pointed out that the word "brother," besides the direct meaning of siblings (Matt 1:2), also signifies fellow citizens (Acts 3:17), any person (Matt 5:22), people of shared interest and rank (Matt 5:4) and all humanity (Matt 25:40; Heb 2:17). It came to mean "not only familial or national relations of people or commonness of their interests but also commonness of their religious views."[197] For Tervits, "brotherhood" in the Christian sense has inner and outer characteristics. Inner is the new birth through Jesus Christ:

> Brotherhood in the Christian understanding is where people are united in the new beginning – new birth. In other words, at the new birth from above, Creator God through Jesus Christ becomes our common Heavenly Father. If this basis is there,

---

194. Bychkov, "Otchetnyi Doklad VSEKhB" (1985), 16.
195. Bychkov, "Otchetnyi Doklad VSEKhB" (1985), 16.
196. Bychkov, "Otchetnyi Doklad VSEKhB" (1985), 16. For a variant reading of these purposes, see K. R., "Ocherednoi Plenum," 59.
197. Tervits, "Bratstvo Liubite," 27.

then such people are a brotherhood – a living organism guided by the Holy Spirit.[198]

The new birth is the foundation from which and the power by which all Christians are connected to God and each other. In this new community, Christ is the centre around which all are united.[199] Each member of the family retains individuality while diversity does not hinder unity:

> Divine miracle – the fruit of the Calvary suffering of our Lord Jesus Christ – is that in spite of the peculiarities of each member of the Christian brotherhood, the victory is won by new life, new longings which establish creative unity because 'all things have been created through him . . . in him all things hold together' – Col 1:16–17.[200]

However, the inner criterion is elusive and unrecognisable. Perhaps for this reason, Tervits introduced the outer characteristic: love-agape.[201] Such love is the fruit of the Holy Spirit, who helps the believer to judge others' views (1 Cor 2:12–15) and distinguish truth from lie (1 John 2:20) and who urges to mutual submission.[202] These works of the Holy Spirit are expressed in "spiritual discipline" and "organisational discipline."[203] The former is related to "the Baptist motto" – "one Lord, one faith, one baptism" (Eph 4:5) – and presupposes "knowing God's love," while the latter presupposes "mutual respect and submission" in growing into total stature in Christ (Eph 4:11–13). Tervits's ideas resemble both Bychkov's unity of brotherhood based on a common confession of faith and church order and Shipkov's insistence on the criterion of love.[204]

The separation of the IG in the 1960s intensified apologetic use of the image of the body of Christ to sustain unity. Thus, Elizaveta Kargel, daughter of Johann Kargel, one of the evangelical pioneers, pointed to literal obedience to God's will expressed in Scriptures, stressing that divisions in Christ's body are

---

198. Tervits, "Bratstvo Liubite," 27.
199. Tervits, "Bratstvo Liubite," 28.
200. Tervits, "Bratstvo Liubite," 28.
201. Tervits, "Bratstvo Liubite," 28.
202. Tervits, "Bratstvo Liubite," 27–28.
203. Tervits, "Bratstvo Liubite," 28.
204. Shipkov, "Bratstvo vo Khriste," 7–8.

not only signs of selfishness and a lack of love to Christ,[205] which cause him to suffer, but are also a sin against the church. The divisions in the church also prevent non-believers from converting to Christ and bring harm to believers.[206] The missiological component was the most outstanding in her letter and some other writings.[207] Sergei Fadiukhin read John 17:21 in the context of Paul's teaching on the church's unity (Col 3:14–16).[208] He based unity on the foundation of God's word (Eph 4:23–24). There is "spiritual unity – inner, unseen unity"[209] and a visible expression of unity in the form of baptism and the Lord's Supper.[210] Dukhonchenko added to this that the unity of the body of Christ is "organic unity. It follows from the fact that every believer in Christ as his personal Savior is born from above, baptised by the Holy Spirit and belongs to the Church. The Holy Spirit acts in the Church in general and in every member, transforming us in Christ's image."[211] This leads to a conclusion that the union of churches was perceived as a form of the church since divisions in the union equate to divisions of the body of Christ.

4.5 Summary

This chapter demonstrates transformations in traditional associational practices in the post-war period. The centralisation and institutionalisation of the union, driven by the necessity to restore it, tune its structure and consolidate dispersed local churches, was enhanced by organised pressure from the state. AUCECB evolved into a denomination with hierarchy, tradition and an administrative structure. The restoration of the union of churches and revitalisation of spiritual life was concentrated around the council of ministers and the ministry of senior presbyters. Good intentions aside, these changes

---

205. Kargel, "O Edinstve Veruiushchikh." On the motif of love as the key driver of unity, see Kargel, "Golos Bratoliubiia."

206. Kargel, "O Edinstve Veruiushchikh," 24.

207. Kargel, "Golos Bratoliubiia," 12; Vasks, "Da Budut Vse Edino," 57; Evangelical Christian Baptist Union, *Evangelskie Khristiane-Baptisty v SSSR*, 12; Dukhonchenko, "Dukhovno-Vospitatel'naia Rabota Sluzhitelei," 56, 59; "Ednist' Khrystyian," 1.

208. Fadiukhin, "Doklad o Edinstve."

209. Fadiukhin, "Doklad o Edinstve," 62.

210. Fadiukhin, "Doklad o Edinstve," 62–63; Klimenko, "Doklad o Prodelannoi Rabote," 59; Dukhonchenko, "Dukhovno-Vospitatel'naia Rabota Sluzhitelei," 53.

211. Dukhonchenko, "Dukhovno-Vospitatel'naia Rabota Sluzhitelei," 52.

jeopardised two historical Baptist values: mission as the driving force and reason for union and freedom of the local church. The leadership of AUCECB focused on survival, maintenance and protectionism. Control over issues that were traditionally under local church authority and the sometimes divisive role of senior presbyters caused dissatisfaction and resistance among local churches. Due to this resistance, the willingness of some AUCECB members and acquiescence from the state, the union managed to gradually restore traditional Baptist associational practices and emphasis on the local church. These events increased suspicion concerning ACs and strengthened the trajectory of local church autonomy. The bond of trust was broken: AUCECB did not trust local churches and controlled everything. Leaders of IG did not trust AUCECB and pushed forward even though it began changing. The leadership of CCECB did not trust fellow ministers and built strong hierarchy.

CHAPTER 5

The Union in Independent Ukraine (1991–2014)

5.1 Introduction

Mikhail Gorbachev, the general secretary of the Communist Party, who came to power in 1985, introduced the programmes of acceleration (*uskorenie*) of the Soviet economy, reconstruction (*perestroika*) and openness (*glasnost'*) of political life in the USSR. These initiatives had tremendous influence on domestic and international politics in the USSR.[1]

By 1989 the USSR withdrew troops from Afghanistan and lost control over the Warsaw Pact bloc which resulted in its disintegration and the demolition of the Berlin Wall, a symbolic act pointing to a new era of relations between East and West.[2] Inside the USSR, the influence of the politburo was restricted and the first semi-democratic elections for the Supreme Soviet occurred. Soviet republics obtained a higher level of autonomy. This led to the so-called "parade of sovereignties"[3] and caused a number of ethnic conflicts in Central Asia and the Caucasus and clashes of the centre with democratic powers in Georgia and Lithuania.[4] In 1990 Lithuania was the first to declare

---

1. See details in Magocsi, *History of Ukraine*, 715–24; Plokhy, *Gates of Europe*, 307–23.
2. Magocsi, *History of Ukraine*, 716.
3. The phrase relates to the attempts to put republican legislation in a place of primacy over USSR legislation and secure economic independence. See Suny, *Revenge*, 146–47; Plokhy, *Gates of Europe*, 315–16.
4. Suny, *Revenge of the Past*, 127–48.

its independence. These processes eventually led to the collapse of the USSR and emergence of new independent states. On 8 December 1991, the representatives of Belarus, Russia and Ukraine signed the Belovezha Accords at a meeting in Belovezha Forest. With this document, the USSR effectively ceased to exist and the Commonwealth of Independent States was created instead.

In Ukraine, the processes of disintegration of the USSR coincided with the revival of Ukrainian culture and the growth of ethnic awareness, as well as aspirations for a democratic and independent state. The Declaration of State Sovereignty of Ukraine (16 July 1990) and the Act of Declaration of Independence of Ukraine (24 August 1991) restored its statehood lost in the 1920s.

Attitude towards religion in the USSR began changing with the approach of the celebration of a millennium of Christianity in Russia (1988).[5] Wide programmes of celebrations stirred interest in Christianity and gave churches a chance to step into the public arena.[6] The disintegration of the USSR impacted AUCECB as well. In 1990, the delegates of the twenty-first assembly of Ukrainian Baptist churches restored the Union of Evangelical Christians-Baptists of Ukraine. Since then this union had existed for four years and was officially registered by the state in 1994 as the All-Ukrainian Union of Associations of Evangelical Christians-Baptists (AUUAECB). The delegates also approved a new constitution. Democratic processes in the USSR in general, and Ukraine in particular, impacted the development of AUUAECB in independent Ukraine. The key feature of this period was that responsibilities for church planting and the edification of believers were handed over to regional associations and the union retained functions of unification and representation on the state and international scene. Religious freedom set the context for equal treatment of religious organisations by the state, for open missionary and social activities by the churches and for more intense ecumenical relations between different Christian denominations.[7] In what follows, I will summarise how ACs are currently represented in organisational

---

5. Pospielovsky, *Pravoslavnaia Tserkov' v Istorii Rusi, Rossii i SSSR*, 360–61; Reshetnikov and Sannikov, *Obzor Istorii*, 219.

6. Franklin, "988–1988: Uses and Abuses of the Millennium."

7. Wanner, *Communities of the Converted*, 131–38; Cherenkov, *FORUM 20*.

structure, associational practices and theological representation. This will set the context for the analysis of semi-structured interviews in chapter 6.

5.2 Organisational Structure

Organisational structures inherited from the Soviet time attracted the justified critique of some Baptist ministers. In the address to the Twenty-Second Congress of AUUCECB, Veniamin Honcharov admitted that reforms of the administrative structure were long overdue.[8] He urged a move towards collegial decisions, the demarcation of responsibilities and authority and clearly approved programmes for departments.[9] Grygorii Komendant, president of AUUCECB (1994–2006), endorsed the transition to collegial decisions,[10] and Serhii Sannikov, first rector of Odesa Theological Seminary (1989–1999), anticipated that reorganisation of the union would make "the spiritual centre in Kyiv truly spiritual and, of course, functional" and unite local churches and associations as one family.[11]

Volodymyr Matviiv, one of the vice-presidents of AUUCECB, who stood against a flat and democratic structure for the union, stated that "among God's people should be theocracy – from top down."[12] Matviiv was concerned for the effectiveness of the union in evangelism and edification. He proposed a ramified structure of the union with an executive board and council of the union.[13] The board consisted of the president, vice-president and executive secretary, who were elected for one term or, as an exception, for two terms. The council was not elected but formed out of the presidents of *oblast* associations, the five heads of the departments (evangelism, publishing, youth, business and international relations) and the members of the board. Matviiv suggested grouping all *oblast* associations into five bigger territorial entities (regional associations) that would comprise several associations. These

---

8. Honcharov, "O Rabote Soiuza EKhB," 2.
9. Honcharov, "O Rabote Soiuza EKhB," 2.
10. "Interv'iu z G.I. Komendantom," 7. In 1998, Oleksandr Nahirniak, the editor-in-chief of the *Slovo very* newspaper, evaluated the collegiality of the executive board positively. See "23-i Z'izd," 24.
11. "Interv'iu z Serhiem Sannikovym," 7.
12. Matviiv, "Menia Bespokoit Sostoianie," 7. This structure resembles that of Timoshenko, discussed in section 3.2.3.
13. Matviiv, "Menia Bespokoit Sostoianie," 7.

could be presided over by senior presbyters of *oblasts* on the basis of annual rotation. Matviiv thought that leaders of these larger units should also be members of the council.[14] He is somewhat inconsistent in this regard. If these leaders are *oblast* senior presbyters and chair the larger units on the basis of rotation, they already belong to the council. If they are heads of these larger units apart from *oblast* associations, then there should be a procedure of elections that imbues them with authority and trust from the churches. If they are appointed by the council or executive board, then this is a return to the infamous AUCECB model.

The proponents of different perspectives were concerned for uniting local churches and associations around the centre in Kyiv and making the union more efficient and helpful for local churches. These concerns marked two decades in independent Ukraine. In general, AUUCECB followed the pattern set by AUCECB: a union comprised of twenty-five *oblast* associations headed by elected regional pastors and pastoral councils. Local churches could join the union only through association. Regional pastors served as a link between the executive board and the regions. The highest organ is the assembly, which meets every four years.[15] The assembly has the right to elect the president and vice presidents (i.e. the executive board), approve members of the council of the union, change the statutes or statement of faith and admit new members to the union. The council of the union consists of all regional pastors, members of the executive board and the heads of the committees. It operates between the assemblies and executes general strategic decisions of the assembly.

On 9–10 October 1996, the Council of the Union decided to implement Matviiv's idea of five larger territorial bodies – regional associations[16] – and

---

14. Matviiv, "Menia Bespokoit Sostoianie," 7.

15. From 2014 on, it met every five years. See "Statut Vseukraïns'koho soiuzu tserkov ievanhel's'kykh khrystyian-baptystiv (2014u)," para. 4.4. For another version of this document, where the word "union" is substituted for "centre," see "Statut Vseukraïns'koho soiuzu tserkov ievanhel's'kykh khrystyian-baptystiv (2014c)." Henceforth referred to interchangeably.

16. These were as follows: Carpathian Regional Association (with 222 churches in the Lviv, Ivano-Frankivs'k, Zakarpat'e and Chernovtsy *oblasts*), Northern Regional Association (with 305 churches in the Kyiv, Zhytomyr, Sumy and Chernihiv *oblasts*), Central Regional Association (with 260 churches in the Poltava, Vinnitsa, Kyrovograd and Cherkasy *oblasts*), Eastern Regional Association (with 249 churches in the Donets'k, Dnipropetrovs'k, Luhans'k and Kharkiv *oblasts*) and Southern Regional Association (with 226 churches in the Odesa, Zaporizhzh'ia, Kherson, Mykolaiv and Crimea *oblasts*). However, these regions did not include

approve the ministers who would be responsible for coordinating the work of local churches in these localities. This move was aimed at the consolidation of churches' work on the grassroots level and to release the Executive Board from an excessive workload by distributing it among vice presidents or regional assistants. However, it is not clear from reports to what extent this scheme was successful.

Transformations of the structure of AUUCECB attracted attention of Ukrainian religious studies scholars. Olena Nazarkina, in her thesis on the Protestant confessions in Ukraine in the 1990s discussed the organisational structure of Baptist and Pentecostal unions. She distinguished two basic types, which she qualified as a "spiritual centre" model and an "association of communities."[17] The "spiritual centre" model represents larger church unions which are characterised by centralised leadership, usually exercised either by an ordained minister or a collegial body. The authority of this leadership encompasses all members of the association and covers both religious and administrative spheres. The "association of communities" is typical for smaller church unions and presupposes leadership only in administrative issues while securing significant independence for local communities in their inner affairs.[18] According to Nazarkina, AUUCECB falls into the first category. She claims that AUUCECB "managed to develop in 1990s the most complex and branched structure," which builds on "the traditions of administration of the church, formed during the Soviet period, and the largest membership."[19] Having analysed the structure of AUUCECB, Nazarkina concludes: "This association became an embodiment of almost total ecclesiasticism [*otsekrovlenie*] of the confession of the Evangelical Christians-Baptists, its breaking away from sectarian forms of organisation."[20]

---

the Khmelnits'kyi, Ternopil', Volyn and Rivne *oblasts*. See "Regionalnye Ob'edineniia," 4. In 2002 and 2006, Komendant reports six regional assistants. See Komendant, "Za Poslednie Chetyre Goda," 16; "Otchet Predsedatelia VSO EKhB," 7, 10. Perhaps, by 2010, regional associations were discontinued since they are not mentioned in the report. See Nesteruk, "Zvitnia Dopovid."

17. Nazarkina, "Protestants'ki Konfesii Ukrainy," 65–73. Later she focuses on the institutionalisation of ECB. See Panych, "Instytutsializatsiia Evangel's'koho Protestantyzmu."

18. Nazarkina, "Protestants'ki Konfesii Ukrainy," 65. She places the union of autonomous churches into this category. See Nazarkina, "Protestants'ki Konfesii Ukrainy," 73–77.

19. Nazarkina, "Protestants'ki Konfesii Ukrainy," 65.

20. Nazarkina, "Protestants'ki Konfesii Ukrainy," 72. For similar conclusions about earlier periods, see Sitarchuk, "Diial'nist' Protestants'kykh Konfesii," 8–9; Goloshchapova,

This analysis is correct in that AUUCECB inherited traditions of administration, a developed organisational structure and a strong role for the executive committee and council of the union. However, Nazarkina's differentiation between "spiritual centre" and "association of churches" is somewhat strained. It is hard to contrast the two, especially with regard to AUUCECB. It is a union of associations of churches, and this union operates through structures that could be called a "spiritual centre."

Ukrainian Pentecostal historian and religious studies scholar Mykhailo Mokienko provided another analysis of ACs in his article on the transformation of the "religious centre" of AUUCECB.[21] By "religious centre," Mokienko understands "central executive-administrative church organ which represents religious association."[22] He places discussion of this transformation in the context of Baptist ecclesiology where the local church is balancing between autonomy and the necessity of being in fellowship with other churches.[23] Reflecting on the recent history of AUUCECB, he argues for a drift from centralisation towards a democratisation of structures and back. Mokienko claims that in the 1990s, AUUCECB slowly moved away from the inherited centralised structure to a more democratic one. The signs of these transformations were the approval of the new statutes, the strengthening of the role of local churches[24] and the election of a new leadership team.[25] Associations received wider autonomy and freedom because of their direct access to local churches and ability to coordinate more effectively their ministry in the regions. However, new cases of separatism and clashes over doctrinal and liturgical issues again raised the question of the necessity of strengthening the religious centre of the union.[26]

"Organisatsiina Budova Baptysts'kykh Hromad," 320. For a perspective on early English Baptists, see Fiddes, "Church and Sect."

21. Mokienko, "Vseukrains'kyi Soiuz Ob'ednan," 633–40.
22. Mokienko, "Vseukrains'kyi Soiuz Ob'ednan," 633.
23. Cf. Reshetnikov, "Ob'edinitel'naia Tendentsiia," 50–60.
24. See Nesteruk, "Zvitnia Dopovid," 9.
25. Mokienko, "Vseukrains'kyi Soiuz Ob'ednan," 637–38.
26. Mokienko, 640. A significant clash around the desire of some churches to leave the Donetsk *oblast* association occurred in the late 1990s and early 2000s. They were dissatisfied with the head of the Donetsk *oblast* association, Stepan Karpenko. Negotiations resulted in a compromise: churches remained in the AUUCECB without being members of the association. Others left and formed Assotsiatsiia Bratskikh Tservei EKhB (Association of Fraternal Churches of ECB) in 2005. See "Edinstvo Dukha," 22.

Mokienko's insight into the fluidity of AUUCECB, as it moved from centralisation to democratisation and back, can be substantiated by an analysis of the statutes of 2002[27] and 2014.[28] Originally, the statutes of 1990 defined Baptist union as the "voluntary association of churches of Evangelical Christians-Baptists and other traditions."[29] However, the statutes of 2002 omitted this and introduced a novel element into the definition. The section "General Provisions" defined AUUCECB as the *"spiritual centre*, which on the voluntary basis unites religious communities (local churches and other religious organisations) of ECB through regional (*oblast*) and local associations, including Autonomous Republic of Crimea, for fraternal fellowship and joint ministry."[30] The section "Union's Structure and Administrative Organs" depicted AUUCECB as a group of churches united through regional associations.[31] The same word, "union," stands for two distinct realities: the national union of churches and the administrative centre or central office of the union.[32] The statutes of 2014 went even further, substituting "union" for "centre" throughout the document:

> *Religious organisation All-Ukrainian Union of Churches of Evangelical Christians-Baptists* (henceforth "Centre") unites on the voluntary basis religious communities and other religious organisations of Evangelical Christians-Baptists through *oblast* and regional associations for the purpose of satisfaction of religious needs in confessing and spreading Christian faith, and acts according to its canonical and institutional structure.[33]

---

27. "Statut Vseukraïns'koho Soiuzu Ob'iednan' Tserkov Evanhel's'kykh Khrystyian-Baptystiv (2002)."

28. "Statut Vseukraïns'koho Soiuzu Tserkov Evanhel's'kykh Khrystyian-Baptystiv (2014c)."

29. "Statut pro Upravlinnia Soiuzom Evanhel's'kykh Khrystyian-Baptystiv Ukraïny (1990)," para. 1.1.

30. "Statut Vseukraïns'koho Soiuzu Ob'iednan' Tserkov Evanhel's'kykh Khrystyian-Baptystiv (2002)," para. 1.1. Emphasis added.

31. "Statut Vseukraïns'koho Soiuzu Ob'iednan' Tserkov Evanhel's'kykh Khrystyian-Baptystiv (2002)," para. 3.1–12.

32. The same confusion was detected in interviews of the leadership of AUUCECB. See section 6.3.1.

33. "Statut Vseukraïns'koho Soiuzu Tserkov Evanhel's'kykh Khrystyian-Baptystiv (2014c)," para. 1.1. Emphasis original.

Equating "union" with the "centre," the document introduced the confusing idea that religious communities could be affiliated with the "centre" not with the "union."[34] Here the "centre" appears to be operating on its own, apart from churches and associations that actually form it and entrust it with authority. Another strange notion is found in the phrase "canonical and institutional structure."[35] Neither the statutes nor any other document define what this means. In fact, this concept is alien for Baptist or Evangelical Christian thinking. Perhaps this phrase was borrowed from the existing statutes of one of the Orthodox churches.[36] Another version of these statutes avoided using "centre" and consistently referred to "union" instead, but still kept the phrase "canonical and institutional structure."[37]

There is an obvious problem with calling AUUCECB the "centre": insufficient distinction between such categories as "national union of churches" and "administrative centre" leads to confusion. In some cases, the "centre" stands for the council, executive board and other officers as an aggregate concept. For instance, Grygorii Komendant, in his report in 1998, referred to the vice presidents and regional assistants as the "spiritual centre of the brotherhood."[38] Such usage could be appropriate when it is made clear that "spiritual centre" and "union of churches" do not coincide. Perhaps calling the union of churches the "spiritual centre" could be justified from the point of view of state officials and legal documents, but it is very confusing from an ecclesiological perspective.

The organisational structure of AUUCECB currently remains within the parameters set earlier. It did pass through democratisation and lost its rigid way of interacting with local churches. Some associational practices served to ensure a supportive and non-imposing role of structures.

---

34. "Statut Vseukraïns'koho Soiuzu Tserkov Evanhel's'kykh Khrystyian-Baptystiv (2014c)," para. 4.1.

35. "Statut Vseukraïns'koho Soiuzu Tserkov Evanhel's'kykh Khrystyian-Baptystiv (2014c)," para. 1.1.

36. See Hovorun, *Scaffolds of the Church*, 73–87. In a personal conversation, Igor Bandura shared that this phrase was imposed by government structures during the presidency of Victor Ianukovich. This encouraged the leadership of the AUUCECB to delay official approval of the statutes for as long as possible to make it inoperative.

37. "Statut Vseukraïns'koho Soiuzu Tserkov Evanhel's'kykh Khrystyian-Baptystiv (2014u)," para. 1.1.

38. Komendant, "Holova VSO EKhB Zvitue," 18–19.

5.3 Associational Practices

AUUCECB uses the system of senior or regional presbyters and holds edifying congresses, conferences of ministers and local church celebrations. These associational practices follow the well-established patterns that proved their effectiveness earlier.

Senior presbyters still operate within the limits set by the congress of AUCECB in 1989: regional councils of ministers assist them in setting agendas, communicating with local churches and resolving sensitive issues. However, some consistent critics such as Sergei Savinskii, a Russian Baptist historian, call to discontinue the system. He admits that originally this system was aimed at the revival of the spiritual life of Baptist churches and their reorganisation in the post-war period. This aim was reached, but revival evoked active resistance from the governmental apparat in the 1960s.[39] Savinskii criticises Levindanto for the legitimisation of an "episcopal system" and the elevation of the status of senior presbyters by calling them "men ruling among the brothers" and "representatives in place of God."[40] Savinskii correctly points out that after 1945 the union of churches was replaced by a council of ministers. However, his views reflect the situation as it was before the 1980s when the processes moved to democratisation.

Representatives of AUUCECB usually participate in the regional congresses, especially when elections of senior presbyters take place. They also work with nomination committees. At the same time, representatives of regional associations usually preside over elections and participate in the ordination of pastors in local churches. This, basically, is a matter of good practice and common sense. There are no documents or publications that evaluate this practice from a theological perspective.

Two other common practices reflect the interconnectedness of local churches. These are the mutual visitations of churches and the practice of greeting guests from other churches during church services. Mutual visitations of churches by groups of ministers or even by whole congregations on special occasions is a typical way to share fellowship and express brotherhood.[41]

---

39. Savinskii, "O Sisteme Starshykh Presviterov," 19.

40. Savinskii, 19; cf. Levindanto, "O Sluzhenii Starshikh Presviterov."

41. See, for example, a report on the visitation of a group of ministers to Mariupol and the churches in the war zone in "Chernivetski Sluzhyteli Vidvidaly Tserkvy." For a report of Vinnitsia Baptist Church's centenary celebration at its mother church in Kyiv, see "Vinnyts'ka Tserkva."

Perhaps the only innovation of AUUCECB's practices was a programme of visitations, the so-called "Union's week in the region."[42] This programme allowed top leadership of the union and well-known and respected ministers to visit local, mostly rural, churches in a given region.[43] Again, reports on visitations never explain what motivates such practices or how they could be interpreted from a theological perspective.

The practice of receiving and sending greetings at the end of Sunday worship is very common among Baptist churches in Ukraine. At the end of the worship service, before the prayer of dismissal, the minister asks if guests from other churches are present and want to greet the church. The guests usually stand up and say, "The church such-and-such is greeting you." When the round of greetings is over, the minister pronounces a formula: "For the greetings we are . . ." and the congregation responds ". . . cordially grateful." Then the minister says, "Bring greetings from our church," and the congregation approves, "Please, do." Then he finishes with the prayer and dismisses the congregation with the phrase "Greet each other." This practice is rooted in the Pauline habit of greeting addressees in the last section of his letters (e.g. Rom 16:3–16; Phil 4:21–22; 2 Tim 4:19–21).[44] Other New Testament letters also contain similar sections (Heb 13:23–24; 1 Pet 5:13–14; 3 John 15). Paul sometimes connects that with the admonition to greet each other with a "holy kiss," which was a typical practice in the early church.[45] The practice of greeting was an expression of the underlining unity that existed among different churches. Philip Hughes sees it as

> part of a still greater unity – unity in Christ of God's people everywhere. Hence Paul conveys to them from Macedonia where he is writing the greetings of *all* the saints, that is, all their fellow-Christians. Even though the majority of the Corinthian and Macedonian Christians have never met and are personally

---

42. On the origin of the programme, see section 6.3.4.

43. For description of a typical visit, see "Tyzhden Soiuzu."

44. For a formal analysis of greetings, see Weima, *Neglected Endings*; Murphy-O'Connor, *Paul*, 102–7; Aune, *Westminster Dictionary*, 269–70. For greetings as expression of personal friendships, see Dunn, *Epistles*, 274–75. Weima points out functions of expressing friendly relations and winning trust in *Neglected Endings*, 114–17.

45. For the practice among Baptists, see Jones, "Kiss of Peace"; Songulashvili, *Evangelical Christian Baptists*, 65–69.

unknown to each other, yet they are united *in Christ*, which is the supreme and transcendental unity of redemption; they are members together in the one body under direction of the one Head; and they *will* meet, together with all the saints of every age and clime, when the unity of Christ and His people has its consummation in everlasting glory hereafter (Rev 7:9ff).[46]

This practice is slowly fading out among new churches.

5.4 Understandings of the Nature of Associations of Churches

Understandings of ACs remain within the framework set by previous generations of Baptist ministers. Reference to the Bible images or theological arguments in favour of ACs are occasional. Pragmatic thinking about ACs dominates confessional publications. This section summarises the use of the major motifs.

5.4.1 Images of the Union

One of the most frequently recurring motifs is the body of Christ. Iakov Dukhonchenko in his summary report to the Twenty-First Congress of AUUCECB (1990) makes a very important statement, stressing the necessity of unity among local churches:

> The Holy Spirit builds the Church as the body of Christ on earth. As members in the body connected not only with the head but also with each other, so believers have fellowship with God and each other. The mark of the true Christian is that he seeks for communion with other believers constituting Christ's Church. The Holy Spirit unites him with the body of Christ. All true believers have this sense of communion for they are born from God's word and the Holy Spirit.[47]

For Dukhonchenko, building the church is the result of the direct work of the Holy Spirit. Even the fact of constituting a church by the believers is the

---

46. Hughes, *Paul's Second Epistle*, 488. Emphasis original.
47. Dukhonchenko, "Zvitnia Dopovid," 2.

consequence of this work. Desire to join other Christians marks true faith, fostered by the Spirit and the word.

In 1994, the twenty-second congress of AUUCECB occurred in Kyiv. Grygorii Komendant, commenting on the presence of many guests from other former Soviet republics, said: "Our brotherhood always valued relations between the unions. That is why we invited representatives from neighbouring and farther countries."[48] During this meeting, the guests referred to the image of the body. Thus, Peter Konoval'chik, the president of the Russian Union of Evangelical Christian-Baptist (1993–2002), expressed hope that cooperation between Baptist unions of Russia and Ukraine would continue because "the Church is one in her essence."[49] Alexander Firisiuk, the president of the Baptist Union of Belarus, explained that Baptists retain the organisational structures they had in the USSR because

> we are not an organisation, we are organism, Church, body of Christ. And an organism does not want to split for it will be invalid then. Therefore, in spite of the external circumstances, the Church of Christ has the feeling of one body, one family. We also need each other for keeping faithfulness to the Gospel.[50]

Four years later, in 1998, Grygorii Komendant, reporting on the life of the union, commented:

> Observing the life of the Brotherhood, I want you to understand that our Brotherhood is not an organisation, it is a living organism – Body of Jesus Christ that consists of many many member-churches. These members are connected in order to function as a unified whole (Eph 4:16). And, in fact, all activities of the centre were directed in order to strengthen these ties. Therefore, we may state that in general [the] Evangelical-Baptist Brotherhood in Ukraine grows in unity of the Spirit and bond of peace.[51]

Komendant thinks of the union and its officers in terms of God's wider picture for the church found in the Epistle to the Ephesians. In his speech at the

---

48. Dolmatova-Agafonova, "25-i S'ezd," 4.
49. "Slovo Hostiam Z'izdu," 7.
50. "Slovo Hostiam Z'izdu," 7; cf. Karev, "Dokald na Rasshirennom Soveshchanii," 37.
51. Komendant, "Holova VSO EKhB Zvitue," 17.

Second Ukrainian Baptist Congress (Kyiv, 6–9 September 2000), Komendant set goals,[52] enumerated the union's key priorities[53] and commented on the divisions among Baptists,[54] but surprisingly omitted the issue of unity among the chief priorities.

Another significant thought, related to the image of the body, is the assertion that common witness presupposes unity of the body of Christ. Iakov Dukhonchenko pointed out: "Witness for Christ is not a privilege of special people but the deed of all Church."[55] Therefore, unity is the warranty of successful witness for Christ.[56] Since witness is the task entrusted to the whole people of God, they all should be one. The gospel calls people from different nations and tribes to join Jesus and form his church. Dukhonchenko hinted that witness is not only a verbal activity but relational, which presupposes life in the body of Christ. Therefore, divisions are a disservice to the gospel and the task of witness. Similarly, Veniamin Honcharov, discussing new opportunities for evangelisation, pointed to the significance of unity for reliable witness:

> Today we should especially think of the meaning of unity of God's people for successful witness to the people of Ukraine and may God help us 'to live in harmony with one another, in accordance with Christ Jesus, so that together you may with one voice glorify the God and Father of our Lord Jesus Christ' (Rom 15:5–6).[57]

5.4.2 Local Church and Union

Local church autonomy remains one of the key ecclesiological categories among Ukrainian Baptists. Thus, Grygorii Komendant, reporting to the delegates, stated:

> To improve the ministry of the Brotherhood today we should think of strengthening the role of local church. Only when local

---

52. Komendant, "V Edinstve Dukha," 5.
53. Komendant, "V Edinstve Dukha," 6.
54. Komendant, "V Edinstve Dukha," 6.
55. Dukhonchenko, "Zvitnia Dopovid," 2.
56. Dukhonchenko, "Zvitnia Dopovid," 2.
57. Honcharov, "O Rabote Soiuza EKhB," 2.

churches will be strong and correctly instructed in the gospel principles, then bigger churches will be helping smaller and the stronger ones – weaker, then every church member will have personal responsibility and specific status in the body of Christ. "For just as the body is one and has many members, and all the members of the body, though many, are one body, so it is with Christ" (1 Cor 12:12). [The] church of Christ is called to continue Jesus's work on earth. It cares for spiritual life through preaching the gospel. As a living organism it also needs constant spiritual renewal, sanctification, spiritual growth and unity in Jesus Christ.[58]

Viacheslav Nesteruk, the next president of the union (2006–2014), picked up this idea and even elevated local church as the highest value:

"Strong [local] church – strong Brotherhood" was said at the last congress. We admit this and approve once again that this is so. All our activity, all our success is concentrated in our churches. All other structures exist only to help [the] church. If they do not help [the] church, they do not accomplish their mission.[59]

The most significant event that stirred intensive discussions on ACs was the symposium "Local Church Autonomy: Relations of the Local Church

---

58. Komendant, "Silnaia Pomestnaia Tserkov," 25. In the neighbouring Russia, Pavel Kirillovykh, deacon of St. Petersburg Baptist Church "Logos," bemoans the rejection of basic elements of Baptist identity and the drift towards an episcopal system (Kirillovykh, "Krizis Identichnosti," 45–49). Kirillovykh points to the following elements: (1) the institution of senior presbyters and their function of overseeing (Kirillovykh, "Krizis Identichnosti," 47–48); (2) the participation of higher rank ministers in ordination (Kirillovykh, "Krizis Identichnosti," 48); (3) senior presbyters are called "bishops" and regional associations are called "local churches" (Kirillovykh, "Krizis Identichnosti," 48); and (4) pastors of local churches are financially dependant on senior presbyters (Kirillovykh, "Krizis Identichnosti," 49). Kirillovykh argues for the principle of local church autonomy as the instrument for restoring Baptist identity in Russia. His critique is a justified reaction to the processes in the Baptist Union. However, he misses a significant part of Baptist traditional practices, especially those related to ordination and the installation of new ministers. Though it is not necessary to have a minister of higher rank, senior presbyters usually represent regional associations or the union. Thus, whether the senior presbyter is "superior" or not could be a matter of perception (or even misinterpretation), unless it is formulated in the statutes or other regulative documents, though actual practices may differ (see Covington, "Investigation," 165.).

59. Nesteruk, "Zvitnia Dopovid," 9. Igor Bandura made a critical remark regarding insufficient efforts in implementing the principle of "strong local church – strong union" (Bandura, "Novye Formy Tserkovnogo Sotrudnichestva," 370).

and the Union" (6–7 December 2007, Kyiv). The symposium was allegedly convened in response to some tensions that occurred during discussions on new structures of the union in AUUCECB.[60] Konstantin Honcharov, pastor of the Irpin' Bible Church, remarked that the symposium was timely for it addressed some tendencies of institutionalisation exemplified in the stereotyped statute of local church, produced and proposed by the working group of AUUCECB.[61] The event gathered scholars and practitioners from the Baptist unions of Ukraine, Russia and Germany. The participants discussed relations between local church and union.

The conference volume arranges presentations into four parts: biblical-theological foundations, historical experience, practical aspects and appendices.[62] This is by far the most comprehensive treatment on the subject available for Ukrainian and Russian readership. It includes thirteen papers by Ukrainian and Russian theologians and Russian and English versions of papers by Uwe Swarat, Christoph Stenschke, Neville Callam, Nigel Wright and William H. Brackney, which they presented at the BWA symposium "Are Baptist Churches Autonomous?" (21–24 March 2007, Elstal, Germany).[63] The appendix contains the BWA Statement on Baptist Identity and Ecclesiology, summary of discussions in small groups and a list of questions for the next symposium.[64] BWA papers and statement place discussions in the wider context of contemporary Baptist ecclesiological conversations. Several presentations during the symposium interacted with BWA papers.[65] Thus, this volume is important because it represents not only local perspectives on the subject of the symposium but also enters into dialogue with the papers presented earlier during the BWA symposium. In what follows I will concentrate on Ukrainian and Russian contributions to the volume.

---

60. Sergei Sannikov in a private e-mail received on 7.03.2017.
61. Honcharov, "Bibleiskoe Obosnovanie Avtonomii," 68.
62. *Avtonomiia Pomestnoi Tserkvi.*
63. Swarat, "Local Churches"; Stenschke, "Issues of Power"; Callam, "Models"; Wright, "Are Baptist Churches Autonomous?"; Brackney, "Historical Theologian."
64. Baptist World Alliance, "Are Baptist Churches Autonomous?"; "Obobshchenie Obsuzhdenii."
65. Nazarkevich, "Poniiattia 'Avtonomnosti' v Istorychnii Perspektyvi." Another paper presented by Sergei Rybikov, at the moment rector of Donetsk Christian University, was not published.

Mikhail Ivanov[66] and Konstantin Honcharov[67] argued for local church autonomy. Both admit that their papers react to restrictions and attacks on this cherished concept.[68] Ivanov represented reaction to the processes among Russian Baptists, while Honcharov reacted to the Ukrainian drift towards centralisation described by Mokienko. Both admit the necessity of ACs but view them as auxiliary bodies that serve local churches.[69]

Mikhail Ivanov, the chair of the Department of Doctrine and Catechisation in the Russian Union of Evangelical Christian-Baptists, discussed local church autonomy against Baptist principles. It is "inner self-government with awareness of inter-church fellowship and cooperation (Rom 16:16). . . . Genuine autonomy presupposes . . . churches with responsible members and ministers who are under the Lordship of Christ."[70] Ivanov thinks that since Baptists are a people of the Bible, "it is hard to imagine that Baptists for centuries would defend as one of the basic teachings that which does not have clear foundation in the Holy Scriptures."[71] The historical experience of Baptists, who placed local church at the centre of their ecclesiology,[72] approves the principle. Autonomy is related to other Baptist principles that reflect the life and polity of local community per se.[73] For Ivanov, local church autonomy is what makes Baptists distinct[74] and "serves as the most crucial factor restraining unhealthy ambitions."[75] However, he agrees that the contemporary situation requires further development of Baptist ecclesiology, especially with regard to the universal church and its nature, and theological rethinking of regional associations and national Baptist unions. Such rethinking, claims Ivanov, "is all the more necessary because Baptists, for the most part, have recognised

---

66. Ivanov, "Avtonomia Tserkvi," 19–25.

67. Honcharov, "Bibleiskoe Obosnovanie Avtonomii," 68–81.

68. Ivanov, "Avtonomia Tserkvi," 19, 24; Honcharov, "Bibleiskoe Obosnovanie Avtonomii," 69.

69. Ivanov, "Avtonomia Tserkvi," 24; Honcharov, "Bibleiskoe Obosnovanie Avtonomii," 79–81.

70. Ivanov, "Avtonomia Tserkvi," 25. He thinks the term "independence" is unsuccessful. This agrees with Paul Fiddes's remark that early Baptists thought of the freedom of the local church as being under the rule of Christ Fiddes, "Christian Doctrine," 209–10.

71. Ivanov, "Avtonomia Tserkvi," 19–20.

72. Ivanov, "Avtonomia Tserkvi," 20.

73. Ivanov, "Avtonomia Tserkvi," 20.

74. Ivanov, "Avtonomia Tserkvi," 25.

75. Ivanov, "Avtonomia Tserkvi," 25.

the need for such structures to function."⁷⁶ Thus, Mikhail Ivanov remains within the trajectory that elevates local church and views ACs functionally. However, his views are open towards transformation evident in a desire to develop understanding of the universal church and reconsider ACs.

Konstantin Honcharov defended local church autonomy on the basis of Scripture. He refers to the Baptist idea of church "gathered by God for mutual life and ministry under the lordship of Christ."⁷⁷ From this he deduces the authority of local ministers to lead the church without external interference. He views the trans-local ministry of Timothy and Titus as helping churches in ordaining ministers to make them "complete."⁷⁸ However, he does not admit that these churches needed external help in this process. He also thinks that the Jerusalem Council (Acts 15) was a council of one church.⁷⁹ He dismisses any attempt to draw a parallel between Acts 15 and other church councils because it was a period of formation of the NT and the apostles were still alive and could announce God's will directly.⁸⁰ However, he misses the fact that both Luke's narrative and the final resolution announced by Peter pointed to the Holy Spirit who acted through those gathered to address the issue the church had encountered. It is also unclear why a decision of one local church should be accepted by another church? Honcharov is correct in supposing that "genuine brotherhood and love are possible only there, where is Christ's freedom and mutual submission to the Bible and its principles."⁸¹

On another pole of discussion were papers by Valerii Antoniuk,⁸² then the executive secretary of AUUCECB, and Taras Dyatlik, academic dean of Donetsk Christian University.⁸³ Antoniuk examined biblical principles for relations among churches. Considering the relations between churches in the apostolic period, he admitted that they were uneasy but always characterised by "understanding of necessity to be together and cooperate for the spread

---

76. Ivanov, "Avtonomia Tserkvi," 25.
77. Honcharov, "Bibleiskoe Obosnovanie Avtonomii," 74. Quotes Kevan, "Baptist Tradition," 123.
78. Honcharov, "Bibleiskoe Obosnovanie Avtonomii," 77.
79. Honcharov, 77. For an alternative, see Fowler, "Churches and the Church," 41–42.
80. Honcharov, "Bibleiskoe Obosnovanie Avtonomii," 77.
81. Honcharov, "Bibleiskoe Obosnovanie Avtonomii," 80.
82. Antoniuk, "Bibliini Pryntsypy Vzaemovidnosyn," 8–18.
83. Dyatlik, "Stremlenie k Avtonomii," 302–16.

of the gospel."[84] This sounds like a pragmatic foundation for cooperation. Turning to the Ukrainian situation, he pointed out that both present context and previous negative experience shaped relations among the churches.[85] For Valerii Antoniuk, the Ukrainian context was shaped by the emergence of a new generation of ministers with alternative views on ACs,[86] the democratisation of Ukrainian society[87] and past experiences of authoritarianism.[88] Though admitting the democratisation of Ukrainian society, he warned against democracy in the church for "it leads to degradation of the Church not to its development"[89] and affirmed "theocratic principle of governance."[90] He concluded: "In the twenty-first century, Christians are called to stay in the context of communal [*sobornyi*] thinking even if they live in the democratic society."[91] His basic thesis reads: "*It is important to emphasise replication of biblical practice of relations among the churches. The Word of God is the foundation for any practice. That is why it is important to return to the roots. Life of Apostolic Church in an example of such practice.*"[92]

He builds this thesis around five principles on which apostolic churches based cooperation: (1) church as the body of Christ; (2) defence of the gospel; (3) missions; (4) social work; and (5) prayer for ministers.[93] His analysis is a mix of theological insights and pragmatic reasoning.[94] I shall highlight the first two and the last of these principles. First, in spite of cultural differences, the apostles understood that churches are the body of Christ and God's instruments in the world. Second, reflecting on the Jerusalem Council, Antoniuk pointed out: "Biblical understanding of the truth is not an individual business

---

84. Antoniuk, "Bibliini Pryntsypy Vzaemovidnosyn," 10.
85. Antoniuk, "Bibliini Pryntsypy Vzaemovidnosyn," 10–12.
86. Antoniuk, "Bibliini Pryntsypy Vzaemovidnosyn," 10.
87. Antoniuk, "Bibliini Pryntsypy Vzaemovidnosyn," 11.
88. Antoniuk, "Bibliini Pryntsypy Vzaemovidnosyn," 11.
89. Antoniuk, "Bibliini Pryntsypy Vzaemovidnosyn," 11.
90. Antoniuk, "Bibliini Pryntsypy Vzaemovidnosyn," 11.
91. Antoniuk, "Bibliini Pryntsypy Vzaemovidnosyn," 11, 17. The term *sobornost'* or *sobornicity* was popularized by Russian Orthodox theologian Aleksei Khomiakov in his influential work *The Church Is One*. See Khomiakov and Zernov, *Church Is One*.
92. Antoniuk, "Bibliini Pryntsypy Vzaemovidnosyn," 9. Emphasis original.
93. Antoniuk, "Bibliini Pryntsypy Vzaemovidnosyn," 12–17.
94. For example, see his appeals to the body of Christ and reflections on helping those weaker, mission as divine call and the accumulation of resources (Antoniuk, "Bibliini Pryntsypy Vzaemovidnosyn," 13, 14).

but a mutual responsibility."[95] This indicates that the gospel and Christian teaching are entrusted to the church as a whole and the local church cannot claim a monopoly on holding the whole understanding of the truth. Finally, prayerful support of each other is a practical expression of the notion of unity based on dependence on Christ.[96] He concludes:

> God's workers are united not so much by one church, one purpose or parachurch structures as by oneness based on real dependency on Jesus Christ (2 Cor 5:14). This is what gives us desire to be co-workers. There are no independent members in the Body of the Church. Thus, ministers of Jesus Christ understand this important connection. Roles and functions are different, but everything is interconnected. The nature of the Church itself does not give us chance to think otherwise. And if the universal Church manifests itself through local church, then our calling is to stand above mercantile interests.[97]

Taras Dyatlik analysed the spiritual, doctrinal, liturgical and administrative aspects of autonomy in the relations of local churches and theological institutions.[98] He used the image of the body of Christ as a hermeneutical key, thinking of relations between local churches, and churches and theological institutions "in terms of relations of members of a human body."[99] For Dyatlik, spiritual autonomy is impossible since all local churches are connected by the Holy Spirit while there is a level of freedom in doctrinal and liturgical issues.[100] Even the administrative autonomy of local churches is limited in such issues as the election and ordination of ministers and the resolution of problems between presbyter and community, between two local churches or in case of heresy.[101] Thus, "the main question is not so much in 'administrative' autonomy as in which form of administration should be used for organizing interaction, mutual coordination, accountability and

---

95. Antoniuk, "Bibliini Pryntsypy Vzaemovidnosyn," 13.
96. Antoniuk, "Bibliini Pryntsypy Vzaemovidnosyn," 17.
97. Antoniuk, "Bibliini Pryntsypy Vzaemovidnosyn," 17.
98. Dyatlik, "Stremlenie k Avtonomii," 304–10.
99. Dyatlik, "Stremlenie k Avtonomii," 303.
100. Dyatlik, "Stremlenie k Avtonomii," 304–5.
101. Dyatlik, "Stremlenie k Avtonomii," 306.

relations between local churches (union, association, alliance etc.)."[102] Taras Dyatlik opines that injudicious or ill-interpreted autonomy puts churches and theological institutions into the state of agony which, in its original meaning, is "struggle, contest, competition."[103] He concludes:

> If local churches exist by themselves, without organic unity with other local churches (groups, associations, unions of churches), not thinking of themselves and others as organic parts of one Church, the body of Christ, they are doomed for agony in the worse sense of the word (the last stage of dying), since deficit of organic unity is compensated by struggle for survival, rivalry for power and influence and other unhealthy phenomena.[104]

For Dyatlik, autonomy contradicts relations in the Trinity where divine persons are unique but still in "organic unity of their divine essence" and their "'freedom' is directed towards being one in each other."[105] Thus, the criterion of unity for the church becomes the touchstone and if striving towards autonomy undermines it then local church goes to agony.

Iurii Reshetnikov, a member of the board of directors of the Ukrainian Association of Religious Freedom, analysed tension between the notions of the unity of the church and the independence of the local church.[106] He asserted that Baptists "maintain a reasonable harmony between independence and the necessity for fellowship and ministry"[107] which results practically in the formation of associations and unions of churches. However, for Reshetnikov, "the idea of independence of a local community enters into a theological contradiction with the notion of unity of the Church as the body of Christ."[108] The independence of the local church leads to the weak social

---

102. Dyatlik, "Stremlenie k Avtonomii," 307.
103. Dyatlik, "Stremlenie k Avtonomii," 310–11.
104. Dyatlik, "Stremlenie k Avtonomii," 313.
105. Dyatlik, "Stremlenie k Avtonomii," 314.
106. Reshetnikov, "Zahal'ni Problemni Pytannia." He uses "independency" and "autonomy" interchangeably. The paper is better argued than his earlier "Ob'edinitel'naia Tendentsiia."
107. Reshetnikov, "Zahal'ni Problemni Pytannia," 318.
108. Reshetnikov, 318. See a similar appraisal in Vandervelde, "Believers Church Ecclesiology," 213–16.

impact of Baptist churches[109] and the lack of a consolidated theological position[110] or even a church calendar.[111]

Traditionally, local church autonomy is rooted in the lordship of Christ over a local community: "Local churches do not recognise authority that could rule or lord over them save Christ, the Head of the Church. Therefore, none of the decisions of the local church could be revised or annulled by any other church organization."[112] However, in practice, decisions depend on a local church minister or a group of influence in the community. For Reshetnikov, unity presupposes the sharing or waiving of some of the authority in favour of the wider church, while some of the ministers want to avoid this and, therefore, argue for independence.[113] However, available resources in Russian do not specify how the independence of the local church and its responsibilities to the union relate to each other.[114]

Reshetnikov delineates the development of the ecclesial structures in the NT and applies these dynamics to the Baptist movement. He agrees with the idea "that new religious movements develop in stages and in their development repeat the same stages as the 'established' religions."[115] NT churches were mostly autonomous, but by the second century they gravitated towards centralisation, simultaneously losing some of their autonomy.[116] Reshetnikov concludes: "there are reasons to state that independence of the communities is typical to the initial stages of a religious movement, and with development of the movement independence is replaced by the idea of unity and consolidation that is manifested in formation of unions with a level of centralisation."[117] The Ukrainian Baptist movement evidences stages of institutionalisation as

---

109. Reshetnikov, "Zahal'ni Problemni Pytannia," 319–20.
110. Reshetnikov, "Zahal'ni Problemni Pytannia," 320–21.
111. Reshetnikov, "Zahal'ni Problemni Pytannia," 321.
112. Reshetnikov, "Zahal'ni Problemni Pytannia," 319. Quotes Vins, *Nashi Baptistskie Printsipy*, 36.
113. Reshetnikov, "Zahal'ni Problemni Pytannia," 319.
114. Reshetnikov, "Zahal'ni Problemni Pytannia," 321–23.
115. Reshetnikov, "Zahal'ni Problemni Pytannia," 324.
116. See Hovorun, *Scaffolds of the Church*, 50–72; Schillebeeckx and Bowden, *Church*, 40–73. See also Fiddes arguing that Baptists do not fit Weber's differentiation of "church" and "sect," turning rather to Troeltsch's concept of "Free Church" (Fiddes, "Church and Sect").
117. Reshetnikov, "Zahal'ni Problemni Pytannia," 324, 334.

seen in the ordination of local presbyters, which is a form of structure, and the formation of Bratstvo and then the union.[118]

On the practical side, Reshetinikov turns to Wieler's three levels of decisions: required, desirable and at the discretion of local churches. He proposes to retain some freedom for the local churches to disagree with the decisions of the general assembly.[119] Sergei Debelinskii shares a similar trajectory when attempting to hold on to the principles of local church autonomy and the interdependence of churches.[120] In particular, he proposes a form of inter-church covenant based on shared beliefs, aimed at mutual spiritual assistance and the spread of the gospel. Such a union is functional and only serves to connect churches. The leadership should be collegial. A local church minister is connected by the pledge with a church and those who ordain him.[121] Though Reshetnikov's suggestion acknowledges the tension between independence and unity, it does not propose a theological solution. He retains local church autonomy and admits the functionality of ACs.

5.4.3 The Ecclesiological Nature of Associations of Churches

The summary of small group discussions in the appendices of the conference volume from the symposium on local church autonomy contains a paragraph on the ecclesiological nature of ACs.[122] This summary does not represent agreed opinion,[123] therefore, it should be treated as tentative. The paragraph answers the question "What is the ecclesiological nature of association or union of churches? Does union or association have an ecclesiological essence?" It only says that "forms of association (interchurch fellowship) have *certain* ecclesiological nature (which should be defined more clearly)."[124] As to the grounds of such fellowships, the paragraph points out that "it is logical that separate churches unite in different forms of interchurch fellowship." It remains within the pragmatic trajectory of understanding of ACs, clarifying that there is need for "transmission of the experience of some local churches

---

118. Reshetnikov, "Zahal'ni Problemni Pytannia," 326–33.
119. Reshetnikov, "Zahal'ni Problemni Pytannia," 334, 335.
120. Debelinskii, "Praktika Avtonomii."
121. Debelinskii, "Praktika Avtonomii," 340–41.
122. "Obobshchenie Obsuzhdenii," 381.
123. "Obobshchenie Obsuzhdenii," 379.
124. "Obobshchenie Obsuzhdenii," 381. Emphasis original.

to others."[125] The text also admits that unions or associations of local churches are necessary, and it points out that the most crucial issue is the nature, form and limits of authority of such structures towards the local church.[126] Perhaps the participants of the discussion groups were not ready to define what that "*certain* ecclesiological nature" is.

5.5 Summary

This chapter demonstrates that AUUCECB inherited structures, practices and unresolved theological issues related to ACs. Initial democratisation of administrative structures somewhat reversed due to clashes between churches and senior presbyters in some regions. This drift hints that circumstances have stronger influence on the structures of ACs than ecclesiological convictions. Associational practices followed the established pattern and were aimed at keeping the balance between local church and the union. They demonstrated "human face" being the expression of organic ties between churches: the participation of senior presbyters in the election and ordination of ministers, representatives of the AUUCECB at regional assemblies and mutual visitations reflect fundamental theological convictions. Unfortunately, none of the practices were analysed from a theological perspective. The representation of the union as the body of Christ and *bratstvo* points to historical continuity: Ukrainian Baptists still think of the union as an ecclesial entity. Discussions on the relations between the local church and the union point to the unresolved issue and unclear thinking about the nature of ACs. The participants of the symposium "Local Church Autonomy: Relations of the Local Church and the Union" (6–7 December 2007, Kyiv) painstakingly tried to avoid throwing away one of the key Baptist values: the centrality of the local church, on which Baptist ecclesiology hangs, as well as the associating of churches which expresses unity in Christ. This is the context for the analysis of oral tradition through semi-structured interviews with key leaders.

---

125. "Obobshchenie Obsuzhdenii," 381.
126. "Obobshchenie Obsuzhdenii," 381.

CHAPTER 6

Exploring Oral Tradition on Associations of Churches

6.1 Introduction

Analysis of practices, organisational structures and theological representations points to regularities in the understanding of ACs by Baptists in the Russian Empire and USSR. However, the picture is incomplete without the inclusion of contemporary understandings of the nature of ACs by Ukrainian Baptists. Oral communicative culture is prevalent among Ukrainian Baptists. Even theologically trained pastors or lecturers at theological institutions rarely have scholarly discussions via printed media. This sets up the method of research interview. Section 6.2 provides general information on the interviewees, interview questions, the actual process of interviewing and the analysis of data. Section 6.3 presents thematic analysis of the data.

6.2 Interviews: A Descriptive Dimension

6.2.1 Interviewees

The interviews fit within the category of elite interviews as proposed by Bill Gillham.[1] Such interviews usually aim to obtain specialist knowledge from the people who are experts in their respective field and typically hold positions

---

1. Gillham, *Research Interviewing*, 54–59.

of power and have access to networks of people and organisations.[2] Gillham suggests interviewing specialist academics, advanced practitioners and expert administrators.[3]

The interviewees in this research project are advanced practitioners. They have been involved in the ministry of Baptist churches and the union for twenty-six years on average. All seven interviewees are long-time ministers in their local churches. Due to their personal talents and ministerial expertise six of seven interviewees served for at least six years as senior pastors in regional associations. Three interviewees served in the capacity of the first vice president of the union and five as the assistants of the president of the union. Three interviewees served as presidents of the union, and one was president at the time the interviews took place. All information obtained through these interviews was insider information.

Traditionally, Ukrainian Baptist churches recognize leaders by their merits in the ministry.[4] The high reputation of interviewees among Ukrainian Baptist churches may point not only to their personal and ministerial qualities but also to the fact that they are good representatives and keepers of the Baptist tradition. The oral nature of the Baptist tradition assumes transmission from one generation to another. Their unique experience and constant involvement in processes on local, regional, national and international levels make these leaders good human sources for this research. However, deep involvement in the various processes of the union could be a disadvantage since it by necessity prevents interviewees from looking critically at the union.

6.2.2 Interview Questions

In semi-structured interviews, questions tend to be more open-ended, focusing on specific information that respondents could provide.[5] The interview initially consisted of fifteen questions organised into four groups.[6] These questions were aimed at obtaining information answering four subsidiary research questions:

---

2. Gillham, *Research Interviewing*, 54.
3. Gillham, *Research Interviewing*, 55–58.
4. Nazarkina, "Protestants'ki Konfesii Ukrainy," 69–70.
5. Merriam, *Qualitative Research*, 89–90.
6. For interview questions and subsidiary questions, see appendix 1.

1. How do the representatives of the AUUCECB understand the nature of ACs?
2. Upon what theological ideas do the representatives of the AUUCECB base this understanding?
3. How is this understanding reflected in the documents, current structures and practices of the AUUCECB?
4. How does this particular understanding of the nature of ACs relate to local church autonomy in the AUUCECB?

The questions were tested twice with people of position and experience similar to the interviewees' and improved in their wording. However, after conducting the first three interviews, it became obvious that some questions needed further amendment. In particular, the operative question OQ10 ("In what way do the organisational forms of your union reflect this particular understanding of the nature of these structures?") was divided into two questions (OQ10: "Could you describe the organisational structure of your union?"; and OQ11: "Do you think that the organisational structure of your union reflects this particular understanding of the nature of these structures?"), and the operative question OQ11 was reformulated and numbered OQ12. As a result of this, all subsequent operative questions were renumbered as OQ13–OQ16. The comparison of the two sets of questions can be consulted in appendix 2.

In spite of the amendment of the questions, the actual process of interviewing demonstrated that almost all respondents had difficulties with answering operative questions OQ6 and OQ7, which deal with the marks of the church and relation of these marks to the ACs. For instance, one of the respondents pointed to Acts 2:42 as the description of the church's marks, another mentioned images of the church, such as those of Christ's body, the bride, the temple of the Spirit, and others insisted on the visible gathering of believers and its statement of faith as the marks of the church. Their responses to operative question OQ6 to some degree predetermined the way they answered operative question OQ7. Only those two who referred to Acts 2:42 and images of the church affirmed that all the marks apply to the AC, while others contended that only some marks, and in a limited sense, relate to the AC.

6.2.3 The Process of Interviewing

Five interviews were conducted in the period of one year (spring 2015–spring 2016), with the two remaining interviews conducted in November 2017. The interviewees received the list of questions well before the actual interview (usually two weeks in advance). They had a chance to get acquainted with the questions and prepare for the interview. Besides that, after one week, the interviewer contacted them via phone or email to clarify whether the questions were clear, or if additional explanation was needed. None of the respondents asked for additional clarification of the questions. Three interviews were conducted through electronic communication software, three in person and one was a written response to the questions. The three electronicly assisted interviews were recorded with the help of recording software, while the three in-person interviews were recorded with a voice recorder. Interviews were transcribed, formatted and saved as separate files. Interviewees could check, amend and approve transcripts. All original files of the interviews and the transcripts were stored on a separate encrypted hard drive, together with the digital copies of informed consent documents from the interviewees.

6.2.4 Analysing Interviews

The analysis of the interviews followed the procedure proposed by Sharan B. Merriam.[7] It consists of three stages: (1) category construction – assigning codes or categories to the bits of information that answer subsidiary research questions; (2) sorting categories and data – refining and grouping categories as regularities emerge in the process of analysis; and (3) naming the categories – refinement or specification of the codes, aligning similar ideas or images together and going to a higher degree of abstraction. The logic of the process goes from discovering to verifying to testing and confirming. It employs different logical operations: inductive analysis at the first stage; inductive-deductive at the second stage; and deductive at the third stage.[8]

The analysis aimed at identifying the segments of data that addressed the subsidiary research questions mentioned above. The major criteria for selection of these segments or "units" were their capacity to answer the questions and their meaningfulness. Merriam points out that the unit should be both

---

7. Merriam, *Qualitative Research*, 175–93.
8. Merriam, *Qualitative Research*, 184.

"heuristic" and stand-alone. By heuristic, she means the relevance of the unit and its ability to "stimulate the reader to think beyond the particular bit of information."[9] Stand-alone means that a unit is subject to explanation "in the absence of any additional information other than a broad understanding of the context in which inquiry is carried out."[10] In this study, units varied from words (images or metaphors of the AC) to word combinations (functions or practices of the AC) to sentences (definitions of the AC or its distinction from local church). At the stage of naming, all data should be organised around categories that help to generalise it and bring it to a higher level of abstraction. This presupposes that the categories must be "responsive to the purpose of the research," "sensitive to the data," "exhaustive to encompass all relevant data," "mutually exclusive" and "conceptually congruent."[11]

Following these instructions, at the first stage all interviews were read and, in the process of reading, initial codes assigned to the units addressing subsidiary questions of the research project. Thus, definitions of "association," "union" and "brotherhood" given by the interviewees clearly differentiated the first two from the last one. "Association" and "union" were labelled as "institution," "legal," "administrative," "structural" and "voluntary," while "brotherhood" was labelled as "fellowship," "spiritual," "symbolic," "biblical" and "non-official." A similar procedure was applied to the rest of the questions.[12]

At the second stage, the initial codes were sorted and grouped around common themes in an attempt of determining regularities emerging out of the data. Thus, in response to the first group of questions, addressing the nature of ACs, a double metaphor of "organism/organisation" emerged together with an intermediary concept of "hybrid." ACs as "hybrid" partially combines organic and organisational elements. The codes related to theological grounds were grouped into pragmatic and biblical/theological, while the shape, decision-making process and regular activities of ACs were organised under a general rubric of practices. The section on practices is more descriptive and aimed at demonstrating whether and how these practices reflect an understanding of the nature of ACs. Different codes which mark the units of data related to local

---

9. Merriam, *Qualitative Research*, 177.
10. Merriam, *Qualitative Research*, 177.
11. Merriam, *Qualitative Research*, 185–86.
12. For table with initial coding, consult appendix 3.

church and AC, and trans-local leadership and AC were grouped together. The section on the leadership of ACs was initially related to the rubric of local church autonomy but in this thematic analysis it is singled out as a separate subsection. In the following thematic analysis, all data is grouped under six headings: (1) the nature of ACs, (2) the necessity of ACs, (3) the biblical and theological grounds of ACs, (4) the practices of ACs, (5) the local churches and ACs and (6) the trans-local leadership of ACs.

6.3 Interviews: A Thematic Dimension

6.3.1 The Nature of Associations of Churches

The understanding of the nature of ACs by the interviwees can be described with a double metaphor of organisation/organism. For all interviewees, "association" (*ob'edinenie*) and "union" (*soiuz*) are distinct from "brotherhood" (*bratstvo*) for they presuppose not only common worship, fellowship and ministry of the churches but also an organisational aspect. "When we speak about 'association' and 'union' we use these terms in a legal sense to describe specific groups of churches," says Igor Bandura.[13] "Brotherhood" is a spiritual reality of church fellowship, united by common confession and shared practice.

6.3.1.1 ACs as organisations

The organisational aspect of ACs is assumed in the way interviewees define association, union and brotherhood, explain their purpose and functions, and interpret association and union through the notion of voluntary society.

"Association" stands for a group of churches in a geographic location.[14] In Ukraine these coincide with administrative-territorial units called *oblasts* (regions).[15] "Union" comprises Baptist churches in Ukraine and its diaspora

---

13. Bandura, Interview 1.A.0, 48–50. Henceforth numbers refer to the lines of the transcript.

14. Shemchyshyn, Interview 1.G.0, 21–22.

15. The English word "region" usually stands for *oblast*, but the interviewees sometimes use the adjective "regional" (*regionalnyi*) to signify a larger geographical area comprising several *oblasts*. Before the Second World War, this structural level of the Baptist union was called *raion*. See Timoshenko, "S'ezd Baptistov v Moskve," 367; Levindanto, "O Sluzhenii Starshego Presvitera," 48; Steeves, "Russian Baptist Union," 82–83.

in Argentina, Australia, Canada, Paraguay, Portugal and the USA.[16] Local churches unite into *oblast* associations and with other sister associations form the AUUCECB. Valerii Antoniuk, the president of the union, explains:

> First is "association," which defines a group of churches in a certain territory. In our contemporary dimension these are *oblast* associations; they can also be regional. The local churches unite together in one region. "Union" [AUUCECB] consists of twenty-five *oblast* associations of churches which are represented by the elected responsible ministers from each association.[17]

Local churches can join the union only via associations. One of the interviewees pointed out that with its new statutes, AUUCECB encountered a serious collision: the official name of the union and its structure and procedures do not coincide. "We changed the name for 'The Union of Churches' but we have not yet developed the mechanism. We do not have the answer for the question whether a single local church can join the Union without joining the regional association."[18] It means that the influence of local churches on the union's affairs is mediated through associations and their representatives on the council or at the general assembly. On the other hand, the union's officials by necessity work with the local churches through senior presbyters and *oblast* presbyters' councils.[19]

Another organisational aspect of ACs is their purpose and function. Here is a brief overview of some elements which will be treated in detail in the section on the necessity of ACs: "Association" and "union" have the same basic purpose "to unite, to help and support local churches"[20] on different levels – *oblast* and national. Through this, ACs give shape to the Baptist movement which otherwise would fall prey to the centrifugal powers of branching and

---

16. See full list at the official website for the AUUCECB, http://www.baptyst.com/prosoyuz/.

17. Antoniuk, Interview 1.D.01, 34–39; see also Bandura, Interview 1.A.0, 52–53.

18. Bandura, Interview 1.A.0, 758–60. One interviewee referred to a conflict in the Donetsk region where a group of churches suspended their membership in the association due to the conflict with the senior presbyter but asked the Union's Council to retain their membership in the Union. See RS, Interview 1.B.0, 621–25; cf. Bandura, Interview 1.A.0, 765–73.

19. Romaniuk, Interview 1.E.0, 68–69.

20. Komendant, Interview 1.C.0, 90–92. see also Antoniuk, Interview 1.D.01, 71–76, 85–86; Romaniuk, Interview 1.E.0, 109–10.

regionalisation. Igor Bandura views this component as necessary: "We understand that any movement should be structured in some way. The structure could be different. It can correspond to the understanding in a certain historical period. It can change, but it helps organise all this, direct it, mobilize resources and distribute them in the best possible way."[21] The elected ministers of the associations and the union represent the local churches before government officials and in interdenominational and international contacts. They work for closer unity and coordination of local churches and mediate conflicts on their levels.[22] Differences in the level of responsibility and authority of the "association" or "union" correspond to their constituency on regional and national levels and beyond: "Let's say that *oblast* association, all its decisions are decisions of a group of approximately one hundred churches. The decisions on the level of the Union are those of, say, 2,500 churches. Therefore, the level of authoritativeness, level of support is much wider in the Union if we compare it with the association."[23]

Interviewees understand ACs as voluntary associations. This is reflected in relations between local churches and ACs[24] and is present in the statutes of AUUCECB.[25] Churches gather around a shared statement of faith, shared practices for confessing Christ and mutual help and support: "regional association is a voluntary union of churches of the *oblast* or region for the sake of common confessing of Jesus Christ and receiving help."[26] The statement of faith and shared practices are consolidating instruments for the union and the litmus test for churches that want to join the union.[27] According to the principle of voluntariness, a local church can freely join or leave, at least in theory, their association or the union. Perhaps such regulation was to some

---

21. Bandura, Interview 1.A.0, 165–70.

22. Bandura, Interview 1.A.0, 81–88 cf. Antoniuk, Interview 1.D.01, 69–74; RS, Interview 1.B.0, 119–21, 141–44.

23. Bandura, Interview 1.A.0, 90–94.

24. Bandura, Interview 1.A.0, 476–79; RS, Interview 1.B.0, 346–49; Komendant, Interview 1.C.0, 575–78; Antoniuk, Interview 1.D.01, 255–56, 316–20, 584–88; Romaniuk, Interview 1.E.0, 60–61, 178–81; Nesteruk, Interview 1.F.0, 634–37; Shemchyshyn, Interview 1.G.0, 12–13, 148–50.

25. Statut Vseukraiins'kogo Soiuzu Tserkov Evangel's'kikh Khrystyian-Baptystiv (2014u), para. 1.1.

26. Romaniuk, Interview 1.E.0, 59–61.

27. Romaniuk, Interview 1.E.0, 682–96.

extent reflecting negative experiences in the USSR after the Second World War when traditional Baptist associational practices declined.[28]

Inclusion of this principle of voluntariness in the statutes may point to the traditional cooperation among churches[29] and the right of a local church to resolve all its internal issues under the lordship of Christ.[30] However, the language and structure of the statutes betray their legal rather than ecclesiological nature. Organisational and judicial terminology overshadow theological and ecclesiological language. Thus, though on the surface the principle of voluntariness seems to comply with Baptist ecclesiology, in reality it almost nullifies the necessity of fellowship with other churches, leaving it to the volition of the congregation or minister. It definitely endangers what belongs to the *esse* of the church. In real practice, the voluntary aspect of associating often deteriorates into arbitrariness which attracts justified critique:

> For instance, in our Statutes two functions [are] mentioned – fellowship and voluntary cooperation. That is all boiled down to this – if we want, we fellowship or do something. Or if we do not want – we do not fellowship or do nothing. In practice this is how things are because local church autonomy, to an extent, presupposes such freedom and self-determination of the local church. . . . Voluntariness should not be understood as capricious "I want this – I don't want that." Voluntariness stems from our freedom in Christ. But the freedom in Christ, if understood correctly, often means that I want because I cannot do otherwise. And I cannot do otherwise not because I am compelled by somebody from above, but because I am a part of this reality, immersed in this reality; if I am a living member of Christ's Body, I cannot do otherwise. If our church is normal and truly autonomous it does mean that we are free, but it also means that we cannot live, exist without other churches. We are not closed. We are voluntarily open. And this is not our choice, this is the expression of our nature.[31]

---

28. See chapter 4; cf. Komendant, Interview 1.C.0, 575–78.
29. Antoniuk, Interview 1.D.01, 253–56.
30. Freeman, *Contesting Catholicity*, 237–38.
31. Bandura, Interview 1.A.0, 485–93.

Here Igor Bandura points to the excesses which result from voluntariness and are contrary to the church as the body of Christ. His proposal to conceive voluntariness as an expression of freedom in Christ and belonging to the body merits further development. Earlier, recollecting on *notae* (marks) with regard to ACs, he pointed to the limits of understanding a group of churches as a voluntary association and proposed thinking of both a local church and a group of churches as the body of Christ.[32] Such rethinking of association and union in terms of the image of the body of Christ, and associating as an expression of the church's nature, may lead beyond the imagery of voluntary association to more lively and plastic relations among the communion of churches.

6.3.1.2 ACs as organisms

The concept of "brotherhood" has absolutely different colouring. While "association" and "union" are defined as legal, administrative and structural entities, the concept of "brotherhood" is viewed as a biblical, spiritual and symbolic definition of a group of churches.[33] This concept is rooted in the Petrine use of the term (1 Pet 2:17) and the early Russian Baptists' self-designation.[34] The interviewees viewed this concept in stark contrast to "association" and "union," for it is devoid of "a function of administrative-organisational form,"[35] does not represent a structure[36] and, in general, is wider and deeper in its scope and meaning.[37] Moreover, "brotherhood" is viewed as a biblical ideal to which AUACECB strives to conform and against which it "evaluates its calling and functions."[38]

Referring to the union of churches as "brotherhood," Ukrainian Baptists see it first as a fellowship or communion of churches.[39] Perhaps this is the most important trait of "brotherhood." One respondent labeled it "a

---

32. Bandura, Interview 1.A.0, 308–16.
33. Bandura, Interview 1.A.0, 50–52; Romaniuk, Interview 1.E.0, 79–80; Nesteruk, Interview 1.F.0, 54–55.
34. See chapters 2 and 4.
35. RS, Interview 1.B.0, 87–89.
36. RS, Interview 1.B.0, 106–7.
37. Bandura, Interview 1.A.0, 100–101.
38. Bandura, Interview 1.A.0, 101–6.
39. Bandura, Interview 1.A.0, 69–70.

spiritual union,"⁴⁰ while another called it "a living fellowship and availability of connections."⁴¹ Thus, "brotherhood" is fraternal relations or fellowship, which is also its core value holding "brotherhood" together.⁴² Since "brotherhood" is devoid of administrative or constitutional ties, the only strings attached are belonging to a family and common heritage, and this presupposes a degree of interdependence of local churches. Valerii Antoniuk emphasises that "brotherhood" is "demonstration of spiritual belonging, interconnectedness and coordination among the churches that commonly share evangelical values and certain theological principles or doctrinal statements."⁴³ This statement leads to the second significant element – common tradition – which connects and holds churches together.

This communion of churches is not only a big family, it is also built around a common theological tradition encompassing a shared confession of faith and shared practices. Igor Bandura clarifies this, explaining that "'brotherhood' . . . is a notion, with which we express communion of churches, united by one attitude, one feeling, one understanding of the Bible and common history, one tradition, they are united by common desire to serve God together, common values, vision and goals."⁴⁴ This tradition both forms a centre of gravity, around which local Baptist churches are united, and defines the demarcating lines making this constellation of churches distinct from other churches. The tradition is not restricted by the walls of one church union. It crosses denominational and even national borders, encompassing all Baptists.⁴⁵ As one interviewee put it:

> In general, speaking about "brotherhood," we presuppose doctrinal unity of all Evangelical Christians-Baptists. And when we say "brotherhood" in a wider sense, then we, probably, include all communities or local churches united by one statement of

---

40. Romaniuk, Interview 1.E.0, 130.
41. RS, Interview 1.B.0, 137.
42. On the fellowship of churches and loose administrative ties as the key principles behind "the Brotherhood of Independent Churches and Missions of Ukraine," see RS, 56–61.
43. Antoniuk, Interview 1.D.01, 65–68.
44. Bandura, Interview 1.A.0, 58–63.
45. RS, Interview 1.B.0, 122–24.

faith. But in this case, it means that this definition includes all Evangelical Christians-Baptists that belong to different unions.[46]

Here "brotherhood" stands for a confessional group[47] and expresses one of the key elements of the church's nature: the fellowship of believers.

Besides spiritual communion and shared tradition, these churches unite around mission. It may sound like a pragmatic reason, helping churches unite their resources for the sake of mission. But participation in mission clearly surpasses pragmatic reasons for unity since it is deeply rooted in the church's nature as a missional community which, in its turn, stems from the *missio Dei*. Valerii Antoniuk succinctly summarises this: "'brotherhood' . . . is rather a biblical definition of a group of local churches that share common evangelical and theological values and cooperate for reaching people and fulfilling the Great Commission of Jesus Christ."[48]

However, not all interviewees saw the concept of "brotherhood" in generic terms. Grygorii Komendant identified it only with "Brotherhood of Independent Churches and Missions of Evangelical Christians-Baptists of Ukraine."[49] Ivan Romaniuk sees all three terms, "association," "union," and "brotherhood" as interchangeable.[50] His statement probably points to the relations that local churches, united in the association or the union, have apart from the formal or legal ties of being members of the same organisational unit. In some other cases, "brotherhood" is applied to a wider group of churches which consist of unions or associations that unite local churches of the same ethnic group. For instance, Ukrainian Baptists in the USA and Canada belong to different unions but still call themselves "Ukrainian Brotherhood."[51]

6.3.1.3 ACs as hybrid

Several interviewees opined that associations and unions cannot be reduced to an administrative or structural reality. Ivan Romaniuk, speaking on the

---

46. RS, Interview 1.B.0, 92–97.
47. RS, Interview 1.B.0, 108–11.
48. Antoniuk, Interview 1.D.01, 39–42.
49. Komendant, Interview 1.C.0, 45–46, 65–67. See the official website of BICMU at http://bibcm.org.
50. Romaniuk, Interview 1.E.0, 88–90; cf. Nesteruk, Interview 1.F.0, 71–79.
51. Romaniuk, Interview 1.E.0, 118–23.

nature of ACs, admitted that there are two types of relations among the Baptist churches:

> We, probably, have this vertical dependence. We also have very good horizontal ties, and they are stronger than the vertical one. Because the vertical is minimal, possibly, in relations with the state or in interchurch or interdenominational relations. But in general fellowship or unity of churches is all on the horizontal level, where we do not have structures that administer this.[52]

The "vertical" dimension of church relations is embodied in the structural and administrative elements of association and union. These bi-directional relations between the centre and periphery are tightly connected to those aspects, which go beyond the capacities of particular local churches, especially in representation on the state, interdenominational and international levels. "Horizontal" are the ties between local churches in geographic proximity or nationwide beyond official denominational structures. This perspective is consonant with explanation provided by Igor Bandura. He referred to two different aspects of the existence of the local church: spiritual and legal.[53] The former presupposes that a local church belongs to other churches and has spiritual communion with them. This belonging stems from the nature of the church.[54] The latter involves the existence of a local church within the Ukrainian legal framework where some issues can be resolved easier if a church is a member of a union.

Thus, ACs exist on two levels: organisational and organic. As organisations, unions and regional associations have offices where certain elected and hired people work for the implementation of their purposes and functions. As organisms, churches interact with each other through and apart from official structures, establishing a network connected "by every supporting ligament" (Eph 4:16). This "hybrid" nature of the structures sometimes causes confusion. Some mistake the "vertical" or "legal" aspects of ACs, represented by the office of senior pastor and the union, for the association or union of churches.[55] They fail to understand that "a regional association is a live interac-

---

52. Romaniuk, Interview 1.E.0, 147–53.
53. Bandura, Interview 1.A.0, 115–34.
54. Bandura, 154–55, 157–58.
55. RS, Interview 1.B.0, 302–16.

tion of the local churches"⁵⁶ and that the "pastoral council and local churches that belong to the regional association, do truly represent all nature of this interaction."⁵⁷ Such misunderstanding can even be seen in the fact that some interviewees labelled ACs as "parachurch structures."⁵⁸ Igor Banura warns against this subtle mistake – separating the administrative structures from associations and the union: "When we talk about structure, about association and union, we do not mean that these are association and the churches, but that this is association of the churches."⁵⁹ This point may help in achieving balance between the "vertical/legal" and "horizontal/spiritual" aspects of local churches and church associations and unions.

6.3.2 The Necessity of Associations of Churches

The necessity of ACs corresponds to two particular aspects of the organisational dimension of these structures – purpose and key functions. These aspects are predominantly pragmatic, though they also allude to theological groundings.

6.3.2.1 The purpose of ACs

One of the reasons for the necessity of ACs is their purpose of enhancing the ministry of local churches.⁶⁰ As will be shown below, the local church takes central place in Ukrainian Baptist ecclesiology, but it is somewhat restricted when it comes to relations with the state, other denominations in Ukraine and beyond, and projects that require rich resources. Igor Bandura commented on this:

> there are very many aspects, which we can do together. This is education, missionary work, publishing, this is doing theology, representation of our churches and protection before the state

---

56. RS, Interview 1.B.0, 309–10.
57. RS, Interview 1.B.0, 314–16.
58. Antoniuk, Interview 1.D.01, 92; Nesteruk, Interview 1.F.0, 30–31. Being asked, he explained that "these are the structures that have the right from the churches to represent their interests before the state and help them in fulfilment of biblical tasks" (Antoniuk, Interview 1.D.01, 100–101). For Nesteruk, union is "a parachurch organisation but which unites churches" (Nesteruk, Interview 1.F.0, 43).
59. Bandura, Interview 1.A.0, 182–86.
60. RS, Interview 1.B.0, 346–49; Antoniuk, Interview 1.D.01, 120–28.

and so on and on. That is, this is what a local church cannot do individually. Even if this church is big. Even if it is influential. Even if it has a good budget. Even if its ministers are not only pastors and good administrators, but they are even gifted theologians, nevertheless, the very sphere of life and ministry of an individual local church cannot provide it with that experience, which could reflect the fullness of Brotherhood's life. And, consequently, without this fullness there is no fullness of theologizing. Therefore, in this regard association and the Union provide opportunity to unite and do together those things, which an individual church either cannot do or, if it can, only in a very limited sense.[61]

Here the limits of a local church encompass not only resources, human and material, but ministry experience and the wisdom that emerges out of it. The limits can only be overcome through belonging to the "fullness of Brotherhood life," which to some extent is embodied in regional associations and the union. Another interviewee put it more emphatically: "They [ACs] not only can, they are created to expand the functions of local churches through their interaction and engaging their potential."[62] The structures are finite and not perfect; they are in the process of constant transformation and adjustment, but one thing is sure: "a structure helps to organise all this, direct all this in a certain way, mobilise resources and distribute them in the best possible way."[63] Here again the structure is a pragmatic instrument to enhance the ministry of a local church, but it also can be treated as a medium, giving access to the experience and wisdom of the wider church. According to Valerii Antoniuk, cooperation has one particular goal, which is "to facilitate churches in their effective fulfilment of the Great Commission of Jesus Christ."[64]

---

61. Bandura, Interview 1.A.0, 194–207.
62. RS, Interview 1.B.0, 203–5.
63. Bandura, Interview 1.A.0, 166–70.
64. Antoniuk, Interview 1.D.01, 111–12; see also Komendant, Interview 1.C.0, 350–54.

6.3.2.2 Functions of ACs

Besides helping local churches, ACs perform on their behalf functions of representation, organization, unification and mediation.

The function of representation encompasses church-state relations and relations with other Christian denominations in Ukraine and abroad. Igor Bandura pointed out that "the state does not build relations with an individual church."[65] Through the elected representatives, churches can lobby many issues common to all religious groups.[66] Individual local church is very restricted in this sense.[67] It can still exist in the Ukrainian legal framework, but its communicative and representational potential will be narrower than that of a union.[68] The union also represents churches in the public arena by communicating their opinion on felt societal issues and witnessing to the gospel. One of the interviewees pointed to the Ukrainian mentality which tends to think of the church as an organisation and not as a local community.[69] Another pointed out that in Ukrainian political circles, people usually associate certain religious organisations with their representatives.[70] From this perspective, the function of representation becomes very significant, although not the most appreciated function.[71]

ACs help organise and unify churches. The organising aspect presupposes the coordinating role of senior presbyter and union officials. One of the interviewees in no uncertain words admitted: "in different areas, churches of the ECB, local churches and communities represent a wide palette of differences. This means that these structures are called to organise interaction of churches on the national or regional scale in order to effectively meet the needs of local churches."[72] In this regard, associations and the union function as coordinating centres that enhance interaction and cooperation among local churches.[73] The ministers in these structures collect information

---

65. Bandura, Interview 1.A.0, 123–24.
66. Bandura, 129–34; RS, Interview 1.B.0, 350–58.
67. RS, Interview 1.B.0, 159–64.
68. Bandura, Interview 1.A.0, 146–50.
69. RS, Interview 1.B.0, 67–69.
70. Komendant, Interview 1.C.0, 197–212.
71. Bandura, Interview 1.A.0, 539–49, 551–58.
72. RS, Interview 1.B.0, 164–69.
73. Antoniuk, Interview 1.D.01, 51–52, 86–87.

from different regions and have the opportunity to transform it into a larger, encompassing vision. They are responsible for working out strategy for the development of churches and their ministry in the country and abroad.[74] Ukraine is a big country and sometimes the geographical remoteness and even isolation of churches can prevent regular contact, and that results in misunderstandings and splits. Grygorii Komendant referred to the necessity of the mutual control of churches: "We all need some form of control, in the right sense of this word, in support. We all control each other and help each other."[75] Ivan Romaniuk added that the work of ACs aims at overcoming the process of the regionalisation of churches.[76] He points out that ACs are "a platform for spiritual unity"[77] and this spiritual unity can express itself through different forms – the informal associations of large churches, younger pastors or younger churches.[78]

It should be noted that the idea of local church autonomy has a significant flaw when it comes to conflict resolution and, especially, when it reaches deadlock.[79] In this regard, ACs function as mediators. This involves the resolution of conflicts inside of local churches as well as between them. Invitation of the representatives of the association or the union by a local church occurs only in those situations "where local church autonomy caused anarchy. Where all brotherly ties are torn apart, where a church is divided into groups, where spirituality destroyed."[80] In all such situations, representatives of a regional association or the union behave as arbiters, who can help with finding a solution and resolving the conflict in a peaceful way and whose involvement is the only way out of conflict.[81] It is not clear on what grounds these arbiters act and why an autonomous local church should accept their judgement. If neither an association nor the union have the power over a local church in

---

74. Romaniuk, Interview 1.E.0, 64–68.
75. Komendant, Interview 1.C.0, 189–91; see also 140–43.
76. Romaniuk, Interview 1.E.0, 170–77.
77. Romaniuk, Interview 1.E.0, 310.
78. Romaniuk, Interview 1.E.0, 311–16.
79. For an example from the Mennonite Brethren, see Dyck, "Moulding the Brotherhood," 48–52.
80. Romaniuk, Interview 1.E.0, 404–6.
81. Bandura, Interview 1.A.0, 633–36; Romaniuk, Interview 1.E.0, 413–24, 429–32.

an organisational sense then there must be something beyond this which serves as a ground for such actions.

6.3.3 Biblical and Theological Arguments for Associations of Churches

The interviewees use of the Bible with regard to ACs is rather sensible and reserved. They avoid direct appeal to passages of Scripture for support of ACs or reading into the NT text their denominational reality.[82] One interviewee even admitted that Scripture does not mention ACs.[83] Another says ironically: "The Bible is good in that one can justify any opinion with it. I know people, who, using the Bible very successfully, claim that there is nothing in it apart from local church and that the Church universal is just a theological construct that does not exist in the Bible."[84] This silence defines their approach to the Scriptures. Instead of directly quoting from the NT, interviewees employed three major approaches to the use of Scriptures: (1) they look at the practices of NT churches that manifest interdependence; (2) they appeal to the texts summoning to unity; and (3) they appeal to or hint at the biblical images of the church related to unity. Such approaches help them to balance local church autonomy and the necessity to go beyond local church to wider Christian community.

Thinking of practices of the NT churches, the interviewees tried to see what theological and ecclesiological reality was behind them, and what allowed the churches to go beyond autonomous existence and encouraged interaction. Valerii Antoniuk pointed to the informal ties between local churches seen in missionary efforts in the book of Acts.[85] For Igor Bandura, interdependence is exemplified by the participation of Macedonian churches in the financial support of Paul's inter-church ministry and their fellow believers in Palestine (2 Cor 8:1–9:13).[86] He contended that, for Paul, the participation of churches is their free obedience to the command of Christ. Another

---

82. Such attempts were not rare among Baptist. See, for example, Anan'in, "Ob'edinenie Obshchin Baptistov," 17–18; Shurden, "Associationalism among Baptists," 79–81.
83. RS, Interview 1.B.0, 369–70.
84. Bandura, Interview 1.A.0, 366–70.
85. Antoniuk, Interview 1.D.01, 275–88.
86. Bandura, Interview 1.A.0, 407–12.

example of practice is the trans-local ministry of Titus[87] or other apostles.[88] From these examples it follows that the NT churches were far from extreme independence or autonomy. Quite the opposite, for these churches fellowship was part of being the church.

Igor Bandura opined that according to Ephesians 4:1–16, the trans-local ministry of apostles and prophets encompasses all existing churches.[89] This means that "the word, entrusted to the apostles, was handed not to a single church but to a group of churches."[90] From this follows that all churches should share the message they receive from the Lord and examine their interpretations and practices against each other.[91] This shared experience expands and corrects local interpretations of the NT message. Through the corrective interaction of different local interpretations emerges what can be called a tradition – "commonness in teaching and practice"[92] – grounded in apostolic authority.[93] This interpretation builds on the notion that a local church is wholly church but is not the whole church.[94]

A classic example of church practice beyond the local church is the meeting of church ministers for different occasions as described in the book of Acts (Acts 15; 20:17–38). Some Baptists traditionally refer to the so-called Jerusalem Council to ground their practice of assembling for the resolution of theological and practical issues. This event is interpreted as a meeting of authoritative church ministers to resolve a theological issue – the coexistence of Jewish and Gentile believers in the same church. While some respondents see a functional similarity between this event and the regional or national assemblies of Ukrainian Baptists,[95] Grygorii Komendant thinks that it was a ministers' meeting of the local church in Jerusalem.[96] He claims that this church played a significant role as the spiritual centre around which other

---

87. RS, Interview 1.B.0, 378–83.
88. Komendant, Interview 1.C.0, 363–65.
89. Bandura, Interview 1.A.0, 371–406.
90. Bandura, Interview 1.A.0, 381–83.
91. Bandura, Interview 1.A.0, 383–85.
92. Bandura, Interview 1.A.0, 402, 404–5.
93. Bandura, Interview 1.A.0, 432–33.
94. See Swarat, "Local Churches," 48.
95. RS, Interview 1.B.0, 371–73; Komendant, Interview 1.C.0, 360–62.
96. Komendant, Interview 1.C.0, 72–74.

churches were united and which set standards in matters of faith and practice. This meeting addressed the issue of Judaizers with the wisdom of authoritative local ministers.[97] What Komendant does not explain is the reason why a decision of one local church, even with such authoritative ministers as apostles and James the brother of Jesus, was accepted by other local churches which were totally autonomous and even independent from each other. This thinking is identical to that of Hiscox.[98] Igor Bandura counterbalances this interpretation by pointing out that the Jerusalem gathering was in fact a meeting of representatives of different churches and their decision was the evidence of unity in the Holy Spirit, who holds the church together, and for this very reason it was gladly accepted by other churches.[99] Another example is a gathering of ministers from Ephesus (Acts 20:17–38) in Miletus. However, this meeting could only serve as an example of Paul's apostolic authority over the church which he planted. This gathering does not include ministers from different churches as in Acts 15.

The only direct reference to Scripture in an attempt to justify the necessity of ACs was Ivan Romaniuk's appeal to John 17:21. He referred to this ecumenical text, commenting that unity is one of the crucial tasks of the church.[100] He adds that the association and union of churches is one of the limited ways of implementing Christ's prayer on unity. In this sense, local churches cannot ignore this important aspect of the church's witness to the world. Appeals to this text were very common in the history of Baptists in the Russian Empire, Soviet Russia and the USSR.[101] Romaniuk's trajectory is in tune with traditional readings of this important text among Russian Baptists.

Some of the interviewees appealed to or implied the scriptural images of the church. The most frequent was the image of the body of Christ.[102] This image will be treated in detail in the paragraph on theological arguments

---

97. See Hiscox, "O Baptistkikh Soborakh," 31; Zhidkov, "Vzgliad Nazad," 9. For critique, see Fowler, "Church and Churches."

98. Hiscox, "O Baptistkikh Soborakh," 32.

99. Bandura, Interview 1.A.0, 413–20.

100. Romaniuk, Interview 1.E.0, 326–28.

101. See details in Geychenko, "On the Use of Scripture."

102. Bandura, Interview 1.A.0, 115–18, 154–58; Antoniuk, Interview 1.D.01, 263–65, 275–78; Romaniuk, Interview 1.E.0, 219–21.

below. Another image of the interdependence of local churches is the image of God's temple.[103]

Theological arguments evolve around nature of the church and indirectly point to the limits of local church. Particularly, that which is built around the image of the body of Christ. This argument starts with the fact that local church does not exist in a vacuum, for it is connected to other churches and this connectedness is an expression of the church's nature.[104] Since a local church is a part of the body, the argument goes, so is a constellation of churches.[105] This train of thought comes to a challenging question:

> [H]ow can I enter into fellowship with the wider Body of Christ? How should I relate to it? How should I cooperate with it? And how could this wider unity in Christ be implemented visually? From this follows an understanding that we need a wider fellowship of churches. How to organise it depends on possibilities and needs. In this case we say that in Ukraine we, as the Union, exist as a brotherhood of churches. We cannot exist otherwise because in that case we cannot long to this fullness of church life. That is, in this sense a single local church, with all its autonomy, cannot realise itself more fully without such fellowship, cooperation, ties, spiritual, first of all, and organisational, structural, with other churches. That is, if Christ wants to accomplish his work through his Church, we all face the question – how we can realise in a visible and active form our unity in Christ.[106]

This understanding of the fundamental unity of the body presupposes that every local church partakes in the church's nature and is its manifestation. So, the question of belonging to the wider fellowship of God's people is rooted in the divine origin of all churches: they are formed of God's daughters and sons and belong to the same Father. However, this spiritual unity, as the quote stresses, needs to be embodied in some visible and tangible form. In the case of Ukrainian Baptists, this is their concept of brotherhood manifested in the form of associations and unions of churches. It is important also to note

---

103. Bandura, Interview 1.A.0, 446–52.
104. Bandura, 154–58; cf. Antoniuk, Interview 1.D.01, 237–38, 260–65.
105. Bandura, Interview 1.A.0, 308–12.
106. Bandura, Interview 1.A.0, 331–44.

that these visual expressions of spiritual unity are transient[107] and represent a very partial attempt to deal with the division within the borders of one denomination.[108] Igor Bandura concludes that such understanding poses a further challenge: the necessity of dealing with other churches to overcome scandalous division in the body of Christ.[109]

Another aspect of the unity of the body is the distribution of spiritual gifts among local churches.[110] No single church holds all spiritual gifts or accumulates all scriptural wisdom, all ministerial experience[111] or all necessary resources for serving God. By cooperation – the sharing of spiritual gifts, resources and mutual support – local churches can partially manifest the fullness of the church.

6.3.4 The Practices of Associations of Churches

Answering questions on the shape and decision-making processes of associations and the union, interviewees referred to the statutes. Traditionally, Ukrainian Baptists have treated the statutes and other documents as transient statements that reflect practice and regulate it.[112] They are often written with government bodies in view and are limited to organisational aspects of ACs. Igor Bandura pointed out that in general a Baptist understanding of local church, associations of churches and the union is wider than the statutes describe them.[113] The structure, decision-making processes and practices of the union reflect the hybrid nature of ACs, where the voice of local churches is balanced by the voice of leadership.

6.3.4.1 The shape of ACs in AUUCECB

Local churches associate with each other on the level of regional associations and the union. The local churches in a given administrative-territorial unit of the country (*oblast*) establish an association of churches. The union comprises all regional associations and sister unions or associations from

---

107. See Bandura, Interview 1.A.0, 166–70.
108. Bandura, Interview 1.A.0, 350–53.
109. Bandura, Interview 1.A.0, 345–49.
110. Bandura, Interview 1.A.0, 158–61.
111. Bandura, Interview 1.A.0, 378–93.
112. See chapter 5.
113. Bandura, Interview 1.A.0, 471–75.

abroad. Both association and union are ecclesial bodies. In this sense, they unite churches and not interested individuals. Association and union as the assemblies of churches or church representatives differ from the offices of the regional associations or union, which are organisational expressions of these church bodies. The former represents the organic relations of the churches while the latter is an organisational component.

Regional association gathers every five years to elect a regional pastor and regional pastoral council. This is the time when local churches can exercise their authority over such matters as defining strategy, electing leadership and approving or amending the statutes. The leadership of an association consists of a senior pastor, his assistants and a pastoral council. These are responsible for spiritual nurturing, mediating conflicts in the churches of the region, developing cooperation inside the region and beyond, and mutual help and live communication with the representatives of the union. The associational assemblies usually precede the general assembly of the union and approve authoritative representatives for this meeting. The general assembly of the representatives of the local churches meets once every five years. It is authorised to elect the president, first vice president and vice presidents of the union, as well as to approve the council of the union. The general assembly can also amend the statement of faith and the statutes. However, all amendments proposed by the Statutes Committee pass through a long process of negotiations and only after approval by the council of the union are they presented to the general assembly.

The executive board of the of the union consists of the president and all vice presidents. The board meets once a month. It is responsible for implementing the decisions of the general assembly and for the operative activities of the union. The council of the union consists of all regional pastors, who automatically join the council, all members of the board, pastors of large churches and some of the most respected senior ministers.[114] The president presides over the council, which meets four times a year. Besides the board and council, there are several specialised committees, the purpose of which are to implement strategic decisions of the general assembly and provide information on the current state of affairs in their respective areas to the

---

114. Principals from the seminaries and theological colleges were not included on the council. This changed in 2019.

board. The committees are groups that unite professionals in different areas of ministry, for instance, missionary work, church planting, youth ministry and women's ministry. Some representatives of the committees are also members of the council.

6.3.4.2 ACs and the decision-making process

The decision-making process among Ukrainian Baptists reflects the essential decentring character of ACs. The general assembly makes major decisions about the life of the union, based on the negotiations and preparatory work of specialised committees and the discussions at regional assemblies. The executive board negotiates issues related to the current life and activity of local churches and proposes decisions to the council of the union for their approval.[115] The regional pastoral council approves decisions at the regional level. One of the shortcomings of this process is that a local church does not have direct input. Its voice could be lost in the process of negotiations and the mediatory structures of regional pastoral councils and approved delegates to the general assembly.

This process presupposes that neither association nor union can impose their decisions on local churches. The local church has the right to approve or disapprove any proposal brought forward by association or union.[116] There is a consensus among interviewees that in the situation when a local church contravenes the association or union, especially in matters of faith or fundamental practices, it cannot stay in the union and should leave it.[117] Formally, such issues are resolved by regional assembly with the mandatory presence of the union representatives.[118] Some of the interviewees could not recall a single case when a local church's membership was withdrawn.[119] One re-

---

115. See RS, Interview 1.B.0, 467–84.

116. Bandura, Interview 1.A.0, 715–19.

117. See, for example, Bandura, 724–28; RS, Interview 1.B.0, 507–14, 595–604; Nesteruk, Interview 1.F.0, 531–34; Shemchyshyn, Interview 1.G.0, 144–47. On the formal exclusion of the local church, see Komendant, Interview 1.C.0, 583–84, 588–90; Antoniuk, Interview 1.D.01, 584–88, 600–605; Romaniuk, Interview 1.E.0, 623–24.

118. See Bandura, Interview 1.A.0, 732–33; RS, Interview 1.B.0, 544–47; Antoniuk, Interview 1.D.01, 593–95; Romaniuk, Interview 1.E.0, 628–33. For an alternative, see Komendant, Interview 1.C.0, 594. On participation of the representatives of the Union, see Bandura, Interview 1.A.0, 627–33, 734–35, 833–36, 850–51.

119. See, for example, Bandura, Interview 1.A.0, 728–30; RS, Interview 1.B.0, 610–11.

spondent explained that in such situations the elected ministers usually tend to use non-confrontational measures of persuasion and negotiation rather than apply the procedure of withdrawal of membership.[120]

In general, relations between local churches and the representatives of ACs are built on the basis of respect, trust[121] and generosity. One interviewee recalled negotiating debates on Christian music:

> I attempted to smooth all these radical manifestations with regard to music or outward appearance. From both sides. Moreover, we agreed that if the church decides on the issues which are not for us the most important ones in the Scriptures, we should be generous enough to allow this church to do so in its walls. And we do not have right to make somebody to behave this way or vice versa.[122]

Igor Bandura pointed out that in some cases strained relations with a local church result from subjective factors or the personal attitude of a local pastor.[123] He emphasised that trustful and generous relations are usually a natural consequence of the spiritual maturity of local pastors as well as of representatives of the union or regional association:

> Here we do not have some administrative strings attached. And we should not have them. Because, on the one hand, this is maturity of the ministers, maturity of individual churches and, on the other, this is spirituality and authority based on personal lived experience of a minster and not on the fact that he is elected, given a position and authority. All this should move towards each other. And, since it moves towards each other, every time we get a new synthesis. In some places better, in some worse. Unfortunately, I do not think it is possible or really needed to set the goal of developing total loyalty, unquestioned

---

120. Bandura, Interview 1.A.0, 804–18, 866–69.
121. For this idea, see Fiddes et al., *On the Way*.
122. RS, Interview 1.B.0, 569–75.
123. Bandura, Interview 1.A.0, 500–504.

obedience, forming some form of hierarchy that would provide opportunities to resolve all issues.[124]

The relations based on trust and generosity do not even presuppose formal consequences for those local churches which avoid participating in financial support of the union and its projects. Ivan Romaniuk clarified: "You know that the day always comes when even the most self-sufficient encounters a problem. And it feels very uncomfortable, when he needs to come and ask – give me even though I have never given. This is concerning finances."[125] The concept of "brotherhood" is manifested in the relations based upon trust and generosity.

6.3.4.3 Regular activities/practices of ACs

The regular activities of associations and union tend to maintain a fine balance between local churches and ACs with the purpose of strengthening bonds of trust. These activities include the routine work of regional and national representatives of ACs and those which encompass all or a majority of local churches and their ministers – congresses, church celebrations and regional and national conferences. Since the purpose of ACs is "to assist every church in fulfilment of her calling"[126] then "approximately half of the regular work of the Union aims at helping [the] individual local church in her ministry."[127]

This involves planned visits of senior pastors to local churches or organised visits of the Executive Board of the Union, members of the Council of the Union and some distinguished ministers into regions called "a week of the Union in the region."[128] Viacheslav Nesteruk, who initiated these visits, sees as their purpose "to help people feel the unity in the brotherhood, to see each other face to face."[129] A typical "week of the Union" is a visit of a group of ministers who participate in different formal and informal meetings of local pastors.[130] These meetings are usually used for discussions, the sharing

---

124. Bandura, Interview 1.A.0, 508–18; see also Bandura, Interview 1.A.0, 774–77.
125. Romaniuk, Interview 1.E.0, 606–8.
126. Bandura, Interview 1.A.0, 535–36.
127. Bandura, Interview 1.A.0, 536–38.
128. Komendant, Interview 1.C.0, 465–72; cf. Bandura, Interview 1.A.0, 637–43.
129. Nesteruk, Interview 1.F.0, 226–27.
130. Nesteruk, 217–27. For a report on a typical visit, see "Tyzhden Soiuzu."

of experience and to inform local pastors on the most crucial strategic moves of the union. Sometimes the visiting team holds a conference on a subject or discusses and resolves particular problems.[131] All the visiting ministers participate in worship services of local churches, especially small rural churches, attempting to cover all or a majority of churches in the region.[132] Such visits certainly help the board to keep a finger on the real situation and get fresh and specific information on church life, particular tendencies, issues or tensions. Local churches and ministers can directly communicate their questions or concerns to the leadership of the union.

The union also receives information from regions and communicates its position on some crucial issues through the representatives at the regional assemblies. Such presence is required by the statutes. Important decisions, such as the election of a regional pastor and pastoral council or strategic planning, should agree with the union[133] and the overall strategy.

The visits by the board and the presence of the representatives are more formal and reflect the organisational aspect of ACs. Other less formal activities embody the organic aspect and strengthen ties between local churches. These are national congresses and church celebrations such as the jubilees of local communities, the ordinations of pastors or the dedications of church buildings. Edifying congresses alternate with the general assembly and usually occur every four years in different regional centres or in Kyiv.[134] As opposed to general assemblies which are more business-like gatherings, congresses provide opportunities for the celebration of unity, fellowship, common prayer and worship, spiritual exhortation and evangelization. The high point is a celebration of the Lord's Supper with all participants.[135] Church celebrations on occasions of ordinations, church jubilees or dedications of new buildings assemble members of other local churches and official representatives of the union. Ivan Romaniuk commented on these occasions:

---

131. Bandura, Interview 1.A.0, 590–626.
132. Komendant, Interview 1.C.0, 466–67.
133. Bandura, Interview 1.A.0, 627–33.
134. The first edifying congress was in Vinnitsa in 1996, the second in Kyiv in 2000, the third in Kyiv in 2004 and the fourth in L'viv in 2012.
135. Cf. Ziubanov, "Trinnadtsatyi S'ezd Sredne-Iuzhnogo Ob'edineniia," 49.

On the one hand, it is a work and a working process, but it is also a working and celebrative process. On the other hand, this is a uniting process, when the leadership or, say, senior pastors who professionally serve in the Union and regional association, attempt to reach closer unity among the churches.[136]

Such events were especially popular for fellowshipping and increasing the ties between the churches during Soviet times when meetings were strictly limited by the atheistic government.[137]

One of the most effective means of uniting the ministers of local churches and shaping their thinking on particular issues is the national pastoral conferences that occur twice a year. They have become regular since 2011, occurring in Kyiv in November and March. They have followed specific plans, developed by the union's pastoral committee. The themes have been "From Stagnation to Spiritual Revival" and "The Way to Spiritual Revival" (2011); "Biblical Preaching in the Church" and "Biblical Counselling in the Church" (2012); and "Missionary Work of Local Church" and "Spiritual Formation of Church Members" (2013). After the Revolution of Dignity, the annexation of Crimea and a proxy war with Russia in the east, the conferences focused on current realities: "The Church in the Context of War" (2014); "Salt and Holiness" and "Discipline of Grace" (2015); "The Church that Impacts Society" (2016).[138] In 2015, the union's council decided to hold one of the events in the regions rather than in Kyiv, particularly in L'viv and Dnipropetrovs'k.[139] Relocation of the conference to the regions allowed it to encompass thrice as many ministers as the conference in Kyiv.[140] The conferences provide good opportunities for transmitting important theological ideas and practical models of ministry to the grassroots ministers and provide a ground for discussions. Ivan Romaniuk opines: "I would say that the biggest work the Union does is the organisation of edifying conferences. As it appears, doctrinal and practical issues, even church-state relations are discussed at these conferences."[141] In addition to

---

136. Romaniuk, Interview 1.E.0, 443–48.
137. See Pilli, *Dance or Die*.
138. Video is available at http://pastoronline.org.ua/ru/resursy/pastorski-konferenciji.
139. RS, Interview 1.B.0, 439–44; Romaniuk, Interview 1.E.0, 463–66.
140. RS, Interview 1.B.0, 444–46, 450–52; Romaniuk, Interview 1.E.0, 474–78.
141. Romaniuk, Interview 1.E.0, 71–74.

these aspects, the conferences gather different generations of ordained and lay ministers, who share their experience, get acquainted with each other, align for common causes in ministry and strengthen the horizontal ties which are so important in the concept of "brotherhood."

6.3.5 Local Churches and Associations of Churches

Local church occupies the central place in Russian and Ukrainian Baptist ecclesiology[142] and in this regard it does not differ from Western Baptist ecclesiology.[143] All interviewees referred to the centrality of local church for Ukrainian Baptists.[144] As one of the interviewees put it: "local churches are the heart of regional association."[145] Another claimed that Jesus "never established any union. He established a church."[146] Perhaps he meant the local church while the biblical text can be read as a reference to the universal church.

Speaking of local church, some of the interviewees preferred the definition of church found in the AUUCECB statement of faith: "A church is a community of born again and baptized by faith Christians, who live in a certain locality and gather together because they share one faith, doctrine and calling by Christ to be light and salt in this world."[147] Others defined local church as "a community" (*hromada*)[148] or "a gathering" (*zibrannia*).[149] Understanding local church as a community of the faithful is a major feature of Ukrainian Baptist ecclesiology.[150] When asked what marks point to the ecclesial nature of these communities of faith, the interviewees pointed to confessing the same statement of faith, regularly gathering for God's worship, the study of

---

142. On this, see Pyzh, "Confessing Community."
143. Thus Steeves, "Russian Baptist Union," 448.
144. For example, Bandura, Interview 1.A.0, 774–77.
145. RS, Interview 1.B.0, 324–25.
146. Komendant, Interview 1.C.0, 621.
147. Bandura, Interview 1.A.0, 226–29; RS, Interview 1.B.0, 214–18.
148. Romaniuk, Interview 1.E.0, 222–27.
149. Komendant, Interview 1.C.0, 222–28; cf. Antoniuk, Interview 1.D.01, 158–60. Antoniuk defined the universal church but claimed that the definition includes the local church too (Antoniuk, 170).
150. Pyzh, "Confessing Community."

Scripture, fellowship, ministry to each other,[151] sharing the Lord's Supper[152] and evangelism and social work in this world.[153] What surprises is the absolute absence of references to the traditional text of Scripture: Matthew 18:20. Only one of the interviewees mentioned "presence of Christ in the church, which is expressed in how the church preaches the Word, how it worships and how it manifests herself as Christ's Body through the ministry of the gifts."[154]

The centrality of the local church counterbalances the possible negative influence of ACs through the voluntariness of membership in regional associations, local church autonomy and the non-imposition of AC decisions on local churches.

The principles of voluntary membership and local church autonomy are related. The former addresses the relations of local church with wider church,[155] while the latter protects the inner life of a faith community.[156] Voluntariness means that a local church makes all major decisions, from membership in a regional association to the acceptance and approval of decisions of the general assembly.[157] Both in theory and practice, local church can exist as an individual community of believers without maintaining formal relations with other churches. Ukrainian legal framework[158] and Baptist ecclesiology allow this.[159] Local church autonomy, on the other hand, is the ability and right of a local church to resolve all the issues related to its inner life and define its forms of ministry without enforcement or interference from outside. Nevertheless, the concepts of the voluntariness and autonomy of the local church do not presuppose arbitrariness or total independence, but only limit the intrusion into the inner life of a community of faith. The interdependence of Baptist communities goes back to the time when they had just emerged

---

151. RS, Interview 1.B.0, 250–57, 265–67.

152. Romaniuk, Interview 1.E.0, 261–65.

153. RS, Interview 1.B.0, 256–57.

154. Bandura, Interview 1.A.0, 260–62.

155. Romaniuk, Interview 1.E.0, 178–85; RS, Interview 1.B.0, 346–49; Komendant, Interview 1.C.0, 576–78; Antoniuk, Interview 1.D.01, 584–87.

156. Romaniuk, Interview 1.E.0, 158–62, 518–22; Antoniuk, Interview 1.D.01, 291–92.

157. Bandura, Interview 1.A.0, 479–93.

158. Bandura, Interview 1.A.0, 125–26.

159. Bandura, Interview 1.A.0, 774–77; Komendant, Interview 1.C.0, 116–17; RS, Interview 1.B.0, 501–6.

in the Russian Empire.¹⁶⁰ The excesses of strong autonomy¹⁶¹ counterbalance appeals to the church as Christ's body or to local church limitations. Igor Bandura formulated this in the certain words:

> From a spiritual point of view, I think, a church, local church as a single autonomous unit, does not exist in vacuum, in principle. Local church autonomy does not presuppose, from our point of view, its isolation, imposed or voluntary. It seems there is something in church's nature that by necessity connects her with other churches.¹⁶²

In another place he comments on the limits of a single local church and uses this as one of the arguments in support of relations with other churches:

> In Ukraine we as the Union exist as a brotherhood of churches. We cannot exist otherwise because in that case we cannot reach this fullness of church life. That is, in this sense a single local church, with all its autonomy, cannot realise itself more fully without such fellowship, cooperation, ties, spiritual, first of all, organisational, structural, with other churches.¹⁶³

Only in communion with other churches can a single local church participate in the fullness of the church and implement its calling to be united with other churches as Jesus united with his Father (John 17:21).

The principles of voluntariness and local church autonomy result in the practice of non-imposition of decisions on a local church.¹⁶⁴ However, some of the interviewees opined that decisions related to the statement of faith are mandatory.¹⁶⁵ We already saw that all decisions are accepted by the churches

---

160. RS, Interview 1.B.0, 181–89.

161. Bandura, Interview 1.A.0, 479–93.

162. Bandura, Interview 1.A.0, 154–61, 308–12; see also Antoniuk, Interview 1.D.01, 237–38, 259–65.

163. Bandura, Interview 1.A.0, 337–42; cf. Bandura, 198–204, 327–31; Antoniuk, Interview 1.D.01, 223–31.

164. Bandura, Interview 1.A.0, 790–92, 804–18.

165. See, for example, RS, Interview 1.B.0, 506–14; Komendant, Interview 1.C.0, 536–39; Antoniuk, Interview 1.D.01, 524–28. On requirements for ministers, see Antoniuk, 529–32; on church discipline, see Antoniuk, 532–34; cf. Romaniuk, Interview 1.E.0, 499–508, 512.

voluntarily, and disciplinary decisions are implemented through the "soft power" of conviction and on the basis of trust.[166]

6.3.6 The (Trans-Local) Leadership of Associations of Churches

Perhaps the least developed element in the Ukrainian Baptist understanding of ACs is the status and role of leaders in these structures. Although they exist and regularly perform their duties and functions for the benefit of associations and the union, their status and role still need to be re-evaluated against the biblical witness and Baptist tradition.

The state of the matter is evident in the tensions over whether this leadership should be predominantly pastoral or organisational/managerial. Igor Bandura defines this as "internal contradiction that needs yet to be resolved."[167] He clarifies that Ukrainian Baptists still differentiate between spiritual and organisational abilities of the leaders and tend to view the latter as "shallow, carnal business-like efficiency, which, though does resolve some issues effectively is, nevertheless, shallow, unspiritual and, as a result, brings no impact."[168] Another interviewee wittily speaks of a choice between "the smart and the handsome," meaning a choice between "spiritual and organisational" aspects of leadership.[169] These commentators admit the necessity of both aspects, though the latter gravitates towards organisational skills, stating that "speaking about functions of these structures I would, first of all, single out the abilities for managerial, leadership and organisational spheres of ministry. But these do not exhaust understanding of the role and responsibilities of the Union and association."[170] Ivan Romaniuk contends that the leaders are "first of all, spiritual persons."[171] This view manifests in the images of servants, used by other interviewees for these leaders. Grygorii Komendant, speaking

---

166. For the influence on the local church via advice, see Shurden, "Associationalism among Baptists," 134–50.

167. Bandura, Interview 1.A.0, 896.

168. Bandura, Interview 1.A.0, 902–4.

169. RS, Interview 1.B.0, 636–42.

170. RS, Interview 1.B.0, 640–43, 654–56.

171. Romaniuk, Interview 1.E.0, 641; cf. Komendant, Interview 1.C.0, 602–3; Antoniuk, Interview 1.D.01, 620–26.

on the role of the leaders, says: "To serve, serve and serve again."[172] Valerii Antoniuk uses the biblical image of servants or slaves "who are called to serve the Church of Jesus Christ."[173] Consequently, their activities are auxiliary or advisory and aimed at caring for the spiritual needs of the churches.[174]

The uncertainty with regard to trans-local leadership is further complicated by the fact that many Ukrainian Baptists almost equate regional and national Baptist leadership and the union, forgetting that associations and AUUCECB represent forms of church fellowship while leaders are just recognised and elected by the churches to work for their good. The leaders receive their status and authority through a process of recognition in the form of elections at regional or national assemblies of churches.[175] They act as the authoritative representatives of the churches, having received their mandate of trust and right to act on their behalf.[176] However, in spite of procedures of elections and the system of counterbalances, the personality factor is still of great importance among Ukrainian Baptists.[177] Igor Bandura admits that ministers and churches often highly esteem strong leaders, who "love the Church, love the Brotherhood, serve devotedly,"[178] and invest them with authority that goes beyond their job description. The problems begin when another leader steps into the same authority and decides to use it differently, to the churches' misfortune.[179]

The ambiguous understanding of leadership in ACs influences their major functions.[180] Leaders are expected to act as servants, working for the benefit of local churches. Therefore, their main activities are pastoral, directed at the development and spiritual nurture of churches, the formation of leaders[181] and

---

172. Komendant, Interview 1.C.0, 603.
173. Antoniuk, Interview 1.D.01, 622–24.
174. Romaniuk, Interview 1.E.0, 654–55.
175. Bandura, Interview 1.A.0, 186–95.
176. Bandura, Interview 1.A.0, 314–16.
177. Bandura, 887–89. On the factor of personality in Ukrainian political culture, see Gatskova, Gatskov, and Institut für Ost- und Südosteuropaforschung, *Political Culture in Ukraine*. See also an interview with the former German ambassador Südemann, "Ukraina Postoianno Torguetsa."
178. Bandura, Interview 1.A.0, 779–80.
179. Bandura, Interview 1.A.0, 781–85.
180. On the ideal set of traits, see Bandura, Interview 1.A.0, 907–26.
181. Romaniuk, Interview 1.E.0, 644–48, 649–50.

the mediation of conflicts.[182] One interviewee pointed out that there is also an opinion that senior presbyters should guard the sound teaching of churches.[183] In this sense their responsibilities approximate those of traditional bishops. Besides spiritual aspects, leaders of ACs engage in organisational aspects of ministry, enhancing the organisational structure of churches[184] and their financial discipline, trying to combine the resources of local churches and ensure that they are aware of and implement the overall strategy of the union.[185] In a sense, almost all activities aim at unifying local churches into one body and eliminating anything that prevents this unity and fruitful cooperation.[186]

6.4 Summary

The opinions of contemporary Ukrainian Baptist leadership manifest significant continuity with the previous tradition. This involves understanding the AC as both organisation and organism, applying to ACs the image of the body of Christ and thinking about unity in the form of the union. A particular case of continuity is the habit of grounding associating and mission pragmatically. This way of seeing the union still plays the most prominent part in advocating for the necessity of the union. Another case relates to the attempts to maintain the balance between the unity of the church in the form of the union and local church autonomy. The interviews also point to several significant problems that need to be resolved. First is confusing the office of the union for the union of churches. In some minds the administrative structure replaces the union itself. Another case of such misunderstanding is thinking of ACs in terms of parachurch structures. A significant problem consists in grounding unity and mission on pragmatic foundations. Within such a pragmatic trajectory, associating becomes something desirable and valuable but not essential for being church in the world. Possible avenues for a positive development of a deeper theological understanding of ACs lead to thinking of the AC as an expression of the body of Christ and the fellowship/

---

182. Komendant, Interview 1.C.0, 609–11.
183. RS, Interview 1.B.0, 331–35.
184. Romaniuk, Interview 1.E.0, 648–49.
185. Komendant, Interview 1.C.0, 465–72.
186. Romaniuk, Interview 1.E.0, 445–48.

communion of churches, participation in mission as a theological motif and voluntariness as an expression of freedom in Christ. These ideas could be both challenged and enriched if they begin dialogue with wider Baptist tradition.

CHAPTER 7

Engaging Wider Tradition: Paul S. Fiddes's Covenant Ecclesiology

7.1 Introduction

In this chapter, I will explore the ecclesiological contributions of Paul S. Fiddes and point to the elements of his ecclesiological thought that are significant for the development of a Ukrainian theology of ACs. In particular, I will focus on the question: Which constructive elements from Paul S. Fiddes may potentially fill the gaps and improve problematic areas in the Ukrainian understanding of ACs? I first summarise the core of Fiddes ecclesiological thought represented by the concepts of covenant, *koinonia* and the body of Christ and its resulting understanding of the church. I also highlight practical implications of covenant ecclesiology[1] on participation in Christ's mission, the theology of trust and pastoral oversight (*episkope*). In the concluding section of this chapter, I shall summarise the results of the previous chapters in terms of recurrent themes, their potential and some of the dead ends of Ukrainian Baptist ecclesiology, and indicate which elements of Fiddes's ecclesiological thought and in what sense are significant for Ukrainian Baptist understanding of ACs.

---

1. Fiddes, *Tracks and Traces*, 254.

7.2 Paul S. Fiddes's Ecclesiological Core

Fiddes's ecclesiological ideas are built around traditional Baptist views of the church which he develops through dialogue with recent theological developments especially those from the ecumenical circles. This produces an interesting and compelling interpretation of traditional Baptist beliefs. In this section I shall first explore theological grounds Fiddes uses for his ecclesiological proposals and then his understanding of the Church.

7.2.1 Thinking Theologically about the Church

Fiddes proposes to look at the Church from a theological perspective which is participation *in* God.[2] This approach presupposes that ecclesiology is intimately connected to sacraments, soteriology and the doctrine of the Trinity.[3] Fiddes suggests that the theme of covenant is potent to open new avenues of theological thinking. Around it he builds his understanding of the Church and AC intertwining it with the NT concepts of *koinonia* and the Body of Christ.[4]

7.2.1.1 Covenant and Covenanting

Covenant takes one of the most significant places in Fiddes' theology. He places it at the centre of Baptist theology since it is related to doing theology in a Baptist way;[5] it was significant in the past and "is gradually being recovered in our day."[6] Moreover, it is definitive for understanding Baptist identity. Fiddes points to the English Separatist covenanting at Gainsborough as the single formative event that had much impact on John Smyth and Thomas Helwys who established the first Baptist church in Amsterdam in 1609.[7] English separatists and, later, early English Baptists, being separated from the established church, claimed continuity with the people of God through

---

2. Fiddes, 66; cf. Haymes, Gouldbourne, and Cross, *On Being the Church*, 3–10.
3. Fiddes, *Tracks and Traces*, 17.
4. Baptist Union of Great Britain, *Nature of the Assembly*, 4; Fiddes, *Tracks and Traces*, 197–227.
5. Fiddes, *Tracks and Traces*, 18–20, 53–56; Fiddes, "Towards a New Millenium," 16–18.
6. Fiddes, *Tracks and Traces*, 17. For a brief justification, see Wright, "Covenant and Covenanting."
7. Fiddes, *Tracks and Traces*, 21–22.

their local covenant and Christ's presence among them.[8] Theologically covenant connects with such important themes as participation in God and his mission in the world, the relation between divine grace and human free will as well as interchurch relations and attitude towards wider society and the whole creation.[9] Fiddes constructs his perspective on covenant by reflecting on biblical roots of covenant, actual practice of covenanting and historical development of the meaning of covenant among Baptists.

Drawing from contemporary OT studies, Fiddes simply labels covenant "agreement or bond"[10] or "an agreement Yahweh makes with his people, a relationship to which the partners have bound themselves".[11] Elsewhere he defines covenant as "an agreement made between members of the church, and between those members and God in Christ".[12] He opines that covenant does not have any contractual nature with regards regard to relations between God and his people,[13] stating that "covenant is about relationship and trust, about 'walking together' which is in some mysterious way part of the very journey of salvation."[14] God initiates these relationships for the benefit of human partakers.[15] Fiddes finds two traditions of describing covenant: promise-covenant and law-covenant.[16] The former is God's promise to grant life and well-being (covenants with Noah, Abraham and David), while the latter is the treaty with the people of Israel through Moses to be their God, which requires obedience to his commands. Regardless of the type, the common denominator of covenants is God's initiative and human response in the form of trust (promise-covenant) or obedience (law-covenant). Difference between the two forms lies in their emphasis not in their essence.[17] Trust and obedience should be in creative tension to avoid distortions. Two forms of covenant in the Bible lead Fiddes to conclude that "no expression of God's

---

8. Fiddes, *Tracks and Traces*, 24.
9. Fiddes, *Tracks and Traces*, 18–20, 23–24, 53–56.
10. Fiddes, "Covenant – Old and New," 10.
11. Fiddes, *Tracks and Traces*, 74.
12. Fiddes, "Covenant and Inheritance," 68.
13. Fiddes, "Covenant – Old and New," 10.
14. Fiddes, *Tracks and Traces*, 9.
15. Fiddes, "Covenants," 124.
16. Fiddes, "Covenant – Old and New," 10–11; Fiddes, "Church, Trinity and Covenant," 47–48; Fiddes, *Tracks and Traces*, 74–75.
17. Fiddes, "Covenant – Old and New," 12, 14–15.

covenant in human words can ever be final."[18] Since God's people are on the way, all covenant formulas are provisional, but "the covenant itself is more fundamental than any particular description of it in human words. What is basic is the initiative which God takes in reaching out towards his rebellious creatures and the response of trust and obedience which he asks from them."[19] These basic elements find fulfilment in the new covenant established by Christ who "fulfills all his *promises* and deals with the results of human failure to keep our *obligations*."[20]

There is a question as to what extent a Baptist understanding of covenant as a local agreement of church members "to walk together" corresponds to the divinely arranged covenants with individuals.[21] Fiddes attempts to resolve this by calling Abraham and David representative leaders of the people, therefore covenants with them also included the people of Israel.[22] In this sense, the OT covenants differ from their Near Eastern analogues, for in the latter gods were invoked as witnesses of the covenant between equal parts, whereas in the former God becomes a covenant partner, and by joining the covenant with God, people also enter the covenant with each other. Thus, the argument goes, the covenant is "no longer simply a human agreement, but a bond made in imitation of the bond made between God and them. Because God had called his people into covenant, they were *also* called into covenant with each other."[23] This important statement throws light on how early English Baptists brought together divine and human dimensions of covenant.

The early English Baptist understanding of covenant, remarks Fiddes, reflects the English Separatist heritage of "conceiving covenant in two dimensions at once, vertical and horizontal; that is, the church was gathered by the members' making a covenant or solemn agreement *both* with God *and* with each other."[24] Summarising the discussion on the meaning of covenant

---

18. Fiddes, "Covenant – Old and New," 16.

19. Fiddes, "Covenant – Old and New," 16.

20. Fiddes, "Church, Trinity and Covenant," 49. Empasis original.

21. For a discussion of the objections, see Fiddes, Kidd, and Quicke, *Something to Declare*, 12–15.

22. Fiddes, "Covenant – Old and New," 10.

23. Fiddes, "Covenant – Old and New," 13. For Scriptural examples of mutuality between human partners, see Kreitzer and Rooke, "Walking in Covenant," 19–20.

24. Fiddes, *Tracks and Traces*, 22. Emphasis original.

among Puritans, Fiddes enlists four uses: (1) a covenant of grace made by God with humanity and angels for their salvation in Jesus Christ; (2) an "eternal covenant" – a transaction between the persons of the Trinity with regard to salvation of the elect through the Son; (3) God's agreement with his church or churches; and (4) the local covenant of members of a particular church.[25] This final usage combines two dimensions and represents a typical seventeenth century Baptist vision of local church as "being joined to the Lord and each other 'by mutual agreement.'"[26] The most important issue is how these different uses relate to each other.

Fiddes points out that both Separatists and early Baptists began combining different uses of the term. Thus, the fusion of the third and fourth uses could already be seen in Robert Browne,[27] who envisioned the human act and promise simultaneously becoming God's act of taking the local church "to be his people," promising to be their God and Saviour.[28] This also had implications for the nature of the authority of the local church, placing it under the direct lordship of Christ, signified by the "seals of the covenant" in electing ministers, administering sacraments and enacting church discipline.[29] John Smyth combined the third and fourth uses of covenant with the first. Fiddes insists that Smyth wrote about the church from the perspective of one eternal covenant which has different dispensations in the Old and New Testaments. Through the covenant, God gives Christ, and with him all the blessings of the covenant, chooses believers and becomes the God of his people. Benjamin Keach seemed to follow the same idea, while John Gill reserved covenant-making only to decisions of the persons of the Trinity and turned local covenant into a contract of mutual obligations.[30] In spite of the diminishing of the Baptist practice of covenanting in the seventeenth century, which was substituted by believer's baptism as the point of entry into

---

25. Fiddes, *Tracks and Traces*, 25–31.
26. Fiddes, *Tracks and Traces*, 31.
27. Fiddes, *Tracks and Traces*, 33. Ascribed to Smyth in Fiddes, 76; cf. White, *English Separatist Tradition*, 128–29.
28. Fiddes, *Tracks and Traces*, 33.
29. Fiddes, *Tracks and Traces*, 33.
30. Fiddes, *Tracks and Traces*, 35–36.

the church,[31] and Gill's ideas of the church as a voluntary society,[32] Fiddes sees potential in developing Smyth's and Keach's ideas of the participation of local covenant in the covenant of grace. He brings it further, connecting local covenant with the inner communion of the Trinity.[33]

Fiddes approaches this task by drawing from Karl Barth's concept of election, which is the actual working of God's word in history, enabling human response to God by the giving of God's grace.[34] He then points out that God's eternal decision ("primal decree") to make covenant with humans through Jesus Christ "eternally shapes the relationships of love within God's own triune being."[35] Since Jesus of Nazareth cannot be distinguished from the person of divine Son, in him "God has elected *humanity* for divine fellowship, and has elected *God's own self* as covenant partner with humanity."[36] Fiddes calls this a "double decree" and concludes that this points to an understanding of the eternal relations within the triune God as "a kind of covenant relationship," though Barth himself avoided such a conclusion, objecting to the image of legal transactions between two divine persons in relation to atonement in federal theology and insisting on a unity of the covenant of grace that does not presuppose any other covenant.[37] Thus, God's election of humanity and himself is rooted in his act of "self-giving in partnership with the world."[38] Following Bruce McCormack, Fiddes calls this "covenant ontology,"[39] which is "the making of covenant with Jesus Christ, the representative human son, as being 'given in' the eternal generation of the divine Son from the Father."[40] He suggests that "double decree" can also be interpreted as "double covenant," which includes God's word of covenant promise in speaking forth the divine Logos and the covenant obedience of the incarnate Christ as the eternal

---

31. Fiddes, *Tracks and Traces*, 30.
32. Fiddes, *Tracks and Traces*, 34–35.
33. Fiddes, *Tracks and Traces*, 35.
34. Fiddes, *Tracks and Traces*, 35.
35. Fiddes, *Tracks and Traces*, 35.
36. Fiddes, *Tracks and Traces*, 35, 78, 162, 252–53. Emphasis original.
37. Fiddes, *Tracks and Traces*, 36.
38. Fiddes, *Tracks and Traces*, 79.
39. Fiddes, *Tracks and Traces*, 36.
40. Fiddes, *Tracks and Traces*, 79.

response of a covenant partner.[41] This allows Fiddes to connect "horizontal" human covenanting with the divine "vertical" aspect of covenant and through this it is absorbed into "inner covenant-making in God."[42] Thus, Fiddes restores an ontological basis for covenanting and goes beyond the pragmatic reasons typical for a voluntary social model.

Fiddes agrees with White that the mutual agreement of members and God's eternal decision are analogous to relations between local and universal church.[43] Therefore,

> Baptist ecclesiology built on the concept of covenant must take a strong view of the church universal. The universal church cannot just be an adding together of many local communities, as Baptists have sometimes depicted it; rather, there is a universal reality which *pre-exists* any local manifestation of it, as God's eternal covenant with humankind pre-exists the local covenant bond. Covenant and catholicity belong together.[44]

Fiddes rooted covenant in the communion of the Triune God which gives him reason to decline interpretations of covenant in terms of voluntarism, although he admits that such interpretations are not groundless.[45] However, they discount God's initiative enabling human response (the church is not only gathering, but gathered) and the direct rule of Christ as opposed to the principle of marketplace choice.[46] Thus, he suggests that "the covenant concept, when grounded *theologically*, is itself thoroughly open to the associating of churches together in the wider forms of cooperation" while the voluntary principle is dangerous.[47]

---

41. Fiddes, *Tracks and Traces*, 79.
42. Fiddes, *Tracks and Traces*, 79.
43. Fiddes, *Tracks and Traces*, 32.
44. Fiddes, *Tracks and Traces*, 32. Emphasis original.
45. Fiddes, *Tracks and Traces*, 40–42.
46. Fiddes, *Tracks and Traces*, 42.
47. Fiddes, *Tracks and Traces*, 44.

7.2.1.2 Koinonia

Fiddes's covenant thinking on church and ACs is closely related to the concept of *koinonia*, which is popular in recent ecclesiology[48] for its capacity to express diverse relations[49] and root them theologically in the vision of the Trinity.[50]

Fiddes turns to *koinonia* in discussing relations within the Trinity.[51] He roots human community in the Trinity,[52] clarifying relations between the local church and the universal church[53] and between churches in response to the ecumenical calling,[54] as well as relations of Christians among each other and with the Lord.[55] He grounds these relations in "the vision of God as three persons, each *hypostasis* a distinct reality because of its relationships to the other two, and united in a communion (*koinonia*) of life so intimate that we are confronted by one Lord."[56] In this vision, divine *koinonia* precedes other communions for "it already exists in God, in the mutual giving and receiving of love between the Father and the Son in the communion of the Spirit."[57] Moreover, it forms other communions, as is formulated in the report of conversations between the BWA and the Roman Catholic Church:

> The One God exists from eternity in a life of relationship, in a communion (*koinonia*) of three Persons, Father, Son and Holy Spirit. Jesus Christ, the eternal Son, is the Word of God as God's

---

48. For *koinonia* in ecumenical discussions, see Fuchs, *Koinonia*. For communion ecclesiology, see Zizioulas, *Being as Communion*; Tillard, *Church of Churches*; VanderWilt, *Church without Borders*; Doyle, *Communion Ecclesiology*; Tillard, *Flesh of the Church*. On the Baptist perspective, see Wright, "Koinonia."

49. Fiddes, Haymes, and Kidd, *Baptists and the Communion of Saints*, 135.

50. Fiddes, "Church's Ecumenical Calling," 39; cf. Baptist Union of Great Britain, *Nature of the Assembly*, 5.

51. Fiddes, *Participating in God*, 11–61; Fiddes, *Tracks and Traces*, 71.

52. Fiddes, *Tracks and Traces*, 76.

53. Fiddes, "Church Local and Universal," 97–100.

54. Fiddes, "Church's Ecumenical Calling," 39–42.

55. Fiddes, Haymes, and Kidd, *Baptists and the Communion of Saints*, 135.

56. Fiddes, *Tracks and Traces*, 71. Harmon calls this "participatory Trinitarism" and defines it as "an understanding of God as essentially relational and communal, *ad intra* and *ad extra* which retrieves the patristic concepts of *perichoresis* and *theosis*, makes social Trinitarian connections between the Triune God and humanity in the image of God" (Harmon, "Trinitarian Koinōnia," 22). Fiddes discards "social Trinitarian connections" because Trinity cannot be envisaged as community and criticizes the model of social Trinity (Fiddes, "Covenant and Participation," 125). For Fiddes, persons "are relations" but do not "have relations." See Fiddes, "Participating in the Trinity," 379–83; Fiddes, "Covenant and Participation," 131.

57. Fiddes, *Tracks and Traces*, 214.

self-communication of self-giving love. Jesus Christ is thus God's self-revelation who draws us into the communion of God's own triune life and into communion (*koinonia*) with each other. This means that the Word of God in the church in the fullest sense is Christ himself who rules as Lord in the grace and power of the Spirit.[58]

This statement points out that Christ not only reveals but draws people into relations with God and each other. As with the covenant, where God takes initiative in opening inter-Trinitarian relations, and the covenanting community responds with obedience and trust, so it is with *koinonia*. God's intentions embrace the whole creation.[59] Covenant allows for greater intentionality.[60]

Since divine *koinonia* precedes all communions, the church should also be thought of as *koinonia* by virtue of its participation in the life of the Trinity through Jesus Christ.[61] This is true with regard to local community and a group of congregations in the area.[62] However, this raises the question how the universal church, local congregation or group of congregations relate to each other. Fiddes discusses that in his article on Catholic and Baptist perspectives on *koinonia*.[63] He draws from the discussions of Leonardo Boff, Joseph Ratzinger and Walter Kasper and from Stanley Grenz's thought. Fiddes agrees that the universal church is not a totality of local churches; rather, "local churches are formed 'out of and in the Church universal,'"[64] though later he affirms the Baptist-Catholic report pointing out that "there is mutual existence and coinherence between the local and universal church of Christ."[65] Kasper calls it "perichoresis of local and universal church: the local churches and the universal church mutually include each other; they share the same existence and they live within each other, in a mysterious unity which is 'constituted

---

58. Catholic Church and Baptist World Alliance, "Word of God," §7, 34.
59. Baptist Union of Great Britain, *Nature of the Assembly*, 5; Fiddes, *Tracks and Traces*, 251; Fiddes, "Covenant and Participation," 127–29.
60. Fiddes, Haymes, and Kidd, *Baptists and the Communion of Saints*, 136–38.
61. Catholic Church and Baptist World Alliance, "Word of God," §11, 36.
62. Catholic Church and Baptist World Alliance, §12, 37.
63. Fiddes, "Church Local and Universal."
64. Fiddes, "Church Local and Universal," 100.
65. Catholic Church and Baptist World Alliance, "Word of God," §12, 37.

after the image of the Trinity.'"[66] Fiddes agrees with Kasper on the *perichoretic* relations between local and universal church and with Ratzinger on priority of the universal church that creates *koinonia*. He attempts to combine both with the theology of the body of Christ where "the local congregation and an assembly of churches are both 'body of Christ' as both make Christ visible in the world; yet Christ in his glorious resurrection body, continuous with his early body must pre-exist both."[67] This brings us to the significance of the theology of the body of Christ for Fiddes's ecclesiology.

7.2.1.3 Body of Christ

The theology of the body of Christ is important for countering an understanding of *koinonia* as invisible or spiritual unity.[68] The image of the body of Christ is a "fundamental image of unity" which presupposes visibility.[69] It first of all describes the universal church, but for Baptists, local community is also the "body of Christ," which is the primary but not the only possible manifestation.[70]

To understand in what way the church is the body of Christ, Fiddes reflects on the three possible meanings of the NT phrase "body of Christ": the body of the church, the body of the communion bread and Jesus's resurrected body.[71] These are "interweaving, overlapping and conditioning each other rather than being simply the same thing."[72] This informs Fiddes's construction of a Baptist perspective on the church as eucharistic community.[73]

The statement that eucharist constitutes the church could only be valid if two truths could be affirmed from a Baptist perspective: that sacraments enable Christ's presence with his people and that sharing the table identifies membership of the church.[74] Fiddes discusses different views of presence

---

66. Fiddes, "Church Local and Universal," 111.
67. Fiddes, "Church Local and Universal," 116.
68. Fiddes, *Tracks and Traces*, 195–96; Fiddes, "Church's Ecumenical Calling," 40–41.
69. Fiddes, *Tracks and Traces*, 197.
70. Fiddes, *Tracks and Traces*, 198–200.
71. Fiddes, *Tracks and Traces*, 67, 150–52.
72. Fiddes, *Tracks and Traces*, 151.
73. Fiddes, *Tracks and Traces*, 157–92.
74. Fiddes, *Tracks and Traces*, 157.

of Christ's body in the elements[75] and points to the irreplaceability of the metaphors of eating and drinking "as they indicate an aspect of receiving the mystery of grace which cannot be otherwise expressed."[76] The presence of Christ through the sacraments is then combined with his presence in the body of the congregation. The overlapping of the "body of Christ" in bread and congregation could be expressed in three ways: communion, story and sacrament. For Baptists, "communion" has the double meaning of communion with Christ and each other, thus Christ is present both through the elements and the congregation.[77] Story is related to a socio-linguistic view that "community is formed by the stories it tells."[78] As the words, symbols and actions of the biblical story enable God's presence, so does remembering that story at the eucharistic liturgy.[79] As a sacrament, the church becomes one of the "doorways into the fellowship of God's triune life."[80]

Fiddes also points out that participation in the Lord's Supper "identifies someone as a member of the church of Christ through its link back to baptism, integrating the three strands of membership, baptism and eucharist."[81] The church as eucharistic community "is formed by the actions of the two sacraments which recall the story of Jesus, and bring it into the present. Only in the church are bread, wine and water means through which Christ promises to be present, and where he can regularly be expected to meet us."[82] Thus, the church, whether local or universal, is the body of Christ because believers are incorporated into Christ through baptism and are assured of the presence and direct rule of Christ among them.[83]

---

75. Fiddes, *Tracks and Traces*, 160–66.

76. Fiddes, *Tracks and Traces*, 166.

77. Fiddes, *Tracks and Traces*, 168.

78. Fiddes, *Tracks and Traces*, 169. See Lindbeck, *Nature of Doctrine*, 102–10; Hauerwas, *Peaceable Kingdom*, 96–102.

79. Fiddes, *Tracks and Traces*, 169.

80. Fiddes, *Tracks and Traces*, 170.

81. Fiddes, *Tracks and Traces*, 174. Eucharist as identification of membership is rooted in understanding of relations of different dimensions of the body of Christ: incarnate, eucharistic, ecclesial and secular. Fiddes draws from social meaning of body (pp. 187–88) and connects this with the idea of relational dwelling of God with his people and our dwelling in God – participation or *perichoresis* (Fiddes, *Tracks and Traces*, 188–89).

82. Fiddes, *Tracks and Traces*, 191.

83. Baptist Union of Great Britain, *Nature of the Assembly*, 5; Fiddes, *Tracks and Traces*, 66–67, 128–29.

Christ makes his presence in the world visible in different forms: through a gathering together of members with gifts bestowed by Christ[84] or in the form of mission and councils.[85] This has implications for local communities associating in wider groupings which is "no more an optional alternative than belonging to Christ."[86]

7.2.2 Church Local, Universal and Wider Union

Fiddes distinguishes between *a church* (local), *the church* (universal) and *being church* (wider union).[87] Though distinct, all three concepts are interrelated and deeply rooted in his understanding of covenant, *koinonia* and the body of Christ: "The church as the community of the new covenant, the sign of God's triune fellowship and as the body of Christ has local, regional and universal form."[88]

7.2.2.1 Local church

Local church, "fellowship of believers" or "gathered church" is a body of believers bound by the covenant,[89] a community of "visible saints."[90] Baptist understanding of the church is based on Christ's promise "where two or three are gathered together in my name, there I am in the midst of them" (Matt 18:20).

Since such a community of believers is gathered around and by the risen Christ himself, it is therefore under his rule:

> Through covenant a local community is under the direct rule of Christ and so has been given the "seals of the covenant" – that is, the power to elect its own ministry, to celebrate the sacraments

---

84. Fiddes, *Tracks and Traces*, 67; cf. Fiddes, *Leading Question*, 20; Baptist Union of Great Britain, *Nature of the Assembly*, 5.
85. Fiddes, *Tracks and Traces*, 207–14.
86. Fiddes, *Tracks and Traces*, 200.
87. Baptist Union of Great Britain, *Nature of the Assembly*, 5; cf. Fiddes, "Daniel Turner," 113–14; Fiddes, "Christian Doctrine," 206.
88. Baptist Union of Great Britain, *Nature of the Assembly*, 5.
89. Baptist Union of Great Britain, *Nature of the Assembly*, 6.
90. Fiddes, "Church and Salvation," 133–34.

of baptism and the Lord's Supper, and to administer discipline (the authority to "bind and loose").[91]

This gives a local community freedom from any "external ecclesiastical authority"[92] and responsibility to find the mind of Christ.[93] Fiddes dissociates such understanding of freedom from the concept of autonomy based in the "freedom of the individual, or in the self-regulation of a voluntary society."[94]

Discussing the nature of leadership, Fiddes states that a local church has some limitation in electing ministers for pastoral oversight: "while the local church is competent by itself to appoint members to the office of *diakonia* (pastoral service), it is not competent alone to appoint members to the office of *episkope* (pastoral oversight) but only in fellowship with the wider Church."[95]

As a community of visible saints, local church is a primary visible expression of the universal body of Christ:

> Wherever two or three are gathered, wherever the body of the communion bread is broken (1 Cor 10:16–17), there is the body of Christ. But the local congregation is always a *"manifestation of the one Church of God on earth and in heaven"*; it derives from the one body. It [is] not then a question of many small bodies making up one large body, by a kind of spiritual arithmetic; the small bodies exist as an "outcropping" of the whole body. Separate churches already relate together because the body exists before us, and we are called to enter it.[96]

However, Fiddes points out that primacy of the local church in manifesting the universal church does not exclude imperfect "visibility" through associations, unions or assemblies of churches.[97] Out of this understanding it

---

91. Fiddes, *Tracks and Traces*, 44; Fiddes, "Church and Salvation," 128.
92. Fiddes, *Tracks and Traces*, 44; Fiddes, "Church and Salvation," 135.
93. Fiddes, *Tracks and Traces*, 52; cf. Fiddes, Haymes, and Kidd, *Baptists and the Communon of Saints*, 130–31.
94. Fiddes, *Tracks and Traces*, 44.
95. Fiddes, *Leading Question*, 33. Fiddes distinguishes pastoral service from pastoral oversight, where the latter is related to the universal church while the former to the local church.
96. Fiddes, *Tracks and Traces*, 198; Emphasis original. Cf. Baptist Union of Great Britain, *Nature of the Assembly*, 6.
97. Fiddes, "Church and Salvation," 135, 136, 137.

follows that "if a local church is under the direct rule of Christ as king then it is necessarily drawn into fellowship with all those who are under Christ's rule and so part of his body."[98] Thus, such fellowships are also under the rule of Christ and manifest the universal body of Christ.

7.2.2.2 Universal church[99]

Universal church for Fiddes comprises believers of all ages, both deceased and living.[100] He admits that historically Baptists believed in the invisible church on earth and in heaven, but this belief did not deny the visibility of the church in wider associations.[101] The invisible church comprised "the total company of all the redeemed, whether they were inside or outside the visible church, and whether they lived in the past, present or future."[102] This distinction stressed the mixed nature of visible church, recognised God's prerogative to enter salvific relations apart from human organisations and elevated the importance of local church as a manifestation of the universal church.[103]

This universal company of believers is not just a conglomerate of many local communities; it "*pre-exists* any local manifestation of it, as God's eternal covenant with humankind pre-exists the local covenant bond."[104] The universal church precedes local church and the latter derives its being from the former: "churches already relate together because the body exists before us, and we are called to enter it."[105] It means that local and universal church are in perichoretic relations with each other.[106]

Fiddes insists that the image of the body of Christ first of all describes the universal church, although local church is also referred to by this title.[107] The image presupposes visibility in this world: "this universal Church must be made visible (and not just remain an invisible, spiritual reality) since one

---

98. Fiddes, *Tracks and Traces*, 44.
99. For the universal church, see Fiddes, "Church and Salvation"; Fiddes, "Daniel Turner."
100. Fiddes, "Church's Ecumenical Calling," 46.
101. Fiddes, "Church's Ecumenical Calling," 46; Fiddes, "Church and Salvation," 133.
102. Fiddes, "Church and Salvation," 134.
103. Fiddes, "Church and Salvation," 135.
104. Fiddes, *Tracks and Traces*, 32, 198. Emphasis original.
105. Fiddes, "Church's Ecumenical Calling," 44.
106. Fiddes, "Learning from Others," 118.
107. Baptist Union of Great Britain, *Nature of the Assembly*, 5.

point of calling the Church the 'Body' of Christ is to express the reality that the Church makes Christ manifest in the world."[108] He admits that the universal church "was visible nowhere in its *completeness*"[109] and criticises Orthodox attempts to equate visibility and indivisibility, since this view overlooks the reality of the tragic visible fragmentation of the church. Fiddes asserts the Baptist view as "a mixture of realism about broken communion, and determination to overcome the scandal of division,"[110] and points to God's humility in accepting the divided church, calling this "a dimension of God's experience of the cross."[111] This brings us to the imperfect but realistic ways of making Christ visible via ACs.

7.2.2.3 Associations of churches

Fiddes's approach to the brokenness of the universal church includes admission of the fact of the scandal of division and the desire to overcome it. The church as covenant community that reflects life in the Trinity and is the body of Christ should be present on every level of society: local, regional, national and international.[112] This corresponds to the three forms of the church: local (*a church*), universal (*the church*) and regional (*being church*).[113] The last one presupposes local communities "being church . . . together in wider union."[114] On regional, national or international levels, "making Christ visible" can only be via the conciliar form of "fellowship of world communions."[115]

This requires rethinking the ecclesiological status of ACs. Historically, Baptists never called their associations "the Baptist Church"[116] but valued the interdependency of local churches. Though associations were established for seemingly pragmatic reasons,[117] these gatherings were thought of as ecclesial.[118]

---

108. Baptist Union of Great Britain, *Nature of the Assembly*, 5.
109. Fiddes, "Church and Salvation," 135. Emphasis original.
110. Fiddes, *Tracks and Traces*, 206, 247.
111. Fiddes, "Church and Salvation," 137.
112. Baptist Union of Great Britain, *Nature of the Assembly*, 10.
113. Baptist Union of Great Britain, *Nature of the Assembly*, 10.
114. Baptist Union of Great Britain, *Nature of the Assembly*, 10.
115. Fiddes, *Tracks and Traces*, 14.
116. Fiddes, *Tracks and Traces*, 15.
117. Baptist Union of Great Britain, *Nature of the Assembly*, 6–7.
118. Baptist Union of Great Britain, *Nature of the Assembly*, 6.

Concepts of covenant, *koinonia* and the body of Christ form a theological basis for union.[119] Thus, the idea of covenant presupposes God's calling of the people into loyal relations for the sake of his mission; as *koinonia* the church participates in the fellowship of the Triune God through Christ and witnesses to the world about these relations; and through the presence and ministry of the Holy Spirit, the church is the body of Christ making him visible in the world.[120]

Fiddes suggests that "a theology of covenant is helpful [for an understanding of ACs], since this holds together what Christ is doing in making himself present in the world through his body, and what his *members* do voluntarily in partnership together."[121] Elsewhere he suggests that "the covenant concept, when grounded *theologically*, is itself thoroughly open to the associating of churches together in the widest forms of cooperation."[122] Fiddes sees danger in the voluntary principle of associating:[123] "Associations and unions of churches are thus not merely task-oriented, but means of exploring the purpose of God in his world."[124] Covenant has both human and divine dimensions that roughly correspond to the concept of "the gathered church."[125] On the human side, members gather together voluntarily, but their gathering is always a response to Christ's action who gathers his church. This could be extended to the fellowship of local churches gathered by Christ.[126] Interpreting ACs through covenant allows a humble view of these structures, for they are always "imperfect signs of a universal church"[127] and a serious attitude towards covenant loyalty.[128] Fiddes admits that ACs have been reduced to pragmatic alliances that do not have ecclesial value and are task-oriented, pragmatic and temporary. He insists on viewing ACs as church unions that

---

119. Baptist Union of Great Britain, *Nature of the Assembly*, 5–6.
120. Baptist Union of Great Britain, *Nature of the Assembly*, 4–5.
121. Baptist Union of Great Britain, *Nature of the Assembly*, 9. Emphasis original.
122. Fiddes, *Tracks and Traces*, 44.
123. Fiddes, *Tracks and Traces*, 44.
124. Fiddes, *Tracks and Traces*, 45.
125. See Parushev, "Gathered, Gathering, Porous."
126. Baptist Union of Great Britain, *Nature of the Assembly*, 8.
127. Fiddes, *Tracks and Traces*, 14.
128. Baptist Union of Great Britain, *Nature of the Assembly*, 9.

presuppose more sustained relations.[129] This means they "have covenant responsibilities for making decisions and prophetic criticisms, for exercising oversight (*episkope*) and for sponsoring mission, no less than local bodies have them, although not in the same way."[130]

Fiddes differentiates between membership in the UK denominational structures and wider denominational and ecumenical groupings. While regional and national assemblies of churches could be called "covenant gatherings,"[131] worldwide bodies lack direct input from local churches. To be "ecclesial," they should meet the criteria for covenanting which are summarised as follows: (1) the involvement of local churches in appointing representatives to assemblies and making corporate decisions; (2) a commitment made by local churches to give weight to the decisions of the larger body; and (3) the involvement of local churches in recognising and appointing *episkope*.[132] "Wider groupings of churches"[133] can express visual unity through sharing God's spiritual gifts and resources in ecumenical mission as well as through conciliar forms of confessing one faith and sharing sacramental life.[134]

7.3 Practical Implications for Associations of Churches

These theological reflections have implications for the authority of ACs with regard to local churches and trans-local leadership through superintendents or regional ministers and mission. Paul Fiddes explicates these under a "theology of trust,"[135] the concept of pastoral oversight and covenant participation in the mission of Christ.

---

129. Fiddes et al., *On the Way*, 22–27.
130. Baptist Union of Great Britain, *Nature of the Assembly*, 10.
131. Baptist Union of Great Britain, *Nature of the Assembly*, 11.
132. Baptist Union of Great Britain, *Nature of the Assembly*, 13–14.
133. Fiddes, "Church and Salvation," 137.
134. Fiddes, *Tracks and Traces*, 207–14; 177–78.
135. Fiddes et al., *On the Way*.

7.3.1 Participation in Christ's Mission

Fiddes's idea of participation in the Trinitarian *koinonia* through Christ allows him to interpret mission theologically.[136] He argues that mission belongs to the being of the church because it belongs to the being of God.[137] Reflecting on mission in terms of participation, Fiddes asserts that by commissioning disciples in John 20:21, Jesus sends them to continue his mission in his way ("as the Father has sent me, so I send you").[138] Sending means that the church's mission is not the imitation of Christ but "*participation* in the Father's own sending forth of the Son."[139] This christological understanding of mission allows seeing it not as a task but as "rooted in the very being of the triune God" in which the church participates.[140] Since mission belongs to the being of God it also belongs to the being of the church.[141] Participation does not mean the church is in some way divine. Adam Glover convincingly demonstrates that participation means that something is "fundamentally dependent on – and derivative of – that in which it participates, and hence that it exists only 'by virtue of something other than itself'"[142] and "always implies both dependence and partiality."[143] In this sense, the mission of a local church is only a partial and dependent expression of the *missio Dei*.

Speaking of mission, Fiddes combines the language of participation with the language of covenant: the eternal generation of the Son is viewed as God's eternal decree to be "God again a second time" – the election of the person of Jesus of Nazareth, and all people with him, which Fiddes views as covenanting.[144] The covenant language presupposes that Christ is a mediator of the covenant who is present and active in his household as prophet,

---

136. Fiddes, *Tracks and Traces*, 249–73.

137. Fiddes, 249. Perhaps, the use of "being" rather than "nature" is intentional because the latter is static while the former is dynamic. This could be seen in his understanding of persons in Trinity as relations. See Fiddes, *Participating in God*, 35–46; Fiddes, "Participating in the Trinity," 379–83; cf. Haymes, "Trinity and Participation," 13.

138. Sharing "in being sent" with the Son, the church also has the characteristic of apostolicity, for apostles are those who were sent. Fiddes, *Tracks and Traces*, 249–52.

139. Fiddes, *Tracks and Traces*, 251. Emphasis original.

140. Fiddes, *Tracks and Traces*, 251.

141. Fiddes, *Tracks and Traces*, 252.

142. Glover, "Partakers of the Promise," 85.

143. Glover, "Partakers of the Promise," 87.

144. Fiddes, *Tracks and Traces*, 252–53.

priest and king.¹⁴⁵ Through his word he calls out and gathers people in the new community. He draws believers into covenant through new birth and incorporation into the body of Christ by virtue of Christ's sacrificial death on the cross. He empowers with spiritual gifts for the edification of the church, and rules in it to make his redeeming presence in the world possible:

> It is risen Christ, standing in the midst of the congregation in the authority of his threefold office, who gives his people the seals of the covenant, and so the right to celebrate the sacraments (as priests), to call some to ministry of the word (as prophets), and to exercise a mutual discipline among each other (sharing the kingly role of Christ).¹⁴⁶

Mission consists then in "making communion and community."¹⁴⁷ Those responding to the call through the apostolic message join in covenant community and God's own life and continue mission in a form of community.¹⁴⁸ Multiple local communities are bound together by mutual covenant commitment since they represent local manifestations of the body of Christ, drawn into it by God's initiative. These relations are significant for witnessing to God's sending of Christ, for finding the mind of Christ and for discovering what God's mission is by listening to all members of the universal body of Christ.¹⁴⁹

7.3.2 Theology of Trust

The concept of trust first appears in Fiddes's small book on the structure and authority of leadership in the local church.¹⁵⁰ Addressing these issues, he treats them in the light of the Bible, wider tradition and Baptist theological heritage,¹⁵¹ attempting "to explore the way that our convictions about leadership in the church ought to be founded upon our doctrine of God."¹⁵²

---

145. Fiddes, "Church and Salvation," 126–28.
146. Fiddes, "Church and Salvation," 128.
147. Fiddes, *Tracks and Traces*, 253.
148. Fiddes, *Tracks and Traces*, 253–54.
149. Fiddes, *Tracks and Traces*, 54–56.
150. Fiddes, *Leading Question*. For abridgement, see Fiddes, "Authority," 59–63.
151. Fiddes, *Leading Question*, 9.
152. Fiddes, *Leading Question*, 9.

God and his dealings with humanity becomes the model for constructing a theology of leadership. Fiddes turns to trust in the third part of the book.

Admitting that for Baptists the church meeting, seeking the mind of Christ, has final authority, Fiddes states that the local church needs to use reliable resources: the authority of spiritual leadership, prophecy, the wider church and Scripture.[153] Reliance on spiritual leadership and the wider church involves a level of trust. Whereas in the case of local church leadership this trust is built on the evidence of serving the congregation,[154] the authority of the wider church is set within the context of covenant relations. Christ's presence in the local body makes it competent to find and implement his mind. "Yet it is not all the Church; the localised Body is a manifestation of the Universal Body and cannot therefore exist in isolation from it, nor . . . can it always find the mind of Christ apart from it," states Fiddes.[155] Thus, local church does not possess all the wisdom of the universal body of Christ. The crucial fact is that the local church is connected to other Baptist churches by association through covenant which itself presupposes mutual trust among the churches.

The question remains how the local church should receive the authority of ACs and decisions made by ACs. Fiddes enlists three different views.[156] According to the first view, the local church is incompetent to find the mind of Christ but may recognise it in the decision of ACs which it must test and may approve. In the second view, the local church admits its incompetence and gives up the right to confirm or block the decisions of ACs, thereby surrendering to them. Paul Fiddes seems to gravitate towards the third view, according to which the local church might normally follow the decisions of ACs because of trust: "as a church might trust the conclusions of its own spiritual leaders (when they have won authority through serving), so a Church Meeting might *normally* follow the decisions of Association and Union Assemblies as a matter of mutual trust and without fierce debate."[157] That is, local church may veto decision of ACs only for a good reason.

---

153. Fiddes, *Leading Question*, 52.
154. Fiddes, *Leading Question*, 52.
155. Fiddes, *Leading Question*, 50; cf. 61.
156. Fiddes, *Leading Question*, 62–63.
157. Fiddes, *Leading Question*, 63. Emphasis original.

Later Fiddes and his colleagues further developed the theology of trust in a small book.[158] There the idea of trust is grounded in the relations God has with his creation, as well as within the Trinity. They read the Bible story from creation through the fall to redemption via the lens of trust. Describing God's relations with his people, they point to God's commitment in covenanting with them:

> The Bible word for this is "covenant." It is what flows naturally out of the heart of God. God takes initiative and, in the calling of a people, makes open commitment of himself to them. He will be their God. If he is jealous for them it is not to fulfil his desire for control but rather that of a lover who longs for the best. Covenant is an expression of grace. It is the way of renewal and freedom and its life blood is faithful trust.
>
> Such is the nature of God's trust that he makes space for the people to respond or not.[159]

God's trust was extended in the coming of Jesus Christ and the new covenant. Jesus as the second Adam trusted God to the very end on the cross.[160] For Fiddes, "the only true way of being church depends on our living in trust," and this trust towards God is based on the fact of Christ's resurrection.[161] Likewise, the early Baptist experience of covenanting is an expression of trust in response to God's calling and commitment to walk in trust with each other in the "gathered church." They could trust each other "because the members of the Christian community all acknowledge a claim upon them that is greater than their claim on each other."[162] Relations of trust presuppose mutual openness and resulting vulnerability.[163]

The idea of covenant and embedded trust helps in the theological understanding of the Baptist practice of associating. An association is a group of local churches "walking together and watching over each other."[164] Such cov-

---

158. Fiddes et al., *On the Way*, 12–13.
159. Fiddes et al., *On the Way*, 14.
160. Fiddes et al., *On the Way*, 14–15.
161. Fiddes et al., *On the Way*, 16.
162. Fiddes et al., *On the Way*, 19.
163. Fiddes et al., *On the Way*, 20.
164. Fiddes et al., *On the Way*, 21.

enant relations are expressed in the gathering of local church representatives to find the mind of Christ and in the willingness of local churches to listen to the association regarding church discipline issues.[165] The tension between the freedom of the local church to decide inner issues under the lordship of Christ and the authority of the association is resolved through appeal to Christ's presence in the association which presupposes the trust of local churches in the possibility that other members of the association could have deeper understandings of Christ's purpose: "A covenant is marked by deep bonds of mutual trust, in which partners are willing to find the mind of Christ together, to allow each other a local liberty, and freely to allow their local liberty to be bounded by the greater discovery of God's purpose."[166] Or as Fiddes says elsewhere: "Local churches have freedom because they exist directly 'under the rule of Christ,' but associations of churches together also stand under the same rule, setting up a tension between local assembly and association that can only be resolved by mutual trust, not hierarchical authority."[167]

Covenant relations in an association or union differ from strategic alliances in that the latter is task-oriented and pragmatic while the former is "'being' together in mutual commitment."[168] The word "union" is a proper expression of the covenant relations of churches for it refers to believers' union with Christ which is rooted in the eternal covenant within the Trinity. Thus,

> A union of churches in trust with each other is thus a reflection of the union of trust within the very being of God. Indeed, it depends upon the trust between the Father and the Son in the triune God. This is why Baptists in the last century who pressed for the forming of a "Baptist Union" frequently appealed to the prayer of Jesus to his Father in John 17, "... *that they may be one, as we are one*" (verse 11). Ideas of "covenant" and "Union" belong together.[169]

---

165. Fiddes et al., *On the Way*, 21–22.
166. Fiddes et al., *On the Way*, 26.
167. Fiddes, "Church Local and Universal," 104–5.
168. Fiddes et al., *On the Way*, 22.
169. Fiddes et al., *On the Way*, 23. Emphasis original.

7.3.3 Pastoral Oversight (*Episkope*) and Associations of Churches

Paul Fiddes develops his understanding of the ministry of oversight against the idea that ministry in general is "all that God seeks to do in, through and amongst his people."[170] The church only participates in the ministry and mission of the Triune God. Fiddes believes that pastoral care (*diakonia*) and pastoral oversight (*episkope*) may have corporate and individual forms.[171] That is, ministry belongs to the whole covenant community for all receive spiritual gifts and all covenanting members promise to be "watching over each other."[172] On the other hand, some are uniquely called to ministry and their calling is recognised by the whole community. This individual ministry of pastors and deacons "focuses" or "sums up" the ministry of the whole community.[173]

Fiddes adheres to the two-fold order where *diakonia* embraces pastoral work within the local church[174] and *episkope* represents ministry beyond the local church.[175] Fiddes points out that NT *episkopoi*, or elders, have certain responsibilities that make them ministers of the wider church: teaching the faith or supervising the teaching,[176] "guarding the tradition of faith, combining this with the role of the earlier teacher who inherited tradition"[177] and representing the wider church in the local church to help it discover a wider perspective on God's mission.[178] Standing in continuity with apostles means not only preserving the faith of the universal church but also challenging the church if needed:

> The *episkopos* is called to stand in the shoes of the apostles, in ensuring that the story of salvation is faithfully transmitted, in

---

170. Baptist Union of Great Britain, *Forms of Ministry*, 16. For other proposals on *episcope*, see Nicholson, "Towards a Theology" and "Towards a Theology (Continued)"; Reynolds, *First among Equals*; Peck, "Episkopé."

171. Fiddes, *Tracks and Traces*, 6, 87; see also Peck, "Episkopé."

172. Fiddes, *Tracks and Traces*, 221.

173. Fiddes, *Tracks and Traces*, 88.

174. Fiddes, *Leading Question*, 32.

175. Fiddes, 30–32; Baptist Union of Great Britain, *Forms of Ministry*, 23. For Baptist perspectives on the three-fold order, see Wright, *Challenge to Change*, 172–90; Wright, "Three-Fold Order"; Teraudkalns, "Episcopacy."

176. Fiddes, *Leading Question*, 30.

177. Fiddes, *Leading Question*, 31; cf. Fiddes, *Tracks and Traces*, 89.

178. Fiddes, "Church Local and Universal," 101.

new words for the new times, and this will at times mean standing over against the congregation with the Word of challenge. It is this ministry which enables the whole church to be "apostolic" in witnessing to the good news of Christ and the forgiveness of sins as the apostles did.[179]

From the scope of these two offices, it follows that candidates are set aside differently. Fiddes insists on the basic principle that "there is one kind of ministry set aside by the local community on its own, and one kind set aside in the bonds of covenant love with other churches."[180] A local church "is not competent alone to appoint members to the office of *episkope* (pastoral oversight) but only in fellowship with the wider Church."[181] In terms of practice, this is expressed in the ordination of pastors by pastors. Fiddes proposes that it does not signify the "receiving of an authority delegated from above downwards through hierarchy of officials" but "continuity with apostolic faith and the recognition of the call of Christ by the body of Christ which is manifest both in and beyond the local church."[182]

The notion of pastoral oversight with regard to ACs comes logically from Fiddes's concept of covenant: "the basic principle that emerges from our particular tradition within the Church of Christ is that *episkope* happens where there is fellowship or covenant."[183] It means that the *koinonia* of God's people precedes and establishes the foundation for the election and installation of ministers.[184] This applies both to local and wider levels. Since all offices fit within the two-fold order, ministry of oversight beyond the local church is an expansion of *episkope* over groups of churches (associations) or a union of churches.[185] Baptists sometimes call them "regional ministers," "superintendents" or "bishops."[186] Different levels of *episkope* do not presuppose a

---

179. Fiddes, *Tracks and Traces*, 104.
180. Fiddes, *Tracks and Traces*, 95.
181. Fiddes, *Leading Question*, 33; Fiddes, *Tracks and Traces*, 91; Fiddes, "Learning from Others," 67.
182. Fiddes, *Tracks and Traces*, 92.
183. Fiddes, *Leading Question*, 44; Baptist Union of Great Britain, *Nature of the Assembly*, 30.
184. Fiddes, *Tracks and Traces*, 222.
185. Fiddes, "Learning from Others," 65.
186. Fiddes, "Church Local and Universal," 101; cf. Reynolds, *First among Equals*, 57–61, 65–67; Teraudkalns, "Episcopacy," 282–83; Wright, "Three-Fold Order," 156. For the

hierarchical principle: "There is no gradation of importance and power, but only a difference in the area of *koinonia*."[187] This wider *episkope* is just "an extension of congregational episcope," where ministers only have "pastoral influence but no executive authority" in other local churches.[188] There are different forms of oversight on the inter-church level: personal (senior ministers), collegial (a team of regional ministers) or communal (the association of churches or general assembly).[189] According to Fiddes, all three forms can be found among Baptists. On the inter-church level, these ministers serve as spiritual advisers, mission leaders, mediators in cases of congregational conflicts and pastors for pastors.[190]

Though in Fiddes's view *episkopoi* are ministers of the wider church, he thinks that Baptists still may learn from other traditions regarding the role of a bishop in expressing and maintaining the unity and continuity of churches.[191] He affirms that apostolicity, understood as succession in the faith and life of the church as a whole and continuity in the orderly transmission of ordained ministry of the word, sacrament and oversight, does not cause any reservations from Baptists.[192] Fiddes disagrees with the idea of succession "as a *sign* of the church's apostolicity," especially if it is understood as a historic line.[193] However, he admits that there is value in seeing the ministers of oversight as a *sign* of apostolicity:

> They might see the meaningfulness of regarding the oversight of their own "regional ministers" as a symbol or sign of apostolic succession. These persons, for instance, *usually* preside over ordinations of ministers, as representing the whole union of churches. It is a way of expressing the fact that the "spiritual

---

study of messengers, see Nicholson, "Office of 'Messenger'"; for superintendents, see Watson, "General Superintendents."

187. Baptist Union of Great Britain, *Nature of the Assembly*, 31.
188. Fiddes, "Church Local and Universal," 101.
189. Fiddes, *Tracks and Traces*, 221–22; Fiddes, "Church's Ecumenical Calling," 57–59.
190. Fiddes, "Learning from Others," 65.
191. Fiddes, "Learning from Others," 66.
192. Fiddes, *Tracks and Traces*, 223; Emphasis original. Fiddes, "Church's Ecumenical Calling," 59. Fiddes's points of reference regarding apostolicity are *Together in Mission and Ministry* and the World Council of Churches' *Baptism, Eucharist and Ministry*.
193. Fiddes, "Learning from Others," 67; Fiddes, *Tracks and Traces*, 223–24; Fiddes, "Church's Ecumenical Calling," 59–60.

overseer" in the local congregation (bishop, pastor) is a representative on the local scene of the wider church, setting its mission in the context of the church in all times and places. While the local congregation is competent to call its own deacons, it has been the historic practice of Baptists for the call of someone to the ministry of word and sacrament to be recognised by a wider group of churches than any one local congregation alone. We might say that this call of Christ should be recognised by as large a segment of the church universal as is possible in the situation of a broken church, and practically this usually means the union or convention of Baptist churches in one country. . . . It would deepen the meaning of ordination for Baptists if the inter-church "overseer" were seen as the guardian of the tradition of the faith, linking the ministry of word and sacraments in the present with the ministry of the whole church in space and time.[194]

Elsewhere, Fiddes admits that the presence of a regional minister during ordination is understood as "a matter of good practice, rather than being essential"[195] and suggests that Baptists could strengthen this idea by simply switching from the participation of a regional minister to having the regional minister preside over the ordination.[196]

7.4 Significance for a Ukrainian Perspective on Associations of Churches

In this final section of the chapter, I shall summarise the results of the previous chapters and tentatively chart the direction in which Fiddes's concepts can be used. Three particular concepts from Fiddes's corpus seem potentially significant for enriching Ukrainian theology of ACs: those are the concepts of covenant, participation and trust. In the next chapter I shall try to demonstrate that these concepts are not totally foreign to Ukrainian Baptist tradition, though they are still inchoate and do not occupy its centre.

---

194. Fiddes, "Learning from Others," 67. Emphasis original.
195. Fiddes, *Tracks and Traces*, 224.
196. Fiddes, *Tracks and Traces*, 225.

7.4.1 Key Themes in Ukrainian Baptist Ecclesiology

In chapters 1–4, I attempted to excavate an understanding of ACs through historical-theological analysis of associational practices, organisational structure and theological representation of ACs in significant theological texts. In chapters 5–6, the historical data was complemented with the analysis of current documents and practices of AUUCECB and the results of semi-structured interviews with key Ukrainian Baptist leaders. Historical-theological analysis of the documents rendered several themes that are permanently present in, and manifest themselves through, the practices, organisational structure and theological representation of ACs utilised by Ukrainian Baptists. The presence of these themes in the theological inventory of Ukrainian Baptists was confirmed by the semi-structured interviews. These themes are (1) mission, (2) unity, (3) associating/fellowship and (4) the centrality of the local church. They are significant for defining Baptist identity as Ukrainian Baptists understand it.[197]

All four themes belong to the rubric of ecclesiology and are related, sometimes indirectly as in the case of the local church, to the practice of associating and the understanding of ACs. They are intertwined, although the local church slightly stands out of the range due to the overstressed emphasis on local church autonomy. If local church is understood as a voluntary society

---

197. The reiterative elements of tradition could be understood in terms of constants or convictions. Stephen B. Bevans and Roger P. Schroeder, analysing the mission of the church, speak of "constants in context." See Bevans and Schroeder, *Constants in Context*, 33–34. These "define Christianity in its missionary nature" (Bevans and Schroeder, 33). The authors build on Andrew F. Walls's concept of "essential continuity," which holds a historical Christian movement together and consists of "the ultimate significance" of the person of Jesus Christ, the use of the Bible by the church, the significance of two of the sacraments and consciousness of the bonds of succession between the church and Israel. See Walls, "Gospel as Prisoner," 6–7. Bevans and Schroeder summarise Walls's constants under the rubrics of "Christology" and "ecclesiology" and add four more: eschatology, salvation, anthropology and culture. See Bevans and Schroeder, *Constants in Context*, 34. These elements are changing when cultural peculiarities sometimes make contextual expressions of Christianity "unrecognizable to others, or indeed even to themselves, as manifestations of a single phenomenon" (Walls, "Gospel as Prisoner," 7). Thus, what is essential for the Christian movement could and does manifest itself in different forms, conditioned by the historical-cultural context and dominant theological tradition. James McClendon Jr. and James M. Smith describe constants through the language of convictions. See McClendon and Smith, *Convictions*, 4–13, 87–91. Conviction is "a persistent belief such that if X (a person or a community) has a conviction, it will not easily be relinquished and it cannot be relinquished without making X a significantly different person or (community) than before" (McClendon and Smith, *Convictions*, 5). Convictions represent and define the identity of a community or a person and apply not only to beliefs but also to affections and actions.

inspired by the modern concept of free association of individuals, it jeopardises Baptist ecclesiology, especially with regard to the interdependence of local churches or the unity of the universal church made visible through associations. Perhaps this could be reversed if Ukrainian Baptists returned to an understanding of local church as deeply rooted in the direct lordship of Christ.

These four themes are related to the biblical texts and images that play a significant role in reflections on ACs: John 17 and Ephesians 4. The former is an important ecumenical text that roots the unity of the church in the unity of the Son and the Father. The latter is a deeply theological text which points to unity but has, nevertheless, been used by Baptists to justify a confessional perspective of it. Two significant and constantly recurring biblical images applied to the AC are those of brotherhood and the body of Christ. Both are related to the idea of unity and have often been used to substantiate the concept of unity in the form of a union. Constant referral to these images prompts the conclusion that they express Ukrainian Baptist self-understanding as a confessional community and a part of the universal people of God.

Among the recurrent themes, three should be mentioned as potentially seminal for rethinking of the ecclesiological nature of ACs: *bratstvo* (brotherhood) as the fellowship/communion of churches; mission as belonging to the nature of the church and related to its unity; and trans-local ministers and their relation to unity.

7.4.2 Covenantal Language and the Practice of Covenanting

The image of *bratstvo* (brotherhood) concerns a wider fellowship/communion of churches. As was demonstrated above, *bratstvo* is a flexible concept: it can define a local community of believers, a regional group of communities, a national union or even a worldwide confessional group. It has been used for expressing the confessional identity of Ukrainian Baptist churches. However, based upon confession of faith and restricted by certain dogmatic boundaries, it has often been a means of exclusion rather than inclusion of others. Therefore, it should be enriched with other ecclesiological language that would help it to overcome a narrow confessional perspective. I suggest that Fiddes's concept of the covenant can be fruitfully merged with the concept of *bratstvo* in the process of rethinking the ecclesiological nature of ACs.

The concept of covenant and covenant ecclesiology is very important and seminal for understanding the ecclesiological nature of ACs. Negatively, it may challenge modes of unity and mission based on pragmatic grounds when unity or mission is just a matter of expediency, needed for the accumulation of resources or the establishment of task-oriented alliances. In such cases unity could easily be dropped off at any time because it is secondary and totally dependent on the volition of separate congregations. Positively, covenant ecclesiology roots both unity and mission in the life of the Trinity providing an ontological basis for communion on the local level and beyond the local level. Moreover, the concept of covenant is flexible and could be used together with the image of *bratstvo*. An attempt at joining these together will be undertaken in the next chapter.

7.4.3 Participation in the Trinity

Fiddes's concept of covenant is tightly connected to the notion of participation in the life of the Trinity. That means that in the process of covenanting, believers not only form a church fellowship (horizontal dimension) but also participate in the Trinitarian *koinonia* (vertical dimension).[198] This move allows Fiddes to start his ecclesiological constructive work with God.[199] In this sense the divine *koinonia* creates ecclesial *koinonia* which in its turn expresses itself in the local congregations and wider ecclesial bodies.[200] On the other hand, local church as the *koinonia* of believers participates in the *koinonia* of divine persons who freely give and receive love.[201] Trinitarian *koinonia* precedes the existence of local fellowship.[202] Moreover, according to Fiddes, God does not limit this fellowship with the church but intends to bring the whole universe into covenant relations, and the church is the witness and the foretaste to this *koinonia*.[203] Even though Russian and Ukrainian

---

198. Fiddes, *Tracks and Traces*, 79; Fiddes, Haymes, and Kidd, *Baptists*, 129–30.
199. Fiddes, "Conversation in Context," 9.
200. Baptist Union of Great Britain, *Nature of the Assembly*, 9.
201. Fiddes, *Tracks and Traces*, 214. Compare this to Anan'in's concept of inner unity as belonging to the one Spirit and being baptised in the Spirit in love (Anan'in, "Ob'edinenie Obshchin Baptistov," 13.
202. Fiddes, "Church's Ecumenical Calling," 53–54.
203. Fiddes, "Church's Ecumenical Calling," 53.

Baptists understood the church to be the result of God's actions,[204] grounding local fellowship in the divine *koinonia* could point to the principal unity and openness of such fellowship.

Participation of a local community in a wider reality that takes its beginning in the Trinity means that "covenant always resists autonomy, not only of single members within the local covenanted congregation, but also of separate congregations joined together in association."[205] Therefore, belonging to a wider fellowship cannot be an option that could or could not be chosen, but a duty which should be done.[206] Unity rooted in the life of the Trinity should be expressed visibly and practically through associating.[207] His understanding of local church as a manifestation of the body of Christ, as *koinonia* and as covenant community has implications for understanding unity and the ecumenical task of the church.[208] The image of "the body of Christ" presupposes visibility since "the members join to make the whole body visible, that is to allow *Christ* to manifest himself in the world, to make himself knowable and tangible through all his members."[209] In the body of Christ, Jews and Gentiles are reconciled,[210] therefore, unity is a fundamental mark of the church as the body of Christ that relates both to the universal and local church.[211] Thus, Fiddes states that Christ should be made visible at every level of human society,[212] and associations, unions and ecumenical bodies are instruments of the unity of the church, though imperfect ones. This aspect of Fiddes's thought would help to overcome the traditional Ukrainian tendency to see participation in the association and union of churches as optional and nonessential. "Walking together in all his ways made known, or to be made known" presupposes that churches united by covenant and mutual trust are on the way towards "fuller *koinonia*."[213] Since they are still

---

204. Pyzh, "Confessing Community," 103–7.
205. Fiddes, Haymes, and Kidd, *Baptists and the Community of Saints*, 130.
206. Fiddes, *Tracks and Traces*, 200.
207. Fiddes, *Tracks and Traces*, 215.
208. Fiddes, *Tracks and Traces*, 66–82, 197–227.
209. Fiddes, *Tracks and Traces*, 67. Emphasis original.
210. Fiddes, *Tracks and Traces*, 68; cf. Mazaev, "O Edinstve," 9.
211. Fiddes, *Tracks and Traces*, 197–98; cf. Fiddes, "Church's Ecumenical Calling," 43–49.
212. Fiddes, *Tracks and Traces*, 200.
213. Fiddes, *Tracks and Traces*, 21, 194–96.

on the way towards the vision of one eschatological gathering of saints, this goal requires all the effort for the sake of overcoming obstacles inhibiting a fuller communion of churches and expression of unity in Christ. Humility and realism are needed when associations and unions of churches are viewed as expressions of one fellowship in Christ.[214]

Ukrainian Baptists believed that mission belongs to the nature of the church and is intimately related to its unity. Unfortunately, unity for the sake of mission was often interpreted pragmatically as desirable, even important, but not essential. That is, churches unite to accumulate resources for the accomplishment of the task set in front of them. If something is inessential, it could be abandoned without significant losses for the church. This pragmatic understanding is contrary to the consensus that unity is one of the *notae* of the church and a recent consensus that mission belongs to the nature of the church.[215] Some local authors put the mission of the church in the wider context of God's redemptive story.[216] These thoughts coupled with Fiddes's concept of participation in the Trinitarian *koinonia* through Christ also allows for interpreting mission theologically. If Vasilii Ivanov was right, and the calling and status of Christians is related through Christ to God's cosmic plan,[217] then this idea resonates with Fiddes's opinion that Christ's commissioning of the disciples in John 20:21 makes them the continuation of his mission in his way.[218] Through Christ, the church participates "in the Father's own sending forth of the Son."[219] Thus, the church only participates in the mission of the Triune God and does not have its own independent mission. This would point to the significance of mission formed in Jesus's way: "as the Father has sent me, so I send you" (John 21:20).

---

214. Fiddes, *Tracks and Traces*, 14.

215. Küng, *Die Kirche*, 313–52; World Council of Churches and Commission on Faith and Order, *Church*, 5–8; Gaillardetz, *Ecclesiology*, 35–131.

216. See sections 2.4.4 and 3.4.3.

217. Ivanov, "Proekt Reorganizatsii."

218. Sharing "in being sent" with the Son, the church also has the characteristic of apostolicity, for apostles are those who were sent. Fiddes, *Tracks and Traces*, 249–52.

219. Fiddes, *Tracks and Traces*, 251.

7.4.4 Trustful Relations

Trans-local ministers emerged when wider church fellowships were being formed. They were considered as ministers of the universal church, although this understanding somewhat fluctuated due to changing external socio-political factors, such as the government's attitude towards religious organisations, and the inner dynamics of the growth and expansion of the union.[220] The presence of senior presbyters at the occasions of the elections and ordinations of local ministers, as well as their work for regional associations and the national union, is understood pragmatically as good practice but could be interpreted theologically as a representation of the universal church at the local level. A theology of trust is helpful for understanding the relations of local churches in associations and unions of churches, the status and role of trans-local ministers and the authority of associations with regard to local churches.

Both concepts – covenant and participation in the life of the Trinity – have intimate relation to the notion of trust.[221] Trust stems from the nature of God who does not coerce but invites. God expresses his trust in the human covenant partners by offering them the opportunity to enter into relations with him. Such relations presuppose vulnerability and openness to pain on the part of God.[222] The same trust and mutual openness to pain should characterise covenant relations in relation to a local community or associations of churches.

Local churches do not have all the resources to know the mind of Christ, therefore, they should have fellowship with other churches in order to listen to a fuller expression of Christ's voice. Within such a framework, a more serious attitude towards covenant loyalty should be emphasised.[223] Since church unions are not pragmatic alliances but ecclesial bodies, such fellowship, then, presupposes sustained relations[224] and "covenant responsibilities for mak-

---

220. Thus, from evangelists and teachers in 1880–1904 (section 2.3.2) to senior presbyters with wider functions in 1905–1935 (section 3.3.2) to denominational functionaries in 1944–1990 (section 4.2.2).

221. Fiddes et al., *On the Way*, 12–27. See also section 7.3.2.

222. Fiddes, "Cross of Hosea Revisited"; Fiddes, "Creation Out of Love"; Fiddes, *Tracks and Traces*, 57–61; Fiddes, "Covenant and Participation," 120–24.

223. Baptist Union of Great Britain, *Nature of the Assembly*, 9.

224. Fiddes et al., *On the Way*, 22–27.

ing decisions and prophetic criticisms, for exercising oversight (*episkope*) and for sponsoring mission, no less than local bodies have them, although not in the same way."[225] The question remains how this theological vision of covenant fellowship could be expressed organisationally. Fiddes suggests extending church meetings as the instrument of searching for the mind of Christ analogically to the associational and general assemblies or councils.[226]

7.5 Summary

This chapter explores Paul S. Fiddes's concept of covenant ecclesiology with the view of using some of its elements for a constructive dialogue with the Ukrainian Baptist understanding of ACs. In particular, Fiddes's concept of covenant could challenge pragmatic models of unity and ground unity and associational life in the life of the Trinity, giving an ontological basis for communion on various levels. Covenant as participation in the life of the Trinity helps to critique the widespread concept of local church autonomy and the optionality of belonging to associations and/or unions of churches. At the same time, it provides a more realistic view of wider associations as provisional on the way towards fuller *koinonia* in the eschaton. Coupled with the language of participation, the image of the church as the body of Christ emphasises the necessity of the visibility of the church's unity, albeit in the partial and imperfect forms of church unions. Finally, covenant presupposes relations of trust and vulnerability not only for human partners with each other but also for God as he opens himself to vulnerable and painful relations. The concept of trust is also important for understanding the relations of churches beyond a local level and for the recognition of the authority of local and trans-local ministers, as well as the decisions made by ACs. In the next chapter I shall tentatively demonstrate how Ukrainian understanding of ACs could be improved through a constructive dialogue with these important elements of wider tradition.

---

225. Baptist Union of Great Britain, *Nature of the Assembly*, 10.
226. Baptist Union of Great Britain, *Nature of the Assembly*, 10–11.

CHAPTER 8

Gathering Puzzles for a Theology of Associations of Churches

8.1 Introduction

In the previous chapters I attempted to reconstruct the understanding of ACs among Baptists in the Russian Empire and USSR (chapters 1–4) and map current understanding of ACs in AUUCECB (chapters 5–6). The historical-theological and qualitative analysis enabled the highlighting of recurring themes related to understandings of the ecclesiological nature of ACs and demonstrated the need to reconsider the understanding of ACs to meet the needs of the context and be resonant with wider tradition. In chapter 7, I introduced the covenant ecclesiology of Paul Fiddes and briefly pointed to the points of contact between covenant ecclesiology and local Baptist tradition. In this chapter, I attempt to bring together Ukrainian understanding of ACs and covenant ecclesiology. First, I will focus on three cases of covenanting that could be touchpoints for local tradition's understanding of ACs and covenant ecclesiology. Then I turn to the local church, since for Baptists this is the strongest ecclesial reality that impacts their understanding of ACs.[1] I will approach local church as an intentional and covenantal community which is free under the rule of Christ but is not autonomous from other churches. Finally, I will proceed to association, rethinking it through elements of covenant ecclesiology, particularly focussing on *bratstvo* as a covenant communion of

---

1. Jones, *European Baptist Federation*, 26–27.

churches that visualise unity in forms of associations and unions, commit to mutual care and participate in Christ's mission.

8.2 Cases of Covenanting

In this section, I turn to the practice of covenanting among Baptists in the Russian Empire and the USSR. I will refer to three cases: the visiting ministers' formal constitution of Tiflis Baptist Church (1879); the pledging of the Luchina community and the Kyiv *guberniia* (province) in response to the invitation to join missionary cause (1883); and the renewal of covenant by Kyiv Autonomous Baptist Church in the context of resistance to the atheistic government (1963). These cases point to influential currents that shaped local Baptist tradition: Tiflis was one of the early Baptist centres in the Russian Empire, which is evident in the correspondence between Ukrainian believers and their fellow-believers in Tiflis and in the decisive voice of Transcaucasian Baptists during the first annual assemblies; German Baptists and Mennonite Brethren influenced the initial stages of the Baptist movement in the Russian Empire and the formation of the "missionary brotherhood"; Kyiv Autonomous Baptist Church was exemplary in bridging AUCECB and CCECB in the 1970s. On the other hand, these cases are snapshots of the ecclesial practices to which Baptist churches turned at significant moments in their lives. As James McClendon demonstrates, the practices of communities of faith reflect the convictions that shape these communities.[2] Therefore, these cases can be sources for understanding their ecclesiological convictions. Finally, these cases show that the language of covenanting was known to local Baptist tradition. It was not well developed and widely practiced, but it was there.

8.2.1 Joining to Constitute a Local Church: A Case of Tiflis Baptist Church

The constitution of Tiflis Baptist Church was partially prompted by a desire to obtain the legal status that was granted to German Baptist communities by the Makovskii Circular.[3] Two German Baptist ministers came to properly constitute Tiflis Baptist Church and ordain its ministers. The event comprised

---

2. McClendon and Smith, *Convictions*, 4–13, 87–91.
3. See section 2.2.1.

one day: constitution of the church occurred at the morning service, and the ministers were ordained at the evening service.[4] The event was described in the protocols of Tiflis Baptist Church.[5] This is the earliest known description of constituting a local church in the Russian Empire.

The protocol provides the gist of the exchange of questions from August Liebig and Johann Kargel and answers from the community. The document describes typical elements of Baptist covenanting.[6] First, the congregants agreed to constitute themselves into community (par. 7).[7] By doing that, they realised that the emergence of their community was God's act, and they were only responding to that (par. 6). It is important to note that they expressed their intention to be constituted into a community of faith to follow the way of salvation and spread the gospel. Second, they acknowledged Christ as their only head (par. 8).[8] This is a very significant element because Christ is the head and foundation of the church. The community emerges by responding to the word of Christ who calls it out of the world and makes it a company of God's people walking in his ways. Third, the community agreed to affirm elected ministers (par. 9) because this meant that the community could function as a normal congregation.[9] Fourth, they agreed to take responsibility for each other by "watching over and admonishing each other."[10] This communal oversight cannot be substituted by the oversight performed by ordained ministers because it represents the very essence of being a community of faith. Finally, the external ministers in this process

---

4. Aleksii Ia. (Dorodnitsyn), *Materialy*, 637.

5. For English text see appendix 4.

6. Consult Keach, *Glory*; cf. Hiscox, *Baptist Directory*, 17; Pendleton, *Church Manual*, 15–17. See also Hiscox, *New Directory*, 52–56. The typical elements: (1) resolution to constitute the church, (2) adoption of covenant and statement of faith, (3) selection of a name for the church and (4) proposal to join the union of churches.

7. See Keach, *Glory*, 5–6. On the importance of formal declaration and adoption of a written covenant by raising the right hand, see Hiscox, *New Directory*, 54.

8. Keach, *Glory*, 6, 54–55.

9. Keach, *Glory*, 8.

10. Aleksii Ia. (Dorodnitsyn), *Materialy*, 640; cf. Keach, *Glory*, 72–73.

should assure the church was established according to God's word[11] and invite it to a wider body.[12]

I suggest that the constitution of Tiflis Baptist Church, as it is described in the protocol, approximates typical descriptions of covenanting. Since Tiflis Baptist Church tried to set a standard for other sister churches,[13] the constitution of Tiflis Baptist Church might serve as an example of the proper way of doing this. It also provides a touchpoint for dialoguing with British Baptists who have a deeper tradition of covenanting.

8.2.2 Pledging for the Sake of Mission: A Case of Luchina Church

The event in the village of Luchina is set within the context of the establishment of "missionary brotherhood" in the Kherson *gubernia*, chaired by "a German pastor," that aimed at "converting the whole Russia with German hymnal and the New Testament."[14] The only missionary brotherhood in the Kherson *gubernia* at this time was that of the Mennonite Brethren, chaired by Johann Wieler. As the protocols of the annual meeting in Rückenau (1882) evidence, some Ukrainians joined the brotherhood and were present there.[15] The Luchina community was invited to join the cause.

The text that contains a description of covenanting reproduces a letter to the diocese magazine where the observer, peasant Ivan Savchenkov, described events that had preceded the series of motivational gatherings aimed at sending a group of church members to Siberia as missionaries, gave a gist of the sermon preached by the local minister, Levko Liber, during one of

---

11. For Pendleton, this is optional. See Pendleton, *Church Manual*, 17. Hiscox calls this "a prudential measure, very proper and well to be continued as a guard against irregularities in doctrine or practice . . . but it is in no sense essential" (Hiscox, *New Directory*, 56). Reading the resolution aloud "makes such a company of disciples, *ipso facto*, a Church of Christ with all the rights, powers, and privileges of any New Testament Church" (Hiscox, *New Directory*, 54). This puts the event within a human horizon.

12. See section 2.2.1.

13. See section 1.3.

14. Savchenkov, "Snariazhenie Shtundistskikh Missionerov," 316. On the Luchina community, see Savchenkov, "Shtundisty s. Luchina." The text, describing the event in Luchina, calls it "Stundist," and the text of the solemn pledge uses the word "Anabaptist," but it would probably not be wrong if we read this as "Baptist."

15. See references in section 2.2.2.

the services, and included the solemn pledge.[16] Besides that, Savchenkov referred to a family conflict experienced by one newly converted peasant, Barklom Didenko. I will only focus on some aspects of the sermon and the text of the "formal pledge."

The sermon drew a parallel between Abraham's obedience to the divine call and the response of the community to go to Siberia.[17] Abraham's story saturated the sermon and gave theological rationale to the Siberian mission, representing it as a response of faith to God's call. As Abraham was approved by being called "God's friend," the response of faith to God's word made these believers "*a brotherhood of God's people.*"[18] As a result of the preaching, one previously secret believer, Barklom Didenko, made a public commitment to live the life of a disciple.[19] This act inspired the community "to pledge faithfulness to Stundist mission."[20] The minister and those who committed to go read "a formal pledge":

> In the name of the Lord God, Amen. We the undersigned, spiritual sons of Christ's faith, undertook for the glory of the Most High and for the benefit of Christ's faith, in the honour and glory of the Lord's name, a journey to Eastern Siberia with the purpose to preach Christ's faith according to the dogmas and teaching of Christians of the Anabaptist confession and to establish *first Stundist colony* there, commit and promise in front of each other in the glory of the Lord's name, united into the brotherly community of God's friends, at no price separate and leave the community, and we pledge to serve the interest of our brotherhood till death. In authentication of this we give our brotherly word and vow before the Lord. Amen.[21]

---

16. For the English text, see appendix 5.
17. Savchenkov, "Snariazhenie Shtundistskikh Missionerov," 316–17. Compare this to the hermeneutical rule formulated by McClendon: "the church now is the primitive church and the church on judgement day" (McClendon, *Ethics*, 30).
18. Savchenkov, "Snariazhenie Shtundistskikh Missionerov," 316. Emphasis original.
19. Savchenkov, "Snariazhenie Shtundistskikh Missionerov," 317.
20. Savchenkov, "Snariazhenie Shtundistskikh Missionerov," 317.
21. Savchenkov, "Snariazhenie Shtundistskikh Missionerov," 317. Emphasis original.

The process of solemn pledging was accompanied with kneeling and ritual kissing.[22] There is no additional information on whether this Siberian mission was accomplished.

First of all, it suffices for our purposes to register the familiarity of Ukrainian believers with the practice of covenanting and that the act of pledging contains some formal elements such as reading a pledge previously written or printed on a sheet of paper.[23] The description of the event significantly differs from the description of the constituting of Tiflis church, but, nevertheless, contains traces of covenantal language and mindsets. Second, this community identified itself as "a brotherhood of God's people," that is, those who obtained such status by responding in faith to God's word and uniting together. This indicates that God initiated their response through his word. Third, they were united by their allegiance to Christ and desire to pursue one goal: "to preach Christ's faith" for the sake of God's glory. This is an expression of certain intent by those who covenanted. Finally, the members made a lifetime commitment to be in "the brotherly community of God's friends." It is also significant that they pledged faithfulness to each other for the sake of shared aims as the ultimate reason of their actions. The document provides a unique description of mutual commitment of members of a local community done in the context of missionary involvement.

8.2.3 Renewing the Covenant: A Case of Kyiv Autonomous Baptist Church

In the 1960s, some evangelical communities opposed the state control and imposition of regulations that restricted the religious activities of churches. A group of believers in Kyiv formed an unregistered community that gathered regularly in semi-underground fashion in 1961–1963. During this period, the community had no fixed membership: anyone could participate in their forest gatherings around Kyiv. Soon, the leadership realised that for normal operation the group should establish church discipline which presupposes membership.[24] They decided to do this through covenanting, which occurred

---

22. Savchenkov, "Snariazhenie Shtundistskikh Missionerov," 317.
23. Savchenkov, "Snariazhenie Shtundistskikh Missionerov," 317.
24. Velichko, *Uzok Put'*.

on 13 August 1963.²⁵ The leadership reasoned that by "this everyone who joins the membership of the church also imposes on himself responsibility – to keep in their further life required rules of discipline accepted in this church and also share in all the church's burdens of ministry and its lot of sufferings for the name of the Lord Jesus Christ."²⁶

The group disassociated from the AUCECB statutes, which were heavily influenced by the Soviet legislation on religious associations.²⁷ They developed an alternative document "The Church Covenant of Kyiv Autonomous Church of ECB" based on their core beliefs and values.²⁸ The text had the status of "inner church statute," though it did not represent comprehensively the church's ministry but only "reflected principal moments of the actual life of the church under the conditions of the state persecutions."²⁹

The covenant contained the following key principles: the church is a voluntary confessing community; Jesus Christ is the head of the church, the Holy Spirit is the guide and the Holy Scripture is the basis of doctrines; sanctification and evangelism are the key tasks of the church; believers relate to each other with brotherly love, charity, patience, self-sacrifice, mutual support and responsibility; and only the church has the right to elect ministers. The covenant also outlined the following practices: openness to fellowship with churches according to Christ's teaching; obedience to the state only in public matters; and matters of church discipline, church registration and the election of ministers – the inner affairs of the church.³⁰ It is obvious that these principles emphasise what was omitted in the AUCECB statutes as a result of state pressure on its leadership.

---

25. The event occurred in the forest near the Ialynka train platform on the Brovary train line, Kyiv region. See Velichko, *Uzok Put'* 61.

26. Velichko, *Uzok Put'* 60.

27. See chapter 4.

28. There are two versions of the document. The first "Proekt Tserkovnogo Zaveta" (A draft of church covenant) is more generic and lacks specifics attaching it to a particular community. It is reproduced by Velichko and CCECB. See Velichko, *Uzok Put'*, 62–65; cf. *Mezhdunarodnyi Soiuz Tserkvei*, 74–77. The second is "Tserkovnyi Zavet" [Church Covenant], which is the actual covenant of Kyiv Autonomous Baptist Church and has a stricter structure, refined content and a handwritten comment: "Received from Kovalenko L. E. on 9 November 1964." I will refer to "Proekt Tsekrovnogo Ustava" as it is published in *Istoriia Evangel'skogo Dvizheniia* 4.0. For the English text, see appendix 6.

29. Velichko, *Uzok Put'*, 61.

30. "Proekt Tserkovnogo Zaveta," 1–3.

It is important to note that in addition to the basic principles, the covenant contained a solemn pledge that clearly follows the biblical tradition of covenant renewal. The text of the pledge reads:

> Therefore, renewing the covenant with the Lord and each other, we:
>
> Trusting not ourselves but the Lord, will put all efforts not to avert from the truth and not commit wilful sin but always go the way of sanctification;
>
> Trusting the Lord, we will seek to entrust all our life without remains in His total disposal, fully relying on His guidance and following Him wherever He leads: to sufferings, persecutions, prison, exile – accepting with joy vilification for Christ's name, defamation, dishonour, despoilment of belongings. . . . Rom 12:1;
>
> Trusting the Lord, we will do our best to love every brother and sister as ourselves and not keeping towards them grievance, egotism, envy, anger, irritation; love Christ's brotherhood, His beloved Church, to be able to "lay your soul for your brothers" and following the example of Macedonian churches participate in the ministry of the church by deed and truth. . . . John 15:12; 2 Cor 8:5;
>
> Trusting the Lord, we will be striving to commit our life to the witness of God's love by personal example and preaching the Christ as the Saviour of sinners. . . . Matt 10:32–33; Rom 1:16; Josh 24:15; 1 John 2:28.[31]

The text, and especially its use of Scripture, echoes biblical tradition for the renewal of covenants.[32] This makes it a unique case in local Baptist tradition.

The document contains some specific elements. First, the church is re-constituted on the basis of covenant. In a way this resembles English Separatists' attempts to re-constitute the church through covenanting in the

---

31. "Proekt Tserkovnogo Zaveta," 4–5. Scripture texts omitted in this paragraph.

32. In epigraph: Eph 4:5; Josh. 24:12, 15, 16, 24; Neh. 9:38, 10:29; Matt. 16:24; in concluding section: Matt. 10:32–33: Rom. 1:16; Josh. 24:15; 1 John 2:28; see "Proekt Tserkovnogo Zaveta," 1, 5.

context of the incomplete reformation of the Anglican Communion.[33] In the case of Kyiv Autonomous Baptist Church, re-constitution or renewal of the covenant occurred against the background of the alleged compromise of AUCECB's leadership with the atheistic government. The preamble points to "mass deviation in our brotherhood from the teaching of our Lord Jesus Christ" as the rationale "to renew the covenant with the Lord and each other."[34] Second, the text uses a covenant formula[35] that refers to the vertical (with God) and horizontal (with each other) dimensions of this act. Third, unlike the Tiflis church, which was constituted in relations with a wider body of believers, Kyiv Autonomous Baptist Church places local church autonomy as the cornerstone. Relations with other churches are possible only if they "support the Truth and are likeminded with us according with the teaching of Jesus Christ."[36] This certainly points to the excluding and protectionist mood of this covenant. Finally, this document represents the only known intentional case of covenanting that closely resembles both biblical tradition and the English Baptist practice of covenanting. The fact that this covenant was included in the programmatic documents of CCECB and the churches affiliated with the autonomous movement points to the significance and/or attractiveness of the practice of covenanting for these churches.

All three cases of covenanting not only throw light on the ecclesial practices of these communities but also provide significant insights into the ecclesiological convictions they held. These insights will inform further attempts to rethink local church and association of churches in dialogue with Paul Fiddes.

8.3 Rethinking Local Church

The cases of covenanting indicate that local church occupies the most significant position in Baptist ecclesiology.[37] This has a significant influence

---

33. See Fiddes, "Covenant and Inheritance," 72–74.
34. "Proekt Tserkovnogo Zaveta," 1.
35. "Proekt Tserkovnogo Zaveta," 1, 5. For a close analysis of covenant formulas in different Bible contexts, see Rendtorff, *Covenant Formula*; cf. McCarthy, *Old Testament Covenant*, 10–34.
36. "Proekt Tserkovnogo Zaveta," 3.
37. See Val'kevich, *Zapiska*, Appendix 3, 2; Pavlov, "Pravda o Baptistakh," no. 46, 361; Baptist [pseudo], "Nashy Nuzhdy"; Baptist [pseudo], "Nashy Nuzhdy (prodolzhenie)"; Ivanov, "Telo Khristovo"; Vins, *Nashi Baptistskie Printsipy*, 20; Odintsov, "O Tserkvi," 4; Mitskevich, "Tserkov, Sviashchennosluzhiteli i Chleny Tserkvi," 30; Mitskevich, "Osnovnye Printsipy," 48–49;

both on theological reflections and local Baptist spirituality.[38] Due to the persecutions of the dominant Orthodox Church and the Soviet government's attempts to control churches through centralised organization, Ukrainian Baptists shifted in their thought and practice towards a stronger emphasis on local church autonomy. The language of autonomy they used significantly influenced their understanding of the ecclesiological nature of ACs. At the same time, their views and practices point to an ecclesial understanding of ACs. In what follows, I shall attempt to demonstrate how the current perspective changes if local church is thought of as intentional covenant community under the lordship of Christ.

8.3.1 Intentional Community

Paul Fiddes insists that covenant communities are intentional and gathered. They are intentional in that members "find their identity and give mutual support in working towards a common goal."[39] Referring to Husserl, he points out that intentionality presupposes a shared memory, which helps to bild corporate identity around shared experience and aim, which are both linked to this memory. Members also perceive each other as participants in this shared experience and aim. This is called "inter-subjectivity of intention" or "co-intention."[40] It is possible to see intentional communities as those that commit to something greater than themselves (shared memory, experience and aim) and to each other (co-intention). However, this intention never comes from communities themselves. Fiddes claims that they are also gathered: first, God himself gathers them through his word; and second, the members agree to gather in a community to follow the Lord.[41]

We can use the language of intentionality to read Ukrainian Baptist ecclesiology. The three cases, mentioned above, are vivid examples of intentional and gathered communities. These communities of faith had shared experience

---

Shatrov, "Tserkov' Khrista"; Dukhonchenko, "Dukhovno-Vospitatel'naia Rabota Sluzhitelei," 54; Pyzh, "Confessing Community."

38. Pyzh, "Confessing Community," 101–54.

39. Fiddes, *Tracks and Traces*, 76–77. See also Keith Jones on intentionality as "commitment to a shared journey of discipleship on the way" (Jones, "Towards a Model," 8n18).

40. Fiddes, *Tracks and Traces*, 77.

41. Fiddes, "Covenant and Inheritance," 69–72; Fiddes, Haymes, and Kidd, *Baptists*, 133–34; Fiddes, *Tracks and Traces*, 42–45, 77–78.

of being saved by Christ and introduced into his new reality, the kingdom of God, which is both already here and not fully yet. The event of constituting (Tiflis) or renewing of covenant (Kyiv) marked the moment after which these communities considered themselves fully established local churches. Even though these gatherings functioned for some time as communities, they were only recognised as such after the acts of intentionality happened.[42]

Such expressions of intentionality could be sometimes understood as mere human efforts to organise into a body of believers – sheer voluntarism. However, the decision to be constituted into church community does not mean that these communities were voluntary societies made of individuals upon own their decision.[43] As is clear in the protocol of constituting Tiflis Baptist Church, the members of the church understood the act of constituting as God's act and their response to it.[44] In this regard, God preceded all human intentions and decisions. The intention of the congregants was a response to the preceding act of God's grace when he spoke forth his word of grace through his Son and drew people into fellowship with him through the work of the Holy Spirit.

Other early documents disclose that Baptist communities in the Russian Empire thought of their communities as tied by mutual obligations. Ukrainian Baptists held to the concept of a visible church which was not strictly distinguished from universal church.[45] They believed it consisted of believers, converted and gathered by the Holy Spirit through God's word. Believers joined the church through baptism, entering close fellowship with Christ and

---

42. This is significant with the view of ecclesiological reductionism when any gathering of Christians is labelled as church on the foundation of Christ's presence. See Colwell, "Integrity and Relatedness," 13.

43. Fiddes, *Tracks and Traces*, 40–45; Fiddes, Haymes, and Kidd, *Baptists and the Communion of Saints*, 133. For a discussion of the non-voluntary nature of Baptist ecclesiology, see Goodliff, "Why Baptist Ecclesiology." For an alternative view, see Brackney, *Voluntarism*; Brackney, *Christian Voluntarism*; Brackney, *Believers Church*, 1–4; Brackney, *A to Z*, 596–97.

44. Aleksii Ia. (Dorodnitsyn), *Materialy*, 638.

45. See Aleksii Ia. (Dorodnitsyn), *Materialy*; "Ispovedanie Very Khristian-Baptistov," 434; cf. Ivanov, "Telo Khristovo"; Kudelia, "Tserkov', Vozniknovenie Ee i Organizatsiia." The only hint of an eschatological body of saints is in the section X on the second coming, see Aleksii Ia. (Dorodnitsyn), *Materialy*; "Ispovedanie Very Khristian-Baptistov," 482. Later, they adopted distinctions between local and universal church. See Vins, *Nashi Baptistskie Printsipy*; Odintsov, "O Tserkvi"; Mitskevich, "Tserkov, Sviashchennosluzhiteli i Chleny Tserkvi," 28; Dukhonchenko, "Dukhovno-Vospitatel'naia Rabota Sluzhitelei," 51–52.

the communion of saints which they expressed through the Lord's Supper.⁴⁶ *Ispovedanie Very Khristian-Baptistov* stated that the

> duty of every person converted to the Lord consists in that he must not stay alone but has to join other disciples of the Lord as with the members of one body (1 Cor 12:12–27), as with the living stones of one house of God (Eph 2:19–22; 1 Pet 2:5) for mutual edification, consolation and help on the way of salvation (1 Thess 5:11, 14; Col 2:18, 19; Jude 20), to abide in the teaching of apostles, in fellowship, in breaking of bread and in prayers (Acts 2:42). Such assembly of the true disciples of Christ, established according to the Word of God, is a Christian church (John 10:27; 8:31).⁴⁷

This text points to the necessity of a converted person joining the community of disciples and supports this by referring to the unity of the body and the image of the church as the temple. Again, intentionality here presupposes the shared experience of conversion that shapes the community's identity. Belonging to the community is important for the continuation of walking the way of salvation together with other disciples of Christ. That is, these disciples have a shared aim that forms their identity. The text also hints at the communal nature of salvation.⁴⁸

Yaroslav Pyzh, analysing the post-Second World War ecclesiology of Soviet Baptists, points out that its key characteristic is that of "confessing community" which is

> a fellowship of believers who submit to the lordship of Jesus Christ and the authority of the Bible, preserve the distinctives of their faith in contrast to the ideology and values of the culture, and maintain doctrinal purity among their members and express their beliefs through communal confession of faith.⁴⁹

---

46. "Ispovedanie Very Khristian-Baptistov," 425.
47. "Ispovedanie Very Khristian-Baptistov," 428. The text seems to assume that individual conversion could happen apart from local community.
48. See Pyzh, "Confessing Community," 89–94.
49. Pyzh, "Confessing Community," 4–5.

For Pyzh, confession of faith is the category that constitutes the community of disciples in response to the acts of God's mercy revealed in the cross and resurrection of Jesus Christ.[50] Confession is intimately related to submission to the lordship of Christ, resulting in the life of a disciple in the community of the faithful which a person joins through water baptism.[51] Believers find their identity and mutual support in serving the same Lord. Pyzh contends that "the gathering of people becomes a church when they are united for the ministry of the Lord and for mutual support."[52] They are united around the common experience of conversion and treat each other as members of one body of Christ who serve the same Lord.

Confession of faith, when it was expressed in a written form, was often considered as the means that drew people together and kept them in unity. It voiced the beliefs of the group to outsiders and instructed insiders.[53] However, as demonstrated above, confessions of faith often divided people instead of uniting them.[54] Perhaps this is why Fiddes insists that the formulation of confessions should be "regarded as the *context* for covenant-making, but never the *required* basis for 'walking together.'"[55] That is, the language of confession as the expression of intentionality accounts well for the community's response to God's act of gathering through God's word. It also lessens emphasis on local church autonomy since the community is gathered by God and cannot be understood to be the result of human volition. The language of confession, though, is less fitting to describe relations between the members of the community. Perhaps this could be improved if the act of confession was understood as a "commitment to a shared journey of discipleship on the way."[56] The image of *bratstvo* traditionally presupposed this latter aspect. Both the language of intentionality and the image of *bratstvo* could be enriched with the language of covenanting.

---

50. Pyzh, "Confessing Community," 103–5.
51. Pyzh, "Confessing Community," 142–45, 158.
52. Pyzh, "Confessing Community," 170.
53. Pyzh, "Confessing Community," 49–51; cf. Fiddes, *Tracks and Traces*, 45. In addition to this, see Anthony Thiselton's comment that confession is both "nailing one's colors to the mast as a self-involving act of Christian identity and commitment" (Thiselton, *Hermeneutics of Doctrine*, 12).
54. See section 3.4.3.3.
55. Fiddes, *Tracks and Traces*, 47. Emphasis original.
56. Jones, "Towards a Model," 8.

8.3.2 Covenant Community

According to Fiddes, covenant is "an agreement made between members of the church, and between those members and God in Christ."[57] This agreement is "about relationships and trust, about 'walking together' which is in some mysterious way part of the very journey of salvation."[58] It is also fundamentally tied to the rule of Christ who draws a church into covenant (vertical dimension) and to the commitment of the members to each other (horizontal dimension).[59] Fiddes also specifies that covenant ecclesiology is connected with two basic tensions: first is the tension between pastoral oversight of the whole community of faith and pastoral oversight of the officers; second is the tension between a local congregation and churches associating together.[60] These, he says, point to the presence of covenant ecclesiology "regardless of whether the word 'covenant' is employed."[61]

Theological and covenantal language have been used in Baptist theology to describe the baptismal experience of a believer. Thus, Thomas Helwys pointed to the vertical (with God) and horizontal (with each other) dimensions of covenanting in baptism:

> That the Church off CHRIST is a company off faithful people 1 Cor. 1.2. Eph. 1.1 separated frō the world by the word & Spirit off GOD. 2 Cor. 6.17. Being knit vnto the LORD, & one vnto another, by Baptisme. 1 Cor. 12.13. Vpon their owne confessiō of the faith. Act. 8.37. and sinnes. Mat. 3.6.[62]

Ukrainian Baptist baptismal language follows this trajectory. For instance, a person's desire to join a local church was described as a desire "to have fellowship with us"[63] or "to be united with us through baptism"[64] or "to unite with

---

57. Fiddes, "Covenant and Inheritance," 68.
58. Fiddes, *Tracks and Traces*, 46.
59. Fiddes, "Covenant and Inheritance," 69–70.
60. Fiddes, "Covenant and Inheritance," 65–68.
61. Fiddes, "Covenant and Inheritance," 66.
62. Lumpkin, *Baptist Confessions of Faith*, 119.
63. Val'kevich, *Zapiska*, Appendix 1, 39.
64. Aleksii Ia. (Dorodnitsyn), *Materialy*, 562.

the community."65 To be baptized is "to enter the covenant with the Lord."66 This is a typical formula that Ukrainian Baptists use to describe the act of baptism. Through baptism, a person united with Christ (vertical dimension) and became a member of Christ's body by joining the visible local church (horizontal dimension).67 Moreover, traditionally the act of baptism was a communal event preceded by collective examination of the candidates, usually a few days before.68 At the day of baptism, all the community gathered at the spot where the baptism was occurring and witnessed the act thereof, participating in prayers and singing. After baptism, ministers prayed over the baptised with laying on of hands, and the community participated in the prayer. Then the Lord's Supper followed and the baptised were welcomed as new members of the church. In addition to baptism, some documents mentioned a pledge of new members, who "upon joining the community pledge themselves to donate for this good cause [mission]."69 The pledge was part of the admission to membership.

On the community level, covenant echoes are found in the three cases mentioned above: Tiflis Baptist Church (1879); the Luchina community (1883); and Kyiv Autonomous Baptist Church (1963). In all three cases, the community is thought of as either the result of God's action (Tiflis) or a response of faith to God's word (Luchina and Kyiv). As Fiddes contends, covenant usually has two aspects: God's initiative and human response.70 Both elements are present in all three cases. This duality – God's initiative/human response – also resonates with the idea of gathered church and intentional community. Covenant stems from the eternal love and fellowship in the Trinity. In that sense, divine *koinonia* creates ecclesial *koinonia* which, in its turn, expresses itself in the local congregations and wider ecclesial bodies:

---

65. Val'kevich, *Zapiska*, Appendix 1, 45, 49, 50, 51, 55. Usually a person joined through baptism, but in some cases, when baptism was performed in adulthood, the church admitted such people on the basis of public profession of faith.

66. Val'kevich, *Zapiska*, Appendix 1, 51; cf. Sannikov, *Podgotovka k Kreshcheniiu*, 193–95; Pyzh, "Confessing Community," 163–64.

67. "Ispovedanie Very Khristian-Baptistov," 428.

68. Aleksii Ia. (Dorodnitsyn), *Materialy*, 679–80.

69. Aleksii Ia. (Dorodnitsyn), *Materialy*, 574, 603, 608.

70. Fiddes, "Covenant – Old and New," 16; Fiddes, *Tracks and Traces*, 75.

> The One God exists from eternity in a life of relationship, in a communion (*koinonia*) of three Persons, Father, Son and Holy Spirit. Jesus Christ, the eternal Son, is the Word of God as God's self-communication of self-giving love. Jesus Christ is thus God's self-revelation who draws us into the communion of God's own triune life and into communion (*koinonia*) with each other.[71]

Fiddes's language of covenant deepens the idea that the church is the result of God's action by connecting it with the life of the Trinity through covenant relations.[72]

Another significant element is that all communities see Jesus Christ as their head and Lord. For Fiddes, "affirmation that Christ alone rules in the congregation is a mark of covenant thinking."[73] In the previous section, we could see that intention to join community under the lordship of Christ could be expressed with the language of confession. Christians confess Christ as their Lord individually and communally and submit to his rule in the continuous life of discipleship. However, it is possible that the language of confession could lead to a mere voluntary understanding of church as a company of those who voluntarily join together on the basis of the similarity of the content of their confession. When Fiddes points to the prominence of Christ with regard to the vertical dimension of covenant – "the rule of Christ, who calls a church into covenant"[74] – he, perhaps, tries to counter such attempts by stressing the idea that Christ is the only mediator of covenant, the one who introduces community into relations with Trinitarian *koinonia* and under whose direct rule a community of faith lives.

These communities commit themselves to relations that presuppose mutual love, admonition and watching over each other (the horizontal dimension of covenant).[75] This horizontal dimension is an expression of intentionality when members of the community deal with each other as those who share the same experience and aim. Besides that, I suggest that the act of constituting

---

71. Fiddes, "Conversation in Context," 9; cf. Baptist Union of Great Britain, *Nature of the Assembly*, 9.

72. Fiddes, *Tracks and Traces*, 214.

73. Fiddes, *Tracks and Traces*, 70.

74. Fiddes, "Covenant and Inheritance," 69.

75. Aleksii Ia. (Dorodnitsyn), *Materialy*, 640; Savchenkov, "Snariazhenie Shtundistskikh Missionerov," 317; Velichko, *Uzok Put'*, 64.

Tiflis Baptist Church contained the tensions between communal and personal pastoral oversight. When Liebig pointed out to the community that "governance and leading should be in the hand of presbyter,"[76] he affirmed personal pastoral oversight; and when he explained that members "have duties to each other. These duties, first of all, consist of mutual love to each other. Everyone should watch over and admonish one another,"[77] he pointed to communal oversight. This type of relationship that presupposes both mutual commitment to oversight and the pastoral ministry to a community is aptly summarised by the image of *bratstvo*, which is typical to Ukrainian and Russian Baptists.

Finally, it should be noted that both the Tiflis and Kyiv churches existed and operated as churches for some time, but only after the act of proper constituting (Tiflis) or the renewing of the covenant (Kyiv) did they turn into regular communities. It is significant that in Tiflis, constituting was done with the presence and active participation of external ministers who also invited the church to join an AC and viewed associating with other churches as the expression of the unity of the Son with the Father for the sake of mission.[78] Here is what Fiddes calls the tension between a local congregation and associating churches. He stresses that unity rooted in the life of the Trinity forms the underlying reality that should be expressed visually and practically through associating.[79] Thus, unity becomes an imperative and irreducible task of the church that expresses its nature. The tension between a local congregation and associating churches will be analysed in the next section.

8.3.3 Freedom under the Lordship of Christ

A local church's right to elect ministers, celebrate sacraments and discipline its members is rooted in the conviction that Christ rules in the local church and gives it all these things as "the seals of the covenant."[80] However, quite often the understanding of that right has gravitated towards the notion of

---

76. Aleksii Ia. (Dorodnitsyn), *Materialy*, 639.

77. Aleksii Ia. (Dorodnitsyn), 640. For discussions on the tension between communal and personal pastoral oversight, see Mazaev, "O Presviterakh"; Pavlov, "Kto Starshe Presviter ili Tserkov"; Akimochkin, "Po Povodu Stat'i"; Mazaev, "Eshche po Povodu Stat'i."

78. Aleksii Ia. (Dorodnitsyn), *Materialy*, 640.

79. Fiddes, *Tracks and Traces*, 215.

80. "A True Confession of Faith" in Lumpkin, *Baptist Confessions of Faith*, 87.

the autonomy or independence of a local church. Paul Fiddes points to a permanent tension between the local church and association of churches.[81] I suggest that the concept of the lordship of Christ over the local church gives freedom to a local church and strengthens its ties with other churches as "outcroppings" of the universal church.

The concept of local church autonomy has been prominent among Baptists in the Russian Empire, the USSR and Ukraine and can be found in major ecclesiological writings and confessional documents. For instance, Russian Baptist pioneer Vasilii Pavlov in the apologetic essay "Pravda o Baptistakh"[82] omitted the universal church[83] and insisted that "every properly constituted local church or community has its own self-government chaired by a presbyter and is not in organic relations with other communities."[84] Iakov Vins[85] wrote that local church was an "autonomous and independent church CORPORATION" if it was "properly constituted and recognised by all the brotherhood."[86] This latter nuance is significant, for it points to the tension

---

81. See Iurii Reshetnikov on the inherent tension between the unity of the church and the independence of the local church. Reshetnikov, "Zahal'ni Problemni Pytannia," 318.

82. Pavlov, "Pravda o Baptistakh," *Baptist* no. 41, 42, 43, 44, 45, 46, 47 (1911). The essay narrated the roots of Baptists (sections 1–8), the beginnings, early missionary work and persecutions of Baptists in Russia (sections 9–16), and their principles, beliefs and practices (sections 17–22). This narrative became standard for Russian Baptist historiography. For the earliest example of historical apology, see Coleman, "Most Dangerous Sect," 28–29. Pavlov's essay assimilated ideas from many authors. See Pavlov, "Pravda o Baptistakh," no. 46, 361–62; cf. Hiscox, *New Directory*, 336. See Pavlov's references to William Jones (1762–1846) on Waldenses, Johan Lorenz von Mosheim (1693–1755) on Dutch Anabaptists, Ludwig Keller (1849–1915) on German Anabaptists and E. T. Hiscox (1814–1901) on church polity. Pavlov built on the concept of "a faithful remnant," which is a persecuted minority who, though not Baptist, held to similar beliefs and practices and suffered for this. See Pavlov, "Pravda o Baptistakh," no. 41, 324. This is a landmarkists' concept of an unbroken historical succession (see Graves, *Old Landmarkism*, 121). On the popularity of successionism in the mid-nineteenth century, see Haykin, "Voluntarism," 48–49.

83. Pavlov, "Pravda o Baptistakh," no. 46, 361–62. This omission resembles E. T. Hiscox, who states that the universal church "represents a conception of the mind, having no real existence in time or place, and not a historical fact, being only an ideal multitude without organisation, without action, and without corporate being" (Hiscox, "Khristianskaia Tserkov," no. 23, 178; cf. Hiscox, *The New Directory*, 24).

84. Pavlov, "Pravda o Baptistakh," no. 46, 361.

85. *Nashi Baptistskie Printsipy* (Our Baptist principles) was prepared for Baptist youth and drew from the works of German Baptists someone F. Friedrich and Pettenhal. See Vins, *Nashi Baptistskie Printsipy*, 3–4.

86. Vins, 20. Emphasis original. Perhaps, for Vins, constitution and recognition was a matter of good practice, not an expression of catholicity (see Ivanov, "Obshchiny i Presvitery," 9). Vins used an unusual word for church: "corporation." It is quite possible that it stands for

between local church and associations of churches. Vins believed that local church could admit new members, exercise discipline and elect ministers because this right was granted by Christ, the only head of the church, and executed through the power of the Holy Spirit.[87] Artur Mitskevich explained that the local church is a community of regenerated believers who recognise "one confession of faith, one church order and hold to the unified views and convictions on basic issues of faith."[88] Churches are independent in accepting or excommunicating members, electing ministers and performing worship services because of Christ's rule.[89]

Fiddes contends that the notion of local church autonomy is not typical for historical Baptist thought.[90] Autonomy is literally "making a law for oneself," which actually contradicts the Baptist insistence on the presence and rule of Christ in the local church.[91] Baptists believed in theocracy not democracy.[92] Christ is present not indirectly through structures but "directly and personally when people gather in the name of Christ, in dependence on the promise."[93] The lordship of Christ in the local community relativizes all human authority that stems from autonomous individuality or human choice. This also means that such community cannot be imposed upon from either ecclesiastical hierarchy or civil powers.[94] On the other hand, other local communities are under the same rule and are called by Christ into fellowship

---

German "Gemeinschaft." Vins opposed using "society" for church, for this was a "stray" word (Vins, *Nashi Baptistskie Printsipy*, 21). For the possible familiarity of Vins (or his sources) with Tönnies's work, see Pyzh, "Confessing Community," 6, n.10; 165–68; cf. Tönnies and Harris, *Community and Civil Society*, 36.

87. Vins, *Nashi Baptistskie Printsipy*, 36–38. Vins admitted the universal church but rejected confessional organisations or national churches, stating that the NT epistles addressed only local churches. Vins, 35; cf. Pavlov, "Pravda o Baptistakh," no. 46, 361–62; Hiscox, "Khristianskaia Tserkov," no. 23, 176; Odintsov, "O Tserkvi," 7.

88. Mitskevich, "Tserkov, Sviashchennosluzhiteli i Chleny Tserkvi," 30. This publication is the basis for the article on the church in the new confession of faith proposed in 1979. P. K. Shatrov repeats it almost verbatim. See Shatrov, "Tserkov' Khrista," 13–15.

89. Mitskevich, "Tserkov, Sviashchennosluzhiteli i Chleny Tserkvi," 30; see also Mitskevich, "Osnovnye Printsipy," 48–49.

90. Fiddes, "Communion and Covenant," 130.

91. Fiddes, "Communion and Covenant," 130; see also Fowler, "Churches and the Church," 29–39; Haymes, Gouldbourne, and Cross, *On Being the Church*, 22–24; Jones, *European Baptist Federation*, 4–5.

92. Haymes, Gouldbourne, and Cross, *On Being the Church*, 41.

93. Haymes, Gouldbourne, and Cross, *On Being the Church*, 197.

94. Fiddes, *Tracks and Traces*, 261; Fiddes, "Communion and Covenant," 130.

with each other on the way to fuller *koinonia*.⁹⁵ Fiddes is convinced that "if a local church is under the direct rule of Christ as king then it is necessarily drawn into fellowship with all those who are under Christ's rule and so part of his body."⁹⁶ This understanding significantly corrects one-sided emphasis on local church autonomy. Churches under the lordship of Christ are called into relations with each other that stem from freedom and are tied by bonds of trust.⁹⁷

Baptists in the USSR attempted to balance the tension between the local church and association. Thus, Artur Mitskevich tried to achieve balance by pointing to the early church,⁹⁸ when the apostles and the Jerusalem church maintained spiritual unity of views and cared for other churches.⁹⁹ He also grounded this balance pragmatically, stating that each local church needed "correct nurturing, resolution of complex inner church issues, training of labourers," the supply of "the books of Holy Scriptures" and help in resolving issues of heresy.¹⁰⁰ Mitskevich stressed that as a believer could not live in isolation from fellow believers so too a local church could not live in isolation from fellow churches,¹⁰¹ and he pointed out that fellowship is fostered by the Holy Spirit who "draws churches towards the holy bonds," towards "unity which connects all local churches into one great living organism."¹⁰²

A particular case of this tension is the issue of authority. Baptists in the Russian Empire tended to elevate local church authority over that of wider

---

95. Fiddes, *Tracks and Traces*, 194–96.
96. Fiddes, *Tracks and Traces*, 44.
97. See section 7.3.2.
98. Mitskevich, "Tserkov, Sviashchennosluzhiteli i Chleny Tserkvi," 31; Mitskevich, "Osnovnye Printsipy," 49; cf. Pyzh, "Confessing Community," 117. See Pyzh on "a balance between the autonomy of the local church and interdependence with larger ecclesial Baptist body" (Pyzh, "Confessing Community," 124; cf. Reshetnikov, "Zahal'ni Problemni Pytannia," 318).
99. Mitskevich, "Tserkov, Sviashchennosluzhiteli i Chleny Tserkvi," 31; see also Pyzh, "Confessing Community," 117–19.
100. Mitskevich, "Tserkov, Sviashchennosluzhiteli i Chleny Tserkvi," 31. The latter aspect obviously goes beyond pragmatic grounds, since protection and transmission of the entrusted deposit of faith belongs to the universal church. Indirectly, this points to the necessity of relations among the churches which have only partial perspectives on the entrusted gospel and teaching. Elsewhere, Mitskevich points to the "commonality of convictions and responsibilities in spreading God's Kingdom, proper nurturing of members and improvement of churches" (Mitskevich, "Osnovnye Printsipy," 49).
101. Mitskevich, "Osnovnye Printsipy," 49.
102. Mitskevich, "Osnovnye Printsipy," 49.

associations. Thus, for Vasilii Pavlov, "communities are superior than the conference."[103] Participants of the Novo-Vasil'evka conference said they did not *"interfere in the inner affairs of a church."*[104] But they agreed that local churches could only be free in dealing with issues related to church practice, while mission and doctrine could not be at the discretion of a single local church apart from the other churches of Bratstvo.[105] The limits of local church authority were also evident in cases of installation and removal of ministers and conflict resolution.[106] This coincides with Fiddes's opinion that "while the local church is competent by itself to appoint members to the office of *diakonia* (pastoral service), it is not competent alone to appoint members to the office of *episkope* (pastoral oversight) but only in fellowship with the wider Church."[107] Perhaps this was why Iakov Vins believed that the advice of the external committee dealing with problems in the local church was binding, for through committee "God's universal Church, gathered for this in its representatives, had its say."[108] For Vins, the committee represented the universal church; therefore, its advice could not be dismissed. A similar way of thinking is expressed in the London Confession of Faith (1644), which in the sections on church discipline specifies that

> although particular Congregations be distinct and severall Bodies, every one a compact and knit Citie in it selfe; yet are they all to walk by one and the same Rule and by all meanes convenient to have the counsell and help one of another in all needfull affaires of the Church, as members of one body in the common faith under Christ their onely head.[109]

---

103. Val'kevich, *Zapiska*, Appendix 1, 38; Aleksii Ia. (Dorodnitsyn), *Materialy*, 623.

104. Aleksii Ia. (Dorodnitsyn), *Materialy*, 581. Emphasis added. See also Val'kevich, *Zapiska*, Appendix 3, 2–4.

105. Aleksii Ia. (Dorodnitsyn), *Materialy*, 580–81. On the idea that NT teaching was entrusted to a group of churches, see Bandura, Interview 1.A.0, 381–83.

106. See section 2.4.2.

107. Fiddes, *Leading Question*, 33. Fiddes distinguishes pastoral service from pastoral oversight, where the latter is related to the universal church while the former relates to the local church.

108. Vins, *Nashi Baptistskie Printsipy*, 41–42.

109. Lumpkin, *Baptist Confessions of Faith*, 168–69.

Here practical mutual "counsell and help" was motivated by being under the same rule, belonging to one body, sharing one faith and being under the lordship of Christ.

Traditional emphasis on the rule of Christ in a local community substantiated the idea that through Christ a church has everything it needs to be church. However, it cannot manifest fully the reality of the people of God.[110] This supposes that a local church is a partial "manifestation" or "outcropping" of the one body of Christ which predates its existence. Thus, a local church, through the mediator of the covenant, Jesus Christ, is related with other churches "because the body exists before us, and we are called to enter it."[111] It stands under the direct rule of Jesus Christ and has responsibility to know his mind. However, no one local church can know everything God wants to reveal, and therefore, each one requires other churches to know the whole counsel of God.[112] On the other hand, upon entering into covenant through Christ, believers not only form a local church (the horizontal dimension of covenant) but also participate in the *koinonia* of the Trinity (the vertical dimension).[113] Through a covenant, local community is tied to a wider reality that takes its beginning in the Trinity, and this means that "covenant always resists autonomy, not only of single members within the local covenanted congregation, but also of separate congregations joined together in association."[114] These covenant relations can also be described with the language of siblingship represented by the image of *bratstvo*.

8.4 Rethinking Association of Churches

As was demonstrated in the previous chapters, Ukrainian Baptists practiced associating from the very beginning of the Baptist movement in the Russian

---

110. See, for example, the BWA statement that "for Baptists, the local church is wholly church but not the whole church" in Baptist World Alliance, "Are Baptist Churches Autonomous?," 376.

111. Fiddes, *Tracks and Traces*, 198; cf. Baptist Union of Great Britain, *Nature of the Assembly*, 6.

112. Fiddes, Haymes, and Kidd, *Baptists and the Communion of Saints*, 130–31; see also Bandura's reflections in section 6.2.3.

113. Fiddes, *Tracks and Traces*, 79; Fiddes, Haymes, and Kidd, *Baptists and the Communion of Saints*, 129–30.

114. Fiddes, Haymes, and Kidd, *Baptist and the Communion of Saints s*, 130.

Empire. Associations emerged as a way to survive, accumulate resources for mission and help each other, and theological justification followed the practice. On the other hand, the practice of associating points to the conviction that local churches should associate with each other. Though ACs were often argued for on pragmatic grounds, occasionally the theological vision of the unity of Christ's body for making Christ known to the world (John 17) came into focus. Ukrainian Baptists used biblical images of *bratstvo* and the body of Christ in regard to associations, insisted on visible expressions of the unity of the church and expressed trans-local ecclesial life through their associational practices (associational assemblies and trans-local ministers). When Dei Mazaev referred to the participants of the congress as "the members of one body," and the union as "the fulness of God's people,"[115] he thought about the union in ecclesial terms. All that points to an understanding of ACs as the embodiment of wider fellowship (*koinonia*). In what follows, I turn to the image of *bratstvo* and expand it through covenantal language in relation to unity, mutual care and mission.

8.4.1 Covenant Brotherhood in Christ

The image of *bratstvo* has been the most common way Ukrainian Baptists have understood and designated themselves. It has often been used in the context of associating and in discussions on the unity of the church. The image describes a community of faith in terms of sibling relations. It was common for the early Christians to address each other as brothers and sisters.[116] The image presupposed kindred relations and mutual care.[117] However, this siblingship is based not on natural kinship but on the common experience of conversion and the confession of Christ as Saviour and Lord.[118] Therefore, Christians enter this new family only through Christ and obtain new relations with God, as their Father, and each other as brothers and sisters. This

---

115. Mazaev, "O Nashikh Nuzhdakh (prodolzhenie)," 8. The same could be said about Pavel Datsko when he promoted the federative model of the union for enhancing growth in "unity of faith and measure of full stature of Christ" (Eph 4:13) and building up the body of Christ through gifts and offices (apostles, prophets, evangelists, pastors and teachers). See Datsko, "O Forme Upravleniia Delami Soiuza," 94–95; cf. Ivanov, "Chto Takoe Baptisty," 3.

116. Aasgaard, *My Beloved*, 114–15; cf. Meeks, *First Urban Christians*, 86–89.

117. Aasgaard, *My Beloved*, 309. Aasgaard argues that Paul uses established sibling roles to inform relations among Christians in the new community.

118. See Tervits, "Bratstvo Liubite," 27–28; Shipkov, "Bratstvo vo Khriste," 5.

condition makes such relations principally open for anyone who converts to Christ and confesses him as Saviour and Lord.

Bratstvo was a flexible concept. It was originally applied to a local community of believers, a regional group of communities, a national union or even a worldwide confessional group.[119] On the other hand, sociologically, Bratstvo was a group that was on the way from sect to church and presupposed gravitation towards ecclesiastical organisation expressed in more mature doctrine, practice and structure, while maintaining characteristics of freedom and simplicity.[120] However, most commonly the image was used to describe associations and unions of churches. This understanding resonates with the original Petrine use of the image in 1 Peter 2:17, when the apostle addressed a group of communities scattered in different geographical locations in Asia Minor.

Baptists in the Russian Empire, the USSR and Ukraine were constantly drawn together into one ecclesial body designated *bratstvo* or *soiuz* (union). Of the three cases of covenanting mentioned above, only the case of Kyiv Autonomous Baptist Church misses the element of commitment to a wider association of churches. To be precise, it rather qualifies relations with other churches on the basis of a similar understanding of doctrine and church practices.[121] The case of Tiflis Baptist Church presupposed relations with wider ecclesial bodies for mutual support and help, for mission and "to fulfil the Saviour's word '*that all be one*' and demonstrate unity to the world."[122] The case of the Luchina community approximates this with regard to a shared missionary goal. Though there are no documented historical precedents of formal covenanting on the associational level, I, nevertheless, suggest that commitment to the Lord and to each other was expressed among Ukrainian Baptists through the language of confession and embodied in the form of the union labelled Bratstvo.

It should be noted that confession of the same faith was the core element around which Bratstvo was formed.[123] The act and practice of confessing

---

119. See relevant subsections in 2.4.2, 3.4.3 and 4.4.2.

120. Wach, *Sociology of Religion*, 137–41.

121. "Proekt Tserkovnogo Zaveta," 3.

122. Val'kevich, *Zapiska*, Appendix 1, 45–47; Aleksii Ia. (Dorodnitsyn), *Materialy*, 640.

123. Klippenstein, "Johann Wieler," 50; cf. Bychkov, "Otchetnyi Doklad VSEKhB 42-Mu S"ezdu," 16; Tervits, "Bratstvo Liubite," 27–28.

Christ is what constitutes a "confessing community," as Yaroslav Pyzh demonstrated when pointing to its significance as a personal act through which believers express their following Jesus as disciples in response to Christ's call.[124] Confession is also a communal response to God's self-revelation.[125] The earliest loose association of Ukrainian Baptist churches emerged in the context of the creation of the confession of faith known as *Pravila Veroispovedania*. Wieler described the event as follows:

> Finally, the brethren decided to make a complete break with the Orthodox Church and form a fellowship of their own according to God's Word. A number of brethren met in Wieler's home especially to seek guidance on this matter through prayer and the reading of God's Word. From this resulted the drawing up of a confession of faith including ten articles which set out the principal points of the Christian faith. It agreed essentially with the statement used by Baptists in Germany. The brethren then submitted copies of the statement to all their groups for discussion and approval. With few exceptions, all the members agreed to form a Baptist fellowship on the basis of this declaration.[126]

Here the representatives of several earliest Ukrainian communities (from villages of Osnova, Ignatovka, Liubomyrka and Poltavka) gathered to establish "a fellowship of their own according to God's word."[127] This was accompanied by the composition of the confessional document that provided the foundation upon which the fellowship rested.[128] This first *bratstvo* comprised characteristics of intentional community. First, they decided to form a fellowship on the basis of their confession of faith (their shared experience), and this could be seen as their commitment to God or even as their response to God who had gathered them through his word (hence, a gathered community). Second, they joined into a fellowship and maintained relations with other similar communities (co-intention of members) through regular visitations, annual assemblies, the work of trans-local ministers and prayers for each

---

124. Pyzh, "Confessing Community," 103–6.
125. Fiddes, *Tracks and Traces*, 8.
126. Klippenstein, "Johann Wieler," 50; cf. Val'kevich, *Zapiska*, Appendix 5, 135.
127. Klippenstein, "Johann Wieler," 50.
128. On covenants and confessions, see Fiddes, *Tracks and Traces*, 45–47.

other. They also cared for those who were imprisoned for the work of evangelism (mutual support in working towards a common goal). Finally, with Wieler's assistance, this fellowship evolved into an association which had mission as its foundational reality and primary goal (shared aim).

However, it should be admitted that this confessional perspective had some restrictions that narrowed *bratstvo* to doctrinal or denominational demarcation lines. I suggest that these restrictions could be overcome if confession is considered, first, as an act of intentionality that presupposes "commitment to a shared journey of discipleship on the way,"[129] and, second, as a communal act within the framework of transmission of faith through community in history. A shared journey of discipleship presupposes commitment to Jesus Christ as the Lord whom different communities of faith follow. This allows for a wider diversity of traditions and forms of expression of this commitment than in the case of allegiance to a fixed body of doctrines. Dei Mazaev referred to the transmission of faith through the community of faith in history when arguing for keeping the name "Baptists" and maintaining unity:

> Apostle Paul addressing Corinthian Christians asked them: "did the word of God originate with you? Or are you the only ones it has reached?" (1 Cor 14:36). These two question marks regarding one of the previous verses in the same chapter: "As in all the churches of the saints" (v. 33), set particular ties between separate churches and even some mutual dependence from each other. Because of these ties and mutual dependence, we, first of all, should say that the Word of God came *not from us* and, secondly, and this is especially important, that it reached *not only us alone* but also many others, and not simultaneously with us, *but much earlier*. We, who were converted in the last days, do not constitute a branch, cut off the root, but are being connected through faith and unity of the spirit with the body of Christ – His Church, and, consequently, participate in the host of those saints who had believed in Christ earlier than we did and earlier than we were built by the Holy Spirit "into God's house."[130]

---

129. Jones, "Towards a Model," 8n18.
130. Mazaev, "Imia 'Baptisty,'" 3; cf. Mazaev, "Edinstvo i Razdelenie," 6.

Here the word of God is something that Baptists in the Russian Empire inherited from and shared with others who preceded them. Mazaev pointed to the continuity of faith through the communion of saints in history as a rationale for keeping both tradition (as Baptists) and unity. Therefore, as a communion of churches that jointly confess Christ and commit to mutual care, fellowship and aim, *bratstvo* stays in continuity with the previous generations of the people of God or, to put it differently, belongs to the wider reality of the universal church. Thus, even within a traditional confessional trajectory, *bratstvo* reaches far beyond denominational demarcation lines both in terms of historical continuity and ecumenical width. However, as we could see in chapter 7,[131] approaching the wider association of churches as covenant community in Christ allows for a deeper theological understanding of being church and introduces a stronger element of catholicity and openness.

First of all, it is Jesus Christ who gathers believers into one body and rules over them. Brian Haymes, Ruth Gouldbourne and Anthony Cross point to the ultimate importance of the conviction that "when people gather in the name of Christ, and Christ, by his own promise is in the midst, there the church is."[132] In this regard, "the church is *manifested* rather than *constituted*,"[133] whether we speak of a local church or wider union. The act of gathering through Christ makes the associating of churches a duty not an option. Elsewhere in this thesis, I stated that Baptists regularly referred to wider associations of churches using the image of the body and the universal church.[134] Bratstvo was a fellowship of churches that shared the same confession of Christ as the Lord and the Son of God, as well as the same experience of faith and goal. For Fiddes, associating is "an obedient response to a divine imperative" because the body pre-exists particular congregations.[135] Local churches just allow this body to become visible through associations of churches. On the other hand, associating could also be seen through the lens of "gathered church": member congregations voluntarily respond to Christ who assembles his church.[136]

---

131. See sections 7.2.1 and 7.2.2.
132. Haymes, Gouldbourne, and Cross, *On Being the Church*, 198.
133. Haymes, Gouldbourne, and Cross, *On Being the Church*, 199. Emphasis original.
134. See sections 3.4.3, 4.4.2, 5.4.1 and 6.3.3. This resonates with Fiddes's observation with regard to English Baptists in Fiddes, *Tracks and Traces*, 197–200.
135. Fiddes, *Tracks and Traces*, 200.
136. Baptist Union of Great Britain, *Nature of the Assembly*, 8.

Thus, particular communities commit themselves to the Lord, responding to his divine call, and to each other, imposing covenant responsibilities to "walk together and watch over each other."

Second, Baptists typically understood a local congregation to be under the rule of Christ, but Fiddes convincingly demonstrates that covenant thinking extends Christ's rule over fellowships of churches too.[137] He turns to the analogical way of thinking, reasoning that "there is the same relation between the particular churches as there is between the particular members of one church."[138] All churches make up one body of Christ and this way of thinking is similar to the Ukrainian Baptist understanding of visible church as a manifestation of the communion of saints.[139] The lordship of Christ over a particular community does give it certain freedom to "find the mind of Christ," but this does not give it the right to ignore the voices of other churches because "a local church is wholly church but is not the whole Church."[140] Hence, these churches are interdependent and under the same rule.

Third, through Jesus Christ as the mediator of covenant a stronger element of catholicity is introduced.[141] Covenant ecclesiology reaches beyond the immediate, human and local level by virtue of participating in Christ. Through Christ, the communion of churches participates in the Trinitarian *koinonia* and the universal body of Christ. Church as covenant community is placed into the larger context of God's cosmic design and purpose by participating in God's mission through Christ and being equipped by the Holy

---

137. Fiddes, *Tracks and Traces*, 42–45, 213–14.

138. Fiddes, *Tracks and Traces*, 199; cf. Jones, *European Baptist Federation*, 8; Mitskevich, "Osnovnye Printsipy," 49.

139. Aleksii Ia. (Dorodnitsyn), *Materialy*, 479–80, 482; "Ispovedanie Very Khristian-Baptistov," 428.

140. Baptist World Alliance, "Are Baptist Churches Autonomous?," 376.

141. Nigel Wright speaks about "open church" in Wright, *New Baptists*, 75–77. Keith Jones and Parush Parushev propose a concept of "porous" communities with regard to membership and worship in Jones, "Towards a Model," and Parushev, "Gathered, Gathering, Porous." Orthodox theologian Cyril Hovorun proposes switching from the metaphor of "borders" of the church to "frontiers," which are penetrable, movable and serve to extend its influence (Hovorun, *Scaffolds of the Church*), 163–79. See also the principle of covenant openness in Fiddes, *Tracks and Traces*, 190–92.

Spirit.¹⁴² Fiddes believes that God intends to bring the whole universe into covenant relations.¹⁴³

Finally, the church in its fullness will only be manifested at the second coming of Jesus Christ.¹⁴⁴ But before this happens, associations of churches could make this coming reality visible, at least partially. Perhaps, the traditional Baptist concept of visible church is helpful here, since it does not draw sharp distinction between universal and local church. As we can see, early Ukrainian Baptist statements of faith applied to visible church images of the body of Christ, God's house and temple, and *sanctorum communio*.¹⁴⁵ Since local church is a manifestation of the universal church that "derives from the one body," then local churches "already relate together because the body exists before us, and we are called to enter it."¹⁴⁶ This has implications for the idea of unity because the image of the body presupposes visibility and tangibility.¹⁴⁷ However, this means that associations of churches are imperfect means of expressing this communion of saints on the way to fuller *koinonia*. This brings us to the theme of visualising the unity of the church.

8.4.2 Visualising Unity in Imperfect Forms

Covenant brotherhood in Christ exists, among other reasons, to make the unity of the church visible through the imperfect forms of associations and unions of churches. Historically, Baptists in the Russian Empire, the USSR and Ukraine related the image of *bratstvo* to the unity of the church.¹⁴⁸ They also believed that unity should be manifested in visible forms. Thus, Tiflis Baptist Church was invited to join the German Baptist Union to implement the unity for which Jesus Christ prayed to his Father and to make it visible to the world.¹⁴⁹ The motif of unity was on Wieler's personal agenda and was in-

---

142. Fiddes, Haymes, and Kidd, *Baptists and the Communion of Saints*, 160.
143. Fiddes, "Church's Ecumenical Calling," 53.
144. Cf. Aleksii Ia. (Dorodnitsyn), *Materialy*, 482.
145. Aleksii Ia. (Dorodnitsyn), *Materialy*, 479–80, 482; "Ispovedanie Very Khristian-Baptistov," 428.
146. Fiddes, "Church's Ecumenical Calling," 44.
147. See section 2.4.4, the subsections on unity and images of the union in 3.4.3, 4.3.3 and 5.3.1, and the subsection on ACs as organisms in 6.3.1.2.
148. Section 4.4.2.
149. Section 2.2.1.

cluded as one of the aims of Bratstvo.[150] In the 1920s, it inspired conversations, albeit with some confessional restrictions, between Baptists and Evangelical Christians aimed at a merger of the two bodies.[151] Unity was envisioned as an implementation of God's will, expressed in Jesus's prayer and exemplified by relations between the Son and the Father (John 17) and related to the church's mission.[152] References to the relations of the divine persons and the understanding of the church as the body of Christ in the discussions on unity will be brought one step further through Fiddes's understanding of associations as a provisional visualisation of the body of Christ.[153]

The image of the body of Christ points to the essential unity that is already in Christ and which should be demonstrated by all members of the body (Gal 3:27–28; Eph 4:1–6), since all believers comprise one body in Christ (Rom 12:3–8; 1 Cor 1:10–30; 12).[154] Christians are called to make this fundamental unity visible to the outer world (John 17:21). This way of thinking was typical of the Baptists in the Russian Empire, the USSR and Ukraine.[155] They understood unity as deeply rooted in the redemptive death of Christ "who laid himself down for the Church,"[156] due to which they became members of one body and were filled with one Holy Spirit.[157] Unity was also understood as a natural expression of being born from above by the Holy Spirit and a sign of the spiritual maturity of those incorporated into the body of Christ and assembled into the temple by the Holy Spirit.[158] Both the constituting of Tiflis Baptist Church and the establishment of Bratstvo reflect the intention of making visible the unity in Christ. In this regard, Alexander Anan'in's remark that Baptist union should "express itself in a visible organization" with "congresses, council, preachers"[159] was fundamentally correct. The parallel Anan'in drew between water baptism and the Lord's Supper as visualisations

---

150. Section 2.4.4.
151. Geychenko, "On the Use of Scripture."
152. Sections 3.4.3, 4.3.3 and 6.2.3.
153. Fiddes, *Tracks and Traces*, 66–67, 197–227.
154. Cf. Aleksii Ia. (Dorodnitsyn), *Materialy*, 580.
155. Section 2.4.5.
156. VSEKhB, *Istoriia Evangelskikh Khristian-Baptistov v SSSR*, 98.
157. VSEKhB, *Istoriia Evangelskikh Khristian-Baptistov v SSSR*, 98.
158. Section 3.4.3.
159. Belousov, "Pervyi Nazidatel'nyi S'ezd," 38. On the necessity of organizational forms, see Bandura, Interview 1.A.0, 165–70.

of invisible reality is exemplary of the view that could be called sacramental.[160] By analogy, his reflections on obligatory visual expressions of unity in the form of the union hint at sacramental thinking about the church[161] and resonate with Fiddes's conviction regarding the visibility of the body of Christ.

Fiddes insists that the body of Christ is a "fundamental image of unity" that presupposes visibility since "the members join to make the whole body visible, that is to allow *Christ* to manifest himself in the world, to make himself knowable and tangible through all his members."[162] This encompasses both the local and universal church.[163] Joining together to make Christ visible betrays intentionality, since members intend each other as participants in a shared experience and aim.[164] The shared experience refers to becoming members of one body in Christ, and the aim is to make this body visible to the world in order to make Christ known.

Fiddes also claims that Christ should be made visible at every level of human society – local, regional and national[165] – therefore, associational forms are proper ways of expressing the body of Christ visibly on regional and national levels. Speaking about wider forms of ecclesial life, Haymes, Gouldbourne and Cross distinguish between "gathering" and "association," where the former refers to events when the people of God gather together in the name of Christ and the church is manifested, while the latter assume organisations.[166] These are related, since gatherings happen as expressions of organisations and organisations emanate from the gathering, enable them to function and depend on them.[167] For Baptists in Russia and Ukraine, associations and unions of churches by necessity had to have organisational components that enabled ACs to perform the mission of the church and that thickened the tangibility of the invisible communion of saints. However, the

---

160. Sannikov, *Znaky Prysutnosti*, 326–28.
161. See Colwell, "Church as Sacrament"; Colwell, *Promise and Presence*, 65–87.
162. Fiddes, *Tracks and Traces*, 67. Emphasis original.
163. Fiddes, *Tracks and Traces*, 197–98; cf. Fiddes, "Church's Ecumenical Calling," 43–49.
164. Fiddes, *Tracks and Traces*, 77.
165. On praxis and the interconnectedness of the church on *micro*, *meso* and *macro* levels, see Van der Ven, *Ecclesiology in Context*, xii.
166. Haymes, Gouldbourne, and Cross, *On Being the Church*, 199.
167. Haymes, Gouldbourne, and Cross, *On Being the Church*, 201, 202–5.

institutional component was never considered the primary element of the ecclesial life of ACs.

The concept of visibility resonates with a major trend in the ecumenical movement: unity as the full communion of churches with different historical and traditional backgrounds.[168] Unity as full communion presupposes not only sharing a common life and mission but also a confession of common faith.[169] The vision of unity as full communion is rooted in the concept of divine *koinonia*. Both on the local and trans-local levels, believers participate in the *koinonia* of divine persons.[170] This divine *koinonia* precedes the existence of human fellowship, and the latter is rooted in the former.[171] The church is the witness and the foretaste to this *koinonia*,[172] but, says Fiddes, "we cannot witness to *koinonia* unless we *embody* it."[173] Unity rooted in the life of the Trinity forms the underlying reality that should be expressed in visual form and in practical ways through associating. Thus, unity becomes an imperative, an irreducible task of the church that expresses its nature. Though appeals to the concept of *koinonia* may lead some to an abstraction of unity as "spiritual unity," or to transposition it into some eschatological future, the image of the body means that it should be expressed here and now in a visible form.[174] Also, this unity cannot be limited by the volition of particular congregations or by confessional or denominational boundaries because it is the *esse* of the church.

For Fiddes, associations, unions and ecumenical bodies are imperfect forms of expression of the unity of the church.[175] He is also convinced that the universal church has never been made fully visible in history.[176] This, by necessity, means two things: on the one hand, the whole catholic church will only be visible in the eschaton; on the other hand, the existing visible forms of the church are fragmentary manifestations of the whole. The universal church

---

168. Fiddes, *Tracks and Traces*, 194–96.
169. Fiddes, *Tracks and Traces*, 195.
170. Fiddes, *Tracks and Traces*, 214.
171. Fiddes, "Church's Ecumenical Calling," 53–54.
172. Fiddes, "Church's Ecumenical Calling," 53.
173. Fiddes, *Tracks and Traces*, 215. Emphasis original.
174. See sections 2.4.4 and 3.4.3.
175. Fiddes, *Tracks and Traces*, 200; see also Jones, *European Baptist Federation*, 2.
176. Fiddes, "Church and Salvation," 135.

is not made of many local churches but "the small bodies exist as 'outcropping' of the whole body,"[177] and this applies to both local churches and communions of churches. Fiddes admits the fact of the brokenness of the church,[178] and he points to God's humility in accepting the divided church, calling this "a dimension of God's experience of the cross."[179] Thus, his understanding of unity in the imperfect forms of associations both admits the reality of division in the church and expresses commitment to making unity in Christ visible.[180] Vasilii Pashkov and Modest Korff, who in 1884 attempted to launch the Russian Evangelical Alliance to implement their vision of Christian unity, believed in unity of the body of Christ but admitted that "if the completion of unity of all the earthly Church does not depend on us, then at least we are obliged to enhance the unity of the Church where the Lord has placed us."[181] Therefore, associations of churches are legitimate expressions of the unity of the church.

8.4.3 Watching Over Each Other

One of the foundational aspects of covenant community is commitment to "walking together." This is also a commitment to mutual care ("watching over each other" or *episkope*) on the way of discipleship. Fiddes contends that "*episkope* happens where there is fellowship or covenant."[182] That is, emergence of a community, whether local or trans-local, leads to the development of spiritual oversight. The genesis of trans-local *episkope* among Ukrainian Baptists follows this basic pattern.

In 1880–1904, in the initial stages of the development of a semi-legal union, trans-local ministers (TLMs) functioned as evangelists, establishing new churches, and teachers, visiting dispersed communities to unify their

---

177. Fiddes, *Tracks and Traces*, 198; Fiddes, "Church's Ecumenical Calling," 44. See also Mazaev pointing out that the church actually pre-exists churches and Russian Baptists are joined to something larger and more ancient than themselves in Mazaev, "Imia 'Baptisty,'" 3.

178. Baptist Union of Great Britain, *The Nature of the Assembly*, 9; Fiddes, *Tracks and Traces*, 205. Another reason is the church's sharing in Christ's dying for the world.

179. Fiddes, "Church and Salvation," 137.

180. Fiddes, *Tracks and Traces*, 206, 247.

181. VSEKhB, *Istoriia Evangelskikh Khristian-Baptistov v SSSR*, 98.

182. Fiddes, *Leading Question*, 44; Baptist Union of Great Britain, *The Nature of the Assembly*, 30.

beliefs and practices.[183] In 1905–1935, the union evolved into a recognised state-wide organization, and besides evangelists and teachers, there emerged senior presbyters who established churches, participated in the election and ordination of ministers, communicated correct understanding of government resolutions and connected regional associations and the union.[184] In 1944–1990, the union was re-established under heavy involvement and control of the Soviet government. Teachers and evangelists disappeared, and senior presbyters assumed the role of denominational functionaries who communicated the decisions of AUCECB to the churches and exercised control.[185] In independent Ukraine (1991–present), senior presbyters lost their controlling function but still connect the wider union and regional associations. This summary demonstrates that the transformation of the functions of TLMs to a degree occurred with changing external circumstances. Nevertheless, whatever the context, TLMs retained several key functions: ensuring the unity of the churches, constituting local churches through the ordination of ministers and supporting communities through pastoral visitations and the mediation of conflicts. Unity and the communities' growth in maturity were, perhaps, among the major goals of TLMs. Thus, Mikhail Ratushny believed that visits to newly planted churches should "unify them into one thought according to the teaching of the Gospel,"[186] and Vasilii Ivanov labelled TLMs as "apostolic care," almost certainly hinting at Apostle Paul's practice.[187]

Speaking about the status of teachers and evangelists, Nikolai Odintsov put them among the ministers of the universal church.[188] The leadership of AUCECB after the Second World War contended that senior presbyters were "overseers."[189] Nikolai Levindanto originally claimed that teachers have the same ministerial status and equal rights "in economy" (*domostroitel'stvo*) as pastors, except authority in local churches.[190] Nevertheless, they still oper-

---

183. Section 2.3.2.
184. Section 3.3.2.
185. Section 4.2.2.
186. Aleksii Ia. (Dorodnitsyn), *Materialy*, 560. Emphasis added.
187. Val'kevich, *Zapiska*, Appendix 3, 26.
188. Odintsov, "O Tserkvi," 6.
189. Section 4.2.2.
190. Levindanto, "O Pravakh Sluzhitelei Tserkvi," 20–21; see also Sapozhnikov, "Sluzhiteli Tserkvi," 7. Later, Levindanto assumed Odintsov's differentiation of local and universal ministers. See Levindanto, "O Sluzhenii Starshikh Presviterov," 49.

ated within the two-fold order of ministry, as does Paul Fiddes.[191] Within this order, presbyters exercise the function of oversight (*episkope*), which is related to the wider church[192] since they carry on and guard apostolic faith and guide the church into the life of the apostolic community.[193] From this status, it follows that ordination for pastoral oversight should be done in the context of wider fellowship, represented by wider fellowship's ministers. This was a typical practice of Baptists in the Russian Empire and the USSR.[194] Yaroslav Pyzh, commenting on the role of senior presbyters after the Second World War, says that it "exemplifies BFSU's understanding of catholicity. The senior pastor exercised authority over the ordination of the pastors for the local churches and served as a guarantee of the unity of local churches and the whole body of the BFSU."[195] This appraisal stresses the unifying function of TLMs, which was typical at every point of their history, which cannot be said about their authority.

In spite of their status, senior presbyters were not vested with authority to rule over local churches or ACs. Rather, their election and recognition stemmed from faithful service and resulted in "trust and favour of God's people towards them as personalities, individual Christians and ministers in economy."[196] They acted as those who receive a mandate of trust and the right to exercise this ministry among churches.[197] It follows that *episkope* cannot be characterised "by ruling but by the gaining and giving of trust. Pastoral oversight can never be a matter of requiring obedience; the only authority can be that of the winning of trust from others, through service offered in imitation of the self-giving of Christ."[198] Thus, trust is a foundational category that characterises covenant relations and serves as a foundation for leadership in associations of churches.

---

191. Fiddes, *Tracks and Traces*, 88–93.

192. Fiddes, *Leading Question*, 30–32; Baptist Union of Great Britain, *Forms of Ministry*, 23.

193. Fiddes, *Tracks and Traces*, 89.

194. "Protokol S'ezda Predstavitelei," 18; cf. *Pervyi Vseurkainskii S'ezd Baptistov*, 13–14; *Pervyi Svobodnyi S'ezd Sibirskogo Otdela*, 42.

195. Pyzh, "Confessing Community," 118–19. BFSU stands for Baptists in the Former Soviet Union.

196. Levindanto, "O Pravakh Sluzhitelei Tserkvi," 20; cf. *Pervyi Svobodnyi S'ezd Sibirskogo Otdela*, 42.

197. Bandura, Interview 1.A.0, 314–16.

198. Baptist Union of Great Britain, *Forms of Ministry*, 26.

8.4.4 Participating in the Mission of God

Mission was the reality out of which unions emerged and a practice that expresses one of the key convictions of this community. Mission formed the foundation on which the union rests and the goal towards which it is directed.[199] Originally, mission pulled local churches together since they had the same self-understanding and desire to serve God, preaching the gospel in their surroundings. This urged Tiflis Baptist Church to form a missionary union and the church in Osnova to seek to join it.[200] It prompted Wieler to establish Bratstvo, where mission was the driving force and constituting principle.[201] At some points, mission was taken as a task to accomplish or a cause that required the accumulation of all available resources.[202] A pragmatic understanding of mission made it a project instead of expressing the very being of the church.[203]

To overcome this inclination towards pragmatism, it is necessary to reconsider the mission of the church in terms of the continuation of Christ's mission and, thus, participation in the *missio Dei*. Occasionally, some local Baptist leaders interpreted mission theologically by putting it in the wider context of God's redemptive actions. Thus, Vasilii Ivanov opined that believers are called to be Christians and adopted as children of God due to Christ's death. Their calling derives from God's cosmic plan of redemption, which is aimed at the renewal of society and the whole of creation.[204] Approaching the calling and mission of Christians from a wider salvific perspective allows Ivanov to shift the point of gravity from mere human activism towards a realisation that believers are partakers in God's mission. Alexander Anan'in also insisted that participation in one mission prompts churches to maintain unity in the form of the union. He pointed to this coming from belonging

---

199. See section 2.4.3.

200. See section 2.2.1.

201. See section 2.2.2; cf. section 3.3.3.

202. This is seen in the constituting of the Missionary Society, which was motivated by pragmatic reasons "to secure more funds from every member of the churches for the spread of the gospel" and was to operate independently from the Baptist union. See Pavlov, "Nashy Sobrania," 15–16.

203. There is a consensus that mission belongs to the nature of the church. See Küng, *Die Kirche*, 313–52; World Council of Churches and Commission on Faith and Order, *Church*, 5–8; Gaillardetz, *Ecclesiology*, 35–84.

204. See section 2.4.3.

to and being baptised by the same Holy Spirit. Here attention is directed to unity shaped by one mission. Both authors emphasise the life of the Spirit as the source of unity and mission.[205]

Paul Fiddes's idea of participation in the Trinitarian *koinonia* through Christ allows us to interpret mission theologically. Ivanov's conviction that the calling and status of Christians is related through Christ to God's cosmic plan is consonant with Fiddes's opinion that the commissioning of disciples in John 20:21 makes them the continuation of Christ's mission in his way.[206] In both interpretations, Jesus Christ is the key person through whom Christians become partakers in God's mission. It means that the church only participates in the mission of the Triune God and does not have its own independent mission. Since Jesus Christ gathers not only local church but, due to his promise in Matthew 18:20, is also present among local churches associating together, then through Jesus Christ associations and unions also participate "in the Father's own sending forth of the Son."[207] Associations as intentional communities share in a common experience and aim. An understanding of being called to and equipped by the Holy Spirit for the same mission is what brings different churches together, uniting them through their mutual commitment to become instruments of the Spirit in this world for the purpose of making Christ known.

Since mission is the movement through which God the Father brings people into communion with him through Christ, then mission is relational *per se*.[208] Due to baptism by the Holy Spirit, Christians become part of the body of Christ and their local communities and associations of churches become the place where the world can meet God. Through Christ, ACs partake in God's own life and continue mission in the form of community.[209] The preaching of the gospel gives people a chance to respond and join communities of the kingdom that comprise covenant fellowships committed to making

---

205. Anan'in, "Ob'edinenie Obshchin Baptistov," 13. However, Anan'in understands mission as the task of the church. On the unity of origin and purpose, see Mazaev, "Edinstvo i Razdelenie," 6.

206. Sharing "in being sent" with the Son, the church also has the characteristic of apostolicity, for apostles are those who were sent. Fiddes, *Tracks and Traces*, 249–52.

207. Fiddes, *Tracks and Traces*, 251.

208. Fiddes, *Tracks and Traces*, 253.

209. Fiddes, *Tracks and Traces*, 253–54.

Christ visible and present in every facet of human society. A local church is wholly church but is not the whole church. Therefore, only by being part of association can local church, with other communities of faith, participate in a more comprehensive witness to God's sending of Christ. Together they can test their understanding of the mind of Christ and discover what God's mission is by listening to the members of the universal body of Christ with whom the local church is united by covenantal ties.[210]

8.5 Summary

This chapter attempts to develop a Ukrainian perspective on the nature of ACs and fix some problematic aspects (local church autonomy; the pragmatic grounds of unity and mission) by engaging with covenant ecclesiology.

A Ukrainian perspective begins with local church as the primary ecclesial reality and interprets it as an intentional covenant community. This approach explains the personal experience of conversion and joining the community, as well as the formation of local church and associations of churches as a response to Christ who gathers his church. It also levels human efforts in the formation of the local church, since the church is manifested rather than constituted. The elements of covenantal language which are present in local baptismal practices and the three shared cases of covenanting root dialogue with covenant ecclesiology in local tradition. This helps to reinterpret the concept of a confessing community as an intentional community and opens avenues for explaining the mutual commitment of believers. Local church as an intentional, covenantal and confessing community recognizes Christ as its only head. This underlies the traditional understanding of local church autonomy, but covenant language points out that the rule of Christ, and participation in the covenant, connects local church with wider ecclesial reality.

Based upon this construction, an association of churches is interpreted as a covenantal brotherhood in Christ. The traditional concept of confession, which was viewed as the foundation for associating, is reinterpreted as a communal act of intentionality that presupposes commitment to a shared journey of discipleship and to confessing one faith. Another aspect of the commitment of associating churches to "walking together" is pastoral

---

210. Fiddes, *Tracks and Traces*, 54–56.

oversight (*episkope*). This office emerges out of fellowship, or covenant, and helps to keep the church in unity and continue apostolic life and mission. The authority of this office is based on the mutual trust between churches and ministers of the covenant fellowship. As an intentional covenant fellowship of churches, brotherhood in Christ is the instrument that makes the body of Christ visible and participates in the mission of Christ. Thus, unity and mission are grounded in covenant relations with the Trinity through Jesus Christ as mediator.

Conclusion

Results

This monograph sought to reconstruct a Ukrainian Baptist understanding of the ecclesiological nature of associations of churches in dialogue with Paul Fiddes's covenant ecclesiology. The first four chapters were devoted to the rediscovery of a historical understanding of the ecclesiological nature of ACs among Baptists in the Russian Empire and the USSR from 1884 to 1990. They focused on the organisational structure, associational practices and theological representation of union retained in the minutes and resolutions of the associational conferences, statutes, official statements, circular letters, confessional texts, publications in church periodicals, memoirs and diaries. Based upon analysis of these sources, I concluded that Baptists in the Russian Empire and the USSR understood associations of churches as ecclesial entities.

The historical analysis facilitated detecting the practice of associating at the earliest stage of the historical development of the Baptist movement in the Russian Empire. It was approximately within a decade after the first conversions, baptisms and formation of the groups of believers into Baptist churches that the representatives of these churches in Ukraine and Transcaucasia began seeking for and practicing associating with similar churches. Though the practical aspects of the survival and mutual support of local churches cannot be totally dismissed, this finding indicates that the practice of associating was in the DNA of those earliest Baptist communities. The practice of associating disclosed a significant theological conviction that local churches should maintain fellowship and be in unity with those who shared the same experience of conversion, confessed one faith and participated in one mission.

The analysis of two associational practices – regular conferences and the ministry of trans-local ministers (evangelists, teachers and senior presbyters) – supports the conclusion stated above. The conferences operated as local church councils where the representatives of the local churches resolved significant issues related to mission and doctrine. The trans-local ministers were treated as the ministers of the universal church, equal to teachers and evangelists (Eph 4:13). They exercised oversight (*episkope*) over the associated churches by encouraging participation in common mission, unity in matters of doctrine and practices, and by helping to resolve conflicts, connect churches together, establish churches and ordain local ministers. Both regular conferences and the ministry of trans-local ministers presupposed the responsibilities of associated churches expressed in intentional fellowship and mutual care.

Organisationally, churches existed in the form of associations that united local churches not individuals. The unsuccessful attempts to introduce the models of the Evangelical Alliance or voluntary association, which presupposed individual membership, indirectly confirmed the conclusion that associations were understood as ecclesial bodies. In these bodies, local churches were primary and the union was derivative. The organisational form of the union transformed over the years, responding to both the inner dynamics of growth and the external legal and political conditions of the country. The exact organisational shape of the union was not sacrosanct and could change to make the ministry of the union more efficient. What was significant and constant was the conviction that unity should be expressed in visible forms. This conviction was rooted in the understanding that visual unity strengthens the witness of the church in this world. However, such understanding did not presuppose that local churches were subject to the authority of wider associations of churches.

The practice of associating and the visualisation of fellowship and unity pointed to significant theological convictions. Theologically, Ukrainian Baptists defined associations of churches as *bratstvo* and the body of Christ. Though the concept of *bratstvo* designated both local communities and wider associations, it was more often applied to the wider associations. These were united upon a common conversion experience, a common confession of faith and shared practices. The concept of *bratstvo* drew on believers' church ecclesiology that brought together concepts of the visible church and the universal church. For Baptists in the Russian Empire and the USSR, associating assumed visible unity of the body of Christ rooted in the Godhead and justified by Christ's High Priestly Prayer (John 17). Unity was the expression of the one body of Christ and a sign of spiritual maturity and health related to the life produced by the Holy Spirit.

Chapters 5 and 6 were aimed at mapping the understanding of the ecclesiological nature of ACs among Ukrainian Baptists during the period of 1991–2014. Both the analysis of current associational practices, organisational structures and theological representation and the semi-structured interviews with key leaders of AUUCECB demonstrated significant continuity with the historical understanding of the nature of ACs. AUUCECB operates as a union of church associations, united by a common confession of faith, a common mission and common practices. The union combines both organic and organisational components. The analysis also detected a shift towards local church autonomy that sharpened the existing tensions between local churches and the union with regard to matters of authority and accountability. The interviews also indicated that some leaders of AUUCECB tend to ground associating and mission pragmatically as the accumulation of resources for more efficient ministry.

Two final chapters (7 and 8) brought together Fiddes's covenant ecclesiology and local understandings of the ecclesiological nature of ACs. Fiddes's concept of covenant, participation in the Trinity and a theology of trust were used to reformulate a Ukrainian Baptist understanding of the local church and ACs.

The local church was reinterpreted as an intentional covenant community under the lordship of Christ. As an intentional community, people commit to something greater than themselves (shared memory, experience and aim) and to each other (co-intention). This community responds to God's initiative in Christ, confessing one faith and committing to communal discipleship. Such a perspective diminishes human efforts in constituting a community of faith, making this act a response to God's initiative. The commitment to the communal confession of faith and discipleship is better expressed through the language of covenanting which is present in a truncated form in the baptismal and ecclesial practices of Ukrainian Baptists.

The emphasis on the lordship of Christ, which has often been used by Baptists to justify local church autonomy, permits both the local church's freedom and the necessity of sharing fellowship with other local churches that are under the same rule of Christ. This idea bridges local church and wider associations of churches by pointing out that a local church is a manifestation of the universal body of Christ that predates it and, due to the presence of Christ, participates in the *koinonia* of the Trinity.

The association of churches was construed as a covenant brotherhood in Christ united by confessing one faith and committed to making visible the unity of the body of Christ in this world, watching over each other and participating in one mission. Within this framework, the confession of faith is reinterpreted as a commitment to a shared journey of discipleship that assumes participation in the wider process of transmitting apostolic faith in history. As a local community is constituted by the presence of Christ, so is a fellowship of churches. Thus, local churches are gathered by Jesus Christ into fellowship that makes the body of Christ visible. Therefore, associations of churches are legitimate expressions of the unity of the church if they are understood as imperfect forms on the way towards fuller *koinonia*. The mutual commitment of churches brings to life the office of oversight (*episkope*) that aims to keep the fellowship in unity, continuing apostolic life and mission. Its authority stems from the mutual trust of the churches and the ministers of the fellowship. As an intentional covenant fellowship, brotherhood in Christ makes the body of Christ visible and participates in Christ's mission in this world.

Contribution of the Monograph

In this monograph, I attempted to explore a subject that has never been studied before. In this sense, it fills a lacuna in the studies of Ukrainian Baptist ecclesiology.

First of all, this study brought together a historical and contemporary understanding of the ecclesiological nature of ACs. For the first time, congress protocols, statutes and publications in denominational periodicals were analysed from an ecclesiological perspective. The monograph also focused attention on documents that contain traces of covenantal language and the practice of covenanting. Second, the monograph indicated that in spite of transformations in organisational forms and leadership models in response to external social-political influences, local Baptist tradition has managed to keep the associational element of its ecclesiological DNA almost unchanged, and it has stayed in continuity with its earlier tradition. Third, this monograph clarified the concept of *bratstvo*, adding an ecclesiological dimension to the already established consensus on its importance for self-identification and for the formation of Baptist structures in the Russian Empire and pointing to its constructive potential for understanding the ecclesiological nature of associations of churches. Fourth, this monograph demonstrated that local tradition was in almost constant dialogue with wider Baptist tradition. The elements of wider Baptist tradition were formative and influential, but the local leadership accepted and adapted those cautiously and critically. Fifth, through research interviews, this monograph for the first time mapped the current understanding of the nature of ACs by those who are considered the keepers of tradition. It also established the continuities and discontinuities within this recent developmental stage of tradition (1944–1990). Sixth, the elements of Fiddes's covenant ecclesiology were used as a conceptual framework for overcoming the intrinsic tensions that local Baptist tradition inherited from the past and for proposing a fresh understanding of the nature of associations of churches that fits the new ecumenical situation in Ukraine.

Areas for Further Study

The monograph employed existing historical documents and studies. This is one of the limits of this study. The major part of the Ukrainian Baptist movement is still in the shadow of the Russian Baptist Union or AUCECB due to the colonial status of Ukraine in the twentieth century. There are a number of studies related to the period of emergence and the existence of the Ukrainian Baptist Union in 1917–1930, but scholars are still far from having a complete picture of the period. I hope that research in now accessible archives may provide new documents and facts that would throw further light on the practices, organisational structures and theological representations of ACs among Ukrainian Baptists.

The mapping of current understanding provided in this monograph might be enhanced and clarified if the opinions of pastors and/or lay leaders of local churches were sought through focus groups. Such a study might provide additional tuning and correction to this account of the nature of ACs.

The present study detected that the foundations that substantiate the authority of ACs within the current model are not clear. The theological grounds of authority and their implications for ACs should be explored further. This issue is related to the problem of reception of decisions. Historically, the dogmatic decisions of the councils became truth not in themselves but through the reception of the church. A Baptist theory and practice of reception should be developed based on ecclesiological grounds. I suggest that this may be pursued in the direction of the lordship of Christ in the community and the practice of "seeking of the mind of Christ."

I hope that this study provides insights for further investigation of these themes in dialogue not only with Baptist tradition but other traditions as well. Only a critical and constructive dialogue with wider tradition will help to identify features (and faults) of local traditions and find new ways of being the church.

APPENDIX 1

Interview Questions and Prompts

QUESTIONS	PROMPTS
RESEARCH QUESTION (RQ)1: HOW DO THE REPRESENTATIVES OF AUUCECB UNDERSTAND THE NATURE OF WIDER ECCLESIAL STRUCTURES?	
Operational Question (OQ)1: In Ukrainian Baptist tradition we use such terms as *ob'edinenie* (association), *souz* (union), and bratstvo (brotherhood). Could you, please, characterize each of them?	What does *ob'edinenie* (association) mean? What does *souz* (union) mean? What does *bratstvo* (brotherhood) mean?
OQ2: Do you think there are distinctions between these structures?	What are the distinctions? What is their purpose? What about their structure? Can you comment on their Essence/Nature?
OQ3: If these structures are necessary, for what purpose?	Could you, please, list their functions?
OQ4: Do you think these structures can do something that local churches cannot?	What specifically? On what level?
RQ2: UPON WHAT THEOLOGICAL IDEAS DO THE REPRESENTATIVES OF THE AUUCECB BAPTIST UNION BASE THIS UNDERSTANDING?	
OQ5: How would you define the church?	Is this a local church or universal?
OQ6: What specific marks or traits does the church have?	

OQ7: Could any of these marks or traits be applied to these structures?	If "yes," which? If "no," why?
OQ8: If you had to explain the necessity of these structures, how would you do this?	Could you suggest biblical, theological or practical reasons?
RQ3: How is this understanding reflected in the documents, current structures, and practices of the AUUCECB?	
OQ9: Do the official documents of your union reflect this understanding of the structures?	What documents?
OQ10: Could you describe the organisational structure of your union?	What authority does every level of the organisational structure have?
OQ11: Do you think that the organisational structure of your union reflects this particular understanding of the nature of these structures?	Could you give an example how practically life of the union embodies the understanding of the nature of ACs you described?
OQ12: As you see it, which regular activities of your union is the best reflection of this particular understanding of the structures?	Representatives' meetings List-bots, circular letters Visitations, Conferences
RQ4: How does this particular understanding of the nature of wider ecclesial structures relate to local church autonomy in the Ukrainian Baptist Union?	
OQ13: What decisions are mandatory for the local churches in your union?	
OQ14: Who makes these decisions?	
OQ15: Could a local church disobey the decisions that are mandatory for the local churches in your union?	
OQ16: What is the role of the leaders in these structures in your union?	Please, list some of their tasks.

APPENDIX 2

Two Versions of the Interview Questions

QUESTIONS v. 1	QESTIONS v. 2
RQ1: How do the representatives of the AUUCECB understand the nature of wider ecclesial structures?	
OQ1: In Ukrainian Baptist tradition we use such terms as ob'edinenie (association), souz (union), and bratstvo (brotherhood). Could you, please, characterize each of them?	OQ1: In Ukrainian Baptist tradition we use such terms as ob'edinenie (association), souz (union), and bratstvo (brotherhood). Could you, please, characterize each of them?
OQ2: Do you think there are distinctions between these structures?	OQ2: Do you think there are distinctions between these structures?
OQ3: If these structures are necessary, for what purpose?	OQ3: If these structures are necessary, for what purpose?
OQ4: Do you think these structures can do something that local churches cannot?	OQ4: Do you think these structures can do something that local churches cannot?
RQ2: Upon what theological ideas do the representatives of the AUUCECB base this understanding?	
OQ5: How would you define the church?	OQ5: How would you define the church?
OQ6: What specific marks or traits does the church have?	OQ6: What specific marks or traits does the church have?

OQ7: Could any of these marks or traits be applied to these structures?	OQ7: Could any of these marks or traits be applied to these structures?
OQ8: If you had to explain the necessity of these structures, how would you do this?	OQ8: If you had to explain the necessity of these structures, how would you do this?
RQ3: How is this understanding reflected in the documents, current structures, and practices of the AUUCECB?	
OQ9: Do the official documents of your union reflect this understanding of the structures?	OQ9: Do the official documents of your union reflect this understanding of the structures?
OQ10: In what way do the organisational forms of your union reflect this particular understanding of the nature of these structures?	OQ10: Could you describe the organisational structure of your union?
OQ11: How is this particular understanding of the structures reflected in the regular activities of your union?	OQ11: Do you think that the organisational structure of your union reflects this particular understanding of the nature of these structures?
	OQ12: As you see it, which regular activities of your union are the best reflection of this particular understanding of the structures?
RQ4: How does this particular understanding of the nature of wider ecclesial structures relate to local church autonomy in the AUUCECB?	
OQ12: What decisions are mandatory for the local churches in your union?	OQ13: What decisions are mandatory for the local churches in your union?
OQ13: Who makes these decisions?	OQ14: Who makes these decisions?
OQ14: Could a local church disobey the decisions that are mandatory for the local churches in your union?	OQ15: Could a local church disobey the decisions that are mandatory for the local churches in your union?
OQ15: What is the role of the leaders in these structures in your union?	OQ16: What is the role of the leaders in these structures in your union?

APPENDIX 3

Initial Coding

QUESTIONS	CATEGORIES
RQ1: How do the representatives of the AUUCECB understand the nature of wider ecclesial structures?	
OQ1: In Ukrainian Baptist tradition we use such terms as ob'edinenie (association), souz (union), and bratstvo (brotherhood). Could you, please, characterize each of them?	**Association, union**: institution, legal, voluntary, territorial, structural administrative. **Brotherhood**: fellowship, biblical, spiritual, confessional, symbolic.
OQ2: Do you think there are distinctions between these structures?	**Association and union (distinctions)**: scope, authority, legitimacy. **Association and union (commonality)**: functions, purpose. **Association and union vs. brotherhood**: structural, administrative body vs. fellowship, spiritual belonging and unity.

OQ3: If these structures are necessary, for what purpose?	**Spiritually**: interdependence, common witness and fellowship as expressions of the church's nature, oversee and protect local churches. **Pragmatically**: cooperation, survival, expansion, movements need structures, help to local churches. **Legally**: representation in church-state, interdenominational and international relations.
OQ4: Do you think these structures can do something that local churches cannot?	Structures are expressions of associations of churches. Structures expand functions of local churches. Structures enhance cooperation. Structures serve as platform for unity. Structures provide for mutual control.
RQ2: Upon what theological ideas do the representatives of the AUUCECB base this understanding?	
OQ5: How would you define the church?	LC: community, gathering, part of UC. UC: Christ's body, invisible gathering.
OQ6: What specific marks or traits does the church have?	**Marks**: gathering in one place, Christ's presence in the Word and sacrament, ministers, common confession (doctrines), regular worship, common practices (Lord's Supper, abiding in God's word, prayers), Acts 2:45.
OQ7: Could any of these marks or traits be applied to these structures?	**Yes**: Lord's Supper at assemblies and congresses, abiding in the word, fellowship and prayers. Association and union more than voluntary, tied through common faith/doctrine, fellowship, practice and leadership.

OQ8: If you had to explain the necessity of these structures, how you would do this?	**Pragmatic**: coexistence, effectiveness in implementation of GC. **Biblical**: trans-local ministry of apostles and prophets (Eph 4); Acts 15; 15:36; 20:17–36: John 17:21; 1 Cor 11:16; 2 Cor 8:1–9:13; Titus 1:5. **Theological**: visible unity and belonging to the fullness of the church's life, assemblage of churches as the way of deeper knowing of revelation and correcting each other, spiritual gifts, unity as necessity.
RQ3: HOW IS THIS UNDERSTANDING REFLECTED IN THE DOCUMENTS, CURRENT STRUCTURES, AND PRACTICES OF THE AUUCECB?	
OQ9: Do the official documents of your union reflect this understanding of the structures?	**Documents**: statement of faith (basis), statutes (functions). **Functions**: fellowship, voluntary cooperation, no administrative imposition. **Goal**: expansion of the gospel teaching.
OQ10a[1]: In what way do the organisational forms of your union reflect this particular understanding of the nature of these structures? OQ10: Could you describe the organisational structure of your union?	Assistance to LC, representation of LC on the state, international and interdenominational levels, visitation, no imposition, council as representative body. **Assembly**: highest **Executive Board**: executive **Council**: representative **Committees**: specialised expert and executive groups

---

1. This is the first version of the question. It was modified after the first three interviews and divided into two questions.

OQ11a: How is this particular understanding of the structures reflected in the regular activities of your union? OQ11: Do you think that the organisational structure of your union reflects this particular understanding of the nature of these structures?	Visits; mediation of conflicts; participation of union's representatives in association assembly; meetings of councils, correspondence. Union as advisory body; mediatory structure.
OQ12: As you see it, which regular activities of your union is the best reflection of this particular understanding of the structures?	Visitation of LC by association and union ministers; participation of the union representative in association meetings; mediatory work; church celebrations; conferences and seminars; financial support.
RQ4: HOW DOES THIS PARTICULAR UNDERSTANDING OF THE NATURE OF WIDER ECCLESIAL STRUCTURES RELATE TO LOCAL CHURCH AUTONOMY IN THE AUUCECB?	
OQ13: What decisions are mandatory for the local churches in your union?	None mandatory (3 persons). Mandatory (4 persons): Statement of faith, biblical requirements to ministers, church discipline. Statement of faith, statutes.
OQ14: Who makes these decisions?	General Assembly: amendments to statutes, confession of faith, election of leadership, strategic steps.
OQ15: Could a local church disobey the decisions that are mandatory for the local churches in your union?	Yes, but may be excluded.
OQ16: What is the role of the leaders in these structures in your union?	**Role**: mediation, care for spiritual, organisational, financial state of LC, advisory. **Qualities**: spiritual vs. organisational. **Images**: servants, slaves of Christ, spiritual persons.

APPENDIX 4

Constitution of the Church[1]

Church's meeting on August 17, 1880. The chair is August Liebig from Odessa.

1) Having opened the meeting with prayer brother A. Liebig asks the community whether all brothers and sisters want to constitute a Baptist community here?

    After the vote it appears that all univocally decided to constitute the community on the same foundation as all our Baptist communities.

2) There were enumerated 20 members present at the meeting.

3) Further the chair asks by which name the community wants to be known.

    Brother Pavlov says that the community already has its stamp on which it is named "1st Tiflis Community of Baptists" and this is the name it should bear in the future.

    Brother I. Kargel supposes that this name may confuse other communities since the word "first" may presuppose existence of another community and, it may happen, that Voronin, for example, gives somebody a testimony on behalf of the second community and such person can, probably, be accepted by the churches.

---

1. For the Russian text, see Val'kevich, *Zapiska*, Appendix 1, 45–47. For a better quality of the text, see Aleksii Ia. (Dorodnitsyn), *Materialy*, 637–40. Pagination follows the text in Aleksii, (Dorodnitsyn).

It was unanimously decided that the community wants to name itself before the government as well as the other churches "The First Tiflis Community of Baptists."

4) Then the chair asks the community whether it recognises itself to be God's work not human work?

All unanimously answer yes.

5) Further the chair asks the community if it wants to have the Bible without apocrypha as the rule and governing principle for its life and doctrines?

The unanimous answer yes follows.

6) The chair. Every community has its own confession of faith which is not put above God's word but serves a token of agreement for the community, expresses its faith in the teaching of God's word. Are you familiar with our confession of faith?

Brother F.M. Mazaev replies that he did not read it.

Brother V. Pavlov explains that the question is not about actual reading of the confession but rather familiarity with its content.

On this brother Feodor Mazaev replies that he knows the teaching of our confession.

Charing brother August Liebig begins to explain some doctrines but having assured that the community is familiar with the content of the confession, leaves it and asks another question.

7) Do brothers and sisters want to immediately unite into a community on the basis of God's word for the spreading of God's word, mutual help on the way of life and exhortation in faith.

Unanimous answer: yes.

8) The chair. Do you acknowledge the Lord Jesus Christ the only supreme Head of the Church and do you reject all visible heads in the Church on earth?

The community unanimously answers: yes.

The chair. Does the community acknowledge that church offices are instituted from God?

The community unanimously answers: yes.

The chair continues: blessed existence of the community is only possible if it has church offices. Therefore, when the presbyter is absent the community should not make any significant decisions.

9) The chair. I heard that in response to the government requirements you elected br. V. Pavlov for a presbyter and br. S.G. Rodionov for a teacher, didn't you?

    The community unanimously: yes.

    The chair. I also heard that you elected Andrei Mazaev and Martin Kalweit for deacons. Thus, do you want to renew, I am not saying to approve, their election and perform laying on of hands over them?

    The community unanimously: yes.

10) The chair continues: We believe that governance and leading should be in hand of presbyter; he must care for bodily and spiritual good of all community; therefore, the community should not make important decisions when he is absent but only when he is present. In case of the extreme need, when the community needs to hold a meeting, it should *unanimously*[2] elect a chair for this time.

    Brother I. Kargel points out that such election of the chair should only happen in case of extreme necessity. Acceptance of Voronin may serve as a warning in this regard. After this there should be other meetings appointed to sort out different cases and that none of the members had excuse that he or she did not know about the meeting. Upon the consultation the community decided to appoint a time for such meetings later.[3]

11) The chair: members of the community also have duties to each other. These duties, first of all, consist of mutual love to each other. Everyone should watch over and admonish one another. Do you agree to act this way?

    The community unanimously: yes.

---

2. Emphasis original.
3. The enumeration of paragraphs misses numbers 11 and 12.

The chair: Do you want to join our German Union of Churches of Baptised Christians in Germany, Denmark, Switzerland, Russia etc.?

Brother V. Pavlov asks to explain the aim of this union.

The chair: The aim of the aforementioned union is, firstly, in support and spread of missionary activity; then for mutual help between the churches and in order to fulfil Saviour's word *"that all be one"* and demonstrate unity to the world. Thus, do you want to join this union?

The community's unanimous response: yes.

The chair: at the future conference the community may send from its side a suggestion to admit it into union.

This ends the meeting at which the community was constituted, and there was a decision reached to perform ordination today in the evening.

Note. Brothers Kargel and Liebig spoke in German and brother V. Pavlov translated into Russian.

The protocol was read and approved by the community at the meeting on August 31st.

Signed: Presbyter *V. Pavlov, Andrei Mazaev,* teacher *S. Rodionov,* M. Kalweit.

APPENDIX 5

Equipping Stundist missionaries for Eastern Siberia[1]

(A letter to the editor of The Kiev Diocesan News)

With the coming of spring, there has been a very lively movement amidst the Stundist brotherhood in the village of Luchina. Almost every day the elder of Luchina Stundist congregation receives couriers from Kherson gubernia with messages, notes, secret orders and verbal directives from the Stundist leaders. There is a rumour that a *special Stundist missionary brotherhood* was established in Kherson gubernia. The purpose of this brotherhood is to entice the whole of Russia into Stundism through the German hymnbook and the New Testament.

In order to achieve this goal, the head of Stundist mission activity, a certain German pastor, recently sent an invitation to all Stundist congregations to participate in the aforementioned missionary work. The Stundist congregation in Luchina received this invitation the other day, and it looks like it went down a treat with these renegades of the Orthodox faith. Almost every day they have solemn meetings at which they enthusiastically and repeatedly read the circular letter of the head of Stundist mission, inviting all the

---

1. For the Russian text, see Ivan Savchenkov, "Snariazhenie Shtundistkikh Missionerov v Vostochnuiu Sibir" [Equipping the Stundist Missionaries to the Eastern Siberia], *Kievskie Eparkhial'nye Vedomosti [Kyiv Diocese Chronicle]*, 1883.

Stundist brothers to move, under the pretence of resettlement, to Eastern Siberia and start a small community, a colony that eventually, because of the tireless efforts of the Stundist brothers, can grow into a mighty *Stundist state* with civil and religious freedom. At one of such meetings, held recently in the house of Stundist Ivan Goncharuk, it was decided to send Liber to the Kiev governor as a representative of the settlers to Eastern Siberia and ask him to help to facilitate their relocation. Liber was very glad to have been chosen and suggested that the brothers should spend the night in prayer. He knelt down before the group of his fellow believers and addressed them with the following speech:

"My beloved brethren! You know already that *we are from God*; he who knows God listens to us; he who is not from God does not listen to us. Therefore, brothers, we are from God, because we listened to our senior brother. We are leaving our home and going to a strange land, getting ready to travel to faraway Eastern Siberia in order to establish a *new homeland*. We are from God, and our obedience will be reckoned to us as righteousness, as it was with Abraham who believed God, and it was reckoned to him as righteousness, and he was called *the friend of God*. And we believed the word of God and became a *brotherhood of God's people*. Abraham, when he was called, obeyed by going out to a place which he was to receive for an inheritance; and he went out, not knowing where he was going. . . . He lived as an alien in the land of promise, as in a foreign land, dwelling in tents with Isaac and Jacob, fellow heirs of the same promise; for he was *looking for* the city which has foundations, whose architect and builder is God. My beloved brethren! We also obey the word of God and go to faraway Eastern Siberia, which we will receive as *an inheritance* like the *promised land* and look forward to the foundation of our own city whose architect and builder is God Himself. We desire a *better* country, that is a heavenly one, therefore God is not ashamed to be called our God; for *He has prepared a city for us*. Therefore, brethren, be renewed in the spirit of your mind and put on *the new self*. Those who sit get up and be careful how you walk, as wise; be filled with the Spirit as bondslaves of Christ, doing the will of God from the heart. Finally, my brethren, be strong in the Lord, and in the strength of His might. Put on the full armour of God, for our struggle is against the world forces of this darkness. Therefore, take up the full armour of God, that you may be able to resist in the evil day, and *having done everything, to stand firm in your faith*. Stand firm therefore, having girded your loins with truth, and having put on the breastplate of righteousness, and having shod your feet with the preparation *to preach our faith*. In addition to all, brethren, take up *the shield of our faith* with which you will be able to extinguish all the flaming missiles of the evil one. And take the helmet of salvation, and *the sword of the Spirit*, which is the word of God. With all prayer and petition pray at all times in the Spirit. And pray on my behalf, that utterance may be given to me in the opening of my mouth, to make known with boldness the mystery of the gospel to the nations that dwell in faraway Siberia, the gospel, for which I am now an ambassador to the authorities, and which I will boldly proclaim, as I should. My brethren, desire earnestly to prophesy. I rejoice that in everything I have confidence in you and pray that God will make you perfect. Brethren, rejoice, be made complete, be comforted. Greet one another with a holy kiss. The grace of the Lord Jesus Christ, and the love of God, and the fellowship of the Holy Spirit, be with you all. Amen."

Having finished his speech, Liber began to exchange kisses with all the members of the future Siberian mission. After that, he instructed all members of his congregation to prepare actively for a long journey to Siberia. At the same time, in order to make it more tempting for the Orthodox, he ordered his audience to slaughter pigs, even those who are not even yearlings, and eat meat, not at home but publicly at the tavern. Barklom Didenko, a peasant from the village of Turbovka and secret follower of this spiteful German teaching, who was also present at this meeting, declared that he would come out of hiding and from then on would not only openly confess the faith of the Stundists, but also go to Siberia as a preacher of Stundist faith. Barklom's declaration was received with rapture. It was immediately decided to start an oath-giving ceremony to show allegiance to Stundist mission. All those preparing for departure for the promised land were to pledge their allegiance, while Liber as a leader and chairman had to read a formal vow, which was immediately done. The fat and pockmarked Liber got on the pew that was next to the table, got on his knees, cleared his throat and, holding a sheet of paper with fat hands that were trembling with agitation, began to read the following:

> In the name of the Lord God, Amen. We the undersigned, spiritual sons of Christ's faith, undertook for the glory of the Most High and for the benefit of Christ's faith, in the honour and glory

of the Lord's name, a journey to Eastern Siberia with the purpose to preach Christ's faith according to the dogmas and teaching of Christians of the Anabaptist confession and to establish first Stundist colony there, commit and promise in front of each other in the glory of the Lord's name, united into the brotherly community of God's friends, at no price separate and leave the community and we pledge to serve the interest of our brotherhood till death. In authentication of this we give our brotherly word and vow before the Lord. Amen.

All the brotherly assembly repeated the pledge and, having given one another a holy kiss, everyone went home. The newly converted Barklom also trudged home despite the dark night, slush and rain.

Barklom came back home as an avowed Stundist, not a secret one. The first thing he did, following the instruction of his elder, was to slaughter his one-year old pig and told his wife to fry some sausages for lunch.

"Have you lost your mind? You must be raving! This is a holy fast. You must have really joined those Stundists," the frightened wife asked Barklom.

"No, sister, I am not a Stundist, but a *brother of God*," Barklom answered meekly to his wife.

"No, dog, you are a devil's brother. That's who you are . . . ," the patriotic wife cried out angrily.

"No, sister, I am a son of God . . . ," Barklom answered even meeker.

"You are the devil himself whose name shouldn't be mentioned here – let the Holy Spirit dwell among us. A swamp demon is in you . . . ," the wife was losing her temper and spitting.

"No, sister, the holy spirit came upon me . . ."

"Shut up! Don't blaspheme or I will break your head with a pestle. If God was with you, you would pray before the holy icons," the wife interrupted Barklom, got on her knees in front of the holy icons and began to say prayers to the Honest Cross and recite the Orthodox creed.

"You can say your prayers to the Blessed Virgin before these boards one *last time*. After that, I will throw them in the trash," Barklom said with a sneer and sat on the bench, waiting for his wife to finish her prayers. The word "last" like an arrow pierced the heart of this pious woman and she decided to keep on praying on her knees until evening and even until after midnight. He had been waiting for a long time, but she was far from finishing her prayer. . . . She intensified the prayer all the more. Finally, the Stundist lost his patience and sprang to his feet like a madman in a frenzy, jumped on the bench behind the table, grabbed the icon of the Mother of God and smashed it against the door. He then stretched out his hand to do the same crazy thing with the icon of the Saviour.

At this moment, he felt a powerful strike of the pestle on his blasphemous hand and immediately stopped his sacrilegious act.

"Insane! Herod! What are you doing? Do you think the Son of God would put up with this mockery?," Barklom's wife, a zealot of Orthodoxy, cried out furiously. Taking advantage of confusion and pain in her husband's hand, she ran out of the house and began to wail and groan, sorrowfully asking for help. The neighbours and relatives heard her yelling and came running. They did not allow the further insult of the holy thing. The neighbours and relatives took all the holy icons were taken from Barklom's house. Barklom's wife took the desecrated icon of the Mother of God, icon of the Saviour and her infant child and, mourning her miserable lot and husband's delusions, went to her mother's place in the village of Lisovka in Skvyra *uezd*.

This is how the preparation for Stundist mission turned out to be a sad incident for the Orthodox Christians.

Peasant Ivan Savchenkov

APPENDIX 6

Church Covenant of the Community of Evangelical Christians-Baptists[1]

"One Lord, one faith, one baptism." (Eph. 4,5)

"Joshua said to all the people . . . choose this day whom you will serve, . . . but as for me and my household, we will serve the Lord. Then the people answered, "Far be it from us that we should forsake the Lord to serve other gods . . . "The Lord our God we will serve, and him we will obey." (Joshua 24,12,15,16,24)

". . . to observe and do all the commandments of the Lord our Lord and his ordinances and his statutes." (Neh. 9,38; 10,29)

". . . If any want to become my followers, let them deny themselves and take up their cross and follow me." (Matt. 16,24)

Since in our Evangelical-Baptist brotherhood a diversion from the teaching of our Lord Jesus Christ is observed, and in result of that many believers turn to the way of wilful sin and loose salvation, we, believers of . . . community of ECB express our desire to reevaluate our lives, renew the covenant with the Lord and each other.

We lay the following as the foundation of our agreement:

---

1. "Proekt Tserkovnogo Zaveta Obshchiny Evangelskikh Khristian-Baptistov (g. Kyiv)" [A Draft of the Church Covenant of the Community of Evangelical Christians-Baptists (Kyiv)], in *Istoria Evangel'skogo Dvizheniia v Evrazii 4.0 [A History of the Evangelical Movement in Eurasia 4.0]* (Odessa: E-AAA, 2005).

1. Our community is a voluntary association of Evangelical Christians-Baptists who confess Jesus Christ as personal Saviour, for "there is no other name under heaven given among mortals by which we must be saved" (Acts 4,12).
2. The only Head of our association is Jesus Christ, the Head of the Church. "He himself is before all things, and in him all things hold together. He is the head of the body, the church" (Col. 1,17–18). Our only Leader is the Holy Spirit, the Spirit of truth who teaches, reminds, admonishes and comforts us. "But the Advocate, the Holy Spirit, whom the Father will send in my name, will teach you everything, and remind you of all that I have said to you" (John 14,26). The only foundation of our teaching is the Word of God, written by God's holy men inspired by the Holy Spirit. (2Pet. 1,19–21), only this Word can prepare for all good work (2Tim. 3, 16–17).
3. Our major goals include:
    a. Sanctification – "For this is the will of God, your sanctification: that you abstain from fornication" (1Thess. 4,3).
    b. Evangelism – "Go therefore and make disciples of all nations, baptizing them in the name of the Father and of the Son and of the Holy Spirit, and teaching them to obey everything that I have commanded you. And remember, I am with you always, to the end of the age" (Matt. 28,19–20).
4. We lay as the foundation of our relations with each other, as the members of one body of the Church of Jesus Christ:
    a. Brotherly love, mercy, longsuffering.

    "I give you a new commandment, that you love one another. Just as I have loved you, you also should love one another" (John 13,34).

    "Love is patient; love is kind; love is not envious or boastful or arrogant or rude. It does not insist on its own way; it is not irritable or resentful; it does not rejoice in wrongdoing, but rejoices in the truth. It bears all things, believes all things, hopes all things, endures all things" (1Cor. 13,4–7).

    b. Self-sacrifice – "Now the man who had been healed did not know who it was, for Jesus had disappeared in the crowd that was there" (John 5,13).

    c. Mutual support and responsibility for each other's' lives. In joy and sorrow respond to all the needs of the Church, be quick to help the people of God, especially there where deprivations and persecutions emerge. To carry all the burdens of the labour and the cross of her sorrows.

"Bear one another's burdens, and in this way you will fulfill the law of Christ" (Gal. 6,2).

5. We admit that the Church herself elects from her own midst ministers that are installed by God through imparting them with the necessary gifts and commitment in ministry (Eph. 4,11–12; Acts 1,20–26), those whose personal qualities should meet the requirements of God's Word. (1Tim. 3; Titus 1). Only the Church and no one else inside or outside of her has the right to elect ministers and this right the Church cannot concede to anybody. Ministers should report to the assembly of the community (the church), that should examine the ministers and also re-elect, remove or recall them. Ministers should not lord over the Church but should provide Christian example through their lives, shepherding the flock (1Pet. 5,3).

6. With regard to attitude towards other communities we will be striving to have brotherly communion with all communities, that withhold the truth and are in one thought with us according to the teaching of our Lord Jesus Christ, we will also provide various support to all who love the Lord.

7. With regard to attitude towards the state we admit that "there is no authority except from God, and those authorities that exist have been instituted by God." (Rom. 13,1) and that we are obliged to obey it in all civil matters on the ground of Rom. 13,7: "Pay to all what is due them—taxes to whom taxes are due, revenue to

whom revenue is due, respect to whom respect is due, honour to whom honour is due."

As to the matters of faith are to obey the instruction of Jesus Christ – Matt. 22,21: "Give therefore to the emperor the things that are the emperor's, and to God the things that are God's." To give what is God's to the Caesar, i.e. to admit the outsiders, extraneous people, godless, to judge the inner church issues and the issues of personal faith is the gravest sin, because this is nothing else as deserting Christ of His right to rule the Church and be her Head. This is also a breach of existing legislation – the decree on separation of the Church from the state and the Constitution of the USSR.

In relation to all the aforementioned issues of inner church life are church's privacy and should not be announced to the extraneous people (1Tim.3,9). The matters of registration, and similar issues related to outer representation, should be decided on the legal basis without interference of the outsiders into inner church life of a community.

Election and ordination of ministers, baptism, performing worship services and so on according the Sacred Scriptures and in accordance with the existing legislation are inner church affairs of the believers themselves and could not be discussed with the outsiders, which is based on 1Cor. 12,28.

We consider all aforementioned necessary to fulfil in our lives first of all because we love the Lord and know that "everyone who does not abide in the teaching of Christ, but goes beyond it, does not have God" (2 John 1,9). And going astray from the truth is the sin that leads to death (James 5,19–20).

Therefore, renewing the covenant with the Lord and each other, we, trusting not ourselves but the Lord, will put all efforts to avert not from the truth and commit no wilful sin but always go the way of sanctification.

Trusting the Lord, we will seek to entrust all our life without remains in His total disposal, fully relying on His guidance and following Him wherever He leads: to sufferings, persecutions, prison, exile – accepting with joy vilification for Christ's name, defamation, dishonour, despoilment of belongings.

"I appeal to you therefore, brothers and sisters, by the mercies of God, to present your bodies as a living sacrifice, holy and acceptable to God, which is your spiritual worship" (Rom. 12:1);

Trusting the Lord, we will do our best to love every brother and sister as ourselves and not keeping towards them grievance, egotism, envy, anger, irritation.

Love Christ's brotherhood, His beloved Church so that be able to "lay your soul for your brothers" and following the example of Macedonian churches participate in the ministry of the church by deed and truth.

"This is my commandment, that you love one another as I have loved you" (John 15:12).

"They gave themselves first to the Lord and, by the will of God, to us" (2 Cor. 8:5).

Trusting the Lord, we will be striving to commit our life to the witness of God's love by personal example and preaching the Christ as the Saviour of sinners.

"Everyone therefore who acknowledges me before others, I also will acknowledge before my Father in heaven; but whoever denies me before others, I also will deny before my Father in heaven" (Matt. 10:32–33);

"For I am not ashamed of the gospel; it is the power of God for salvation to everyone who has faith, to the Jew first and also to the Greek" (Rom. 1:16);

"Choose this day whom you will serve, . . . as for me and my household, we will serve the Lord" (Josh. 24:15);

". . . so that when he is revealed we may have confidence and not be put to shame before him at his coming" (1 John 2:28).

Praise to Him! Amen!

Bibliography

Minutes, Statutes, Statements of Faith

"Instruktivnoe Pis'mo Starshim Presviteram VSEKhB" [Instructional Letter to the Senior Presbyters of AUCECB]. In *Almanakh po Istorii Russkogo Baptizma* [Almanac on the History of Russian Baptism], 3:321–27. Bibliia dlia vsekh, 2004.

"Instruktsiia dlia Upolnomochennykh VSEKhB" [Instruction for Plenipotentiaries AUCECB]. In *Istoriia Evangel'skogo Dvizheniia v Evrazii* [History of the Evangelical Movement in Eurasia]. Odessa: E-AAA, 2005. CD-ROM 4.0.

"Izveshchenie ob Obrazovanii Orgkomiteta" [Notification on Establishment of Organisational Committee]. In *Istoriia Evangel'skogo Dvizheniia v Evrazii* [History of the Evangelical Movement in Eurasia], CD-ROM, 1.1. Odessa: E-AAA, 2004.

"Izveshchenie o Vsesoiuznom Soveshchanii Sluzhitelei Tserkvei Evangel'skikh Khristian-Baptistov" [Notice on All-Union Consultation of the Ministers of the Churches of Evangelical Christians-Baptists]. In *"Bratskii Listok" Soveta Tserkvei EkhB: Sbornik, 1965–2000* ["Fraternal Leaflet" of the Council of Churches of ECB: A Collection, 1965–2000], 33–40. Moscow: Sovet Tserkvei EkhB, 2001.

Mezhdunarodnyi soiuz tserkvei evangelskikh khristian-baptistov. Ob osviashchenii. Veroucheniye. Ustav MSTs EkhB [International Union of Churches of Evangelical Christians-Baptist. On Sanctification. Doctrines. Statutes of ICC EkhB]. N.p.: Khristianin, 2006.

Ob'edinennyi S'ezd (Evangelskikh Khristian I Baptistov) Kavkazskogo Raiona [United Congress (of Evangelical Christians and Baptists) of Caucasus District]. Kislovodsk: Pechatnoe Delo, 1918.

"Obrashchenie Rukovoditelei Evangelskikh Khristian i Baptistov" [Appeal of the leaders of Evangelical Christians and Baptists]. In *Istoriia Evangelskogo*

Dvizheniia v Evrazii [History of the Evangelical Movement in Eurasia], CD-ROM, 4.0. Odessa: E-AAA, 2005.

"Obrashchenie VSEKhiB k Brat'iam i Sestram 29.06.1946" [Appeal of AUCECB to the Brothers and Sisters 29.06.1946]. In *Istoriia Evangelskogo Dvizheniia v Evrazii* [History of the Evangelical Movement in Eurasia], CD-ROM, 4.0. Odessa: E-AAA, 2005.

"Otchet o Rabote Orgkomiteta, 22.09.1962" [Report on Organisational Committee's Work, 22.09.1962]. In *Istoriia Evangel'skogo Dvizheniia v Evrazii* [History of the Evangelical Movement in Eurasia], CD-ROM, 4.0. Odessa: E-AAA, 2005.

Otchet Vserossiiskogo s'ezda evangel'skikh khhristian baptistov [Report of All-Russian council of Evangelical Christians Baptists Moscow, 27 May–6 June, 1920].

Pervyi Svobodnyi S'ezd Russkikh Baptisov Vsei Rossii v g. Vladikavkaze s 20 po 27 Aprelia 1917 [First Free Congress of Russian Baptists of Russia in the City of Vladikavkaz from 2[0t]h to 2[7t]h April 1917]. Baku, 1917.

Pervyi Svobodnyi S'ezd Sibirskogo Otdela Russkogo Soiuza Baptistov [First Free Congress of the Siberian Department of Russian Baptist Union]. Omsk: Zemlia i Volia, 1918.

Pervyi Vseurkainskii S'ezd Baptistov [First Ukrainian Congress of Baptists]. Kiev: Dnepr, 1918.

Piatyi Vseurkainskii S'ezd Khristian Baptistov [Fifth Ukrainian Congress of Christians Baptists]. 1928.

"Pismo VSEKhB o Pravilakh Prepodavaniia Krescheniia (1951)" [An AUCECB Letter on Rules of Baptizing (1951)]. In *Istoriia Evangel'skogo Dvizheniia v Evrazii* [History of the Evangelical Movement in Eurasia], CD-ROM, 4.0. Odessa: E-AAA, 2005.

"Pismo VSEKhB Presviteram Obshchin o Poriadke Provedeniia Bogosluzhenii (1950)" [An AUCECB Letter to Local Presbyters on the Order of Worship Services]. In *Istoriia Evangel'skogo Dvizheniia v Evrazii* [History of the Evangelical Movement in Eurasia], CD-ROM, 4.0. Odessa: E-AAA, 2005.

"Pismo VSEKhB Starshim Presviteram o Poriadke Rassylki Tsirkuliarnykh Pisem (1946)" [An AUCECB Letter to Senior Presbyters on Sending of Circular Letters (1946)]. In *Istoriia Evangel'skogo Dvizheniia v Evrazii* [History of the Evangelical Movement in Eurasia], CD-ROM, 4.0. Odessa: E-AAA, 2005.

"Pismo VSEKhB Starshim Presviteram o Sobliudenii Polozheniia (1957)" [A AUCECB Letter to Senior Presbyters on Obeying the Statutes (1957)]. In *Istoriia Evangel'skogo Dvizheniia v Evrazii* [History of the Evangelical Movement in Eurasia], CD-ROM, 4.0. Odessa: E-AAA, 2005.

"Pismo VSEKhB Starshim Presviteram po Voprosu o Rukopolozhenii (1945)" [An AUCECB Letter to Senior Presbyters on the Issue of Ordination (1945)].

Bibliography

In *Istoriia Evangel'skogo Dvizheniia v Evrazii* [History of the Evangelical Movement in Eurasia], CD-ROM, 4.0. Odessa: E-AAA, 2005.

"Plenum Soveta Vseukrainskogo Soiuza Khristian-Baptistov" [Plenum of the Council of All-Ukraininan Union of Christians-Baptists]. *Baptist Ukrainy* [Ukrainian Baptist], no. 10 (1927): 57–58.

"Polozhenie o Soiuze Evangel'skikh Khristian i Baptistov (1944)" [Statutes on the Union of Evangelical Christians and Baptists]. *Bratskii Vestnik* [Brotherly Herald], no. 1 (1945): 33–34.

"Polozhenie o Soiuze Evangel'skikh Khristian-Baptistov (1948 g.)" [Statutes of the Union of Evangelical Christians-Baptists (1948)]. In *Istoriia Evangel'skogo Dvizheniia v Evrazii* [History of the Evangelical Movement in Eurasia], CD-ROM, 4.0. Odessa: E-AAA, 2005.

"Polozhenie o Soiuze Evangel'skikh Khristian-Baptistov (1960 g.)" [Statutes of the Union of Evangelical Christians-Baptists (1960)]. In *Istoriia Evangel'skogo Dvizheniia v Evrazii* [History of the Evangelical Movement in Eurasia], CD-ROM, 4.0. Odessa: E-AAA, 2005.

"Poslanie Prezidiumu VSEKhB" [Address to the Presidium of AUCECB]. In *Istoriia Evangel'skogo Dvizheniia v Evrazii* [History of the Evangelical Movement in Eurasia], CD-ROM, 1.1. Odessa: E-AAA, 2004.

Pravlenie, V. S. O. B. "Ot Soiuza k Obshchinam" [From the Union to Communities]. *Baptist Ukrainy*, no. 5 (1926): 52–54.

"Proekt Tserkovnogo Zaveta Obshchiny Evangelskikh Khristian-Baptistov (g. Kyiv)" [A Draft of the Church Covenant of the Community of Evangelical Christians-Baptists (Kyiv)]. In *Istoria Evangel'skogo Dvizheniia v Evrazii 4.0* [A History of the Evangelical Movement in Eurasia 4.0], CD-ROM, 4.0. Odessa: E-AAA, 2005.

"Proekt Ustava Russkikh Evangel'skikh Khristian Baptistov No. 1" [Project of Statutes of Russian Evangelical Christians Baptists No. 1]. *Baptist*, no. 35 (1910): 278–80.

"Proekt Ustava Russkikh Evangel'skikh Khristian Baptistov No. 2" [Project of Statutes of Russian Evangelical Christians Baptists No. 2]. *Baptist*, no. 35 (1910): 281.

"Proekt Ustava Soiuza Russkikh Evangel'skikh Khristian Baptistov" [Project of Statutes of the Union of Russian Evangelical Christians Baptists]. *Baptist*, no. 44 (1910): 350–51.

"Protokol Ocherednogo Zasedaniia Missionerskogo Obschestva (13 maia 1909, Odessa)" [Minutes of a Regular Meeting of the Missionary Society, 13 May 1909]. *Baptist*, no. 10 (1909): 18–19.

"Protokol S'ezda Predstavitelei Baptistskikh Obshchin" [The Minutes of the Congress of the Representatives of Baptist Communities]. *Baptist*, no. 22 (1909): 15–18.

"Protokol Uchreditel'nogo S'ezda Missionerskogo Obschestva Evangel'skikh Khristian-Baptistov 5-7 Maia 1907, Rostov-na-Donu" [Minutes of the Constitutive Meeting of the Missionary Society of the Russian Evangelical Christians-Baptists (5-7 May 1907, Rostov-on-Don)]. *Baptist*, no. 2 (1907): 23-24.

"Protokol Zasedanii Konferentsii Predstavitelei Obshchin Russkikh Evangel'skikh Khristian-Baptistov, Proiskhodivshykh v Mae 1907 g. v Rostove na Donu" [Minutes of Sessions of the Conference of Representatives of the Communities of Evagelical Christians–Baptists held in May 1907 in Rostov-on-Don]. *Baptist*, no. 2 (1907): 20-22.

"Protokol Zasedanii Pervogo Ocherednogo Sobraniia Chlenov Missionerskogo Obshchestva Russkikh Evangel'skikh Khristian-Baptistov, Proiskhodivshykh v Balashove, Saratovskoi Gubernii s 30 Iiunia po 2 Iiulia" [Minutes of Sessions of the First Regular Meeting of the Members of Russian Evangelical Christians-Baptist Missionary Society Held in Balashov, Saratov Region 30 June–2 July]. *Baptist*, no. 2 (1907): 23-24.

"Protokol Zasedanii S'ezda" [The Minutes of the Congress Sessions]. *Baptist*, no. 8 (1908): 16-18.

Protokoly i Materialy Pervogo S'ezda Volgo-Kamskogo Soiuza Baptistov v Samare, s 1-go po 7-oe Iiunia 1927 g [Minutes and materials of the First Congress of Volga-Kama Union of Baptists in Samara 1-7 June 1927]. Trotsk: Izd. N.V. Odintsova, 1928.

'Statut pro Upravlinnia Soiuzom Evanhel's'kykh Khrystyian-Baptystiv Ukraïny (1990)' [Statute of All-Ukrainian Union of Churches of Evangelical Christians-Baptists (1990)]. Soiuz Evanhel's'kykh Khrystyian-Baptystiv Ukraïny, 3 Zhovtnia 1990 [Union of Churches of Evangelical Christians-Baptists of Ukraine, 3 October 1990]. Personal Archive of Oleksandr Geychenko.

'Statut Vseukraïns'koho Soiuzu Ob'iednan' Tserkov Evanhel's'kykh Khrystyian-Baptystiv (2002)' [Statute of All-Ukrainian Union of Associations of Churches of Evangelical Christians-Baptists (2002)]. Soiuz Ob'iednan' Tserkov Evanhel's'kykh Khrystyian-Baptystiv, 31 Travnia 2002 [Union of Associations of Churches of Evangelical Christians-Baptists, 31 May 2002]. Personal Archive of Oleksandr Geychenko.

'Statut Vseukraïns'koho Soiuzu Tserkov Evanhel's'kykh Khrystyian-Baptystiv (2014u)' [Statute of All-Ukrainian Union of Churches of Evangelical Christians-Baptists (2014u)]. Soiuz Tserkov Evanhel's'kykh Khrystyian-Baptystiv, 12 Chervnia 2014 [Union of Churches of Evangelical Christians-Baptists, 12 June 2014]. Personal Archive of Oleksandr Geychenko.

'Statut Vseukraïns'koho Soiuzu Tserkov Evanhel's'kykh Khrystyian-Baptystiv (2014c)' [Statute of All-Ukrainian Union of Churches of Evangelical

Christians-Baptists (2014c)]. Soiuz Tserkov Evanhel's'kykh Khrystyian-Baptystiv, 12 Chervnia 2014 [Union of Churches of Evangelical Christians-Baptists, 12 June 2014]. Personal Archive of Oleksandr Geychenko.
"Ustav Evro-Aziatskoi Federatsii Soiuzov EKhB" [Statutes of Euro-Asian Federation of the Unions of ECB]. *Bratskii Vestnik*, no. 3 (1993): 72–75.
"Ustav Soiuza Evangel'skikh Khristian-Baptistov (1963 g.)" [Statutes of the Union of Evangelical Christians-Baptists (1963)]. In *Istoriia Evangel'skogo Dvizheniia v Evrazii* [History of the Evangelical Movement in Eurasia], CD-ROM, 4.0. Odessa: E-AAA, 2005.
"Ustav Soiuza Evangel'skikh Khristian-Baptistov (1979)" [The Statutes of the Union of Evangelical Christians-Baptists (1979)]. *Bratskii Vestnik*, no. 1–2 (1980): 58–65.
"Ustav Soiuza Evangel'skikh Khristian-Baptistov SSSR" [Constitution of the Union of Evangelical Christians-Baptists of USSR]. *Bratskii Vestnik*, no. 6 (1966): 50–53.
"Ustav Soiuza Evangel'skikh Khristian-Baptistov" [Statutes of the Union of Evangelical Christians-Baptists]. *Bratskii Vestnik*, no. 3 (1990): 82–94.
"Ustav Soiuza Tserkvei Evangel'skikh Khristian-Baptistov v SSSR" [Statutes of the Union of Churches of Evangelical Christians-Baptists] In *"Bratskii Listok" Soveta Tserkvei EKhB: Sbornik, 1965–2000* ["Fraternal Leaflet" of the Council of Churches of ECB: A Collection, 1965–2000], 44–48. Moscow: Sovet Tserkvei EKhB, 2001.
IV Vserossiiskii S'ezd Evangel'skikh Khristian Baptistov s 1 po 9 Sentiabria 1910 g. v S.-Peterburge [All-Russian Congress of Evangelical Christians-Baptists 1–9 September 1910 St. Petersburg]. St. Petersburg: Izdanie Russkikh Baptistov, 1910.
26 Vsesoiuznyi s'ezd baptistov S.S.S.R.: protokoly i materialy [26th All-Union congress of Baptists of U.S.S.R.]. Moscow: Izdanie Federativnogo Soiuza Baptistov, 1927.
Zapis' zasedanii plenuma soveta soiuza baptistov SSSR, sostoiavshegosia v Moskve 5–12 dekabria 1925 goda [Records of the meetings of plenum of the Union of Baptists of USSR, occurred in Moscow 5–12 December 1925]. Moscow: Soiuz Baptistov SSSR, 1926.

Interviews

Antoniuk, Valerii. Interview 1.D.0. Interview by Oleksandr Geychenko. Transcript, 3 September 2015.
Bandura, Igor. Interview 1.A.0. Interview by Oleksandr Geychenko. Transcript, 1 February 2015.

Komendant, Grygorii. Interview 1.C.0. Interview by Oleksandr Geychenko. Transcript, 22 June 2015.

Nesteruk, Viacheslav. Interview 1.F.0. Interview by Oleksandr Geychenko. Transcript, 30 November 2017.

Romaniuk, Ivan. Interview 1.E.0. Interview by Oleksandr Geychenko. Transcript, 21 November 2015.

R. S. Interview 1.B.0. Interview by Oleksandr Geychenko. Transcript, 2 June 2015.

Shemchyshyn, Vladimir. Interview 1.G.0. Interview by Oleksandr Geychenko. Transcript, 30 November 2017.

Collections of Historical Documents

Aleskii Ia. (Dorodnitsyn). *Materialy dlia Istorii Religiozno-Ratsionalisticheskago Dvizheniia na Iuge Rossii vo Vtoroi Polovine XIX-go Stoletiia* [Materials for the History of the Religious-Rationalistic Movement in the South of Russia in the Second Half of the 19th Century]. Kazan: Tsentr. tipografia, 1908.

Beznosova, O. V., ed. *Evangel'skoe Dvizhenie v Rossiiskoi Imperii, 1850–1917: Ekaterinoslavskaia Guberniia, Sbornik Dokumentov i materialov* [The Evangelical Movement in the Russian Empire, 1850–1917: The Ekaterinoslav Province, Collection of Documents and Materials]. Dnepropetrovsk: Samencorn, 2006.

Bonch-Bruevich, V., ed. *Materialy k Istorii i Izucheniiu Russkogo Sektantstva i Raskola* [Materials for the History and Study of Russian Sectarianism and Old Believers]. Vol. 1. St. Petersburg: Tipographia V.M. Vol'fa, 1908.

Holovashchenko, S. *Istoriia Evangel'sko-Baptistskogo Dvizheniia v Ukraine: Materialy i Dokumenty* [History of the Evangelical-Baptist Movement in the Ukraine: Materials and Documents]. Odessa: Bogomyslie, 1998.

Val'kevich, Viktor L. *Zapiska o Propagande Protestantskikh Sekt v Rossii i v Osobennosti na Kavkaze* [A Memorandum on the Propaganda of Protestant Sects in Russia And in Particular in the Caucasus]. Tiflis: Tip. Kantseliarii glavnonachalstvuiushchago grazhdanskoi chastiu na Kavkaze, 1900.

Confessional Periodicals

Baptist [Baptist]

"A. E. Leushkin" [A. E. Leushkin]. *Baptist*, no. 2 (1925): 23.

Akimochkin, S. "Po Povodu Stat'i 'Kto Starshe Presviter ili Tserkov'" [On the Article "Who has Seniority, the Presbyter or the Church"]. *Baptist*, no. 18 (1909): 19–20.

Anan'in, A. S. "Ob'edinenie Obschin Baptistov" [Union of Baptist Communities]. *Baptist*, no. 11–12 (1926): 12–19.

Balikhin, F. P. "Mysli po Voprosam Programmy S'ezda" [Thoughts on the Congress's Programme]. *Baptist*, no. 14 (1912): 11.

Baptist [pseudo]. "Nashy Nuzhdy" [Our needs]. *Baptist*, no. 13 (1912): 7–9.

———. "Nashy Nuzhdy (prodolzhenie)" [Our needs (continued)]. *Baptist*, no. 14 (1912): 12–16.

———. "S'ezd Plenuma Soveta Vserossiiskogo Soiuza Baptistov, 10–15 Dekabria 1924 goda" [A Consutation of Plenum of the Council of the All-Russian Baptist Union. 10–14 December 1924]. *Baptist*, no. 2 (1925): 4–5.

Belousov, S. V. "Pervyi Nazidatel'nyi S'ezd Baptistov v Omske" [First Edifying Baptist Congress in Omsk]. *Baptist*, no. 6–7 (1925): 35–39.

"Chetvertyi Vseukrainskii S'ezd Baptistov v Khar'kove" [The Fourth All-Ukrainian Congress of Baptists in Khar'kov]. *Baptist*, no. 4–5 (1925): 1–4.

Clifford, John. "Vsemirnyi Soiuz Baptistov, Ego Proiskhozhdenie, Zhachenie" [World Baptist Union, its origin and meaning]. *Baptist*, no. 30 (1911): 233–34.

"Edinaia tserkov' Bozhiia" [One Church of God]. *Baptist*, no. 1–4 (1914): 11–13.

Fetler, V. A., I. V. Neprash, and D. I. Mazaev. "Nazidatel'nye S'ezdy dlia Veruiushchikh [Edifying Congresses for Believers]." *Baptist*, no. 6 (1912): 9–11.

Filadelfiiskii, I. "Polozhennoe Nachalo" [The Foundation Laid]. *Baptist*, no. 9 (1927): 24–25.

Hiscox, Edward T. "Khristianskaia Tserkov" [The Christian Church]. *Baptist*, no. 23 (1910): 177–178.

———. "Khristianskaia Tserkov" [The Christian Church]. *Baptist*, no. 24 (1910): 185–187.

———. "Khristianskaia Tserkov" [The Christian Church]. *Baptist*, no. 25 (1910): 193–195.

———. "Khristianskaia Tserkov" [The Christian Church]. *Baptist*, no. 26 (1910): 201–204.

———. "Khristianskaia Tserkov" [The Christian Church]. *Baptist*, no. 27 (1910): 209–210.

———. "Obvinenie na Presvitera" [An Accused Minister]. *Baptist*, no. 40 (1911): 314–16.

———. "O Soiuzakh" [On the Unions]. *Baptist*, no. 49–52 (1911): 396–99.

Ivanov, Vasilii V. "Chto Takoe Baptisty i Ikh Soiuz" [What Are the Baptists and Their Union]. *Baptist*, no. 16 (1909): 1–3.

———. "Kniga Episkopa Aleksiia" [Bishop Aleksii's Book]. *Baptist*, no. 9 (1908): 23–27.

———. "Obshchiny i Presvitery" [Churches and Presbyters]. *Baptist*, no. 21–24 (1914): 8–11.

———. "O Soiuze" [On the Union]. *Baptist*, no. 40 (1911): 316–17.
———. "O Soiuze (okonchanie)" [On the Union (continued)]. *Baptist*, no. 50 (1910): 398–99.
———. "Polozhenie Baptistov" [Status of Baptists]. *Baptist*, no. 9 (1911): 69–71.
———. "Telo Khristovo" [Body of Christ]." *Baptist*, no. 20 (1912): 5–9.
———. "Zabota o Vsekh Tserkvakh" [Anxiety for All the Churches]. *Baptist*, no. 1 (1912): 7–10.
Kudelia, I. "Tserkov', Vozniknovenie Ee i Organisatsiia" [Church, Its Origins and Organisation]. *Baptist*, no. 11 (1928): 1–3.
Levindanto, N. A. "Blagochinie Pomestnykh Tserkvei Ili Dukhovnaia Disciplina" [Local Church Discipline]. *Baptist*, no. 3 (1927): 1–9.
———. "O Pravakh Sluzhitelei Tserkvi (v Poriadke Obsuzhdeniia)" [On the Rights of Church Ministers (a Proposal)]. *Baptist*, no. 4 (1928): 20–21.
Mazaev, D. I. "Edinstvo i Razdelenie" [Unity and division]. *Baptist*, no. 2 (1909): 6–8.
———. "Eshche po Povodu Stat'i 'Presviter ili Sovet'" [Once More about the Article "Presbyter of Council"]. *Baptist*, no. 15 (1912): 5–8.
———. "Imia 'Baptisty'" [The name "Baptists"]. *Baptist*, no. 1 (1907): 2–4.
———. "K Protokolu" [On the Minutes]. *Baptist*, no. 13 (1909): 19–20.
———. "Nechto o S'ezde" [Something about the Congress]. *Baptist*, no. 1 (1917): 13–14.
———. "Ne ta Doroga!" [Wrong Way!]. *Baptist*, no. 34 (1911): 268–69.
———. "O Nashikh Nuzhdakh" [On Our Needs]. *Baptist*, no. 17 (1912): 8–12.
———. "O Nashikh Nuzhdakh (prodolzhenie)" [On Our Needs (continued)]. *Baptist*, no. 18 (1912): 7–10.
———. "O Presviterakh" [On Presbyters]. *Baptist*, no. 5 (1907): 12–15.
Mazaev, G. I. "O Edinstve" [On Unity]. *Baptist*, no. 6 (1909): 8–10.
"Na Nive Bozhiei" [In the God's Fields]. *Baptist*, no. 4–5 (1925): 34–35.
Odintsov, N. V. "O Tserkvi" [On the Church]. *Baptist*, no. 9–10 (1926): 4–7.
O[dintsov], N. "S'ezd Baptistov v S.-Peterburge" [Baptist Congress in St. Petersburg]. *Baptist*, no. 38 (1910): 301–4.
Pavlov, V. G. "Besedy 'Baptista'" [Conversations of "The Baptist"]. *Baptist*, no. 35 (1910): 275–76.
———. "K Reorganisatsii Nashego Soiuza" [On Reorganisation of Our Union]. *Baptist*, no. 5 (1908): 26–30.
———. "Kto Starshe Presviter ili Tserkov" [Who has Seniority, the Presbyter or the Church]. *Baptist*, no. 6 (1908): 21–23.
———. "Nam Pishut. Pis'ma s Puti" [Our Correspondence. Letters from Travels]. *Baptist*, no. 23 (1909): 21–23.
———. "Nashy Sobrania i Torzhestva" [Our Gatherings and Celebrations]. *Baptist*, no. 2 (1907): 13–20.

———. "Pravda o Baptistakh" [The Truth about Baptists]. *Baptist*, no. 41 (1911): 322–25.

———. "Pravda o Baptistakh" [The Truth about Baptists]. *Baptist*, no. 42 (1911): 329–33.

———. "Pravda o Baptistakh" [The Truth about Baptists]. *Baptist*, no. 43 (1911): 337–38.

———. "Pravda o Baptistakh" [The Truth about Baptists]. *Baptist*, no. 44 (1911): 345–47.

———. "Pravda o Baptistakh" [The Truth about Baptists]. *Baptist*, no. 45 (1911): 353–56.

———. "Pravda o Baptistakh" [The Truth about Baptists]. *Baptist*, no. 46 (1911): 361–63.

———. "Pravda o Baptistakh" [The Truth about Baptists]." *Baptist*, no. 47 (1911): 369–70.

———. "O Souzakh. (Ot Perevodchika)" [On the Unions. (A Translator's Note)]. *Baptist*, no. 49–52 (1911): 399.

"Raionnyi S'ezd Evangel'skikh Khristian-Baptistov v Peskakh" [District Congress of Evangelical Christians-Baptists in Peski]. *Baptist*, no. 8 (1908): 19–20.

Sapozhnikov, F. "Sluzhiteli Tserkvi i Ikh Rukopolozhenie" [Church Ministers and Their Ordination]. *Baptist*, no. 2 (1927): 5–10.

Shipkov, G. I. "Bratstvo vo Khriste" [Brotherhood in Christ]. *Baptist*, no. 1 (1927): 4–8.

———. "Bratstvo vo Khriste (continued)" [Brotherhood in Christ]. *Baptist*, no. 2 (1927): 1–5.

"Spisok Otdelov, Raionov Soiuza Baptistov i Ikh Adresa" [A List of Departments and Regional Associations of the Baptist Union and Their Addresses]. *Baptist*, no. 3 (1925): 22.

Timoshenko, M. "S'ezd Baptistov v Moskve" [Baptist congress in Moscow]. *Baptist*, no. 45 (1911): 359–60.

———. "S'ezd Baptistov v Moskve (Den' Shestoi)" [Baptist Congress in Moscow (Day Six)]. *Baptist*, no. 46 (1911): 367–68.

———. "Soglasovannost' Raboty (k Voprosu o Edinstve Soiuza Baptistov)" [Harmony of Work (On the Unity of the Baptist Union)]. *Baptist*, no. 6–7 (1925): 25–29.

———. "Soiuz Baptistov i Ego Deiatel'nost (v Poriadke Obsuzhdeniia)" [The Baptist Union and its Activity (a Proposal)]. *Baptist*, no. 11–12 (1926): 20–21.

"26-i Vsesoiuznyi S'ezd Baptistov SSSR" [26th Congress of Baptists of USSR]. *Baptist*, no. 3 (1927): 23–25.

"Voprosy po Domostroitelstvu" [Questions on Economy]. *Baptist*, no. 3 (1928): 23.

Baptist Ukrainy [Ukrainian Baptist]

Aleshko, P. G. "Aven-Ezer (Zasedanie Soveta V.S.O.B. 24–27 Sentiabria 1926)" [Aven-Ezer (Meeting of the Council of UUAB 24–27 September 1926)]. *Baptist Ukrainy*, no. 6 (1926): 52–58.

———. "O Zasedanii Soveta Vseukrainskogo Soiuza Khristian-Baptistov" [On the Meeting of the Council of All-Ukrainian Union of Christians-Baptists]. *Baptist Ukrainy*, no. 5 (1927): 49–54.

Datsko, P. Ia. "Soiuz Baptistov i Ego Deiatel'nost" [The Baptist Union and Its Activity]. *Baptist Ukrainy*, no. 5 (1926): 41–43.

Dranyi, A. "S'ezd Zaporozhskogo Oblastnogo Ob'edinenia" [Congress of Zaporozhe Regional Association]. *Baptist Ukrainy*, no. 5 (1928): 50–51.

Kmeta-Efimovich, Ivan A. "Zhyvye Kamni. Ocherki Istorii Baptisma na Iuge Ukrainy" [Living Stones: Outlines of the History of Baptists in the South of Ukraine]. *Baptist Ukrainy*, no. 10 (1927): 12–15.

Kostiukov, A. P. "Ot Pravleniia Vseukrainskogo Soiuza Baptistov" [From the Executive Board of the All-Ukrainian Union of Baptists]. *Baptist Ukrainy*, no. 1 (1926): 31–32.

———. "K Zasedaniiu Soveta Vseukrainskogo Soiuza Baptistov" [For the Meeting of the Council of All-Ukrainian Baptist Union]. *Baptist Ukrainy*, no. 1 (1926): 32–34.

———. "Vsem Obshchinam, Gruppam i Otdel'nym Chlenam Tserkvi Khristovoi" [To All Communities, Groups and Individual Members of the Church of Christ]. *Baptist Ukrainy*, no. 6 (1927): 43–48.

Krashtan, E. "Godovoi Prazdnik" [Annual Celebration]. *Baptist Ukrainy*, no. 2 (1927): 55–57.

"Na Nive Bozhiei" [In the God's Fields]. *Baptist Ukrainy*, no. 1 (1926): 43–47.

"Pervyi S'ezd Tsentral'nogo Soiuza Baptistov" [The First Congress of the Central Baptist Union]. *Baptist Ukrainy*, no. 8 (1928): 30–33.

Sinitsyn, V. I. "Tserkov Khristova" [Church of Christ]. *Baptist Ukrainy*, no. 1 (1927): 19–23.

Siora, E. "Oblastnaia Dukhovnaia Konferentsiia v Kremenchuge" [Regional Spiritual Conference in Kremenchug]. *Baptist Ukrainy*, no. 4 (1928): 49–54.

Tret'iakov, P. "S'ezd v Konotope" [Assembly in Konotop]. *Baptist Ukrainy*, no. 5 (1927): 54–55.

Ziubanov, N. "Na Nive Bozhiei: Vpechatleniia o S'ezde Sredne-Iuzhnogo Raiona" [On God's Filed: Impressions on the Congress of Mid-South District]. *Baptist Ukrainy*, no. 2 (1926): 44–47.

———. "Trinnadtsatyi S'ezd Sredne-Iuzhnogo Ob'edineniia Kh. B. (Dnepropetrovsk 26–30.X.27)" [Thirteenth Congress of Sredne-Iuzhnyi Association of Ch. B. (Dnepropetrovsk 26–30.X.27)]. *Baptist Ukrainy*, no. 4 (1928): 47–49.

Bratskii Listok [Brotherly Leaflet]

"Izveshchenie o Vsesoiuznom Soveshchanii Sluzhitelei Tserkvei Evangel'skikh Khristian-Baptistov" [Notice on All-Union Consultation of the Ministers of the Churches of Evangelical Christians-Baptists]. In *"Bratskii Listok" Soveta Tserkvei EKhB: Sbornik, 1965-2000* ["Fraternal Leaflet" of the Council of Churches of ECB: A Collection, 1965-2000], 33-40. Moscow: Sovet Tserkvei EKhB, 2001.

Bratskii Vestnik [Brotherly Messenger]

"Avtoritetnost' Vsesoiuznogo Soveshchaniia" [On Authority of All-Union Consultation]. *Bratskii Vestnik*, no. 2 (1945): 18-20.

Bychkov, A. M. "Otchetnyi Doklad VSEKhB 42-Mu S'ezdu" [A Report of AUCECB to the 42nd Congress]." *Bratskii Vestnik*, no. 1-2 (1980): 14-34.

———. "Otchetnyi Doklad VSEKhB 43-Mu S'ezdu EKhB" [Report Presented to the 43rd Congress of ECB]. *Bratskii Vestnik*, no. 3 (1985): 15-34.

Chernopiatov, M. P. "Presviterskoe Soveshchanie v Kurske" [Consultation of Ministers in Kursk]. *Bratskii Vestnik*, no. 1 (1969): 72.

Dukhonchenko, Ia. K. "O Dukhovnom Vospitanii Veruiushchikh" [On Spiritual Formation of Believers]. *Bratskii Vestnik*, no. 5 (1975): 65-69.

———. "Ob Izmeneniiakh v Ustav VSEKhB" [On the Amendments of the Statutes of AUCECB]. *Bratskii Vestnik*, no. 1-2 (1980): 36-42.

———. "Dukhovno-Vospitatel'naia Rabota Sluzhitelei Tserkvi v Dele Ukrepleniia Edinstva Khristian" [Edifying Work of the Ministers for the Cause of Strengthening Christian Unity]. *Bratskii Vestnik*, no. 1 (1983): 50-61.

Fadiukhin, S. P. "Doklad o Edinstve" [Address on Unity]. *Bratskii Vestnik*, no. 6 (1966): 61-67.

"Izveshcheniia VSEKhB" [AUCECB Alerts]. *Bratskii Vestnik*, no. 2 (1945): 42-44.

"Izveshcheniia VSEKhB" [AUCECB Alerts]. *Bratskii Vestnik*, no. 2 (1947): 61-62.

Kadaeva, V. "Zasedanie Soveta Soiuza Evangel'skikh Khristian-Baptistov" [Meeting of the Council of the Union of Evangelical Christians-Baptists]. *Bratskii Vestnik*, no. 1 (1992): 51-62.

Karev, A. V. "Eshche Odin Shag v Dele Edinstva" [One More Step for the Cause of Unity]. *Bratskii Vestnik*, no. 3 (1945): 7-8.

———. "Dokald Na Rasshirennom Soveshchanii VSEKhB" [Address at the Extended Consultation of AUCECB]. *Bratskii Vestnik*, no. 5 (1948): 32-37.

———. "Dokald General'nogo Secretaria VSEKhB" [Address of the Secretary General of AUCECB]. *Bratskii Vestnik*, no. 6 (1966): 15-36.

Kargel, E. I. "O Edinstve Veruiushchikh" [On the Unity of Believers]. *Bratskii Vestnik*, no. 5 (1965): 23-25.

Kargel, M. I. "Golos Bratoliubiia" [The Voice of Brotherly Love]. *Bratskii Vestnik*, no. 4 (1966): 12-14.

Klimenko, A. E. "Doklad o Prodelannoi Rabote Prezidiuma Za 1976 God" [A Report on the Work Done by the Presidium in 1976]. *Bratskii Vestnik*, no. 2 (1977): 56–65.

———. "Otvetstvennost Presviterov i Starshykh Presviterov" [Responsibility of Presbyters and Senior Presbyters]. *Bratskii Vestnik*, no. 1 (1985): 41–50.

Kolesnikov, N. A. "O Vospitanii Veruiushchikh v Pravil'nom Otnoshenii k Svoim Khristianskim Obiazannostiam" [On Formation of Believers in the Right Attitude towards Their Christian Duties]. *Bratskii Vestnik*, no. 3 (1974): 68–73.

Kovalenko, L. E. "Otkrytoe Pis'mo Sovetu Tserkvei po Voprosu Edinstva" [Open Letter to the Council of Churches on the Issue of Unity]. *Bratskii Vestnik*, no. 5 (1970): 74–76.

K. R. "Ocherednoi Plenum VSEKhB" [Ordinary Plenum of AUCECB]. *Bratskii Vestnik*, no. 4 (1989): 58–68.

Levindanto, N. A. "Pamiati Deia Ivanovicha Mazaeva" [In Memory of Dei Ivanovich Mazaev]. *Bratskii Vestnik*, no. 2–3 (1953): 95–98.

———. "O Sluzhenii Starshikh Presviterov" [On the Ministry of Senior Presbyters]. *Bratskii Vestnik*, no. 1 (1956): 48–52.

Mitskevich, Artur I. "O Vospitanii Veruiushchikh v Pravil'nom Otnoshenii k Svoim Khristianskim Obiazannostiam" [On Formation of Believers in the Right Attitude towards Their Christian Duties]. *Bratskii Vestnik*, no. 4 (1974): 54–59.

———. "Tserkov, Sviashchennosluzhiteli i Chleny Tserkvi" [Church, Ministers and Members of the Church]. *Bratskii Vestnik*, no. 2 (1965): 28–34.

———. "Osnovnye Printsipy Evangelskikh Khristian-Baptistov" [Basic Principles of Evangelical Christians-Baptists]. *Bratskii Vestnik*, no. 1 (1966): 44–55.

M[otorin], I. I. "Edinstvo Veruiushchikh" [Unity of Believers]. *Bratskii Vestnik*, no. 1 (1946): 19–22.

———. "Pervyi S'ezd Russkikh Veruiushchikh po Voprosu Edinstva" [First Congress of Russian Believers on the Issue of Unity]. *Bratskii Vestnik*, no. 2 (1946): 24–26.

Nahirniak, Alexandr. "Dei Ivanovich Mazaev" [Dei Ivanovich Mazaev]. *Bratskii Vestnik*, no. 1 (2008): 31–42.

"Obrashchenie Uchastnikov Dukhovno-Nazidatel'nogo S'ezda Soiuza EKhB Ko Vsemu Bratstvu Evangel'skikh Khristian-Baptistov" [Resolution of the Participants of the Spiritual-Edifying Congress of ECB towards All the Brotherhood of Evangelical Christians-Baptists]. *Bratskii Vestnik*, no. 1 (1993): 77–79.

"Obrashchenie Uchastnikov Rasshirennogo Soveta" [Resolution of the Participants of the Meeting of Extended Council]. *Bratskii Vestnik*, no. 1 (1992): 63–64.

Orlov, M. A. "Soobshchenie o Sisteme Upolnomochennykh" [Address on the System of Plenipotentiaries]. *Bratskii Vestnik*, no. 1 (1944): 35–36.

Shatrov, P. K. "Tserkov' Khrista v Svete Ucheniia Sviashchennogo Pisaniia" [Church of Christ in the Light of the Holy Scriptures]. *Bratskii Vestnik*, no. 2 (1977): 13–15.
Somov, K. V. "Odno Stado i Odin Pastyr" [One Flock and One Shepherd]. *Bratskii Vestnik*, no. 5 (1964): 31–34.
Tervits, Ia. "Bratstvo Liubite" [Love Brotherhood]. *Bratskii Vestnik*, no. 5 (1986): 27–29.
"Tretii Den' S'ezda" [Third Day of the Congress]. *Bratskii Vestnik*, no. 2 (1970): 73–75.
Vasks, A. P. "Da Budut Vse Edino (Ev. Ioan. 17:21)" [May All Be One (John 17:21)]. *Bratskii Vestnik*, no. 6 (1966): 54–58.
"Vsesoiuznyi S'ezd Evangel'skikh Khristian-Baptistov v Moskve, Sostoiavshyisia c 15 Po 17 Oktiabria 1963 Goda" [All-Union Congress of Evangelical Christians-Baptists in Moscow on 15–17 October 1963]. *Bratskii Vestnik*, no. 6 (1963): 7–54.
"Vystuplenie Starshego Presvitera po Ukraine A. L. Andreeva" [Address of Senior Presbyter of Ukraine A. L. Andreev]. *Bratskii Vestnik*, no. 6 (1963): 34–37.
Zhidkov, Ia. I. "Neskol'ko Slov o Rabote VSEKhB" [Few Words about AUCECB Work]. *Bratskii Vestnik*, no. 1 (1946): 32–36.
———. "Otradnoe v Zhizni Nashego Bratstva" [Gratifying Things in the Life of Our Brotherhood]. *Bratskii Vestnik*, no. 3 (1946): 10–11.
———. "Nash Otchet" [Our Report]. *Bratskii Vestnik*, no. 1 (1947): 13–18.
———. "Preobrazhenie" [Transfiguration]. *Bratskii Vestnik*, no. 4 (1947): 8–12.
———. "Vzgliad Nazad" [A Look Back]. *Bratskii Vestnik*, no. 1 (1948): 5–10.
———. "Tserkov Khristova i Ee Poriadki" [Church of Christ and Its Orderliness]. *Bratskii Vestnik*, no. 5 (1956): 5–7.

Gost' [Guest]

"Edinstvo Dukha v Soiuze Mira" [Unity of the Spirit in the Bond of Peace]. *Gost'* [Guest], no. 1(15) (2006): 22.
Savinskii, Sergei. "O Sisteme Starshykh Presviterov" [On the System of Senior Presbyters]. *Gost'* [Guest], no. 5(14) (2005): 18–19.

Evangel'skaia Niva/Evangel's'ka Nyva [Gospel Field]

"23-i Z'izd Evangel's'kikh Krystyian-Baptistiv Ukrainy" [23rd Congress of Evangelical Christians-Baptists of Ukraine]. *Evangel's'ka Nyva*, no. 2 (1998).
Dolmatova-Agafonova, Iuliia. "25-i S'ezd Vseukrainskogo Soiuza EKhB" [25th Congress of Al-Ukrainian Union ECB]. *Evangel'skaia Niva*, no. 2 (2006): 2–18.
Komendant, Grygorii."Holova VSO EKhB Zvitue" [The President of AUAECB Reports]. *Evangel's'ka Nyva*, no. 2 (1998): 15–20.

———. "V Edinstve Dukha" [In the Unity of the Spirit]. *Evangel'skaia Niva*, no. 3 (2000): 4–6.

———. "Za Poslednie Chetyre Goda . . . (Otchet Predsedatelia VSO EKhB G. I. Komendanta)" [Over the Last Four Years . . . (A Report of the President of AUUECB G. I. Komendant)]. *Evangel'skaia Niva*, no. 2 (2002): 16–17.

———. "Silnaia Pomestnaia Tserkov' – Silnoe Bratstvo: Otchet Predsedatelia VSO EKhB" [Strong Local Church – Strong Brotherhood: A Report of the President of AUAECB]. *Evangel'skaia Niva*, no. 1 (2006): 24–25.

———. "Otchet Predsedatelia VSO EKhB G.I. Komendanta" [A Report of the President of AUUECB]. *Evangel'skaia Niva*, no. 2 (2006): 7, 10.

Nesteruk, Viacheslav. "Zvitnia Dopovid" [Summary Report]. *Evangel's'ka Nyva*, 2010.

Khrystyians'ke Zhyttia [Christian Life]

Dukhonchenko, Ia. K. "Zvitnia Dopovid" [Summary Report]. *Khrystyians'ke Zhyttia*, February 1990.

"Ednist' Khrystyian – Zaporuka Navernennia Svitu" [Unity of Christians is a Guaranty of Conversion of the World]. *Khrystyians'ke Zhyttia*, April 1989.

Honcharov, V. F. "O Rabote Soiuza EKhB v 1989–1994" [On the Work of the Union of ECB in 1989–1994]. *Khrystyians'ke Zhyttia*, March 1994.

"Interv'iu z Serhiem Sannikovym" [Interview with Serhii Sannikov]. *Khrystyians'ke Zhyttia*, Autumn 1994.

"Slovo Hostiam Z'izdu" [Guests of the Congress Speaking]. *Khrystyians'ke Zhyttia*, n. d., 2-3/1994 edition.

Protestant [Protestant]

Kornilov, N., and A. Rudenko. "Beseda s Ia. K. Dukhonchenko" [Interview with Ia. K. Dukhonchenko]. *Protestant*, 1989.

Mel'nikov, A. "Tsentralizatsiia ii Edinstvo?" [Centralisation or Unity?]. *Protestant*, 1990.

———. "V Plenu u Proshlogo" [Captured by the Past]. *Protestant*, 1990.

Rudenko, A. "Preodolet Administrativnyi Gypnoz" [To Overcome Administrative Hypnosis]. *Protestant*, 1989.

Savinskii, S. N. "K Voprosu o Structure Soiuza EKhB" [On the Issue of the Structure of the Union of ECB]. *Protestant*, 1989.

Slovo Very [Word of Faith]

"Interv'iu z G. I. Komendantom" [Interview with G. I. Komendant]. *Slovo Very*, 1994.

Matviiv, V. N. "Menia Bespokoit Sostoianie Dela Bozh'ego v Ukraine" [I Am Concerned for the State of God's Work in Ukraine]. *Slovo Very*, 1993.
"Regionalnye Ob'edineniia" [Regional Associations]. *Slovo Very*, December 1996.

Memoirs

Fadiukhin, S. P. "Vospominaniia o perezhytom. Chast' II: Otkrovenie griadushchego" [Memoirs of the Past. Part II: Revelation of the Things to Come]. In *Almanakh po Istorii Russkogo Baptizma, Vypusk 3* [Almanac on the History of Russian Baptism, Issue No. 3], 111–319. St. Petersburg: Bibliia dlia vsekh, 2004.

Liubomyrenko, B. *Z Khrystom v Ukraini: Spogady viruiuchogo za roky 1941–1943* [With Christ in Ukraine: Memoirs of a Believer of Years 1941–1943]. Winnipeg: Doroga Pravdy, 1973.

Nyshchyk, S. *Shliakh viry* [Way of Faith]. Winnipeg: Doroga Pravdy, 1975.

Shaptala, M. *Kak eto bylo: Istoriia vozniknoveniia nezavisimogo dvizheniia EKhB* [How All It Was: A History of Emergence of Independent Movement of ECB]. Cherkassy: Smyrna, 2011.

Tserkov' dolzhna ostavat'sia tserkov'iu. Neobratimye desatiletiia: 1917–1937 gody v istorii evangel'skogo i baptistskogo dvizheniia [The Church Should Remain the Church. The Irreversible Decades: 1917–1937 in the History of Evangelical Christian and Baptist Movement]. N.p.: Mezhdunarodnyy sovet tserkvey yevangel'skikh khristian-baptistov, 2008.

Velichko, N. K. *Uzok Put', Vedushchii v Zhizn': Kratkaia Istoriia Kievskoi Nezavisimoi Tserkvi Evangel'skikh Khristian-Baptistov "Khram Spaseniia" 1961–2011* [Narrow is the Way Leading to Life: A Short History of Kyiv Independent Church of Evangelical Christians-Baptists "The Temple of Salvation" 1961–2011]. Kyiv: n.p., 2011.

Vins, G. *Tropoi vernosti* [Following the Path of Faithfulness]. 2nd expanded and corrected ed. St. Petersburg: Biblia dla Vsekh, 1997.

Published Works in Russian and Ukrainian

Aleskii Ia. (Dorodnitsyn). *Iuzhno-Russkii Neobaptizm, Izviestnyi pod Imenem Shtundy: Po Offitsialnym Dokumentam* [South-Russian Neo-Baptism Known by the Name of Stunda: According to Official Documents]. Stavropol-Kavkazskii: Tipo-lit. TM Timoçfeeva, 1903.

———. *Vnutrenniaia Organisatsiia Obshchin Iuzhno-Russkikh Neobaptistov, Shtundistov, to zhe* [Inner Organisation of the Communities of Russian Neo-Baptists, Same Stundists]. Kazan: TSentr. tip, 1908.

Antoniuk, V. S. "Bibliini Pryntsypy Vzaemovidnosyn Mizh Tserkvamy" [Biblical Principles of Relations among Churches]. In *Avtonomiia Pomestnoi Tserkvi: Materialy Simposiuma* [Local Church Autonomy: Proceedings of Symposium], 8–18. Odessa: E-AAA, 2009.

Avtonomiia Pomestnoi Tserkvi: Materialy Simposiuma [Local Church Autonomy: Proceedings of Symposium]. Odessa: E-AAA, 2009.

Bandura, Igor. "Novye Formy Tserkovnogo Sotrudnichestva: Izuchenie Opyta" [New Forms of Church Cooperation: Learning from Experience]. In *Avtonomiia Pomestnoi Tserkvi: Materialy Simposiuma* [Local Church Autonomy: Proceedings of Symposium], 362–70. Odessa: E-AAA, 2009.

Beznosova O. V. "Nemetskie propovedniki-missionery i ih rol' v rasprostranenii protestantizma v Ukraine" [German Preachers-missionaries and their Role in Expansion of Protestantism in Ukraine]. In *Malochislennye natsional'nosti iuga Ukrainy. Istoria i sovremennost': tezisy k Oblastnoi nauchno-prakticheskoi konferentsii 19–20 sentiabria 1990 g.* [Ethnic Minority Groups of Southern Ukraine. History and Present: Theses to Regional Scholarly and Practical Conference 19–20 September 1990], 21–22. Zaporozh'e: ZDU, 1990.

———. "Do pytannia zarodzhennia protestantyzmu v seredovyshche pravoslavnoho naselennia Katerynoslavs'koi hubernii v druhii polovyni XIX – pochatku XX st." [On the Issue of Origin of Protestantism among Orthodox Population of Katerynoslav Region in the Second Half of XIXth – Beginning of XXth cent.]. In *Rehional'ne i zahal'ne v istorii: tezy mizhnarodnoi naukovoi konferencii, prysviachenoi 140-richchiu narodzhennia D. I. Yavornyts'kogo* [Regional and Universal in History: Papers of the International Scholarly Conference in Honour of 140th Anniversary of D. I. Yavornycky], 252–254. Dnipropetrovs'k: Porohy, 1995.

———. "Istoriografiia suspil'no-relihiinyh ruhiv v Ukraini v druhii polovyni XIX st." [Historiography of Social and Religious Movements in the Second Half of the Nineteenth Cent.]. In *Suchasni problemy sotsial'no-humanitarnykh nauk: materialy naukovoi konferentsii* [Contemporary Issues of the Social Science and Humanities: Papers of the Scholarly Conference], 76–78. Dnipropetrovs'k: DDU, 1995.

———. "Rol' nemetskikh kolonistov i mennonitov v rasprostranenii protestantizma sredi pravoslavnogo naseleniia Ukrainy vo vtoroi polovine XIX v." [The Role of German Colonists and Mennonites in the Expansion of Protestantism among Orthodox Population of Ukraine in the Second Half of the Nineteenth Century]. In *Voprosy germanskoi istorii: mezhvuzovskii sbornik nauchnykh trudov* [The Issues of German History: An Intervarsity Compendium of Scholarly Works], 76–86. Dnepropetrovsk: DGU, 1996.

———. "K voprosu o religioznom vzaimovliianii nemtsev-kolonistov i ukrainskogo naseleniia iuga Ukrainy v XIX st." [On the Issue of Mutual

Influence of German Colonists and Ukrainian Population of the South of Russia in the Nineteenth Cent.] In *Etnografichni doslidzhennia naselennia Ukrainy: materialy pershoi vseukrains'koi etnologichnoi konferentsii studentiv ta molodyh vchenyh. L'utyi 1996 r.* [Ethnographic Studies of Ukrainian Population: Papers of the First National Ethnological Conference of the Students and Younger Scholars. February 1996], 39–41. Odesa: n.p., 1996.

———. "K voprosu o religioznom vliianii nemetskikh kolonistov na pravoslavnoe naselenie Ukrainy. Missionerskaia deiatel'nost' I. I. Vilera" [On the Issue of Religious Influence of German Colonists on Orthodox Population of Ukraine: A Missionary Work of I. I. Viler]. In *Ukraina-Germaniia: ekonomicheskoe i intellektual'noe sotrudnichestvo v XIX-XX st.* [Ukraine-Germany: Economic and Intellectual Cooperation in XIX–XX centuries. Vol. I], 18–26. Dnepropetrovsk, NGAU, 1998.

———. "Mennonitskaia obshchina-tserkov' v tsarskoi Rossii: osobennosti ustroistva i otnoshenii s gosudarstvom v kolonistskii period (1786–1874)" [The Mennonite Community-church in Tsarist Russia: Specifics of Polity and Relations with the State in the Colonists' Period (1786–1874)]. In *Rossiiskoe gosudarstvo, obshchestvo i etnicheskie nemtsy: osnovnye etapy i kharakter vzaimootnoshenii (XVIII–XXI vv.): materialy XI Mezhdunarodnoi nauchnoi konferentsii (Moskva, 1–3 noiabria 2006 g.)* [Russian State, Society and Ethnic Germans: Major Stages and the Nature of Relations (XVIII–XXI Centuries: Proceedings of XIth International Scholarly Conference (Moscow, 1–3 November 2006)], 90–100. Moscow: MSNK-press, 2007.

Borodyns'ka, L. I. "Dosvid Ob'ednavchykh Protsesiv Spilnot Evangel'skikh Khrystyian i Baptystiv u Pershii Polovyni XX st." [Experience of Merging of Communities of Evangelical Christians and Baptists in the First Half of the Twentieth Cent.]. In *Naukovi Zapysky Natsional'nogo Universytetu Ostroz'ka Academia. Istorychne Religieznavstvo* [Proceedings of the National University Ostroh Academy. Historical Religious Studies], no. 11 (2014): 49–60.

"Bratskii Listok" Soveta Tserkvei EKhB: Sbornik, 1965–2000 ["Fraternal Leaflet" of the Council of Churches of ECB: A Collection, 1965–2000]. Moscow: Sovet Tserkvei EKhB, 2001.

Cherenkov, Michael. *FORUM 20. Dvadtsat Let Religioznoi Svobody i Aktivnoi Missii v Postsovetskom Obschestve. Itogi, Problemy, Perspectivy Evangel'skikh Tserkvei. Materialy k Discussiam* [FORUM 20. Twenty Years of Religious Freedom and Active Missionary Work in the Post-Soviet Society. Results, Problems, Prospects of Evangelical Churches. Materials for Discussions]. Kyiv: Dukh i Litera, 2011.

Corrado, Sharyl. *Filosofia Sluzheniia Polkovnika Pashkova* [The Philosophy of Ministry of Colonel Vasiliy Pashkov]. St. Petersburg: Bibliia dlia vsekh, 2005.

Datsko, P. Ia. "O Forme Upravleniia Delami Soiuza Baptistov SSSR" [On the Form of the Governance of the Baptist Union of USSR]. In *26 Vsesoiuznyi S"ezd Baptistov S.S.S.R.: Protokoly i Materialy* [26th All-Union Congress of Baptists of USSR], 93–98. Moscow: Izdanie Federativnogo Soiuza Baptistov, 1927.

Debelinskii, S. N. "Praktika Avtonomii: Plusy i Minusy" [Practice of Autonomy: Pros and Cons]. In *Avtonomiia Pomestnoi Tserkvi: Materialy Simposiuma* [Local Church Autonomy: Proceedings of Symposium], 337–42. Odessa: E-AAA, 2009.

Dement'ev, A. *Aven-Ezer: Evangelskoe Dvizhenie v Primor'e (1898–1990 gody)* [Aven-Ezer: Evangelical Movement in Primor'e (1898–1990)]. Vladivostok: Russkii ostrov, 2011.

"Deiatel'nost' Pashkova v Sele Astrakhanke Tavricheskoy Gubernii" [Pashkov's Activity in the Village of Astrakhanka, Tavrida Province]. In *Istoriia Evangel'skogo Dvizheniia v Evrazii 1.1.* [History of the Evangelical Movement in Eurasia 1.1.]. CD-ROM. Odessa: E-AAA, 2004.

Domashovets', Hrygorii. *Narys Istorii Ukrainskoi Evangelsko-Baptystskoi Tserkvy* [Essay on History of Ukrainian Evangelical-Baptist Church]. Irvington: n.p., 1967.

Dyatlik, T. N. "Stremlenie k Avtonomii kak Vozmozhnyi Put' k Agonii: K Voprosu o Vzaimootnosheniiakh Mezhdu Pomestnymi Obshchinami i Bogoslovskimi Vuzami" [Striving towards Autonomy as Possible Way to Agony: On the Issue of Relations Between Local Churches and Theological Institutions]. In *Avtonomiia Pomestnoi Tserkvi: Materialy Simposiuma* [Local Church Autonomy: Proceedings of Symposium], 302–16. Odessa: E-AAA, 2009.

Dyck, Johannes. "Stanovlenie evangel'sko-baptistskogo bratstva v Rossii (1860–1887): Novye fakty iz arkhiva V. A. Pashkova i ikh osmyslenie" [Development of Evangelical-Baptist Brotherhood in Russia (1860–1887): New Facts from V. A. Pashkov Archive and their Evaluation]. In *Materialy Nauchno-bogoslovskoi konferentsii RS EKhB "140 let rossiiskomu baptismu. Proshloe, nastoyashee, perspektivy"* [The Proceedings of the Scholarly Conference "140 Years of Russian Baptism: Past, Present, Prospects"], 7–23. Moscow: RS EKhB, 2008.

———. "Zavisimost' nezavisimosti: obshchina v zhyzni evangel'skogo bratstva v Rossii v period ego stanovleniia (1870–1887)" [Dependence of Independence: A Community in Life of Evangelical Brotherhood in the Period of Its Development (1870–1887)]. In *Avtonomiia pomestnoi tserkvi. Materialy pervogo simpoziuma "Vzaimootnosheniia pomestnoi tserkvi i soiuza" 6–7 dekabria 2007 g. v Kievskoi tserkvi "Dom Evangeliia"* [Local Church Autonomy: The Proceedings of the 1st Colloquium "Relations of the Local Church and the Union" (6–7 December 2007, Kyiv Church "Dom Evangelia"], 275–294. Odessa: EAAA, 2009.

Honcharov, K. V. "Bibleiskoe Obosnovanie Avtonomii Pomestnoi Tserkvi" [Biblical Foundations of Local Church Autonomy]. In *Avtonomiia Pomestnoi Tserkvi: Materialy Simposiuma* [Local Church Autonomy: Proceedings of Symposium], 68–81. Odessa: E-AAA, 2009.

Evangelical Christian Baptist Union. *Evangelskie Khristiane-Baptisty v SSSR: Na Russkom i Angliiskom Iazykakh* [Evangelical Christians Baptists in the USSR: In Russian and English]. Moscow: Izdanie Vsesoiuznogo Soveta Evangelskih Khristian-Baptistov, 1979.

Fiddes, Paul S. "Ekkleziologiia koinonii u katolikov i baptistov: germenevtika, perikhorezis i individual'nost'" [Koinonia Ecclesiology among Roman Catholics and Baptists: Hermeneutics, Perichoresis and Personhood]. *Stranitsy: Bogoslovie, Kul'tura, Obrazovanie* [Pages: Theology, Culture, Education] 18, no. 2 (2014): 250–69.

———. "'Obshchenie v mire i dlia mira': Bogoslovskaia kritika zakliuchitel'noi chasti dokumenta 'Tserkov': na puti k obshchemu videniiu' (dokument no. 214 komissii Vsemirnogo soveta tserkvei 'Vera i tserkovnoe ustroistvo')" ["Koinonia in and for the World": A Theological Critique of the Final Part of "The Church: Towards a Common Vision" (Paper No. 214 of Faith and Order Commission of WCC]. *Stranitsy: Bogoslovie, Kul'tura, Obrazovanie* [Pages: Theology, Culture, Education] 18, no. 4 (2014): 587–601.

Goloshchapova, Ie. O. "Dynamika Tchysel'nosti Hromad Evanhel'skykh Khrystyian-Baptystiv Pivdennoii Ukraiiny u 1920–30-ti rr." [A Dynamics of Membership of the Communities of Evangelical Christians-Baptists of Southern Ukraine in 1920–1930s]. *Naukovi Pratsi Istorychnoho Fakul'tetu Zaporiz's'koho Natsional'noho Universytetu* [Scholarly Works of the Faculty of History of Zaporizhzia National University], no. 27 (2009): 147–55.

———. "Organizatsiina Budova Baptysts'kykh Hromad u 1920-ti rr. (na Materialakh Pivdennoii Ukraiiny)" [Organizational Shape of Baptist Communities in 1920s (On Materials of South Ukraine]. *Naukovi Pratsi Istorychnoho Fakul'tetu Zaporiz'koho Natsional'noho Universytetu* [Scholarly Works of the Faculty of History of Zaporizhzia National University], no. 29 (2010): 153–60.

———. "Osnovni Vektory Diial'nosti Pivdennoukrains'kikh Baptysts'kykh Hromad u Konteksti Sotsial'no-Politychnoi Sytuatsii u 1920–30-kh rr." [Major Vectors of Activities of South-Ukrainian Baptist Communities in the Context of Social-Political Situation in 1920–30s]. *Naukovi Pratsi Istorychnoho Fakul'tetu Zaporiz'koho Natsional'noho Universytetu* [Scholarly Works of the Faculty of History of Zaporizhzia National University], no. 31 (2011): 255–62.

———. "Baptysty Ukrainy v Umovakh Suspil'nykh Transformatsii 20-30-kh rr. XX st.: Isoriographichnyi Aspekt" [Baptists of Ukraine in the Conditions of Societal Transformations in 1920–1930s: A Historiographical Aspect].

Naukovi Pratsi Istorychnoho Fakul'tetu Zaporiz'koho Natsional'noho Universytetu [Scholarly Works of the Faculty of History of Zaporizhzia National University], no. 32 (2012): 318–24.

Hartfeld, Hermann. *Nauchnoe Issledovanie Kontekstualizatsii Bogoslovskikh Doktrin v Zhizni Tserkvei Evangel'skikh Khristian-Baptistov pod Rukovodstvom Vsesoiuznogo Soveta EKhB v Byvshem Sovetskom Soiuze* [Scientific Investigation into Contextualization of Theological Doctrines in the Life of Churches of Evangelical Christians-Baptists under the Leadership of All-Union Council of ECB in the Former Soviet Union]. Cherkassy: Stefanus, 1995.

Iasevich-Borodaevskaia, V. I. *Bor'ba za Veru: Istoriko-Bytovye Ocherki i Obzor Zakondatelystva po Staroobryadchestu i Sektantstvu* [Battle for Faith: Historical and Everyday Essays and the Survey of the Law on Old-Believers and Sectarians]. St. Petersburg: n.p., 1912.

Iuzov, I. *Russkie Dissidenty: Starovery i Dukhovnye Khristiane* [Russian Dissidents: Old-Believers and Spiritual Christians]. St. Petersburg: Tipografia A.M. Kotormina, 1881.

"Ispovedanie Very Khristian-Baptistov, Izdannoe F.G. Pavlovym v Rostove na Donu (1906)" [Confession of Faith of the Christians-Baptists]. In *Istoria Baptizma. Sbornik. Vyp. 1* [History of Baptism. A Compendium. Issue no. 1], 421–34. Odessa: Odessa Theological Seminary, 1996.

Ivanov, M. V. "Avtonomia Tserkvi i Baptistskie Printsipy" [Local Church Autonomy and Baptist Principles]. In *Avtonomia Pomestnoi Tserkvi: Materialy Simposiuma* [Local Church Autonomy: Proceedings of the Simposium], 19–25. Odessa: E-AAA, 2009.

Kalinicheva, Z. V. *Sotsialnaia Sushchnost Baptizma (1917–1929 gg)* [Social Character of Baptism (1917–1929)]. Leningrad: Nauka, 1972.

Kirillovykh, Pavel V. "Krizis Identichnosti u Evangelskikh Khristian-Baptistov: Chetvertyi Printsip Baptizma i Poiavlenie Episkopal'noi Formy Upravleniia" [Identity Crisis among Evangelical Christians-Baptists: Fourth Baptist Principle and Emergence of Episcopal Form of Polity]. In *Materialy Mezhdunarodnoi Nauchno-Practicheskoi Konferentsii "105 Let Legalizatsii Russkogo Baptisma" (5–7 Aprelia 2011)* [Proceedings of the International Scholarly and Practical Conference "105 Years since Legalisation of Russian Baptists], 45–49. Moscow: RS EKhB, 2011.

Klibanov, A. I. *Istoria Religioznogo Sektantstva v Rossii* [A History of Religious Sectarinaism in Russia]. Moscow: Nauka, 1965.

Kmeta-Efimovich I. A. "100-letnii iubilei evangel'skikh khristian-baptistov (v SSSR i v rasseianii) 1867–1967" [A Centenary Jubilee of Evangelical Christians-Baptists in USSR and in Descent]. In *Stoletie evangel'skikh khristian-baptistov* [A Centenary of Evangelical Christians-Baptists]. Ashford, 1967.

Kostiukov, A. P. "Doklad Pravleniia Vseukrainskogo Soiuza Baptistov" [Address of the Executive Board of the All-Ukrainian Union of Baptists]. In *26 Vsesoiuznyi S'ezd Baptistov S.S.S.R.: Protokoly i Materialy* [26th All-Union Congress of Baptists of USSR], 61–69. N.p.: Izdanie Federativnogo Soiuza Baptistov, 1927.

Kriuchkov, G. K. *Velikoe Probuzhdenie XX Veka* [The Great Revival of the 20th Century]. N.p.: Khristianin, 2008.

Kuksenko, Sergey I. "Konfessional'nye issledovaniia istorii baptisma v USSR I SSSR" [Faith-Based Study of the History of Baptists in Ukraine and USSR]. *Vestnik SPbGUKI* [Herald of SPbGUKI]. 1, no. 18 (2014): 184–87.

105 Let Legalizatsii Russkogo Baptizma: Materialy Mezhdunarodnoi Nauchno-Prakticheskoi Konferentsii [105 Years of Legalization of Russian Baptism: Proceedings of International Scholarly and Practical Conference]. Moscow: Russian Union of Evangelical Christians-Baptists, 2011.

Mitrokhin, L. N. *Baptizm: Istoriia i Sovremennost': Filosofsko-Sotsiologicheskie Ocherki* [Baptism: History and Modernity; Philosophical and Sociological Essays]. St. Petersburg: Izd-vo Russkogo Khristianskogo gumanitarnogo in-ta, 1997.

Mitskevich, Artur I. *Istoriia Evangelskikh Khristian-Baptistov* [History of Evangelical Christians-Baptists]. Moscow: Russian Union of Evangelical Christians-Baptists, 2007.

Mokienko M. M. "Vseukrains'kii soiuz ob'ednan' evangel's'ykh khrystyian-baptystiv: transformatsiia religiinogo tsentru" [All-Ukrainian Union of Evangelical Christians-Baptists: a Transformation of Religious Centre]. In *Istoria religii v Ukraini: naukovyi shchorichnyk. Knyga I* [The History of Religions in Ukraine: An Annual Scholarly Compendium. Book I], 633–40. Lviv: Logos, 2007.

Nazarkevich, Yaroslav I. "Poniiattia 'Avtonomnosti' v Istorychnii Perspektyvi (na Dosvidi Velykoi Brytanii, SShA ta Kanady)" [Concept of Autonomy in a Historical Perspective (Based on the Experience of Great Britain, USA and Canada)]. In *Avtonomia Pomestnoi Tserkvi: Materialy Simposiuma* [Local Church Autonomy: Proceedings of the Symposium], 222–34. Odessa: E-AAA, 2009.

"Obobshchenie Obsuzhdenii Diskussionnykh Grupp Uchastnikov Simposiuma 'Avtonomny li Baptisty?' (6–7 Dekabria 2007, Kyiv, Ukraina)" [A Summary of Conversations of the Discussion Groups of Participant of the Symposium "Are Baptist Autonompus?" (6–7 December 2007, Kyiv, Ukraine)]. In *Avtonomia Pomestnoi Tserkvi: Materialy Simposiuma* [Local Church Autonomy: Proceedings of the Symposium], 379–81. Odessa: E-AAA, 2009.

Panych, O. I. 'Instytutsializatsia evangelskogo protestantyzmu d Ukraini (199-ti – 2000-ni roky) [Institutionalization of the Evangelical Protestantism in

Ukraine (1990s – 2000s)]. Українське релігієзнавство [Ukrainian Religious Studies], no. 77 (2016): 55–66.

Pashchenko, V., and Roman A. Sitarchuk. "Deiaki Aspekty Derzhavno-Tserkovnykh Vidnosyn u 20-30-ti rr. XX st. (na Prykladi Hromad Baptystiv ta Evangel's'kykh Khrystyian Poltavshchyny)" [Some Aspects of the State-Church Relations in 1920–30s (On the Example of the Communities of Baptists and Evangelical Christians of Poltava Region)]. *Z Arkhiviv VUChK-GPU-KGB* [From the Archives of VUChK-GPU-KGB], no. 20 (2003): 278–86.

Plett, I. I. *Zarozhdenie Tserkvei EKhB: Zakavkaz'e, Ukraina, Peterburg* [The Origin of the Churches of ECB: Transcaucasia, Ukraine, Petersburg]. N.p.: Khristianin, 1994.

Pospielovsky, Dimitry V. *Pravoslavnaia Tserkov' v Istorii Rusi, Rossii i SSSR. Uchebnoe Posobie* [Orthodox Church in the History of Rus', Russia and the USSR: A Handbook]. Moscow: BBI, 1996.

Potapova, N. V. *Evangel'skoe Khristianstvo i Baptism v Rossii 1917–1922 (Na Materialakh Dal'nego Vostoka: Monographiia. V dvukh tomakh* [Evangelical Christianity and Baptism in Russia in 1917–1922 (on the Materials of the Far East): Monograph. In Two Volumes]. Vol. 1. Iuzhno-Sakhalinsk: Izdatel'stvo SakhGU, 2014.

Prokhanov, I. S. "Izlozhenie Evangel'skoi Very ili Verouchenie Evangel'skikh Khristian, Sostavlennoe I.S. Prokhanovym (1910)" [Exposition of Evangelical Faith or Statement of Faith of Evangelical Christians Composed by I. S. Prohanov (1910)]. In *Istoria Baptizma. Sbornik. Vyp. 1* [History of Baptism. A Compendium. Issue no. 1], edited by S. V. Sannikov, 435–58. Odessa: Odessa Theological Seminary, 1996.

Prugavin, Aleksandr Stepanovich. *Raskol Vverkhu: Ocherki Religioznykh Iskanii v Privilegirovannoi Srede* [Schism in the Above: Essays on Religious Seeking among the Nobility]. St. Petersburg: Obshchestvennaya Pol'za, 1909.

Reshetnikov, Iu. *Ukrainskie Baptisty i Rossiiskaia Imperiia* [Ukrainian Baptists and the Russian Empire]. Odessa: Bogomyslie, 1997.

———. "Ob'edinitel'naia tendenziia i separatism v istorii otechestvennogo baptizma" [A Unifying Tendency and Separatism in the History of Local Baptism]. *Ukrainskoe Religiovedenie* [Ukrainian Religious Studies] 13 (2000): 50–60.

———. "Zahal'ni Problemni Pytannia Evangel's'ko-Baptysts'koi Ekreziologii: Ednist' Soiuzu chy Nezalezhnist' Hromady" [General Problematic Issues of Evangelical-Baptist Ecclesiology: Unity of the Union or Independence of Community]. In *Avtonomia Pomestnoi Tserkvi: Materialy Simposiuma* [Local Church Autonomy: Proceedings of the Symposium], 317–36. Odessa: E-AAA, 2009.

Reshetnikov, Iu., and S. V. Sannikov. *Obzor Istorii Evangelsko-Baptistskogo Bratstva na Ukraine* [Survey of the History of Evangelical-Baptist Brotherhood in Ukraine]. Odessa: Bogomyslie, 2000.

Rozhdestvenskii, Arsenii. *Iuzhnorusskii Shtundizm: Issledovanie Sviashchen. Arseniia Rozhdestvenskogo* [South-Russian Stundizm: A Sudy of Arsenii Rozhdestvenskii]. St Petersburg: Tip. Dep. udelov, 1889.

Sannikov, S. V. *Podgotovka k Kreshcheniiu v Tserkvakh Evangel'skoi Traditsii* [Preparation to Baptism in the Churches of Evangelical Tradition]. 7th ed. Kyiv: Knigonosha, 2016.

Sannikov, Serhii. *Znaky Prysutnosti. Khreshchennia v Konteksti Baptysts'koi Sakramentalogii* [Signs of Presence: Baptism in the Context of Baptist Sacramentalism]. Kyiv: Dukh i Litera, 2019.

Savinskii, S. N. *Istoriia Evangelskikh Khristian-Baptistov Ukrainy, Rossii, Belorussii (1867–1917)* [History of Evangelical Christians-Baptists of Ukraine, Russia and Belorus (1867–1917]. St. Petersburg: Bibliia dlia vsekh, 1999.

———. *Istoriia Evangelskikh Khristian-Baptistov Ukrainy, Rossii, Belorussii (1917–1967)* [History of Evangelical Christians-Baptists of Ukraine, Russia and Belorus (1917–1967)]. St. Petersburg: Bibliia dlia vsekh, 2001.

Savchenkov, Ivan. "Shtundisty s. Luchina, Skvirskogo uezda, Kievskoi Gubernii" [Stundists of the Village Luchina, Skvira District, Kiev Province]. *Kievskie Eparkhial'nye Vedomosti* [Kyiv Diocese Chronicle], no. 3 (1883): 65–70.

———. "Snariazhenie Shtundistskikh Missionerov v Vostochnuiu Sibir" [Equipping the Stundist Missionaries to the Eastern Siberia]. *Kievskie Eparkhial'nye Vedomosti* [Kyiv Diocese Chronicle], no. 15 (1883): 316–17.

Sinichkin A. V. "Dialog mezhdu VSEKhB i STsEKhB v 1961–1972." [A dialogue of VSEKhB and STsEKhb in 1961–1972] *Put' Bogopoznaniya* 10 (2004): 40–80.

———. "Dialog mezhdu VSEKhB i STsEKhB v 1961–1972" [A dialogue of VSEKhB and STsEKhb in 1961–1972]. *Put' Bogopoznaniya* 11 (2005): 68–127.

———. *Vozrozhdenie Vopreki Bezbozhiiu* [Revival in Spite of Godlessness]. Korosten: Dukhovnoe Vozrozhdenie, 2015.

Sitarchuk, Roman A. "Represii shchodo Protestants'kykh Tserkov ta ikh Kerivnykiv u 30-ti rr. XX st." [Repressions towards Protestant Churches and Their Leaders in 1930s]. *Naukovi Zapysky Vinnyts'kogo Derzhavnogo Pedagogichnogo Universytetu* [Proceedings of the Vinnytsia State Pedagogical University], no. 20 (2012): 97–101.

Stricker, Gerd. *Russkaia Pravoslavnaia Tserkov' v Sovetskoe Vremia (1917–1991). Materialy i Dokumenty po Istorii Otnoshenii mezhdu Gosudarstvom i Tserkov'iu* [Russian Orthodox Church during the Soviet Time (1917–1991): Sources and Documents on the History of Relations between the State and the Church]. Vol. 1. Moscow: Propilei, 1995.

Traditsiya Podgotovki Sluzhitelei v Bratstve Evangelskikh Khristian-Baptistov: istoriia i Perspektivy [Traditioin of Training of Ministers in the Brotherhood of Evangelical Christians-Baptists]. Moscow: Russian Union of Evangelical Christians-Baptists, 2013.

Ushinskii, A. D. *O Prichinakh Poiavleniia Ratsionalisticheskikh Uchenii Shtundy: I Nekotorykh Drugikh Podobnykh Sekt v Sel'skom Pravoslavnom Nasilenii i o Merakh Protiv Rasprostranenia Ucheniia Etikh Sekt* [On the Causes of Emergence of the Rationalistic Teachings of Stunda; And Some Other Similar Sects among the Rural Orthodox People and the Measures Against Their Spreading]. Kiev: Tip. S.V. Kul'zhenko, 1884.

Vins, Ia. Ia., ed. *Nashi Baptistskie Printsipy* [Our Baptist Principles]. Kharbin: Tipo-litografiia i tsinkografiia L.M. Abramovicha, 1924.

VSEKhB. *Istoriia Evangelskikh Khristian-Baptistov v SSSR* [History of Evangelical Christians-Baptist in the USSR]. Moscow: VSEKhB, 1989.

Zhabko-Potapovych L. *Khrystovo svitlo v Ukraini: v 2 tomakh* [Christ's Light in Ukraine in 2 Vols.]. Vinnipeg-Chester: N. p., 1952.

Published Works in English

Aasgaard, Reidar. *My Beloved Brothers and Sisters!: Christian Siblingship in Paul.* Journal for the Study of the New Testament. Supplement Series. Early Christianity in Context, no. 265. London: T&T Clark International, 2004.

Acheraïou, Amar. *Questioning Hybridity, Postcolonialism and Globalization.* New York: Palgrave Macmillan, 2011.

Andronoviene, Lina. "As Songs Turn into Life and Life into Songs: On the First-Order Theology of Baptist Hymnody." In *Currents in Baptistic Theology of Worship Today*, edited by Keith G. Jones and Parush R. Parushev, 129–41. Prague: International Baptist Theological Seminary of the European Baptist Federation, 2007.

Anglican Communion Office, and Baptist World Alliance. *Conversations around the World, 2000–2005: The Report of the International Conversations between the Anglican Communion and the Baptist World Alliance.* London: The Anglican Communion Office, 2005.

Ashcroft, Bill, Bill Ashcroft, Gareth Griffiths, and Helen Tiffin. *Postcolonial Studies: The Key Concepts*, 2017.

Aune, David E. *The Westminster Dictionary of New Testament and Early Christian Literature and Rhetoric.* Louisville Westminster John Knox Press, 2010.

Baptist Union of Great Britain. *The Nature of the Assembly and the Council of the Baptist Union of Great Britain.* Didcot: Baptist Union of Great Britain, 1994.

———. *Forms of Ministry Among Baptists: Towards an Understanding of Spiritual Leadership; a Discussion Document.* Didcot: Baptist Union of Great Britain, 1996.

———. *Covenant 21.* Didcot: The Baptist Union of Great Britain, 2001.

Baptist Union of Great Britain and Ireland. *Believing and Being Baptized: Baptism, So-Called Re-Baptism, and Children in the Church; a Discussion Document.* Didcot: Baptist Union of Great Britain, 1996.

———. *Baptist Union Documents, 1948-1977.* Edited by Roger Hayden. London: Baptist Historical Society, 1980.

Baptist Union of Great Britain, Faith and Unity Executive Committee, and Council for Christian Unity. *Pushing at the Boundaries of Unity: Anglicans and Baptists in Conversation.* London: Church House, 2005.

Baptist World Alliance. "Are Baptist Churches Autonomous? Statement from the Baptist World Alliance Symposium on Baptist Identity and Ecclesiology." In *Avtonomia Pomestnoi Tserkvi: Materialy Simposiuma* [Local Church Autonomy: Proceedings of the Symposium], 376–78. Odessa: E-AAA, 2009.

———. "Extended Response from the Baptist World Alliance to a Common Word between Us and You (26 December 2008)." In *A Common Word between Us and You*, edited by au:Mu'assasat Āl al-Bayt lil-Fikr al-Islāmī, 5th-year Anniversary Edition, 213–34. MABDA – English Monograph Series 20. Amman: The Royal Aal Al-Bayt Institute for Islamic Thought, 2012.

Bebbington, David W. *Baptists through the Centuries: A History of a Global People.* Waco: Baylor University Press, 2010.

Beeson, Trevor. "Russia's Reform Baptists and the WCC." *The Christian Century* 92, no. 7 (26 February 1975): 187–88.

Bennett, Frank Russell. *The Fellowship of Kindred Minds: A Socio-Theological Study of the Baptist Association.* Atlanta: Southern Baptist Convention, Home Mission Board, 1974.

———. 'The Nature of the Baptist Association'. *Review & Expositor* 77, no. 2 (1980): 177–84.

Best, Ernest. *A Critical and Exegetical Commentary on Ephesians.* Edinburgh: T & T Clark, 2004.

Bevans, Stephen B. *Models of Contextual Theology.* Maryknoll: Orbis Books, 2003.

Bevans, Stephen B., and Roger P. Schroeder. *Constants in Context: A Theology of Mission for Today.* Maryknoll: Orbis Books, 2009.

Birch, Julian. "Initsiativniki of the Ukraine." *Religion in Communist Lands* 3, no. 6 (November 1, 1975): 20–24.

Boiter, Albert. "Law and Religion in the Soviet Union." *The American Journal of Comparative Law* 35, no. 1 (1987): 97–126. https://doi.org/10.2307/840164.

Bolshakoff, Serge. *Russian Nonconformity: The Story of "Unofficial" Religion in Russia.* Philadelphia: Westminster Press, 1950.

Bourdeaux, Michael. *Religious Ferment in Russia: Protestant Opposition to Soviet Religious Policy.* New York: St. Martin's Press, 1968.

———. "Baptists in the Soviet Union Today." *Baptist History and Heritage* 10, no. 4 (October 1, 1975): 220–232.

Brachlow, Stephen. *The Communion of Saints: Radical Puritan and Separatist Ecclesiology (1570–1625).* Oxford: Oxford University Press, 1988.

Brackney, William H. *Voluntarism: The Dynamic Principle of the Free Church.* Wolfville: Acadia University, 1992.

———. *Christian Voluntarism: Theology and Praxis.* Grand Rapids: Eerdmans, 1997.

———, ed. *The Believers Church: A Voluntary Church; Papers of the Twelfth Believers Church Conference: Held at McMaster Divinity College, October 17–19, 1996.* Kitchener: Pandora Press, 1998.

———. *A Genetic History of Baptist Thought: With Special Reference to Baptists in Britain and North America.* Macon: Mercer University Press, 2004.

———. "An Historical Theologian Looks Anew at Autonomy." In *Avtonomia Pomestnoi Tserkvi: Materialy Simposiuma* [Local Church Autonomy: Proceedings of the Symposium], 257–74. Odessa: E-AAA, 2009.

———. *The A to Z of the Baptists.* Lanham: Scarecrow Press, 2009.

Briggs, John H. Y. *A Dictionary of European Baptist Life and Thought.* Studies in Baptist History and Thought 33. Milton Keynes: Paternoster, 2009.

Callam, Neville. "Models of the Church in the New Testament." In *Avtonomia Pomestnoi Tserkvi: Materialy Simposiuma* [Local Church Autonomy: Proceedings of the Symposium], 165–78. Odessa: E-AAA, 2009.

Carter, David, and Paul Fiddes. "Baptist Ecclesiology." *Ecclesiology* 1, no. 3 (1 May 2005): 87–100. doi:10.1177/1744136605052782.

Catholic Church, and Baptist World Alliance. "The Word of God in the Life of the Church: A Report of International Conversations between the Catholic Church and the Baptist World Alliance 2006–2010". *American Baptist Quarterly* 31, no. 1 (2012): 28–122.

Cheprasov, Timofei. "Political and Religious Factors in the Emergence of the Baptist Movement in the Russian Empire." *Baptistic Theologies* 2, no. 2 (September 1, 2010): 46–58.

Clarke, Anthony, ed. *For the Sake of the Church: Essays in Honour of Paul S. Fiddes.* Centre for Baptist History and Heritage Studies 3. Oxford: Regent's Park College, 2014.

———, ed. *Within the Love of God: Essays on the Doctrine of God in Honour of Paul S. Fiddes.* New York: Oxford University Press, 2014.

Clarke, Anthony John, and Paul S. Fiddes, eds. *Flickering Images: Theology and Film in Dialogue.* Regent's Study Guides 12. Oxford: Regent's Park College, 2005.

Clements, Keith, Paul S. Fiddes, Roger Hayden, Brian Haymes, and Richard L. Kidd. *A Call to Mind: Baptist Essays towards a Theology of Commitment*. London: Baptist Union, 1981.

———. *Bound to Love: The Covenant Basis of Baptist Life and Mission*. London: Baptist Union, 1986.

Coleman, Heather J. *Russian Baptists and Spiritual Revolution, 1905–1929*. Bloomington: Indiana University Press, 2005.

———. "Baptist Beginnings in Russia and Ukraine." *Baptist History and Heritage* 42, no. 1 (December 1, 2007): 24–36.

Collins, Paul M., and Barry A. Ensign-George, eds. *Denomination: Assessing an Ecclesiological Category*. Ecclesiological Investigations 11. London: T & T Clark, 2011.

Colwell, John. *Promise and Presence: An Exploration of Sacramental Theology*. Bletchley: Paternoster, 2005.

———. "The Church as Sacrament: A Mediating Presence." In *Baptist Sacramentalism 2*, edited by Anthony R. Cross and Philip E. Thompson, 48–60. Studies in Baptist History and Thought 25. Eugene: Wipf & Stock, 2009.

———. "Catholicity and Confessionalism." *Baptist Quarterly* 43, no. 1 (1 January 2009): 4–23. https://doi.org/10.1179/bqu.2009.43.1.002.

———. "Integrity and Relatedness: Some Critical Reflections on Congregationalism and Connexionalism." *Baptist Quarterly* 48, no. 1 (2 January 2017): 11–22. https://doi.org/10.1080/20514530.2016.1255408.

Doerksen, Victor G. "Eduard Wüst and Jerusalem." *Mennonite Quarterly Review* 56, no. 2 (April 1, 1982): 169–178.

———. "A Second Menno? Eduard Wüst and Mennonite Brethren Beginnings." *Mennonite Quarterly Review* 74, no. 2 (April 1, 2000): 311–325.

Doyle, Dennis M. *Communion Ecclesiology: Vision and Versions*. Maryknoll: Orbis Books, 2000.

Dulles, Avery. *Models of the Church*. New York: Image Books, 2002.

Duncan, Peter J. S. "Rebounding Identities: The Politics of Identity in Russia and Ukraine." *Religion, State & Society* 38, no. 3 (September 1, 2010): 305–8.

Dunn, James D. G. *The Epistles to the Colossians and to Philemon: A Commentary on the Greek Text*. New International Greek Testament Commentary. Grand Rapids: Eerdmans, 2014.

Durnbaugh, Donald F. *The Believers' Church: The History and Character of Radical Protestantism*. Scottdale: Herald Press, 1985.

Dyck, Johannes. "Fresh Skins for New Wine: On the Structure of the First Russian Baptist Congregations in South Russia." In *Eastern European Baptist History: New Perspectives*, edited by Sharyl Corrado and Toivo Pilli, 34–51. Prague: International Baptist Theological Seminary, 2007.

Ellis, Christopher J. "Understanding Worship: Trends and Criteria." In *Currents in Baptistic Theology of Worship Today*, edited by Keith G. Jones and Parush R. Parushev, 25–40. Praha, Czech Republic: International Baptist Theological Seminary of the European Baptist Federation, 2007.

———. "Worship at the Heart of Life." In *Currents in Baptistic Theology of Worship Today*, edited by Keith G. Jones and Parush R. Parushev, 41–57. Praha, Czech Republic: International Baptist Theological Seminary of the European Baptist Federation, 2007.

Van Engen, Charles Edward. *God's Missionary People: Rethinking the Purpose of the Local Church*. Grand Rapids: Baker Book House, 1991.

Epp, Peter. "A Brief History of the Omsk Brotherhood." *Journal of Mennonite Studies* 30 (2012): 113–32.

European Baptist Federation. *What Are Baptists?: On the Way to Expressing Baptist Identity in a Changing Europe*. EBF, 1993.

Fiddes, Paul S. "God and History." *Baptist Quarterly* 30, no. 2 (1983): 74–90.

———. "Ministry and Ordination." *The Fraternal* 211 (July 1985): 11–19.

———. "Covenant – Old and New." In *Bound to Love: The Covenant Basis of Baptist Life and Mission*, 9–23. London: Baptist Union, 1985.

———. *A Leading Question: The Structure and Authority of Leadership in the Local Church*. London: Baptist Publications, 1986.

———. *The Creative Suffering of God*. Oxford: Oxford University Press, 1988.

———. *Past Event and Present Salvation: The Christian Idea of Atonement*. London: Darton, Longman & Todd, 1989.

———. "The Atonement and the Trinity." In *The Forgotten Trinity*, edited by Alasdair I. C. Heron, 103–22. Vol. 3 of *A Selection of Papers Presented to the BCC Study Commission on Trinitarian Doctrine Today*. London: BCC/CCBI, 1991.

———. "The Cross of Hosea Revisited: The Meaning of Suffering in the Book of Hosea." *Review & Expositor Review & Expositor* 90, no. 2 (1993): 175–90.

———. "Authority in People-Pastor Relationships." In *The Papers of the Study and Research Division of the Baptist World Alliance 1990-1995*, edited by L. A. (Tony), 59–63. Vol. 1 of *Baptist Faith and Witness*. Birmingham, AL: Samford University, 1995.

———. "The Understanding of Salvation in the Baptist Tradition." In *For Us and for Our Salvation: Seven Perspectives on Christian Soteriology*, edited by Rienk L. Lannooy, 15–37. Utrecht-Leiden: Interuniversitair Instituut voor Missiologie en Oecumenica (IIMO) Research Pub., 1995.

———. "Church, Trinity and Covenant. An Ecclesiology of Participation." In *Gemeinschaft Am Evangelium. Festschrift Für Wiard Popkes*, edited by E. Brandt, P. Fiddes, and J. Molthagen, 37–54. Leipzig: Evangelische Verlagsanstalt, 1996.

———. "'Walking Together': The Place of Covenant Theology in Baptist Life Yesterday and Today." In *Pilgrim Pathways: Essays in Baptist History in Honour of B. R. White*, 47–74. Macon: Mercer University Press, 1999.

———. *Believer's Baptism: An Act of Inclusion or Exclusion?* Hertfordshire: Hertfordshire Baptist Association, 1999.

———. *Freedom and Limit: A Dialogue between Literature and Christian Doctrine*. Macon: Mercer University Press, 1999.

———. "Towards a New Millennium: Doctrinal Themes of Strategic Significance for Baptists." In *The Papers of the Study and Research Division of the Baptist World Alliance 1995-2000*, edited by L. A. (Tony) Cupit, 13–22. Vol. 2 of *Baptist Faith and Witness*. McLean: Baptist World Alliance, 1999.

———. *Participating in God: A Pastoral Doctrine of the Trinity*. Louisville: Westminster John Knox Press, 2000.

———. "Theology and a Baptist Way of Community." In *Doing Theology in a Baptist Way*, edited by Paul S. Fiddes, 19–38. Oxford: Whitley Publications, 2000.

———. *The Promised End: Eschatology in Theology and Literature*. Oxford: Blackwell, 2001.

———. "Creation out of Love." In *The Work of Love: Creation as Kenosis*, 167–91. Grand Rapids: Eerdmans, 2001.

———. "Baptism and the Process of Christian Initiation." *The Ecumenical Review* 54, no. 1 (2002): 48–65.

———. "The Church and Salvation: A Comparison of Baptist and Orthodox Thinking." In *Ecumenism and History: Studies in Honour of John H.Y. Briggs*, edited by Anthony R. Cross, 120–48. Studies in Christian History and Thought. Carlisle: Paternoster Press, 2002.

———. "Baptism and the Process of Christian Initiation." In *Dimensions of Baptism: Biblical and Theological Studies*, edited by Stanley E. Porter and Anthony R. Cross, 280–303. JSNT Supplement Series 234. London: Sheffield Academic Press, 2002.

———. "Receiving One Another: The History and Theology of the Church Covenant [at New Road Baptist Church, Oxford], 1780." In *A Protestant Catholic Church of Christ: Essays on the History and Life of New Road Baptist Church, Oxford*, edited by Rosie Chadwick, 65–105. Oxford: New Road Baptist Church, 2003.

———. "Faith and Baptism in the New Testament and Christian Doctrine." In *Dialog Zwischen Der Europäischen Baptistischen Föderation Und Der Gemeinschaft Evangelischer Kirchen in Europa Zur Lehre Und Praxis Der Taufe*, edited by Wilhelm Hüffmeier and Tony Peck, 134–45. Frankfürt am Main: Verlag Otto Lembech, 2005.

———. "Participating in the Trinity." *Perspectives in Religious Studies* 33, no. 3 (September 2006): 375–91.

———. "Learning from Others: Baptists and Receptive Ecumenism." Paper presented to the Society for Ecumenical Studies, "Receptive Ecumenism: The Call to Ecumenical Learning," St. Mary's Catholic Church, Cadogan Street, Chelsea, November 2007. http://sfes.faithweb.com/0711fiddesreceptiveecumenism.pdf.

———. *Tracks and Traces: Baptist Identity in Church and Theology*. Studies in Baptist History and Thought 13. Eugene: Wipf & Stock, 2007.

———. "Learning from Others: Baptists and Receptive Ecumenism." *Louvain Studies* 33, no. 1/2 (2008): 54–73. https://doi.org/10.2143/LS.33.1.203.4336.

———. "Ex Opere Operato: Re-Thinking a Historic Baptist Objection." In vol. 2 of *Baptist Sacramentalism*, edited by Anthony R. Cross and Philip Edward Thompson, 219–38. Studies in Baptist History and Thought 25. Milton Keynes: Paternoster Press, 2008.

———. "Concept, Image and Story in Systematic Theology." *International Journal of Systematic Theology* 11, no. 1 (2009): 3–23.

———. "Covenants, Theology Of." In *A Dictionary of European Baptist Life and Thought*, 124–26. Studies in Baptist History and Thought 33. Milton Keynes: Paternoster Press, 2009.

———. "Daniel Turner and a Theology of the Church Universal." In *Pulpit and People: Studies in Eighteenth Century Baptist Life and Thought*, edited by J. H. Y. Briggs, 112–27. Studies in Baptist History and Thought 28. Eugene: Wipf & Stock, 2009.

———. "Church and Sect: Cross-Currents in Early Baptist Life." In *Exploring Baptist Origins*, edited by Anthony R. Cross and Nicholas J. Wood, 33–60. Centre for Baptist History and Heritage Studies 1. Oxford: Regent's Park College, 2010.

———. "Christian Doctrine and Free Church Ecclesiology: Recent Developments among Baptists in the Southern United States." *Ecclesiology* 7, no. 2 (2011): 195–219. https://doi.org/10.1163/174553111X559454.

———. "A Conversation in Context: An Introduction to the Report *The Word of God in the Life of the Church*." *American Baptist Quarterly* 31, no. 1 (2012): 7–27.

———. "Ethnography and Ecclesiology: Two Disciplines, Two Worlds?" In *Perspectives on Ecclesiology and Ethnography*, edited by Peter Ward, 13–35. Studies in Ecclesiology and Ethnography 1. Grand Rapids: Eerdmans, 2012.

———. "The Church's Ecumenical Calling: A Challenge to Baptists and Pentecostals." In *The Many Faces of Global Pentecostalism*, edited by Harold D. Hunter and Neil Ormerod, 36–61. Cleveland: CPT Press, 2013.

―――. "Baptists and 1662: The Effect of the Act of Uniformity on Baptists and Its Ecumenical Significance for Baptists Today." *Ecclesiology* 9, no. 2 (2013): 183–204. https://doi.org/10.1163/17455316-00902004.

―――. "The Church Local and Universal: Catholic and Baptist Perspectives on Koinonia Ecclesiology." In *Revisioning, Renewing, and Rediscovering the Triune Center: Essays in Honor of Stanley J. Grenz*, edited by Derek J. Tidball, Brian S. Harris, and Jason S. Sexton, 97–120. Eugene: Cascade Books, 2014.

―――. "Praying with Mary and All the Saints." In *Baptists and the Communion of Saints: A Theology of Covenanted Disciples*, 73–102. Waco: Baylor University Press, 2014.

―――. "Communion and Covenant." In *Baptists and the Communion of Saints: A Theology of Covenanted Disciples*, 127–56. Waco: Baylor University Press, 2014.

―――. "God and Story in the Church and in Doctrine." *Ecclesial Practices* 2, no. 1 (2015): 5–22.

―――. *Seeing the World and Knowing God: Hebrew Wisdom and Christian Doctrine in a Late-Modern Context*. Oxford: Oxford University Press, 2015.

―――. *The Trinity in Worship and Preaching*. London: London Baptist Preachers' Association, 1991.

―――. "Versions of Ecclesiology." *Ecclesiology* 12, no. 3 (13 October 2016): 331–53. https://doi.org/10.1163/17455316-01203006.

―――. "Covenant and Participation: A Personal Review of the Essays." *Perspectives in Religious Studies* 44, no. 1 (2017): 119–37.

―――. "A Fourth Strand of the Reformation." *Ecclesiology* 13, no. 2 (23 May 2017): 153–59. https://doi.org/10.1163/17455316-01302002.

―――. "Covenant and Inheritance of Separatism." In *The Fourth Strand of the Reformation: The Covenant Ecclesiology of Anabaptists, English Separatists, and Early General Baptists*, 63–92. Centre for Baptist History and Heritage Studies 17. Oxford: Regent's Park College, 2018.

Fiddes, Paul S., ed. *Faith in the Centre: Christianity and Culture*. Regent's Study Guides 9. Oxford: Regent's Park College, 2001.

―――, ed. *Reflections on the Water: Understanding God and the World through the Baptism of Believers*. Regent's Study Guides 4. Oxford: Regent's Park College, 1996.

―――, ed. *Sharing the Faith at the Boundaries of Unity: Further Conversations between Anglicans and Baptists*. Centre for Baptist History and Heritage Studies 12. Oxford: Regent's Park College, 2015.

―――, ed. *Under the Rule of Christ: Dimensions of Baptist Spirituality*. Regent's Study Guides 14. Oxford: Regent's Park College, 2007.

Fiddes, Paul S., William H. Brackney, and Malcolm B. Yarnell. *The Fourth Strand of the Reformation: The Covenant Ecclesiology of Anabaptists, English Separatists and Early General Baptists*. Oxford: Centre for Baptist History and Heritage, 2018.

Fiddes, Paul S., and Alec Gilmore. *Charismatic Renewal: A Baptist View; A Report Received by the Baptist Union Council with Commentary*. London: Baptist Publications, 1980.

Fiddes, Paul S., Brian Haymes, and Richard Kidd. *Baptists and the Communion of Saints: A Theology of Covenanted Disciples*. Waco: Baylor University Press, 2014.

Fiddes, Paul S., Brian Haymes, Richard L. Kidd, and Michael J. Quicke. *On the Way of Trust*. Oxford: Whitley Publications, 1997.

Fiddes, Paul S., Brian Haymes, Richard Kidd, and Michael J. Quicke. *Doing Theology in a Baptist Way*. Oxford: Whitley Publications, 2000.

Fiddes, Paul S., Richard L. Kidd, and Michael J. Quicke. *Something to Declare: A Study of the Declaration of Principle*. Edited by Richard L. Kidd. Oxford: Whitley Publications, 1996.

Fiddes, Paul S., and Malkhaz Songulashvili. "A Dialogue between the Orthodox Church of Georgia and the 'Evangelical Christians-Baptists' of Georgia (1979–1980) with Its Wider Baptist Context." *International Journal for the Study of the Christian Church* 13, no. 3 (2013): 222–54.

Fonseca Molina, Josué. "A Response to the Report of International Conversations between the Catholic Church and the Baptist World Alliance." *American Baptist Quarterly* 31, no. 1 (2012): 123–37.

Fountain, David G. *Lord Radstock and the Russian Awakening*. Southampton: Mayflower Christian, 1988.

Fowler, Stanley K. "Churches and the Church." In *Recycling the Past or Researching History? Studies in Baptist Historiography and Myths*, edited by Philip Edward Thompson and Anthony R. Cross, 25–49. Studies in Baptist History and Thought 11. Milton Keynes: Paternoster, 2005.

Franklin, Simon. "988–1988: Uses and Abuses of the Millennium." *The World Today* 44, no. 4 (1988): 65–68.

Freeman, Curtis W. *Contesting Catholicity: Theology for Other Baptists*. Waco: Baylor University Press, 2014.

Friesen, Peter M, and J. B Toews. *The Mennonite Brotherhood in Russia (1789–1910)*. Fresno: Board of Christian Literature, General Conference of Mennonite Brethren Churches, 1980.

Fuchs, Lorelei F. *Koinonia and the Quest for an Ecumenical Ecclesiology: From Foundations through Dialogue to Symbolic Competence for Communionality*. Grand Rapids: Eerdmans, 2008.

Gaillardetz, Richard R. *Ecclesiology for a Global Church: A People Called and Sent*. Theology in Global Perspective. Maryknoll: Orbis Books, 2010.

Garrett, James Leo. *Baptist Theology: A Four Century Study*. Macon: Mercer University Press, 2009.
Gatskova, Kseniia, Maxim Gatskov, and Institut für Ost- und Südosteuropaforschung. *Political Culture in Ukraine*, 2015. http://nbn-resolving.de/urn:nbn:de:101:1-201511107482.
Gaustad, Edwin S. *Baptists, the Bible, Church Order and the Churches: Essays from Foundations, a Baptist Journal of History and Theology*. New York: Arno Press, 1980.
George, Timothy. "The Sacramentality of the Church: An Evangelical Baptist Perspective." In *Baptist Sacramentalism*, edited by Anthony R. Cross and Philip E. Thompson, 21–35. Studies in Baptist History and Thought 5. Eugene: Wipf & Stock, 2006.
George, Timothy, and David S. Dockery. *Baptist Theologians*. Nashville: Broadman Press, 1990.
Geychenko, Oleksandr. "On the Use of Scripture in Discussions on Unity among Russian Baptists." *Baptist Quarterly*, 10 July 2017, 1–14. https://doi.org/10.1080/0005576X.2017.1343914.
Gillham, Bill. *The Research Interview*. London; New York: Continuum, 2005.
———. *Research Interviewing: The Range of Techniques*. Maidenhead: Open University Press, 2005.
Glover, Adam. "'Partakers of the Promise': Participation between Covenant and Ontology." *Perspectives in Religious Studies* 44, no. 1 (2017): 83–101.
Goodliff, Andy. "Why Baptist Ecclesiology Is Non-Voluntary." *Baptistic Theologies* 6, no. 2 (November 2014): 1–13.
Graves, James Robinson. *Old Landmarkism: What Is It?* Memphis: Baptist Book House, 1880.
Gsovski, Vladimir. "Legal Status of the Church in Soviet Russia." *Fordham Law Review* 8, no. 1 (n.d.): 1–28.
Guy, Laurie, and Paul S. Fiddes. *Making Sense of the Book of Revelation*. Macon: Smyth & Helwys Pub., 2009.
Haight, Roger. *Comparative Ecclesiology*. Vol. 2 of *Christian Community in History*. London: Bloomsbury, 2014.
———. *Ecclesial Existence*. Vol. 3 of *Christian Community in History*. London: Bloomsbury, 2014.
———. *Historical Ecclesiology*. Vol 1 of *Christian Community in History*. London: Bloomsbury, 2014.
Hanch, Kate. "Participation in God; Owned by Love: Paul Fiddes in Dialogue with Julian of Norwich." *Perspectives in Religious Studies* 44, no. 1 (2017): 69–82.
Harmon, Steven R. *Baptist Identity and the Ecumenical Future: Story, Tradition, and the Recovery of Community*. Waco: Baylor University Press, 2016.

———. "The Ecumenical Dimensions of Baptist Denominational Identity." In *Denomination: Assessing an Ecclesiological Category*, edited by Paul M. Collins and Barry A. Ensign-George, 34–49. Ecclesiological Investigations 11. Londong: T & T Clark International, 2011.

———. "Trinitarian *Koinōnia* and Ecclesial *Oikoumenē*: Paul Fiddes as Ecumenical Theologian." *Perspectives in Religious Studies* 44, no. 1 (2017): 19–37.

Harris, Marvin. "History and Significance of the EMIC/ETIC Distinction." *Annual Review of Anthropology* 5, no. 1 (1976): 329–50. https://doi.org/10.1146/annurev.an.05.100176.001553.

Hauerwas, Stanley M. *The Peaceable Kingdom: A Primer In Christian Ethics*. Notre Dame: University of Notre Dame Press, 2011.

Haykin, Michael A. G. "Voluntarism in the Life and Ministry of William Fraser (1801–1883)." *Baptist Quarterly* 39, no. 6 (2015): 263–75.

Haymes, Brian. "Trinity and Participation: A Brief Introduction to the Theology of Paul S. Fiddes." *Perspectives in Religious Studies* 44, no. 1 (2017): 7–18.

Haymes, Brian, Ruth M. B. Gouldbourne, and Anthony R. Cross. *On Being the Church: Revisioning Baptist Identity*. Studies in Baptist History and Thought 21. Milton Keynes: Paternoster Press, 2008.

Heier, Edmund. *Religious Schism in the Russian Aristocracy 1860–1900: Radstockism and Pashkovism*. The Hague: Nijhoff, 1971.

Healy, Nicholas M. "Traditions, Authorities and the Individual Christian." *Pro Ecclesia* 18, no. 4 (2009): 371–74.

Heron, Alasdair I. C., British Council of Churches, and Council of Churches for Britain and Ireland, eds. *The Forgotten Trinity*. Vol. 3 of *A Selection of Papers Presented to the BCC Study Commission on Trinitarian Doctrine Today*. London: BCC/CCBI, 1991.

Hiscox, Edward T. *The Baptist Directory*. New York: s.n., 1859.

———. *The New Directory for Baptist Churches*. Philadelphia: Judson Press, 1894.

Hobbs, Herschel H., and Edgar Young Mullins. *The Axioms of Religion*. Nashville: Broadman Press, 1978.

Holmes, Stephen R. "Reflections on the Word of God in the Life of the Church: A Report of International Conversations between the Catholic Church and the Baptist World Alliance, 2006–2010." *American Baptist Quarterly* 31, no. 1 (2012): 138–53.

Holmes, Stephen R., Paul D. Molnar, Thomas H. McCall, Paul S. Fiddes, and Jason S. Sexton. *Two Views on the Doctrine of the Trinity*. Grand Rapids: Zondervan, 2014.

Hovorun, Cyril. *Meta-Ecclesiology: Chronicles on Church Awareness*. New York: Palgrave Macmillan, 2015.

———. *Scaffolds of the Church: Towards Poststructural Ecclesiology*. Eugene: Cascade Books, 2017.

Hudson, Winthrop Still. 'The Associational Principle among Baptists'. *Foundations* 1, no. 1 (January 1958): 10–23.

———. 'Stumbling into Disorder'. *Foundations* 1, no. 2 (April 1958): 45–71.

———. 'Documents on the Association of Churches'. *Foundations* 4, no. 4 (October 1961): 332–39.

———. 'Prolegomena to a Theology of Church Order'. *Foundations* 8, no. 2 (April 1965): 101–16.

Hughes, Philip Edgcumbe. *Paul's Second Epistle to the Corinthians: The English Text with Introduction, Exposition and Notes*. Grand Rapids: Eerdmans, 1967.

Humphreys, Fisher. "E. Y. Mullins." In *Baptist Theologians*, edited by Timothy George and David S Dockery, 330–50. Nashville: Broadman Press, 1990.

Jantz, Harold. "A Pietist Pastor and the Russian Mennonites: The Legacy of Eduard West." *Direction* 36, no. 2 (September 1, 2007): 232–246.

Jones, Keith G. *A Believing Church: Learning from Some Contemporary Anabaptist and Baptist Perspectives*. Didcot: Baptist Union of Great Britain, 2006.

———. *The European Baptist Federation: A Case Study in European Baptist Interdependency, 1950-2006*. Studies in Baptist History and Thought 43. Milton Keynes: Paternoster Press, 2009.

———. *From Conflict to Communion: Some Strategies and Possibilities in Local and Regional Inter-Church Life*. Didcot: Baptist Union of Great Britain, 2007.

———. *A Shared Meal and a Common Table: Some Reflections on the Lord's Supper and Baptists*. Praha, Czech Republic: International Baptist Theological Seminary of the European Baptist Federation, 2004.

———. "Towards a Model of Mission for Gathering, Intentional, Convictional Koinonia." *Journal of European Baptist Studies* 4, no. 2 (January 2004): 5–13.

Keach, Benjamin. *The Glory of a True Church, and Its Discipline Display'd Wherein a True Gospel-Church Is Described: Together with the Power of the Keys, and Who Are to Be Let in, and Who to Be Shut Out*. London: s.n., 1697.

Khomiakov, A. S, and Nicolas Zernov. *The Church Is One: (A Classic of Russian Orthodox Theology)*. London: Fellowship of St. Alban and St. Sergius, 1968.

Klippenstein, Lawrence. "Johann Wieler (1839–1889) among Russian Evangelicals: A New Source of Mennonites and Evangelicalism in Imperial Russia." *Journal of Mennonite Studies* 5 (1987): 44–60.

———. "Russian Evangelicalism Revisited: Ivan Kargel and the Founding of the Russian Baptist Union." *Baptist History and Heritage* 27, no. 2 (1 April 1992): 42–48.

Kreider, Robert S. "The Anabaptist Conception of the Church in the Russian Mennonite Environment, 1789–1870." *The Mennonite Quarterly Review* 25, no. 1 (January 1951): 17–33.

Kreitzer, L. Joseph, Paul S. Fiddes, Ian M. Randall, Michael A. G. Haykin, and William H Brackney. *William Kiffen and His World*. Oxford: Regent's Park College, 2010.

Küng, Hans. *Die Kirche*. Serie Piper 161. München: Piper, 1977.

Lannooy, R., ed. *For Us and for Our Salvation: Seven Perspectives on Christian Soteriology*. Utrecht-Leiden: Interuniversitair Instituut voor Missiologie en Oecumenica (IIMO) Research Pub., 1995.

Latimer, Robert Sloan. *Dr. Baedeker and His Apostolic Work in Russia*. London: Morgan and Scott, 1907.

Leskov, N. S., and James Y. Muckle. *Schism in High Society: Lord Radstock and His Followers*. Nottingham: Bramcote Press, 1995.

Lindbeck, George A. *The Nature of Doctrine: Religion and Theology in a Postliberal Age*. Louisville: Westminster John Knox Press, 2009.

Little, Franklin H. "The Concept of the Believer's Church." In *The Concept of the Believer's Church: Addresses from the 1968 Louisville Conference*, edited by James Leo Garrett, 27–32. Scottdale: Herald Press, 1969.

Lumpkin, William Latane. *Baptist Confessions of Faith*. Valley Forge: Judson Press, 1969.

Lyubashchenko, Viktoriya. "Protestantism in Ukraine: Achievements and Losses." *Religion, State & Society* 38, no. 3 (1 September 2010): 264–89.

MacIntyre, Alasdair C. *After Virtue: A Study in Moral Theology*. 2nd ed. Notre Dame: University of Notre Dame Press, 1984.

Magocsi, Paul R. *A History of Ukraine: The Land and Its Peoples*. Toronto: University of Toronto Press, 2012.

Martin, Gordon W. *The Church: A Baptist View*. London: Baptist Publications, 1976.

May, Lynn E. *The Work of the Baptist Association: An Integrative Study (CC-SR 12)*. Vol 2. Nashville: Southern Baptist Convention, 1969.

McBeth, Leon. *The Baptist Heritage*. Nashville: Broadman Press, 1987.

McCarthy, Dennis J. *Old Testament Covenant: A Survey of Current Opinions*. Atlanta: Knox, 1976.

McClendon, James William. *Biography as Theology: How Life Stories Can Remake Today's Theology*. Philadelphia: Trinity Press International, 1990.

———. *Doctrine*. Vol. 2 of *Systematic Theology*. Nashville: Abingdon Press, 1994.

———. *Ethics*. Vol. 1 of *Systematic Theology*. Nashville: Abingdon Press, 2002.

McClendon, James William, and James M. Smith. *Convictions: Defusing Religious Relativism*. Valley Forge: Trinity Press International, 1994.

McClendon, James William, and Nancey C. Murphy. *Witness*. Vol. 3 of *Systematic Theology*. Nashville: Abingdon Press, 2000.

McGlothlin, William Joseph. *Baptist Confessions of Faith*. Philadelphia: American Baptist Publication Society, 1911.

Meeks, Wayne A. *The First Urban Christians: The Social World of the Apostle Paul.* New Haven: Yale University Press, 1983.
Merriam, Sharan B. *Qualitative Research: A Guide to Design and Implementation.* Rev. and expanded edition. San Francisco: Jossey Bass, 2009.
Moltmann, Jürgen. *The Church in the Power of the Spirit: A Contribution to Messianic Ecclesiology.* London: SCM Press, 1992.
Mostowlansky, Till, and Andrea Rota. "A Matter of Perspective?" *Method and Theory in the Study of Religion* 28, no. 4–5 (17 November 2016): 317–36. https://doi.org/10.1163/15700682-12341367.
Mullins, Edgar Young. *The Axioms of Religion: A New Interpretation of the Baptist Faith.* Philadelphia: American Baptist Publication Society, 1908.
———. *Baptist Beliefs.* Louisville: Baptist World Publishing Company, 1912.
Murphy-O'Connor, J. *Paul the Letter-Writer: His World, His Options, His Skills.* Collegeville: Liturgical Press, 1995.
'News in Brief'. *Religion in Communist Lands* 8, no. 4 (1 January 1980): 320–32. https://doi.org/10.1080/09637498008430971.
Nichols, Gregory L. *The Development of Russian Evangelical Spirituality: A Study of Ivan V. Kargel (1849-1937).* Eugene: Pickwick Publications, 2011.
Nicholson, J. F. V. "The Office of 'Messenger' amongst British Baptists in the Seventeenth and Eighteenth Centuries." *Baptist Quarterly* 17, no. 5 (1 January 1958): 206–25. https://doi.org/10.1080/0005576X.1958.11750994.
———. "Towards a Theology of Episcope amongst Baptists." *Baptist Quarterly* 30, no. 6 (1 January 1984): 265–81. https://doi.org/10.1080/0005576X.1984.11751654.
———. "Towards a Theology of Episcope amongst Baptists (Continued)." *Baptist Quarterly* 30, no. 7 (1 January 1984): 319–31. https://doi.org/10.1080/0005576X.1984.11751662.
Niebuhr, H. Richard. *The Social Sources of Denominationalism.* Reprint of 1929 edition. New York: Meridian Books, 1958.
Parsons, Michael. "An Understanding of Covenanted Church: Is There a Contemporary Relevance?" *Journal of European Baptist Studies* 7, no. 3 (May 2007): 5–15.
Parushev, Parush R. "Carrying Out the Theological Task in a Baptistic Way." *Baptistic Theologies* 6, no. 1 (2014): 53–71.
———. "Gathered, Gathering, Porous: Reflections on the Nature of Baptistic Community." *Baptistic Theologies* 5, no. 1 (2013): 35–52.
Payne, Ernest Alexander. *The Fellowship of Believers: Baptist Thought and Practice Yesterday and Today.* London: Kingsgate Press, 1952.
———. "The Baptists of the Soviet Union." *Ecumenical Review* 7, no. 2 (1 January 1955): 161–68.

Peek, Stephanie. "Sacrifice, Service, and Radical Inclusion: Participating in the Divine Critique according to the Gospel of Mark." *Perspectives in Religious Studies* 44, no. 1 (2017): 39–52.

Pendleton, J. M. *Church Manual, Designed for the Use of Baptist Churches*. Philadelphia: American Baptist Publication Society, 1867.

Penner, Peter. "Baptist in All but Name: Molotschna Mennonite Brethren in India." *Mennonite Life* 46, no. 1 (1 March 1991): 17–23.

Pierson, Arthur T. *The Keswick Movement in Precept and Practise*. New York: Funk & Wagnalls company, 1903. Microform.

Pilli, Toivo. *Dance or Die: The Shaping of Estonian Baptist Identity under Communism*. Studies in Baptist History and Thought 37. Milton Keynes: Paternoster, 2008.

Plokhy, Serhii. *The Gates of Europe: A History of Ukraine*. New York: Basic Books, 2017.

Pospielovsky, D. "Forty-First All-Union Congress of the Evangelical Baptists of the Soviet Union." *St. Vladimir's Theological Quarterly* 19, no. 4 (1 January 1975): 246–253.

———. *A History of Marxist-Leninist Atheism and Soviet Antireligious Policies*. Vol. 1 of *A History of Soviet Atheism in Theory and Practice, and the Believer*. Basingstoke: Macmillan Press, 1987.

———. *Soviet Antireligious Campaigns and Persecution*. Vol. 2 of *A History of Soviet Atheism in Theory and Practice, and the Believer*. Basingstoke: Macmillan Press, 1988.

———. *Soviet Studies on the Church and the Soviet Response to Atheism*. Vol. 3 of *A History of Soviet Atheism in Theory and Practice, and the Believer*. Basingstoke: Macmillan Press, 1988.

Prabhu, Anjali. *Hybridity: Limits, Transformations, Prospects*. Albany: State University of New York Press, 2007.

Puzynin, Andrey P. *The Tradition of the Gospel Christians: A Study of Their Identity and Theology during the Russian, Soviet, and Post-Soviet Periods*. Eugene: Pickwick Publications, 2011.

Randall, Ian M. "'Council and Help': European Baptists and Wider Baptist Fellowship." *Journal of European Baptist Studies* 11, no. 1 (September 2010): 25–35.

Rendtorff, Rolf. *The Covenant Formula: An Exegetical and Theological Investigation*. Edinburgh: T & T Clark, 1998.

Reynolds, Geoffrey G. *First among Equals: A Study of the Basis of Association and Oversight among Baptist Churches*. N.p.: Berkshire, Southern, Oxfordshire, and East Gloucestershire Baptist Associations., 1993.

Rowe, Michael. "Democracy Versus Authority in Moscow." *Christianity Today* 24, no. 3 (February 8, 1980): 76.

———. "The 1979 Baptist Congress in Moscow: A Western Observer Reports." *Religion in Communist Lands* 8, no. 3 (1 September 1980): 188-96.

———. "Soviet Baptists Engage in Perestroika." *Religion in Communist Lands* 18, no. 2 (1 June 1990): 184-87.

———. "USSR Baptist Congress." *Religion in Communist Lands* 13, no. 3 (1 December 1985): 333-34.

Sawatsky, Walter. "Russian Evangelicals Hold a Congress." *Religion in Communist Lands* 3, no. 1-3 (1 January 1975): 12-15. https://doi.org/10.1080/09637497508430714.

———. "Call for Union of Baptists and Mennonites Issued by a Russian Baptist Leader." *Mennonite Quarterly Review* 50, no. 3 (1 July 1976): 230-39.

———. *Soviet Evangelicals since World War II*. Kitchener: Herald Press, 1981.

Schillebeeckx, Edward, and John Bowden. *The Church with a Human Face: A New and Expanded Theology of Ministry*. London: SCM, 1985.

Schillebeeckx, Edward, and Cornelius Ernst. *Christ the Sacrament of Encounter with God*. London: Sheed & Ward, 1964.

Schreiter, Robert J. *Constructing Local Theologies*. Maryknoll: Orbis Books, 1985.

———. *The New Catholicity: Theology Between the Global and the Local*. Maryknoll: Orbis Books, 1997.

Shurden, Walter B. 'The Development of Baptist Associations in America, 1707-1814'. *Baptist History and Heritage* 4 (January 1969): 31-39.

———. 'Baptist Associations: The Annual Meetings Prior to 1814'. *Baptist History and Heritage* 10, no. 4 (October 1975): 233-37.

———. 'Associational Principle, 1707-1814: Its Rationale'. *Foundations* 21, no. 3 (July 1978): 211-24.

———. 'Church and Association: A Search for Boundaries'. *Baptist History and Heritage* 14, no. 3 (July 1979): 32-40, 61.

———. 'The Advance of Baptist Associations across America'. *Baptist History and Heritage* 14, no. 4 (October 1979): 56-57.

———. 'The Historical Background of Baptist Associations'. *Review & Expositor* 77, no. 2 (1980): 161-75.

———. 'The Authority of a Baptist Association'. *Baptist History and Heritage* 40, no. 1 (2005): 6-7.

———. '"Minutes of the Philadelphia Baptist Association"'. *American Baptist Quarterly* 27, no. 1 (2008): 34-38.

———. 'Baptist Associations and the Turn toward Denominational Cooperation: 1640s-1707'. In *Turning Points in Baptist History: A Festschrift in Honor of Harry Leon McBeth*, 63-73. Macon: Mercer University Press, 2008.

Smyth, John, and William Thomas Whitley. *The Works of John Smyth, Fellow of Christ's College, 1594-8*. 2 vols. Cambridge: Cambridge University Press, 1915.

Songulashvili, Malkhaz. *Evangelical Christian Baptists of Georgia: The History and Transformation of a Free Church Tradition*. Waco: Baylor University Press, 2015.

Stenschke, Christoph. "Issues of Power, Authority and Interdependence from a Biblical Perspective." In *Avtonomia Pomestnoi Tserkvi: Materialy Simposiuma* [Local Church Autonomy: Proceedings of the Symposium], 116–48. Odessa: E-AAA, 2009.

Suny, Ronald Grigor. *The Revenge of the Past: Nationalism, Revolution, and the Collapse of the Soviet Union*. Stanford: Stanford University Press, 2004.

Swarat, Uwe. "Local Churches and Wider Ecclesial Structures from the Perspective of Reformation Ecclesiology." In *Avtonomia Pomestnoi Tserkvi: Materialy Simposiuma* [Local Church Autonomy: Proceedings of the Symposium], 42–55. Odessa: E-AAA, 2009.

Tanner, Kathryn. *Theories of Culture: A New Agenda for Theology*. Minneapolis: Fortress Press, 1997.

Teraudkalns, Valdis. "Episcopacy in the Baptist Tradition." In *Recycling the Past or Researching History: Studies in Baptist Historiography and Myths*, edited by Philip Edward Thompson and Anthony R. Cross, 272–93. Studies in Baptist History and Thought 11. Milton Keynes: Paternoster, 2005.

Thiselton, Anthony C. *Hermeneutics of Doctrine*. Grand Rapids: Eerdmans, 2015.

Tillard, Jean-Marie Roger. *Church of Churches: The Ecclesiology of Communion*. Collegeville: Liturgical Press, 1992.

———. *Flesh of the Church, Flesh of Christ: At the Source of the Ecclesiology of Communion*. Collegeville: The Liturgical Press, 2001.

Toews, J. A. "Baptists and Mennonite Brethren in Russia (1790–1930)." In *Mennonites and Baptists: A Continuing Conversation*, edited by Paul Toews, 81–96. Winnipeg: Kindred Press, 1993.

Together in Mission and Ministry: The Porvoo Common Statement with Essays on Church and Ministry in Northern Europe; Conversations between the British and Irish Anglican Churches and the Nordic and Baltic Lutheran Churches. London: Church House, 1996.

Tönnies, Ferdinand, and José Harris. *Community and Civil Society*. Cambridge: Cambridge University Press, 2001.

Tracy, David. *The Analogical Imagination: Christian Theology and the Culture of Pluralism*. New York: Crossroad, 1987.

Trotter, A. *Lord Radstock: An Interpretation and a Record*. London: Hodder and Stoughton, 1914.

Vandervelde, George. "Believers Church Ecclesiology as Ecumenical Challenge." In *The Believers Church: A Voluntary Church. Papers of the Twelfth Believers Church Conference Held at McMaster Divinity College, October 17–19, 1996*, edited by William H Brackney, 199–216. Studies in the Believers Church Tradition 1. Kitchener: Pandora Press, 1996.

Van der Ven, J. A. *Ecclesiology in Context*. Grand Rapids, MI: Eerdmans, 1996.

VanderWilt, Jeffrey T. *A Church without Borders: The Eucharist and the Church in Ecumenical Perspective*. Collegeville: Liturgical Press, 1998.

Wach, Joachim. *Sociology of Religion*. Chicago: University of Chicago Press, 1944.

Walls, Andrew F. "The Gospel as Prisoner and Liberator of Culture." In *The Missionary Movement in Christian History: Studies in the Transmission of Faith*, 3–15. Maryknoll: Orbis Books, 1996.

Wanner, Catherine. *Communities of the Converted: Ukrainians and Global Evangelism*. Ithaca: Cornell University Press, 2007.

Ward, Roger. "Editorial Introduction: Trinity and Participation; Engaging and Celebrating Paul Fiddes." *Perspectives in Religious Studies* 44, no. 1 (2017): 3–5.

Wardin, Albert W. "August G. A. Liebig: German Baptist Missionary and Friend to the Mennonite Brethren." *Journal of Mennonite Studies* 28 (1 January 2010): 168–86.

———. "Baptist Immersions in the Russian Empire: Difficult Beginnings." *Journal of European Baptist Studies* 10, no. 3 (2010): 37–44.

———. "Baptist Influences on Mennonite Brethren with an Emphasis on the Practice of Immersion." *Direction* 8, no. 4 (1 October 1979): 33–38.

———. "Continental European Baptists in the Twentieth Century." *Baptist History and Heritage* 7, no. 4 (1972): 205–10.

———. "How Indigenous Was the Baptist Movement in the Russian Empire?" *Journal of European Baptist Studies* 9, no. 2 (2009): 29–37.

———. "Mennonite Brethren and German Baptists in Russia: Affinities and Dissimilarities." In *Mennonites and Baptists: A Continuing Conversation*, edited by Paul Toews, 97–112. Winnipeg: KS USA, 1993.

———. "Penetration of the Baptists into the Russian Empire in the Nineteenth Century." *Journal of European Baptist Studies* 7, no. 3 (2007): 34–47.

———. "Historiography of Baptists in Russia." In *Materialy Mezhdunarodnoi nauchno-practicheskoi konferentsii "105 let legalizatsii russkogo baptisma"* (5–7 aprelia 2011) [Papers of International Scholarly and Practical Conference "105th Anniversary of Legalization of Russian Baptism" 5–7 April 2011], 50–56. Moscow: RS EKhB, 2011.

———. *On the Edge: Baptists and Other Free Church Evangelicals in Tsarist Russia, 1855–1917*. Eugene: Pickwick Publications, 2013.

Watson, E. C. *The Baptist Association*. Nashville: Convention Press, 1975.

Weima, Jeffrey A. D. *Neglected Endings: The Significance of the Pauline Letter Closings*. Journal for the Study of the New Testament. Supplement Series 101. JSOT Press, 1994.

White, B. R. *The English Baptists of the Seventeenth Century*. Didcot: Baptist Historical Society, 1996.

———. *The English Separatist Tradition*. Oxford: Oxford University Press, 1971.

Wilmington, David M. "Distinctly Harmonious: Creaturely Participation in the Trinity (in the Key of Fiddes)." *Perspectives in Religious Studies* 44, no. 1 (2017): 103–17.

Winter, Sean. "Tracks and Traces." *Baptist Quarterly* 41, no. 7 (1 July 2006): 439–46. https://doi.org/10.1179/bqu.2006.41.7.005.

World Council of Churches. *Baptism, Eucharist and Ministry*. Geneva: WCC, 1995.

World Council of Churches, and Commission on Faith and Order. *The Church: Towards a Common Vision*. Geneva: WCC, 2013.

Wright, Nigel. "Are Baptist Churches Autonomous?" In *Avtonomia Pomestnoi Tserkvi: Materialy Simposiuma* [Local Church Autonomy: Proceedings of the Symposium], 202–21. Odessa: E-AAA, 2009.

———. *Challenge to Change: A Radical Agenda for Baptists*. Eastbourne: Kingsway, 1991.

———. "Covenant and Covenanting." *Baptist Quarterly* 39, no. 6 (1 April 2002): 287–90. https://doi.org/10.1179/bqu.2002.39.6.005.

———. *Free Church, Free State: The Positive Baptist Vision*. Milton Keynes: Paternoster Press, 2005.

———. "'Koinonia' and Baptist Ecclesiology: Self-Critical Reflections from Historical and Systematic Perspectives." *Baptist Quarterly* 35 no. 8 (1994): 363–75.

———. *New Baptists, New Agenda*. Carlisle: Paternoster Press, 2002.

Zhuk, S. I. *Russia's Lost Reformation: Peasants, Millennialism, and Radical Sects in Southern Russia and Ukraine, 1830–1917*. Washington: Woodrow Wilson Center Press, 2004.

Zizioulas, John D. *Being as Communion: Studies in Personhood and the Church*. Contemporary Greek Theologians 4. Crestwood: St. Vladimir's Seminary Press, 1985.

Dissertations

Baraniuk, Fiodor V. "A Missiological Assessment of the Impact of Western Mission Agencies upon the Development of Baptist Union Churches in Russia since November of 1989." PhD diss., Mid-America Baptist Theological Seminary, 2004. ProQuest (AAT 3138626).

Belyea, Gordon Lansdowne. "Living Stones in a Spiritual House: The Priesthood of the Saint in the Baptist Sanctorum Communio." ThD diss., Wycliffe College and University of Toronto, 2012.

Beznosova, Olga V. "Pozdnee protestantskoe sektantstvo yuga Ukrainy, 1850–1905" [Late Protestant Sectarianism in the South of Ukraine, 1850–1905]. PhD diss., Dnepropetrovsk State University, 1997.

Billingham, John. "Divine Authority and Covenant Community in Contemporary Culture." PhD diss., University of Oxford, 2014.

Blane, Andrew. "The Relations between the Russian Protestant Sects and the State, 1900–1921." PhD diss., Duke University, 1964. ProQuest (AAT 302159365).

Bokova, O. A. "Teologia rossiiskikh evangel'skikh khristian-baptistov na rubezhe XX i XXI vekov: avtoreferat dis. . . . kandidata filosofskikh nauk" [A Theology of Russian Evangelical Christians-Baptists at the Brink of 20th and 21st Centuries: Author's Abstract of PhD diss.]. PhD diss., St. Petersburg Gosudarstvennyi Universitet, 2011.

Breyfogle, Nicholas B. "Heretics and Colonizers: Religious Dissent and Russian Colonization of Transcaucasia, 1830–1890." PhD diss., University of Pennsylvania, 1998.

Carlson, Gordon William. "Russian Protestants and American Evangelicals since the Death of Stalin: Patterns of Interaction and Response." PhD diss., University of Minnesota, 1986. ProQuest (AAT 8625875).

Chalandeau, Alexander de. "The Theology of the Evangelical Christians-Baptists in the USSR, as Reflected in the *Bratskii Vestnik*." PhD diss., University of Strasbourg, 1978. ProQuest (AAT 3466419).

Coleman, Heather Jean. "The Most Dangerous Sect: Baptists in Tsarist and Soviet Russia, 1905–1929." PhD diss., University of Illinois at Urbana-Champaign, 1998. ProQuest (AAT 304451630).

Copson, S. L. "Association Life of the Calvinistic Baptists of Northern England, with Reference to the History of the Churches from 1648 to 1732." PhD diss., University of Oxford, 1987. ProQuest (AAT 301486106).

Corrado, Sharyl. "The Philosophy of Ministry of Colonel Vasiliy Pashkov." Master's thesis, Wheaton College, 2000.

Covington, Randy Wayne. "An Investigation into the Administrative Structure and Polity Practiced by the Union of Evangelical Christian-Baptists of Russia." PhD diss., Southwestern Baptist Theological Seminary, 2004. ProQuest (AAT 305100280).

Durasoff, Steve. "The All-Union Council of Evangelical Christians-Baptists in the Soviet Union 1944–1965." PhD diss., New York University, 1968. ProQuest (AAT 302318472).

Dyck, Johannes. "Moulding the Brotherhood: Johann Wieler (1839–1889) and the Communities of the Early Evangelicals in Russia." ThM thesis, University of Wales, 2007.

Ensign-George, Barry. "Denomination: Intermediary Ecclesial Structure within the Unity of the Church." PhD diss., Southern Methodist University, 2013. ProQuest (AAT 1416425006).

Esselman, Thomas E. "The Principle of Functionality in Ecclesiology." PhD diss., University of St. Michael's College, 1990. ProQuest (AAT 219924564).

Fiddes, Paul S. "The Hiddenness of Wisdom in the Old Testament and Later Judaism." DPhil diss., University of Oxford, 1975.

Goloshchapova, Ie. O. "Hromady Evnagel'skikh Khrystyian-Baptistiv v Umovakh Suspil'nykh Transformatsii 20–30kh rr. XX st." [Communities of Evangelical Christians-Baptists in the Conditions of Social Transformations of 1920–30s]. PhD diss. abstract, Zaporiz'skyi Natsional'nyi Universytet, 2010.

Greenfeld, L. "Eastern Orthodox Influence on Russian Evangelical Ecclesiology." MTh thesis, University of South Africa, 2002. http://hdl.handle.net/10500/16876.

Ivanov, M. V. "Sovremennye tendentsii v bogoslovii rossi'skikh evangel'skikh khristian-baptistov: avtoreferat dis. . . . kandidata filosofskikh nauk" [Contemporary Tendencies in the Theology of Russian Evangelical Christians-Baptists: Author's Abstract of PhD Diss.]. Moscow: Rossiiskaia Akademiia Narodnogo Khoziaistva i Gosudarstvennoy Sluzhby pri Prezidente RF, 2012.

Kashirin, Alexander. "Protestant Minorities in the Soviet Ukraine, 1945–1991." PhD diss., University of Oregon, 2010. ProQuest (AAT 748974224).

Kuznetsova, Miriam R. "Early Russian Evangelicals (1874–1929): Historical Background and Hermeneutical Tendencies Based on I. V. Kargel's Written Heritage." PhD diss., University of Pretoria, 2009. http://upetd.up.ac.za/thesis/available/etd-07302010-165055/.

Long, Esther Grace. "Identity in Evangelical Ukraine: Negotiating Regionalism, Nationalism, and Transnationalism." PhD diss., University of Kentucky, 2005. ProQuest (AAT 304992386).

Mask, E. Jeffrey. "At Liberty under God: A Baptist Ecclesiology." PhD diss., Emory University, 1990. ProQuest (AAT 303916929).

McCarthy, Mark Myers. "Religious Conflict and Social Order in Nineteenth-Century Russia: Orthodoxy and the Protestant Challenge, 1812–1905." PhD diss., University of Notre Dame, 2004. ProQuest (AAT 305137823).

Mulcahy, Eamonn. "The Cause of Our Salvation: Soteriological Causality according to Some Modern British Theologians, 1988–1998." PhD diss., Pontifical Gregorian University, 2007.

Nazarkina, Olena I. "Protestants'ki konfesii Ukrainy v 90-ti roky XX st.: baptysts'ki ta p'iatydesyatnyc'ki techii" [The Protestant Confessions in Ukraine in the 90s of the 20th Century: Baptist and Pentecostal Movements]. PhD diss., Donetsk National University, 2003.

Nesdoly, Samuel J. "Evangelical Sectarianism in Russia a Study of the Stundists, Baptists, Pashkovites, Evangelical Christians, 1855-1917." PhD diss., Queen's University, Canada, 1971. ProQuest (AAT 302563178).

Pankhurst, Jerry Glen. "The Orthodox and the Baptists in the USSR: Resources for the Survival of Ideologically Defined Deviance." PhD diss., University of Michigan, 1978. ProQuest (AAT 302878292).

Popov, Alexander. "The Evangelical Christians-Baptists in the Soviet Union as a Hermeneutical Community: Examining the Identity of the All-Union Council of the ECB (AUCECB) through the Way the Bible Was Used in Its Publications." PhD diss., International Baptist Theological Seminary, Prague, 2010. ProQuest (AAT 884998092).

Potots'kii, V. P. "Rozvytok Relihiinoho Sectantstva v Kharkivs'kii Hubernii (1861-1917): Avtoreferat" [Development of the Religious Sectarianism in Kharkiv Hubernia (1861-1917): Thesis Abstract]. PhD diss., V. N. Karazin Kharkiv National University, 2004.

Prokhorov, Constantine. "Russian Baptists and Orthodoxy, 1960-1990: A Comparative Study of Theology, Liturgy, and Traditions." PhD diss., International Baptist Theological Seminary, Prague (Czech Republic), 2011. http://search.proquest.com/dissertations/docview/906771696/abstract/A34534F870B646A1PQ/5.

Pyzh, Yaroslav. "The Confessing Community as the Ecclesiological Core of the Baptists in the Soviet Union, 1960-1990." PhD diss., Southwestern Baptist Theological Seminary, 2012. ProQuest (AAT 1285507583).

Renihan, James M. "The Practical Ecclesiology of the English Particular Baptists, 1675-1705: The Doctrine of the Church in the Second London Baptist Confession as Implemented in the Subscribing Churches." PhD diss., Trinity Evangelical Divinity School, 1997. ProQuest (AAT 304385162).

Reshetnikov, Iu. "Stanovlennia ta diferentsiatsiia evangel'skogo rukhu v Ukraini" [Formation and Differentiation of the Evangelical Movement in the Ukraine]. PhD diss., G. S. Skovoroda Philosophy Institute of National Academy of Sciences of Ukraine, 2000.

Rogers, David. 'A Critical Analysis of the History of Southern Baptist Approaches to Interdenominational Cooperation in International Missions'. PhD diss, Southeastern Baptist Theological Seminary, 2015.

Shurden, Walter B. "Associationalism among Baptists in America, 1707-1814." ThD diss. New Orleans Baptist Theological Seminary, 1967.

Sitarchuk, Roman A. "Diial'nist' Protestants'kykh Konfesii u Radians'kii Ukraini v Konteksti ii Derzhavnoi Polityky (20-30 rr. XX st.)" [Activity of Protestant Confessions in Soviet Ukraine in the Context of its State Politics (1920-30)]. PhD diss. abstract, Instytut Filosofii im. H. S. Skovorody Natsional'noi

Akademii Nauk Ukrainy [H. S. Skovoroda Institute of Philosophy. National Academy of Science of Ukraine], 2011.

Steeves, Paul D. "The Experience of the Russian Baptists, 1922 to 1929." Master's thesis, University of Kansas, 1972.

———. "The Russian Baptist Union, 1917–1935: Evangelical Awakening in Russia." PhD diss., University of Kansas, 1976. ProQuest (AAT 302817810).

Surer, Jan M. "Colonel V. A. Pashkov and the Late Nineteenth-Century Protestant Movement in Russia." MPhil thesis, University of Oxford, 1999.

———. "Religion, Authority, and the Individual: The Russian Orthodox Church and Stundist Sectarianism in Kiev Province, 1870–1917." PhD diss., Brandeis University, 2012. ProQuest (AAT 1019056177).

Thompson, Philip Edward. "Toward Baptist Ecclesiology in Pneumatological Perspective." PhD diss., Emory University, 1995. ProQuest (AAT 304261519).

Tyson, Samuel Daley. 'Dependent Independence: Toward a Theology of Southern Baptist Associationalism'. Ph.D., The Southern Baptist Theological Seminary, 2017.

Waldrop, Michael Wayne. 'Toward a Theology of Cooperation: A Historical, Biblical, and Systematic Examination of the Compatibility of Cooperation and Autonomy among Local Baptist Churches'. Ph.D., Mid-America Baptist Theological Seminary, 2009.

Wamble, Hugh. "The Concept and Practice of Christian Fellowship: The Connectional and Inter-denominational Aspects Thereof, among Seventeenth Century English Baptists." PhD diss. Southern Baptist Theological Seminary, 1955. ProQuest (AAT 301928369).

Wilkins, Dennis Ray. 'Southern Baptist Intercongregational Collaboration'. Ph.D., Southwestern Baptist Theological Seminary, 2010.

Yuchkovski, Alexander. "A Comparison of the Evangelical Movement in Russia in the 1920s and the 1990s." PhD, Middlesex University, 2015.

CD-ROMs

Baptist Ukrainy 1926–1928 [Ukrainian Baptist 1926–1928]. Odessa: EAAA, 2013. CD-ROM.

Bratskii Vestnik 1945–1993 [Brotherly Herald 1945–1993]. Odessa: EAAA, 2008. CD-ROM.

Istoriia evangel'skogo dvizheniia v Evrazii 1.1 [History of the Evangelical Movement in Eurasia 1.1.]. Odessa: EAAA, 2001. CD-ROM.

Istoriia evangel'skogo dvizheniia v Evrazii 2.0. [History of the Evangelical Movement in Eurasia 2.0.]. Odessa: EAAA, 2002. CD-ROM.

Istoriia evangel'skogo dvizheniia v Evrazii 3.0. [History of the Evangelical Movement in Eurasia 3.0.]. Odessa: EAAA, 2003. CD-ROM.

Istoriia evangel'skogo dvizheniia v Evrazii 4.0. [History of the Evangelical Movement in Eurasia 4.0.]. Odessa: EAAA, 2005. CD-ROM.
Istoriia evangel'skogo dvizheniia v Evrazii 5.0. [History of the Evangelical Movement in Eurasia 5.0.]. Odessa: EAAA, 2006. CD-ROM.

Web-Based Resources

'Fiddes, Rev. Prof. Paul Stuart'. In *Who's Who*, Online ed. Published online December 1, 2007. Accessed June 1, 2018. http://www.ukwhoswho.com/view/10.1093/ww/9780199540884.001.0001/ww-9780199540884-e-245556.

Baptist Union of Great Britain. 'Baptists and Life in Covenant' by Paul S. Fiddes. Accessed September 6, 2017. http://www.baptist.org.uk/Articles/457297/Baptists_and_life.aspx.

Regent's Park College (webpage). 'Professor Paul Fiddes (profile)'. Accessed 11 July 2018. http://www.rpc.ox.ac.uk/people/professor-paul-fiddes/.

Rukh 'Za Zdorovu Tserkvu' (blog). 'Dlia Chogo Neobhindyi Rukh "Za Zdorovu Tserkvu" [Why the Movement "For Healthy Church" Needed?]' by Valeriy Antonyuk, posted September 26, 2008. http://zerkva.blogspot.com/2008/09/blog-post_26.html.

Rukh 'Za Zdorovu Tserkvu' (blog). 'Opys Tsinnostei Rukhu "Za Zdorovu Tserkvu" [Description of Values of the Movement "For Healthy Church"]' by *Rukh 'Za Zdorovu Tserkvu'*, posted November 21, 2008. http://zerkva.blogspot.com/2008/11/blog-post_21.html.

Rukh 'Za Zdorovu Tserkvu' (blog). 'Prezentatsiia Rukhu "Za Zdorovu Tserkvu" [Presentation of the Movement "For Healthy Church"]' by pastor Mykola Romanyuk, posted, September 25, 2008. http://zerkva.blogspot.com/2008/09/blog-post_25.html.

Stüdemann, Dietmar. "Dytmar Shtiudemann: Ukrayna Postoianno Torhuetsia" [Dietmar Steudemann: Ukraine is constantly bargaining], 21 December 2009. Online-media "Infromatsiine Agenstvo 'Glavkom',' Media Identificator R40-01991. Accessed July 25, 2017. http://glavcom.ua/publications/45-ditmar-shtjudemann-ukraina-postojanno-torguetsja.html.

VSTs EKhB. 'Chernivetski Sluzhyteli Vidvidaly Tserkvy v Zoni ATO [Ministers from Chernivsti Visited Churches in the Anti-Terrorist Operation Zone]'. The official webpage of AUUCECB, 2 July 2017. Accessed July 20, 2017. http://old.baptyst.com/index.php?option=com_content&view=article&id=4547%3Acherniveczki-sluzhiteli-vidvidali-czerkvi-v-zoni-ato&catid=75&Itemid=1&lang=ua.

VSTs EKhB. 'Pro Souiz EKhB - Vseukraiins'kii Soiuz Tserkov Evangel's'kykh Krystyian-Baptystiv [About the Union of ECB - All-Ukrainian Union of Churches of Evangelical Christians-Baptists]". The official webpage of AUUCECB. Accessed 4 June 2018. http://www.baptyst.com/pro-soyuz/.

VSTs EKhB. 'Startuvala Strategichna Konferentsiia Komitetiv VSTs EKhB [The Strategic Conference of the Committees of VSTs EKhB Has Begun]". The official webpage of AUUCECB. VSTs EKhB. Accessed 27 August 2018. http://old.baptyst.com/index.php?option=com_content&view=article&id=2575%3Astartuvala-strategchna-konferenczya-komtetv-vscz-xb&catid=13%3As-&Itemid=53&lang=ua.

VSTs EKhB. 'Tyzhden Soiuzu na Khersonshchyni 5–10 grudnia 2006 [Week of the Union in Kherson Region 5–10 December 2006]". The official webpage of AUUCECB. Published December 14, 2006. http://old.baptyst.com/index.php?option=com_content&view=article&id=173&catid=78%3A-&lang=ua.

VSTs EKhB. 'Vinnyts'ka Tserkva Sviatkuvala v Kyevi Svoe 100-richchia [Vinnitsa Church Celebrates in Kyiv its Centenary]". The official webpage of AUUCECB. Accessed 21 June 2018. http://www.baptyst.com/vinnytska-tserkva-svyatkuvala-v-kyyevi-svoye-100-richchya/.

Fariseevka (blog) [Pharisee-town (blog)]. 'Kakim Sudom Sudite [See How You Judge]' by B. M. Zdorovets. Published November 20, 2002. http://pharisai.at.ua/publ/21-1-0-172.

Fariseevka (blog) [Pharisee-town (blog)]. 'Kakim Sudom Sudite 2 [See How You Judge 2]' by B. M. Zdorovets. Published November 20, 2002. http://pharisai.at.ua/publ/21-1-0-173.

Langham Literature, with its publishing work, is a ministry of Langham Partnership.

Langham Partnership is a global fellowship working in pursuit of the vision God entrusted to its founder John Stott –

> *to facilitate the growth of the church in maturity and Christ-likeness through raising the standards of biblical preaching and teaching.*

Our vision is to see churches in the Majority World equipped for mission and growing to maturity in Christ through the ministry of pastors and leaders who believe, teach and live by the word of God.

Our mission is to strengthen the ministry of the word of God through:
- nurturing national movements for biblical preaching
- fostering the creation and distribution of evangelical literature
- enhancing evangelical theological education

especially in countries where churches are under-resourced.

Our ministry

Langham Preaching partners with national leaders to nurture indigenous biblical preaching movements for pastors and lay preachers all around the world. With the support of a team of trainers from many countries, a multi-level programme of seminars provides practical training, and is followed by a programme for training local facilitators. Local preachers' groups and national and regional networks ensure continuity and ongoing development, seeking to build vigorous movements committed to Bible exposition.

Langham Literature provides Majority World preachers, scholars and seminary libraries with evangelical books and electronic resources through publishing and distribution, grants and discounts. The programme also fosters the creation of indigenous evangelical books in many languages, through writer's grants, strengthening local evangelical publishing houses, and investment in major regional literature projects, such as one volume Bible commentaries like the *Africa Bible Commentary* and the *South Asia Bible Commentary*.

Langham Scholars provides financial support for evangelical doctoral students from the Majority World so that, when they return home, they may train pastors and other Christian leaders with sound, biblical and theological teaching. This programme equips those who equip others. Langham Scholars also works in partnership with Majority World seminaries in strengthening evangelical theological education. A growing number of Langham Scholars study in high quality doctoral programmes in the Majority World itself. As well as teaching the next generation of pastors, graduated Langham Scholars exercise significant influence through their writing and leadership.

To learn more about Langham Partnership and the work we do visit **langham.org**

www.ingramcontent.com/pod-product-compliance
Lightning Source LLC
Chambersburg PA
CBHW061705300426
44115CB00014B/2564